Holistic Mission

Weighed in the Balances

Holistic Mission

Weighed in the Balances

E.S. Williams

Belmont House Publishing

London

Holistic Mission: Weighed in the Balances
is published by Belmont House Publishing

First published May 2016

ISBN 0 9548493 9 6

Scripture quotations from the King James Authorised Version, unless otherwise indicated.

Published by Belmont House Publishing
36 The Crescent
Belmont
SUTTON
Surrey SM2 6BJ

Website www.belmonthouse.co.uk

A Catalogue record for this book is available from the British Library.

Printed and bound in Great Britain by
Marston Book Services Limited, Oxfordshire

Sincere thanks to the Christian brothers and sisters who commented on the text and helped with proof-reading.

Holistic Mission: Weighed in the Balances

Table of Contents

Introduction   viii

1. Holistic Mission   1

2. John Stott Changes his Mind   20

3. Higher Criticism of the Bible   33

4. Higher Criticism in the UK and USA   50

5. The Social Gospel of Walter Rauschenbusch   68

6. Edinburgh 1910   81

7. J. Gresham Machen Battles the Modernists   102

8. Scopes Monkey Trial   117

9. World Council of Churches   122

10. The New Evangelicals   145

11. Berlin 1966   162

12. Lausanne Congress on World Evangelization   172

13. The Post-Lausanne Battle   188

14. Radicals Take Up the Fight   208

15. A Short History of Missiology   219

16. Ralph Winter: The Missionary Statesman   231

17. Missiology of Christopher Wright   252

18. Contextualizing the Gospel   268

19. Edinburgh Centenary Celebration 2010   284

20. Lausanne III: Cape Town 2010   302

21. Concluding Remarks   319

   Index   338

Introduction

The purpose of this book is to warn of the rise of a heresy in the Christian Church that is known by the term 'holistic mission'. Its advocates assert that the Great Commission of the Church, 'must be understood to include social as well as evangelistic responsibility, unless we are to be guilty of distorting the words of Jesus'. At the heart of holistic mission is the belief that socio-political action and evangelism are, 'a partnership like two blades of a pair of scissors or two wings of a bird'. The effect of the holistic model is to make social reform part of the evangelical mandate, and the Great Commission is understood to include both social action and evangelism. The mission of the Church is to build the Kingdom of God on earth.

Holistic mission is the product of a politically-motivated reinterpretation of Scripture, which by degrees has come to dominate the thinking and activity of much of the modern evangelical movement, as many churches, para-church organisations and mission societies now unquestioningly embrace holistic ministry. It is deeply heretical because it redefines the very meaning of the gospel itself—the priority of the gospel is no longer the salvation of sinners, but the transformation of society.

In effect, holistic mission has undermined the proclamation of the true gospel, distorted the interpretation of the Scriptures, and morphed missionary outreach into primarily a socio-political enterprise that seeks to improve whole societies through good works. Preaching salvation from sin through the atoning death of Christ is no longer regarded as a priority.

Holistic mission is supported by some of the most well-known names in evangelicalism, including Billy Graham and John Stott, and is routinely taught in the Bible seminaries and mission institutions of the evangelical world. Over the past 40 years or so it has developed a massive influence that can hardly be exaggerated——through conferences, books, periodicals and the work of numerous Christian missiologists operating in the fields of the social sciences and anthropology. It now has all the unstoppable qualities of the proverbial juggernaut.

This book endeavours to trace holistic mission from its roots far back in the nineteenth century; then on through higher criticism, liberal theology, and the social gospel. It then catalogues how it took shape in the post-war period with the founding of the World Council of Churches and the new evangelical movement, followed by the Lausanne movement for World Evangelization, and culminating in the rapid growth of academic missiology in Bible seminaries around the world at the present day.

While holistic mission regards itself as the authentic expression of biblical Christianity, it unashamedly associates with the enemies of the Faith once for all delivered to the saints (Jude 3). It boldly promotes ecumenism and looks favourably upon the Roman Catholic Church. Simultaneously, it fiercely rejects biblical fundamentalism as anti-intellectual and culturally-conditioned. The biblical doctrine of separating from false teaching is being replaced by the 'new' approach of contextualizing the gospel to make it culturally relevant.

The net result has been the tragic loss of the true gospel of salvation in a welter of unbiblical activity, conference papers and socio-political initiatives. It must inevitably continue to grow worse and worse, but for the grace and restraining hand of God.

The following chapters document the insidious development of holistic mission from its beginnings in sheer unbelief; on through the folly of ecclesiastical compromise; culminating in the deliberate and conscious rejection of what the people of God have always regarded as true biblical evangelism.

In his short letter to the Church, Jude exhorts believers to 'earnestly contend' for the Faith once for all delivered to the saints (Jude 3). The emphatic expression 'earnestly contend' translates the Greek word *epagonizomai*, from which we get the English verb to agonise. The word 'earnestly' is added to convey the full force of the command that we should agonise over the defence of our precious Faith. It is in this spirit that I write this book.

ES Williams

Chapter 1

Holistic Mission

What is the true mission of the Church of Jesus Christ? This is a question that has troubled the Church over the last century, as many prominent church leaders have sought to promote the idea that the authentic mission of the Church is holistic and includes socio-political action. In 1974, when the Rev John Stott, a highly regarded evangelical minister, confidently asserted that evangelism and social action are a *partnership*, 'like two blades of a pair of scissors or two wings of a bird', the result was a paradigm shift in evangelical thinking. Whereas for centuries the Church had believed that its mission was to preach the gospel of salvation from sin, this is no longer the case. An increasing focus on social activity has caused the traditional gospel to recede into the background, as a cloud of uncertainty and confusion descends over the Church.

We begin our evaluation of holistic mission with the story of how John Stott (1921-2011) changed his mind about the mission of the Church. An Anglican minister at All Souls, Langham Place, London, his reputation amongst Anglicans and throughout the international evangelical constituency was legendary. As a man of immense influence he was destined to play a pivotal role in developing the concept of holistic mission within the Church.

Stott was perhaps the most highly regarded Christian intellectual of the twentieth century. His reputation as a sound evangelical was beyond question. So it came as a great surprise when after three decades as a preacher and church leader, he actually changed his mind about the *mission* of the Church.

This is what happened. Back in 1966 at the World Congress on Evangelism in Berlin, organised by Billy Graham, John Stott, as a renowned Bible teacher, was asked to give a biblical account of the Church's mission to a large gathering of evangelicals. Expounding three accounts of the

Great Commission from the Gospels of John, Matthew and Luke, he presented the orthodox biblical understanding of the Church's mission. Stott concluded that 'the cumulative emphasis seems clear. It is placed on preaching, witnessing and making disciples, and many deduce from this that the mission of the church, according to the specification of the risen Lord is exclusively a preaching, converting and teaching mission.'[1] What Stott had done at Berlin was simply to present the orthodox understanding of the Great Commission that was widely believed by evangelical Christians. The thrust of Stott's message was crystal clear: the Great Commission of the risen Christ 'is exclusively a preaching, converting and teaching mission'.

Less than a decade later, at the International Lausanne Congress on World Evangelization in 1974, Stott had radically changed his mind.

> Today, however, I would express myself differently. It is not just that the commission includes a duty to teach converts everything Jesus had previously commanded... and that social responsibility is among the things which Jesus commanded. I now see more clearly that not only the consequences of the commission but the actual commission itself must be understood to include social as well as evangelistic responsibility, unless we are to be guilty of distorting the words of Jesus.[2]

He was emphasising what has become known as the 'holistic model' of the Great Commission. The *Lausanne Covenant*, largely written by Stott, expressed 'penitence both for our neglect of our Christian social responsibility and for our naive polarization in having sometimes regarded evangelism and social concern as mutually exclusive... we affirm that evangelism and socio-political involvement are both part of our Christian duty.'[3] In his book, *Christian Mission in the Modern World* (1975), Stott promotes the Johannine version of the Great Commission. He writes:

> The crucial form in which the Great Commission has been handed down to us (though it is the most neglected because it is the most costly) is the Johannine. Jesus had anticipated it in his prayer in the upper room when he said to the Father: "As thou didst send me into the world, so I have sent them into the

world" (John 17.18). Now, probably in the same upper room but after his death and resurrection, he turned this prayer-statement into a commission and said: "As the Father has sent me, even so I send you" (John 20.21). In both these sentences Jesus did more than draw a vague parallel between his mission and ours. Deliberately and precisely he made his mission the *model* of ours, saying "*as* the Father has sent me, even *so* I send you"[4] (Stott's emphasis).

The Johannine Commission

Stott was advocating a new understanding of the Great Commission in which Jesus and his mission became the model for the Church's mission. This approach, which focuses on continuity between Christ's incarnate earthly ministry and the contemporary ministry of the Church, became known as the 'incarnational model' of the Great Commission. A feature of those who follow the incarnational model is the desire to establish *shalom* (peace, social harmony) in today's world by actions which promote social and political justice.[5]

David Hesselgrave, Professor of Missiology at Trinity Evangelical Divinity School in Deerfield, Illinois, explained Stott's position.[6] He writes:

Stott holds John 20.21 to be the most important statement of the Great Commission. When Jesus said '*As* the Father sent me, even *so* I send you,' Stott sees Jesus clearly making his mission a model for the church's mission (as in Luke 4.18-19). That means that socio-political action (deed) is a more or less equal partner with evangelism (Word) in Christ's mission and our own. Accordingly, the church's mission today consists of 'everything the church is sent into the world to do.'[7] Stott goes so far as to say that, since the church is to be salt and light, it is the failure of the church if a community deteriorates socially or physically.[8]

Hesselgrave makes the point that 'in liberation theology and missiology, incarnationalism has been used to support all kinds of social and political activities, including participation in violent revolution.'[9]

Stott based his understanding of the Great Commission on one verse of Scripture, entirely ignoring the ministry and writings of the apostle Paul. This one verse (John 20.21) has been used by Stott and others to create the so-called 'incarnational model' of the Great Commission, which has become the bedrock of the holistic movement.

Stott correctly asserts that Jesus came to serve, but he gives a novel interpretation:

> So he gave himself in selfless service for others, and his service took a wide variety of forms according to men's needs. Certainly he preached, proclaiming the good news of the kingdom of God… But he served in deed as well as in word, and it would be impossible in the ministry of Jesus to separate his works from his words. He fed hungry mouths, and washed dirty feet… He supplies us with the perfect model of service… it seems that it is in our servant role that we can find the rich synthesis of evangelism and social action.[10]

Yet Stott's emphasis on the servant role of Jesus is misleading, for at the heart of the gospel is the Cross. Jesus Christ came to die for the sin of his people. He is the Lamb of God who takes away the sins of the world (John 1.29).

Stott teaches that the Lord Jesus gave two instructions—a Great Commission *and* a Great Commandment to love our neighbour. He says that if 'we truly love our neighbour we shall not stop with evangelism… if we love our neighbour as God made him, we must inevitably be concerned for his total welfare, the good of his soul, his body and his community. Moreover, it is this vision of man as a social being, as well as a psychosomatic being, which obliges us to add a *political* dimension to our social concern'[11] (Stott's italics). We should be involved in 'the quest for better social structures in which peace, dignity, freedom and justice are secured for all men. And there is no reason why, in pursuing this quest, we should not join hands with all men of good will, even if they are not Christians. To sum up, we are sent into the world, like Jesus, to serve.'[12]

He is advocating that in order to deliver his political dimension, it is perfectly acceptable for Christians to join forces with unbelievers. But does John's Gospel teach the kind of incarnational model advocated by

Stott? The answer is a clear no! Stott is reinterpreting the text to support his own agenda. So how should we understand John 20.21?

Joel James and Brian Biedebach, two long-term missionaries to Africa, comment on Stott's hermeneutics:

> The Father's authoritative sending of Jesus into the world is a dominant theme in John's gospel. In light of this, no complicated explanation of John 20.21 need be sought: as the Father authoritatively sent the Son, and as the Son submissively obeyed, so Jesus now authoritatively sends His disciples. The issue is authority and obedience, not the content of the mission. Much of Jesus' mission—such as His substitutionary death—was irreproducible by man. Additionally, Stott's view of John 20.21 fails to give proper regard to the fact that, in the context, forgiveness of sin is the only thing mentioned, not social action (20.23).[13]

Andreas Kostenberger, Professor of New Testament and Biblical Theology at Southeastern Baptist Theological Seminary in Wake Forest, North Carolina, comments:

> The Fourth Gospel does not therefore appear to teach the kind of 'incarnational model' advocated by Stott and others. Not the way in which Jesus came into the world (i.e. the incarnation), but the nature of Jesus' relationship with his sender (i.e. one of obedience and utter dependence), is presented in the Fourth Gospel as the model for the disciples' mission.[14]

Stott is wrong to contend that the focus of Christ's ministry was on serving. The focus of his ministry was *not* to heal the sick and meet the needs of the poor. He was sent into the world to save his people from their sins. He was lifted up on the Cross of Calvary so believers could have eternal life (John 3.14-15). The main purpose of his ministry was to preach the gospel and call sinners to repentance and faith. At times his deeds of compassion were a distraction from preaching the gospel (Mark 1.40-45). And while the Lord performed many miracles of healing out of compassion, their main purpose was to demonstrate his divine authority, and to point to his identity as the long-awaited Messiah, the Son of God.

John wrote his Gospel so that his readers might 'believe that Jesus is the Christ, the Son of God; and that believing ye might have life through his name.'(John 20.31). This was the supreme purpose of John's Gospel.

Holistic Mission

There is no doubt that the 1974 International Congress on World Evangelization was a watershed event, for it was at this Congress that the evangelical mind was opened to the idea that the mission of the Church is indeed holistic, involving socio-political action. When Stott promoted the idea that evangelism and social action are a *partnership*, 'like two blades of a pair of scissors or two wings of a bird', he produced a paradigm shift in evangelical thinking about the mission of the Church. He found it 'exceedingly strange that any followers of Jesus Christ should ever have needed to ask whether social involvement was their concern'. He pointed out that the gospel preached during the Evangelical Revival on both sides of the Atlantic, 'inspired people to take up social causes in the name of Christ'. He contended that during the nineteenth century, 'not only Britain and America but also through the agency of missionaries in Africa and Asia, the gospel of Jesus Christ produced the *good fruit* of social reform' (my italics).[15] Stott inadvertently makes the crucially important point—the gospel of salvation preached by the evangelicals of the eighteenth and nineteenth centuries produced the *good fruit* of social reform. That is, good works are the inevitable *fruit* of the Christian life. But it is a serious mistake to go on and claim that social reform is an integral part of the evangelical mandate.

Stott's concept of holistic mission was written into article 5 of the *Lausanne Covenant*:

> Evangelism and socio-political involvement are both part of our
> Christian duty... The message of salvation implies also a message
> of judgement upon every form of alienation, oppression and
> discrimination ... the salvation we claim should be transforming
> us in the totality of our personal and social responsibilities.[16]

In his exposition of the *Lausanne Covenant*, Stott made socio-political action a Christian *duty*. He wrote:

It is our duty to be involved in socio-political action; that is both in social action (caring for society's casualties) and in political action (concerned for the structures of society itself).[17]

A paper entitled 'Holistic Mission', produced by the Lausanne movement in 2004, focuses on the needs of the poor and oppressed.

Holistic mission is the task of bringing the whole of life under the lordship of Jesus Christ… The mission of the church is, therefore, comprehensive in its means and in its impact… God has made an unbreakable link between faith in Himself and the outworking of that faith in seeing that justice is done to the poor and oppressed. Not surprisingly, therefore, the poor figure prominently in any discussion of holistic mission. The pursuit of justice for the poor is not the whole of holistic mission but it is a key component.[18]

Latin American theologian Rene Padilla, a prominent delegate at Lausanne, writes that the concept of holistic mission 'has become increasingly accepted among evangelicals, especially in the Two-thirds World, since the International Congress on World Evangelization, held in Lausanne, Switzerland, in 1974.'[19]

Dr Las Newman, Chairman of the Oxford Centre for Mission Studies in the UK, is deeply committed to the holistic gospel. He writes in the foreword to *Holistic Mission: God's Plan for God's People* (2010):

One of the most important developments in contemporary Christian missiology is the recovery of a theology of mission in the late twentieth century that integrates faith and life, word and deed, proclamation and presence. This holistic understanding of Christian mission is deeply rooted in the biblical theology of the Judeo-Christian faith… Because the Christian gospel of the kingdom of God is universally transformative, strong and holistic, it challenges the *status quo* everywhere it is proclaimed. In proclaiming the gospel our Lord in his earthly ministry, practiced and modelled a holistic approach in ministry.

Here we must notice Newman's confident assertion that Jesus Christ practised and modelled a holistic approach in ministry. This remarkable claim, which has no biblical warrant, is an article of faith for the holistic movement. We are asked to accept that the earthly ministry of Jesus was holistic, and therefore Stott's affirmation, 'we are sent into the world, like Jesus, to serve'.

Newman goes on: 'The church today is still challenged to authenticate the gospel in contexts where colonialism has left a legacy of structural poverty, economic underdevelopment, and disempowered and marginalized peoples. Thank God that an authentic biblical understanding of Christian mission as holistic and integrated is being restored, and that mission thinkers and practitioners now universally embrace holistic ministry as the truly transformative Gospel.'[20]

As we shall see in this book, the political agenda of the holistic movement is never far from the surface. The Church must learn to deal with the colonial legacy, which according to the holistic mindset is the cause of the structural poverty and economic underdevelopment of marginalised people.

We now consider a few examples of holistic ministry, in order to demonstrate how far it has departed from biblical truth. We need to understand that the terms 'holistic' mission and 'integral' mission are interchangeable. (South American theologians, like Rene Padilla and Simon Escobar, preferring the latter term.)

The Church of England

The Church of England, the church John Stott served his whole life, commissioned the report, *Holistic Mission: Social Action and the Church of England*, launched in 2013 at Lambeth Palace, with keynote remarks from the Archbishop of Canterbury, Lord Justin Welby. The launch set out the case for the Church's role as an enabler of holistic social action, claiming that the Church is the key to unlocking a revolution in both voluntary and statutory public service provision.

According to the Report, the mission of the Church 'should be understood as building up the life of the Kingdom on earth'. The Church's social mission 'is indivisible from its spiritual mission... The Church considers social action to be part of its mission and service, reflecting in particular the gospel and "God's call to the poor".' The Church of England has a grand vision for society; it seeks not just to ameliorate a damaged society, 'but to fundamentally reorder the systemic nature of contemporary injustice and so genuinely heal the world'.[21]

The Report reminds its readers that the former Archbishop of Canterbury, Dr Rowan Williams, 'welcomed the role of other religions, particularly Muslims and Sikhs, in the regeneration of the post-industrial English city. This holistic approach to Christian social action in urban communities can be seen across England.'[22]

Bright Hope International

Bright Hope International, a para-church Christian organisation, 'envisions a world where under-resourced, local, in-country churches transform their communities and bring Hope to the extreme poor'. The website explains: 'We have found building into an already existing unit like the church is more effective in life transformation and helping lift the extreme poor out of their situation than trying to establish something new. At Bright Hope we believe in the power of a holistic approach and have a three-tiered development model centered around: feeding programs, clean water initiatives, orphans and vulnerable children care, medical assistance, crisis and disaster response.' Bright Hope appeals to Christians for financial support. The vision is for community betterment through feeding programmes, clean water and medical care.

Micah Network Declaration on Integral Mission

Micah Network, a coalition of evangelical churches and agencies from around the world, convened a meeting in 2001 in Oxford, England, of leaders from a hundred Christian organisations from 50 countries involved with the poor, to consider the cause of the Kingdom of God among the poor. The outcome was the Micah Declaration on Integral Mission.

The Declaration recognised that thousands die in the poor countries of the world because of the evil alliance of injustice and apathy, and called the attention of the Church and the world to this daily outrage against human beings made in the image of the creator. 'Perhaps the most critical social task for the church in our generation is to offer a compelling alternative to the unjust imbalances in the world economic order and the values of its consumer culture. God is calling us to build global twin towers of justice and peace. We need to create a coalition of compassion.'[23]

The Micah Declaration offers this definition: 'Integral mission or holistic transformation is the proclamation and demonstration of the gospel. It is not simply that evangelism and social involvement are to be done alongside each other. Rather, in integral mission our proclamation has social consequences as we call people to love and repentance in all areas of life... Justice and justification by faith, worship and political action, the spiritual and the material, personal change and structural change belong together. As in the life of Jesus, being, doing and saying are at the heart of our integral task.'[24]

Integral mission means treating the poor and marginalised with respect. 'We welcome welfare activities as important in serving with the poor. Welfare activities, however, must be extended to include movement towards values transformation, the empowerment of communities and co-operation in wider issues of justice... We object to any use of the word "development" that implies some countries are civilised and developed while others are uncivilised and underdeveloped...'

The best way for the Church to address poverty is 'by working with the poor and other stakeholders like civil society, government and the private sector with mutual respect and a recognition of the distinctive role of each partner. We offer the Micah Network as one opportunity for collaboration for the sake of the poor and the gospel.'[25]

The Micah Declaration asserts that integral mission is the concern of every Christian. 'There is a need for integral discipleship involving the responsible and sustainable use of the resources of God's creation and the transformation of the moral, intellectual, economic, cultural and political dimensions of our lives... Wealthy Christians – both in the West and in the Two-Thirds World – must use their wealth in the service of others...'[26]

All Nations Christian College

All Nations Christian College, a missionary training institution in Hertfordshire, England, referring to the influence of the Micah Declaration, makes the point that great numbers of individuals and churches have adopted a holistic or integral approach to church life and ministry, working with the whole person and the whole community. 'At a time when integral mission has passed from the avant-garde to become almost conventional wisdom, there is more than ever the need to explore its implications, and to learn the achievements and the challenges of working in an integral way.'[27]

To help Christians gain a more complete understanding of integral mission, All Nations has a number of training options, both residential and online, including a Masters degree in Contemporary Mission Studies, and another in Development with Mission.

World Vision

World Vision is an international partnership of Christians whose mission is to follow Jesus Christ 'in working with the poor and oppressed to promote human transformation, seek justice and bear witness to the good news of the Kingdom of God'.[28]

World Vision pursues this mission through an integrated, holistic commitment to transformational development that is community-based and sustainable, focused especially on the needs of children, and through emergency relief that assists people afflicted by conflict or disaster. It develops 'partnerships with churches to contribute to spiritual and social transformation'.[29]

World Vision says it follows the example of Jesus, serving those who are suffering from poverty and injustice, regardless of colour, belief, or gender, as part of God's plan to redeem, reconcile, and restore the world.

The local church is seen 'as a primary agent of bringing peace, justice, and love to a broken world. The integrated "word" and "deed" dimensions of God's mandate, as evidenced through the church's integral, or transformational, mission are necessary to bringing reconciliation and restoration to God, others, and the environment.'

Tear Fund

Tear Fund believes integral mission is the Church living out its faith in Jesus in every aspect of life. 'At Tearfund, integral mission is how we operate. People need material things to survive, and we choose to work through church-based partners who help people access these things. But our partners won't stop there. Local churches know the needs of their communities, and have the potential to change lives

– bringing new perspectives, helping heal emotional scars, offering hope and togetherness. This is, in our experience, the most powerful and effective way to help people make lasting changes in their lives and escape poverty… And when the local church operates as part of the global church, its capacity and influence on behalf of poor people is a mighty force for change.'[30]

Holistic Mission on the Mission Field

In an essay on holistic mission, Brethren historian Dr Harold H. Rowdon writes, 'The concept is in fact nothing more – nor less than one which does full justice to every aspect of God's mission to the world… Holistic mission, then, is concerned with wholes—the whole of God's mission to the whole world, the whole of the church's God-given task, and the whole of human need… Let us not worry too much about the ugly term. Let us make sure it is being practised. And the last word must be given to a British missionary who is engaged in social work in Peru.'[31] She wrote:

> Sometimes my time is spent visiting hospitals, schools, lawyers and different organizations in an attempt to get help; sometimes I might sit with an anxious mother in a hospital waiting room and help her fill in forms; sometimes I might sit a child on my knee, wipe away his tears and give him a cuddle. Whatever I might do, concrete 'results' are rarely seen. *I've not seen anyone converted*, and my attempts to sort out people's problems are often thwarted. I do not feel that this is necessarily the most important factor. These children and their families need to know that someone is willing to take their part; that someone cares. After all, how else will they ever know that God cares? (my italics)

Impact of Holistic Mission on the Mission Field

Two men who have been missionaries in Africa for twenty years, draw attention to the impact holistic mission is having on the mission field. Joel James, Pastor of Grace Fellowship Ministry in Pretoria, and Brian Biedebach, Pastor of International Bible Fellowship Church in

Lilongwe, Malawi, have written an article, entitled, 'Regaining Our Focus: A Response to the Social Action Trend in Evangelical Missions', to draw attention to problems they have encountered on the mission field. They write: 'Today churches and missionaries are being told that to imitate the ministry of Jesus they must add social justice to their understanding of the church's mission. As pastors and missions committees embrace the idea that social action and gospel proclamation are "two wings of the same bird," the kind of work that they send their missionaries to do changes, and this has a negative effect on world missions.'[32]

They insist that as a consequence of holistic mission evangelical missions in Africa are changing for the worse. 'In the past, the bulk of the theologically conservative missionaries in Africa came to do church planting and leadership training. No longer. Today many of the new missionaries being sent are focused on social relief, with the church tacked on as a theological addendum. By all appearances there has been a mega-shift in evangelical missions away from church planting and leadership training and toward social justice or social action... As a result, the evangelical church in the West is commissioning and sending a generation of missionaries to Africa whose primary enthusiasm is for orphan care, distributing medicine, combating poverty, and other social action projects. For the most part, these new missionaries value the church, but in many cases they seem to view the church primarily as a platform from which to run and fund their relief projects.'[33]

According to the article, recent key voices in evangelical circles enthusiastically promoting social action in missions include John Stott, Tim Keller, and popular emergent authors.[34]

What has been the effect of all this in Africa? 'It's an oversimplification, but the result is the wrong missionaries doing the wrong things... Fewer and fewer of the kinds of missionaries who will make a long-term difference in Africa—Bible translators, church planters, and leadership trainers—are being sent.'[35]

The authors encourage preachers who are committed to proclamation-focused missions to speak out, 'offering the church something better than they're getting from the social justice bloggers and the popular missional authors. It won't be easy. Who wants to be (unfairly) branded as being against orphans or clean water? We don't. But the price of silence is high: the church is poised to lose a generation of missionaries to secondary work such as building schools and digging wells. And if history has anything to say about the matter, we might lose the gospel too...'[36]

The Ideology of Holistic Mission

The central idea of holistic mission is the belief that the great problems facing mankind are poverty and political oppression. Church leaders are persuaded that people are more open to the gospel when their physical needs have been ameliorated. Therefore the church needs to engage in social programmes. Initially, some tried to find a compromise by arguing that the mission of the Church is evangelism with social action added on, and some even conceded the evangelism should have priority. But with the passage of time, and much debate and many books and many conferences, the movement for the *primacy* of social action has gained ground. By the time of the Centenary World Mission Conference in Edinburgh 2010, the debate had been firmly decided in favour of social activism, and the mission of the Church was triumphantly declared to be holistic. This means the gospel message and the mission of the Church is not only about the salvation of souls, it *intrinsically* includes social transformation, not as an add-on but as an *essential* component at its very foundation, in practice taking precedence.

This new approach to mission is far removed from the traditional understanding of the Great Commission, which focused on preaching the gospel of Christ in order that precious souls (that is, individual people), by the grace of God, might be saved from their sins and receive the hope of eternal life through faith in Christ. What is more, the presentation of the holistic model is set out in intellectualised, complex jargon, far removed from the simplicity of the true gospel. Men have interposed their carnal wisdom between the sinner and the Saviour.

The Protestant Church of the recent past passionately believed that 'the purpose of nineteenth-century missions was evangelism; the goal was the conversion of the heathen. Both in scale and results it was the great century of Christian expansion.'[37] The missionary endeavours of the nineteenth century were greatly blessed by God, as the true gospel of Jesus Christ was proclaimed in many countries across the globe. New churches were planted in China, Africa, the Americas, the Pacific and Asia. The commitment of missionaries like Hudson Taylor, William Carey, Adoniram Judson, David Livingston and hundreds of other lesser known men and women, were a cause for rejoicing, as their labours for Christ and preaching of the gospel was blessed with much fruit.

How has this unbiblical perversion of the gospel of salvation come about? How was it possible that the World Missionary Conference of 2010 was a celebration of the holistic gospel? In this study we shall examine the events and ideas that led, in the second half of the twentieth century, to this significant change in the meaning of the Great Commission and the mission of the Church, a change that has effectively distorted the message of the gospel and changed the practice of missionary organisations worldwide. We shall uncover the real purpose of holistic mission (also known as integral mission) and reveal deep flaws in the concept; we shall also seek to understand the true nature of the Great Commission.

The True Mission of the Church

To gain a true understanding of the Church's mission we need to examine the ministry of the apostle Paul, whom our Lord appointed to be his 'chosen vessel' (Acts 9.15). On the Damascus road, the risen Christ said to Paul:

> I have appeared unto thee for this purpose, to make thee a minis-
> ter and a witness both of these things which thou hast seen, and
> of those things in the which I will appear unto thee; delivering
> thee from the people, and from the Gentiles, unto whom now
> I send thee, to open their eyes, and to turn them from darkness
> to light, and from the power of Satan unto God, that they may
> receive forgiveness of sins, and inheritance among them which
> are sanctified by faith that is in me (Acts 26.16-18).

Here we learn from Christ himself the *true* mission of the Church. The apostle Paul, God's chosen vessel, minister and witness, *is sent by Christ* to the Jews and Gentiles to open their *spiritual* eyes, and to turn them from *spiritual* darkness to the light of the gospel. So there is no doubt that Paul's mission is to witness to the *spiritual* needs of men and women, to open their *spiritually* blind eyes to the light of the gospel, to entreat them to repent of their sins and turn to God, that they may receive forgiveness. Paul, in obedience to the heavenly vision, preached the gospel of Christ to people in Damascus, Jerusalem, Judea and then to the Gentiles across the Roman Empire. His message was to repent and turn to God, and do works fit for repentance (Acts 26.20). Those who repent and are turned to God demonstrate the genuineness of their conversion by good works. It is clear that good works are the *fruit* of repentance, and not part of the Church's mission to the unbelieving world. Moreover, despite the oppressive Roman occupation, Paul did not agitate for socio-political transformation in Damascus, Jerusalem or Judea. His mission was to preach the gospel of Christ—the need for repentance and forgiveness, that sinners might turn to God.

If the holistic model was in the mind of Christ, then he would surely have made that plain to his chosen apostle when he was commissioned on the Damascus Road. Surely Christ would have commanded his chosen apostle to *unequivocally* write into the New Testament the dual salvation and socio-political mission of the Church to the world, so that it could be read by all succeeding generations of believers. The Roman Empire, notorious for its cruelty and oppression, was in great need of social trans-formation. But Christ's gospel was all about spiritual transformation.

The book of Acts provides a record of Paul's ministry as the *pattern* Christian missionary. As guided by the Holy Spirit, Paul preached Christ in numerous towns and cities across Asia Minor and then on to Macedonia, Athens, Corinth and Rome. In every town, Paul went into the synagogue to preach salvation through Christ. When there was no synagogue, Paul took every opportunity to preach the gospel of salva-tion, even in the open air. Paul said to the Romans, 'as much as in me is, I am ready to preach the gospel… for it is the power of God unto salvation to every one that believeth' (Romans 1.15-16).

He wrote to the Corinthian Church, 'For Christ sent me not to bap-tize, but to preach the gospel: not with wisdom of words, lest the cross of Christ should be made of none effect. For the preaching of the cross… is the power of God… it pleased God by the foolishness of preaching to save them that believe' (1 Corinthians 1.17-18, 21). In defending his apostleship, Paul wrote: 'For though I preach the gospel, I have nothing to glory of: for necessity is laid upon me; yea, woe is unto me, if I preach not the gospel!' (1 Corinthians 9.16). By examining Paul's ministry, recorded in Acts and his letters to the churches, we gain a clear understanding of the true mission of the Church. Paul was Christ's chosen vessel to preach the gospel to the Gentiles, to kings and to the children of Israel (Acts 9.15). Paul's missionary endeavours, struggles and sufferings form the definitive pattern for the Church of Christ for all time. Believers are instructed to follow his example (Philippians 3.17; 1 Corinthians 11.1).

Following his resurrection, the Lord Jesus opened the minds of the disciples that they might understand the Scriptures and then explained the Church's mission in the world. He said to the disciples, 'Thus it is written, and thus it behoved Christ to suffer, and to rise from the dead the third day: And that repentance and remission of sins should be preached in his name among all nations, beginning at Jerusalem' (Luke 24.46-47). And Matthew 28.18-20 provides a clear statement of the Great Commission, understood throughout Church history as the spiritual transformation of sinners.

The mission of the Church is to preach Christ among all nations. The gospel message is repentance and remission of sins. 'This is a faithful saying, and worthy of all acceptation, that Christ Jesus came into the world to save sinners' (1 Timothy 1.15). God commends his love toward us, in that, 'while we were yet sinners, Christ died for us. Much more then, being now justified by his blood, we shall be saved from wrath through him' (Romans 5.8-9).

So the holistic mission of the modern Church and the mission mandate given to the apostle Paul by the risen Christ, stand in direct opposition to one another. The first seeks socio-political transformation; the second offers salvation from sin and a personal relationship with God.

Apologia for this Book

The key aim of this book is to show that the old and discredited social gospel has reappeared in the guise of holistic mission, and is being embraced throughout the Christian Church worldwide—among many local churches, para-Christian organisations, Bible seminaries, missionary societies, missiologists and theologians. While the intention is to demonstrate that holistic mission is a heresy, this is not a negative book, as some might say. Today many people regard all attempts to expose error in the Church as being negative, or as attacking other Christians. We often hear the plea that Christians should only promote the positive aspects of their Faith and avoid all that appears to be negative or controversial. Exposing false teaching is regarded as being judgmental and unloving. But this is an unbiblical way of thinking, for Christ came into the world to declare the truth of God (John 18.37), and those who follow Jesus Christ are commanded to earnestly contend for the truth of the gospel (Jude 3). This means opposing every teaching that distorts the Gospel of Truth. Exposing error is not being unloving, but is an essential and expected part of growing in the knowledge and truth of God. The Lord Jesus warned his disciples: 'Beware of false prophets, which come to you in sheep's clothing, but inwardly they are ravening wolves... by their fruits ye shall know them. Not every one that saith unto me, Lord, Lord, shall enter into the kingdom of heaven; but he that doeth the will of my Father which is in heaven. Many will say to me in that day, Lord, Lord, have we not prophesied in thy name? and in thy name have cast out devils? and in thy name done many wonderful works? And then will I profess unto them, I never knew you: depart from me, ye that work iniquity' (Matthew 7.15, 20-23).

As Christians we are to test everything, and then to cling to that which is good and expose that which is false (1 Thessalonians 5.21). We need to understand that as God's people we are involved in a spiritual battle against the forces of darkness, whose purpose is to deceive the Church.

We now proceed to examine John Stott's change of mind about the meaning of the Great Commission. How was it possible for a highly regarded Christian leader, who had studied God's Word over several decades, who had written numerous books on Christian theology, and who had taught in theological seminaries across the world, to have been so wrong regarding the mission of the Church that he needed to change his mind? Chapter 2 examines this question in some detail.

(Endnotes)

1 John Stott, *Christian Mission in the Modern World*, IVP Books, 1975, p25
2 Ibid. p25
3 The *Lausanne Covenant*, paragraph 5, Christian Social Responsibility
4 John Stott, *Christian Mission in the Modern World*, pp25-26

5   David Hesselgrave, *Paradigms in Conflict*, Kregel publications, 2005, p145

6   Ibid. pp146-147

7   Hesselgrave cites Stott in *Christian Mission in the Modern World*, p30

8   Hesselgrave cites Stott in *Christian Mission in the Modern World*, p32

9   *Paradigms in Conflict*, pp148-149

10   *Christian Mission in the Modern World*, pp26-27

11   Ibid. p32

12   Ibid. p32

13   Joel James and Brian Biedebach, 'Regaining Our Focus: A Response to the Social Action Trend in Evangelical Missions', *The Master's Seminary Journal,* Spring 2014, p48

14   Andreas Kostenberger, *The Mission of Jesus and the Disciples According to the Fourth Gospel,* Eerdmans Publishing, 1998, p217.

15   John Stott*, Issues Facing Christians Tod*ay, Marshall Pickering, 1990, p6

16   The *Lausanne Covenant*, paragraph 5, https://www.lausanne.org/content/covenant/lausanne-covenant

17   The Lausanne Covenant: An Exposition and Commentary by John Stott, 1975, Lausanne Committee for World Evangelization, Occasional paper, C. The Doctrine of Salvation

18   Holistic Mission, Occasional Paper No. 33, produced by the Issue Group on this topic at the 2004 Forum for World Evangelization hosted by the Lausanne Committee for World Evangelization in Pattaya, Thailand, 2004, 'A New Vision, a New Heart, a Renewed Call, Volume 1', edited by David Claydon, introduction by Dewi Hughes, p9

19   Ibid. Rene Padilla, Holistic Mission, p11

20   *Holistic Mission: God's Plan for God's People*, edited by Brian Woolnough and Wonsuk Ma, 2010, foreword by Las G. Newman

21   *Holistic Mission: Social action and the Church of England*, July 2013, James Noyes and Phillip Blond, p9

22   Ibid. p15

23   Micah Declaration on Integral Mission, September 2001, http://www.micahnetwork.org/sites/default/files/doc/page/mn_integral_mission_declaration_en.pdf

24   Ibid.

25   Ibid.

26   Ibid.

27   All Nations website, http://www.allnations.ac.uk/downloadlibrary/SC%20UIM%20course%20flyer%20final.pdf

28   World Vision mission statement, http://www.wvi.org/vision-and-values-0

29   World Vision International, Vision and values, http://www.wvi.org/vision-and-values-0

30   Tear Fund website, http://www.tearfund.org/en/about_us/how_we_work/why_the_church/

31   Harold Rowdon, *Into All the World*, p32 and p40 http://biblicalstudies.org.uk/pdf/cbr/40_032.pdf

32   Joel James and Brian Biedebach 'Regaining our Focus: A Response to the Social Action Trend in Evangelical Missions', p29

33   Ibid. p29

34   Ibid. p31

35   Ibid. p49

36   Ibid. p50

37   The Re-forming Tradition: Presbyterians and Mainstream Protestantism, edited by Milton J. Coalter, John M. Mulder, Louis B. Weeks, p167

Chapter 2

John Stott Changes his Mind

When the man considered by many to have been the leading evangelical of our day changes his mind about the meaning of the Great Commission, the evangelical movement needs to sit up and take notice, for John Stott's ministry still has a large impact on the Church. His legacy will continue to shape evangelicalism through his many books and his seminal work in the Lausanne movement. And so we must ask: Was it possible that for centuries evangelicals had not really understood what Scripture actually teaches about the mission of the Church? Or was John Stott's change of mind a profound error that is distorting the mission of the Church? For some, to even raise such questions is unthinkable, for to them Stott embodies all that it best in biblical Christianity.

In an attempt to justify his change of mind, Stott sought to persuade us that the gospel of the evangelical movement has *always* been holistic. In his ground-breaking book, *Issues Facing Christians Today* (1984), he wrote that during the nineteenth century, 'not only in Britain and America but also through the agency of missionaries in Africa and Asia, the gospel of Jesus Christ produced the good fruit of social reform. But then something happened, especially among evangelical Christians.' At some point during the first 30 years of the twentieth century 'a major shift took place which the American historian Timothy Smith has termed "The Great Reversal", and which David Moberg, Professor of Sociology at Marquette University, investigates in his book with that title'.[1]

Referring to Moberg's sociological research, Stott explains 'the origins of the evangelical renunciation of social responsibility'. At the beginning of the twentieth century evangelicals were concerned about the social gospel that was being propagated by the American theologian Walter Rauschenbusch, and this concern 'hindered the development of an evangelical social programme',[2] Stott argues that when Rauschenbusch politicised the Kingdom of God, 'it is understandable (if regrettable) that, in reaction to him, evangelicals concentrated on evangelism and personal philanthropy, and steered clear of socio-political action'.[3] This change has been labelled the 'Great Reversal'.

To make the point that evangelicals who emphasise personal salvation tend to be selfish and uncaring, Stott quotes Moberg's social research: 'The general picture that emerges from the results presented… is that those who place a high value on salvation are *conservative*, anxious to maintain the status quo, and *unsympathetic or indifferent* to the plight of the black and the poor… Considered all together, the data suggest a portrait of the religious-minded as a person having a *self-centred preoccupation* with saving his own soul, an *other-worldly orientation*, coupled with an indifference toward or even a tacit endorsement of a social system that would *perpetuate social inequality* and *injustice*'[4] (my italics). In large agreement with Moberg's sociological analysis, Stott mentions situations 'in which the church has acquiesced in oppression and exploitation, and has taken no action against these evils, nor even protested against them'.[5]

From the above it seems that Stott does not regard personal salvation as of first importance. He accepts Moberg's unfounded assertion that conservative Christians, who place a high value on salvation from sin, are 'unsympathetic or indifferent to the plight of the black and the poor'. He asserts that the Church has acquiesced in oppression and exploitation. What is clear is that Stott's promotion of the so-called 'Great Reversal' is deeply political. Equally clear is Stott's dislike of conservative Christians who do not follow his socio-political agenda. In *Essentials: A Liberal-Evangelical Dialogue* (1988), Stott provides a list of 'eight tendencies of the mind-set styled fundamentalism' from which he wishes to dissociate himself, accusing fundamentalists of 'some extreme right-wing political concerns'.[6]

Stott concludes that not all evangelicals mislaid their social conscience at the beginning of the twentieth century. 'Some soldiered on, deeply involved in social as well as evangelistic ministries, and thus retained this indispensable outworking of the gospel, without which evangelicalism loses part of its authenticity. *But most turned away.* Then during the 1960s, the decade of protest, when young people were rebelling against the materialism, superficiality and hypocrisy of the adult world they had inherited, the evangelical mainstream recovered its morale, and the process of "Reversing the Great Reversal" (as Moberg entitles his final chapter) got under way'[7] (my italics).

The Great Reversal

The sociological theory of the Great Reversal is an attempt to explain and defend what would become known as the holistic mission movement. The argument for the Great Reversal is developed by sociologist Moberg in his book, *The Great Reversal: Evangelism Versus Social Concern* (1972). The book attempts to associate the ideas of the modern holistic movement with the evangelicals of the eighteenth and nineteenth centuries. It discusses why the evangelical Church, which, according to Moberg, had been the leader in social reforms prior to the twentieth century, discontinued its involvement in social action early in the twentieth century.

In his analysis Moberg mentions two opposing camps—the evangelicals and the social reformers. 'The evangelistic camp holds that the Christian has but one task – the winning of souls to Christ. The only important goal in life is to be a "fisher of men"… Trophies for Christ are sought in somewhat the same way a big-game hunter in Africa stalks his exotic prey.'[8] It is not difficult to detect Moberg's dislike of evangelicals who focus on winning souls to Christ, for in his eyes they behave like cruel big-game hunters! But Moberg has presented a caricature of evangelicals. In the other camp are social reformers, such as Walter Rauschenbusch, who believed that 'Christians as citizens and as children of God should step into the political and social arena to cope with problems of injustice and suffering.'[9]

Moberg recognises problems with both positions for neither, in his view, are fully biblical. The theme developed by *The Great Reversal* is that there is a more excellent way. 'There was a time when evangelicals had a balanced position that gave proper attention to both evangelism and social concern, but a great reversal early in this century led to a lopsided emphasis upon evangelism and omission of most aspects of social involvement. Since that time their shortcomings in regard to the fulfilment of Christian social responsibility have been very apparent. Sociological analysis of evangelism can help to shed light on this complex subject.'[10] Moberg's more excellent way is a holistic balance between evangelism and social concern. The so-called Great Reversal in the early part of the twentieth century is a *sociological* interpretation of the battle between the modernists and traditional Christianity—in reality, a spiritual battle for the very truth of the gospel, which we deal with in chapter 7.

According to Moberg, 'the false dichotomy between evangelism, which stresses personal salvation, and social concern, which emphasises the regeneration of society, has hampered the work and witness of evangelicals and other Protestants'.[11] He does not appear to understand that the true gospel, which stresses personal salvation, regenerates the heart of man. He does not understand that society is improved through the good deeds of born-again Christians who are zealous for good works, which are the inevitable *fruit* of the true gospel (Titus 2.14).

Moberg claims that when a church engages in social action community leaders become aware of its existence. 'Social concern thus promotes evangelism.'[12] He tells of his excitement when he and his wife visited the Church of the Saviour in Washington DC, January 1971. Their visit coincided with a sermon by its minister, Gordon Crosby, 'which summarized progress toward significant social reforms in numerous areas of the city's welfare programs and political life that had resulted from the diligent and persistent but quiet work of the mission group of the congregation. A sense that I was hearing a contemporary report of a new chapter of the Acts of the Apostles overwhelmed me as I listened.'[13]

Some examples of evangelistic efforts combined with social involvement are recorded in Moberg's book. He relates 'the inspiring story of the establishment of *Freedom Now* by the Rev Fred A. Alexander to awaken white fundamentalists to their sinful racism and to stimulate corrective Christian action; its subsequent development into the highly significant magazine, *The Other Side*, which shares Christian perspectives, action, and information about the forgotten Americans who are hungry, defeated, miserable, discriminated against, and ignored.'[14]

It is difficult to avoid the obvious conclusion that *The Great Reversal* is a polemic with a clear political agenda. Yet John Stott, in *Issues Facing Christians Today*, fully accepts Moberg's sociological analysis of the Great Reversal. He writes:

'One of the most notable features of the world-wide evangelical movement during the last ten to fifteen years has been the recovery of our temporarily mislaid social conscience. For approximately fifty years (c 1920-1970) evangelicals were preoccupied with the task of defending the historical biblical faith against the attacks of liberalism, and reacting against its "social gospel". But we are convinced that God has given us social as well as evangelistic responsibilities in his world. Yet the half-century of neglect has put us far behind in this area. We have a long way to catch up.'[15]

However, Rev Melvin Tinker, an Anglican vicar and author, has a different perspective on the so-called Great Reversal. He writes: 'A different perspective on these developments asks whether the liberalism which Evangelicals were busy defending themselves against in the 1930s has in fact entered into the mainstream of the evangelical movement by the back door. This verdict of history might be termed "The Great Betrayal".'[16] Tinker is correct in identifying the liberalism that lies behind the proponents of the Great Reversal. And Tinker is not alone in his criticism of those who promote holistic mission. Arthur Johnston of Trinity Evangelical Divinity School, Deerfield, Illinois, expressed the concern that evangelicals, far from rediscovering their heritage, are in danger of losing it.[17]

To place the Great Reversal in context we need to recognise that the social reforms of the nineteenth century took place in the wake of the revivals of the eighteenth century. We must ask the crucial question. Did the evangelicals of the Great Awakening follow a holistic approach to the mission of the Church as Stott wants us to believe?

The Evangelical Revival

The discerning historian understands the profound influence of the evangelical revival associated with the preaching of George Whitefield and John Wesley on the social, moral and religious condition of the country. The reawakening of evangelical Christianity in England in the second half of the eighteenth century was an event that was to have national and international repercussions. According to J.C. Ryle in *Christian Leaders of the 18th Century*: 'The men who wrought deliverance for us, a hundred years ago, were a few individuals, most of them clergymen of the Established Church, whose heart God touched about the same time in various parts of the country... They were simply men whom God stirred up and brought out to do his work, without previous concert, scheme or plan... The movement of these gallant evangelists shook England from one end to the other ... They held, with St Paul, that a minister's first work is "to preach the gospel".' A true Christian must always be known by his fruits, and these fruits must be plainly manifest and unmistakable in all the relations of life. 'They never shrunk from declaring, in plainest terms, the certainty of God's judgment and of wrath to come, if men persisted in impenitence and unbelief; and yet they never ceased to magnify the riches of God's kindness and compassion, and to entreat all sinners to repent and turn to God before it was too late... These were the doctrines by which they turned England upside down, made ploughmen and colliers weep till their dirty faces were seamed with tears, arrested the attention of peers and philosophers, stormed the strongholds of Satan, plucked thousands like brands from the burning, and altered the character of the age.'[18]

George Whitefield was an extremely gifted preacher – one of the greatest ever, especially in the open air. His powerful and eloquent presentation of the full gospel of Christ, however, caused offence to the establishment, and church leaders soon openly denounced him. Unperturbed, he turned to preaching in the open air. In this way he reached thousands who would never have dreamt of attending a place of worship. From 1739 to his death in 1770, Whitefield preached the gospel in virtually every town and city throughout England, Scotland and Wales. 'When churches were opened to him he gladly preached in churches; when only chapels could be obtained, he cheerfully preached in chapels. When churches and chapels alike were closed, or were too small to contain his hearers, he was ready and willing to preach in the open air. For thirty-one years he laboured in this way, always proclaiming the same glorious gospel, and always, as far as man's eye can judge, with immense effect.'[19] Ryle describes the effectiveness of

Whitefield's ministry: 'He was the first to see that Christ's ministers must do the work of fishermen. They must not wait for souls to come to them, but must go after souls, and "compel them to come in". He did not sit tamely by his fireside, like a cat on a rainy day, mourning over the wickedness of the land. He went forth to beard the devil in his high places. He attacked sin and wickedness face to face, and gave them no peace. He dived into holes and corners after sinners. He hunted out ignorance and vice wherever they could be found.'[20]

The ministry of John Wesley the preacher and Charles Wesley the hymn writer also had a massive impact on the spiritual and moral awakening of England. J.W. Bready in *England, Before and After Wesley* (1939), explains how the conversion of John Wesley, the one-time don of Oxford, which 'strangely warmed' his heart toward God, produced 'a succession of results destined finally to change the whole trend of social history throughout the British Empire and the English-speaking world. Nor was the impact of this prophet, who claimed "the world for his parish," confined even within those spacious limits. Millions, of many colours, climes and tongues, inhabiting the four corners of the earth, have lived richer, happier, nobler and more serviceable lives because, in 1738, fire from off the altars of God purged and illumined the soul of a downcast and disillusioned English priest.'[21] J.W. Bready comments on John Wesley's ministry:

> As a prophet of God and an ordained ambassador of Christ, *he did not conceive it his task to formulate economic, political and social theories*; nor did he judge himself competent so to do. His calling he believed was far more sacred, and more thoroughgoing: it was to lead men into contact with spiritual reality, to enable them to possess their souls and enter the realms of abundant life. For if once men, in sufficient numbers, were endowed with an illumined conscience and spiritual insight they, collectively as well as individually, would become possessors of the "wisdom that passeth knowledge"; and *in that wisdom social problems gradually would be solved*[22] (my italics).

Dr Donald Drew, a professor of history who was on Francis Schaeffer's Swiss L'Abri staff for nearly six years, summarised Bready's book in an unpublished lecture. Drew commented: 'Wesley's central understanding of Christianity was individual redemption leading to social regeneration. He believed that the main purpose of the Bible is to show sinners their way back to God by the atoning sacrifice of Christ. This and this only he preached. But he understood also that *social changes are an inevitable by-product* and a useful piece of evidence of conversion. Therefore, because of the preaching, the high moral principles enshrined in Scripture slowly began to take root in people's minds. Wesley knew that God's Word calls for *the salvation of individual souls* but also gives us firm ordinances for national existence and a common social life. Under God, this was his goal, and he never lost sight of it'[23] (my italics).

Wesley saw his priority as preaching the gospel of salvation from sin. He understood that the Christian life entailed doing good works, loving one's neighbour, being a hard-working honest citizen. It was the spiritual awakening that flowed from the gospel preaching of John Wesley and George Whitfield – preaching that emphasised sin and called for repentance and faith in Christ alone – which provided the moral climate and spiritual impetus for social reforms. In other words, social reform followed the preaching of the gospel. The men and women who came to Christ in their hundreds of thousands, were eager for good works. Henry Carter, author of *The Methodist Heritage* (1951), comments: 'To Wesley a scheme of reconstructing society which ignored the redemption of the individual was unthinkable.'[24]

The Cambridge Social History of Britain describes how evangelical Christianity has left its mark not only in Britain but throughout the Protestant world. In the Anglican Church the early evangelicals were not much concerned with ritual and sacraments or with church government, for they believed that no one should be allowed to intervene between God and man. 'Doctrines mattered more – the Bible as the Word of God, original sin, salvation by faith, the atoning sacrifice of Christ, God's forgiveness – even if they were neither new nor theologically sophisticated. But it was experience, and above all the experience of conversion – the "big change" – that was at the heart of evangelicalism: evangelicals were born-again Christians. They were also intensely moralistic. Describing themselves as "serious" they saw life as a perpetual battle between right and wrong, in which every action, no matter how small, was to be subjected to moral scrutiny. The result was a religion not only of prayer and Bible reading but of active good works – not because good works were of the slightest help to anyone seeking salvation, but because God required them, because they might be taken as evidence of divine favour, and because they might help bring others to God. Evangelicals consequently were tireless do-gooders, organising and campaigning for a bewildering array of moral, philanthropic and missionary causes. The aims of the evangelicals could hardly have been more ambitious: to convert Britain, to roll back the Catholic Church and ultimately to carry their version of Christianity to every nation on earth…. The evangelicals called for self-discipline, hard work and moral rectitude; their obsession with the use of time, their fetish of early rising and their strict accountability to God for every waking moment; their condemnation of idleness and frivolity: all these found a positive response in the middle-classes…'[25]

The evangelicals introduced to Britain a 'new moral economy' of sobriety, self-control, sexual restraint and respectability, which challenged both the hedonism of the aristocracy and the egalitarianism and violence of the French Revolution. In the 1790s, when evangelicals (dissenting as well as Anglican) launched the modern missionary movement, they expected nothing less than the rapid and imminent conversion of the entire world.[26] The Victorian age was self-consciously religious. Britain's greatness, Victorians believed – its prosperity, social stability, political liberties, and Empire – was rooted in Christian (i.e. Protestant) faith.[27]

In *Victorian People and Ideas* (1973), Richard Altick argues that 'Evangelicalism is chiefly important in the history of English culture for the moral tone it lent society down to the last quarter of the century.'[28] The evangelical ethos was diffused through most of the nation, and brought a morality that could be summed up in the single word 'respectability'. The practical outworking of the evangelicals' faith was to influence public morality. They believed that public morality depended upon private virtue. In their zeal to save the souls of the lost, 'they sought to impose their standards of right living (of whose absolute authority, residing in divine inspiration, they had no doubt) upon society as a whole'.[29]

A feature of the evangelicals was a love of reading that did much to widen the reading public. According to Richard Altick, 'Theirs was a veritable religion of print, resting as it did upon the Bible as the inerrant word of God. Daily communication with the Bible was necessary for salvation, for without its inspiration one could not achieve the faith requisite for divine grace. The ability to read therefore was highly prized, and the Evangelicals nurtured it in their educational activities. The large market they formed for improving literature encouraged the development of the cheap production and distribution techniques that revolutionised the Victorian book trade.'[30] The evangelical witness had a profound influence on the prose of the day, which was replete with biblical language and stories. 'From earliest childhood, consequently, on all levels of society, both at home and at school, the Victorians were accustomed to biblical language and biblical stories to an extent almost inconceivable today.'[31]

It was in the middle classes that the Victorian religious boom had the biggest impact. A religious census of 1851 showed that half of the population attended church on the Sunday of the census. Over half of the children aged between five and fifteen attended Sunday school or were enrolled with a Sunday school. And Sunday school was a significant factor in developing the social and moral ethos of Victorian society. Children were taught respect for authority, to obey their parents and the difference between right and wrong.

In the year 1859 a religious revival began in the United Kingdom, affecting every county in Ulster, Scotland, Wales and England, adding over a million new converts to the evangelical churches. The revival was associated with a great social uplift, and gave an effective impulse to home and foreign missionary activity.[32] Edwin Orr, writing in *The Second Evangelical Awakening in Britain*, concludes 'that the fifty years following 1859 constituted a distinct and definite period of the expansion of the Christian Church, in fact, a Second Evangelical Awakening comparable to its noted predecessor'.[33] While the preaching of Wesley and Whitefield moved a vast number of human beings, the second Evangelical Awakening moved an even greater number. 'Evangelistically, the Awakening of 1859 revived the older agencies raised up by the evangelical revival of the previous century. It also created new organisations of a permanent character, and increased the efforts of all Christians to fulfil the Great Commission to preach the gospel to every creature, at home and abroad... Socially, the awakening gave birth to a litter of active religious and philanthropic societies, which accomplished much in human uplift, the welfare of children, the reclamation of prostituted women, of alcoholics, of criminals, and the development of social virtues.'[34]

The Great Betrayal

John Stott's attempt to equate the evangelical Christianity of the two great awakenings in the eighteenth and nineteenth centuries with the holistic movement of today is not only a complete failure, but a *betrayal* of the legacy of evangelical Christianity. The fact that he resorts to the sociological research of Moberg to defend his change of mind about the Great Commission tells us much about his misguided ministry. The Great Reversal is an attempt to cover over the way the true gospel is surreptitiously being replaced by the social gospel of the holistic movement.

Traditional evangelicals, past and present, believed that man's greatest need is salvation from sin, not social improvement. A sinner, dead in his trespasses and sins, needs to be turned to Christ in genuine repentance that leads to salvation. By God's grace, a sinner is saved through faith in Christ and born again of God's Spirit. New birth in Christ radically changes a man's heart and fits him for good works. Social improvement is the *inevitable fruit* of the true gospel, not part of the evangelical mandate. We must conclude that those who promote the Great Reversal are, in fact, betraying the true evangelicals of the eighteenth and nineteenth centuries by implying that their gospel of salvation is similar to the social gospel of the holistic movement. Nothing, of course, could be further from the truth.

At the root of all false teachings is a flawed use of Scripture. When Stott changed his mind about the Great Commission, and experienced his own 'great reversal', it was because of a flawed interpretation of the John 20.21, which he used to develop an 'incarnational model' of mission (see previous chapter). The strategy of the enemy of souls has always been to cast doubt on the interpretation of God's Word. 'Did God really say…?' We therefore need to continue our study of the holistic movement by examining the so-called 'higher criticism' of God's Word as it impacted the Church in the second half of the nineteenth century.

(Endnotes)

1 John Stott, *Issues Facing Christians Today*, Hodder & Stoughton, 1984, p6

2 Ibid. p6

3 Ibid. pp7-8

4 John Stott, quoting David Moberg in *Issues Facing Christians Today*, p8

5 *Issues Facing Christians Today*, p8

6 *Essentials: A Liberal Evangelical Dialogue*, David Edwards and John Stott, Intervarsity Press, 1988, p91

7 *Issues Facing Christians Today*, p9

8 David O. Moberg, *The Great Reversal – Evangelism versus Social Concern*, British edition 1973, p20

9 Ibid. p23

10 Ibid. pp25-26

11 Ibid. p150

12 Ibid. p159

13 Ibid. p171

14 Ibid. p172

15 *Issues Facing Christians Today*, preface to first edition, pxi

16 'Reversal or Betrayal? Evangelicals and Socio-political Involvement in the Twentieth Century', *Churchman* 113/3 1999, Melvin Tinker

17 Arthur P. Johnston, *World Evangelism and the Word of God* (Bethany Fellowship 1974) and *The Battle for World Evangelism* (Wheaton Illinois: Tyndale House 1978)

18 J.C. Ryle, *Christian Leaders of the 18th Century*, Banner of Truth, 1990, pp 22, 23, 28

19 Ibid. p40

20 Ibid. p48

21 J. Wesley Bready, author of *England: Before and After Wesley*, Hodder & Stoughton, 1939. http://seedbed.com/feed/england-before-and-after-wesley/

22 J. Wesley Bready, *England Before and After Wesley*, Hodder & Stoughton, 1939, p 257

23 Dr Donald Drew in an unpublished article summarises the volume by J.W. Bready titled, "England Before and After Wesley", published in 1939, cited from the Disciple Nations Alliance

24 Cited in J. Wesley Bready *England Before and After Wesley* (Hodder & Stoughton 1939) p203

25 *The Cambridge Social History of Britain 1750-1950*, edited by F.M.L. Thompson, Cambridge University Press, 1990, pp321-22

26 Ibid. p326

27 Ibid. p328

28 Richard D. Altick, *Victorian People and Ideas*, J.M. Dent & Sons, London, 1973, p167-68

29 Ibid. p181

30 Ibid. p191
31 Ibid. p193
32 J. Edwin Orr, *The Second Evangelical Awakening in Britain*, Marshall, Morgan & Scott, London, 1953, p5
33 Ibid. p262
34 Ibid. p264

Chapter 3

Higher Criticism of the Bible

In our study of holistic mission we need to recognise that the true antecedent to the holistic movement is the social gospel of Walter Rauschenbusch (discussed in chapter 5), and not nineteenth-century evangelicals, as claimed by John Stott. And behind Rauschenbusch's social gospel was a flawed view of Scripture that came from the so-called 'higher criticism' of the Bible that had developed what it called a new 'scientific' way of interpreting the Scriptures. The edifice of higher criticism was built on ideas of rationalism, which held that truth is determined by reason, not by revelation.

Higher criticism is defined in the Concise Oxford Dictionary of the Christian Church (2006):

> The critical study of the literary methods and sources used
> by the authors of… biblical books, in distinction from textual
> (lower) criticism, which is concerned solely with recovering
> the text as it left its author's hands.

Behind this seemingly innocuous definition lies a world of unbelief, and a subtle attack on the integrity and reliability of the Bible.

The phrase 'higher criticism' became popular in Europe from the mid-eighteenth century to the early twentieth century. It originally referred to the work of German biblical scholars of the Tübingen School (a German theological seminary notorious for rationalistic scepticism), such as David Friedrich Strauss (1808–1874) and Ludwig Feuerbach (1804–1872). The scholars of higher criticism built on the tradition of enlightenment thinkers such as John Locke, David Hume and Immanuel Kant.[1] David Strauss set the tone for the higher criticism in his epoch-making *Life of Jesus,* published in 1835. He boldly asserted that the supernatural elements of gospel history were unhistorical myth, that the miracles described in the Bible were not historical truth. The impact of this book was monumental; so much so that the phrase 'Tübingen School' became virtually synonymous with unbelief.

The higher criticism was to have a massive influence on the way the Church, and especially church leaders, regarded the Bible. It was also to form the bedrock of modernist liberal theology. The ideas of higher criticism developed in an era dominated by evolutionary thought, and were profoundly influenced by the philosophy of the Enlightenment (an eighteenth-century intellectual movement which elevated human reason to the place of the final arbiter of truth). Evolutionary thinking was applied by Charles Darwin to biology and by Karl Marx to economics. In theology, the 'scientific' study of the Scriptures produced not God's thoughts about man but man's thoughts about God. The result was not God's revealed religion but an invented, man-made liberal version of the Christian Faith.[2]

Some in the Christian world responded to the rise of rationalism by attempting to reconcile faith and human reason. They supported the notion that the Bible should be read with an open mind and a critical attitude. The result of these unfamiliar new ways of thinking was the development of a *liberal theology* in Germany, which sought to diminish belief in the supernatural while at the same time elevating the value of rational thinking.[3]

Theological Liberalism

In common parlance the word 'liberal' means open-minded, tolerant of other opinions. In theology it means something akin to this, but the open-mindedness and tolerance are applied to biblical doctrine and historic Christian beliefs. The term 'conservative' represents the opposite tendency in theology—that is, adherence to biblical doctrine and historic Christian beliefs. The characteristics of theological liberalism include the following: 1) A desire to adapt doctrine to perceived modern views of what is reasonable and acceptable; 2) Scepticism regarding the miraculous elements of the Faith; 3) An acceptance of evolutionary thought as normative; 4) A rejection of an inerrant and infallible Bible—it may contain God's Word, but it is not the Word of God and so can be treated like any other book; 5) An emphasis on earthly social improvement, rather than spiritual salvation; 6) A denial of the Fall, original sin, and the penal substitutionary doctrine of the atonement; 7) An over-emphasis on God's love that avoids God's holiness; 8) An optimistic view of human nature that avoids reference to hell and eternal punishment.

Modernism and Liberalism

In the confusion of a rapidly changing world in the second half of the nineteenth century, liberal-minded churchgoers argued that the Christian religion needed to adapt to modern ideas in order to survive. Darwin's new theory of evolution, for example, appeared to be challenging the most basic doctrines of the Faith. Free-thought philosophers were openly challenging the veracity of Scripture. In response to these ideas many started to believe that adaptation was the surest way to make Christianity acceptable to a modern world.

As the ideas of modernism arose in Western society in the second half of the nineteenth and early twentieth centuries, some liberal theologians developed techniques of criticism that profoundly challenged the authority and accuracy of the Bible. Ernestine van der Wall, Professor of the History of Christianity at Leiden University in the Netherlands, writes: 'All in all the new scientific approach to the Bible caused men and women to ask themselves whether the Bible was merely a collection of myths, legends, and folklore, whether there was a kernel of history in it – and if so, what that kernel contained.'[4]

In the 1880s George Harris, Professor of Systematic Divinity at Andover Theological Seminary, the oldest graduate school of theology in the United States, claimed that Protestants were wrong to insist on the infallibility and inerrancy of the Bible, for to do so violated the spirit of the Reformation. Professor Harris was so deeply committed to the ideas of higher criticism that he wrote: 'It would be difficult to find an intelligent person who holds to the inerrancy of all parts of the Bible, or who is disturbed by the modifications and readjustments of criticism. Indeed, it is great relief to know that some statements are not true.'[5]

A central pillar of modernism was the belief that human reason, armed with the scientific method, is the only reliable means of attaining knowledge about life and the universe. Modernists asserted that reason, not the Bible, is the final authority in questions of life and faith. Liberal

Christians, influenced by the ideas of modernism, tried to reconcile historical Christianity with the findings of modern science and philosophy. A feature of liberal Christianity was a low view of the Bible—liberals held that the Bible, while it contains God's word, is not without error, and so it must be read just like any other book; its historical context and authorship must be interpreted through critical analysis. The early chapters of Genesis are reduced to poetry or myth, and while there is a message, these chapters must not be taken literally. This free and easy interpretation of Genesis makes room for the flawed theology of theistic evolution, which is a hallmark of liberal Christianity. Theistic evolutionists of our day are the grandchildren of the higher criticism. Most liberals do not believe that humanity inherited original sin from Adam and Eve or that Satan actually exists. It follows that mankind is not seen as totally depraved, and human beings are viewed as inherently good-natured.

Understanding Higher Criticism

By the second half of the nineteenth century the ideas of higher criticism had gained a strong foothold in the USA. In his essay, 'The Fundamentals, Higher Criticism and Archaeology', Dr Mark Elliott makes the point that modernist views on higher criticism were not confined to a few elite universities. 'Support for the historical and critical study of the Scriptures would not be the sole preserve of scholars; eventually it spread into the churches. Based upon a later survey, Walter F. Peterson believed that by 1910 approximately 25% of Protestant ministers were supportive of higher criticism… For years, traditional religious principles had been losing ground to liberalism. Higher criticism and its general findings were studied at most major universities and seminaries. Liberal Protestants adopted its basic hypotheses. Many traditionalists were persuaded that they must attempt something dramatic to reaffirm Christian truth and counter the seduction of biblical criticism and other modernist tendencies.'[6]

The Fundamentals – a Testimony to the Truth

Concerned about the inroads of modernist thought and the ideas of higher criticism, a group of conservative Christians saw the need to defend orthodox Christian doctrines. The outcome was *The Fundamentals – a testimony to the truth*, a book that contained around 90 essays defending the Christian Faith, published by the Bible Institute of Los Angeles between 1910 and 1915. Two Christian laymen funded and distributed the book across America and beyond free of charge. Sixty-four different authors from mainline Protestant denominations wrote essays affirming conservative Protestant beliefs, especially those of the Reformed tradition. These essays are widely considered to be the foundation of a modern and resurgent orthodox Christianity, which later became known as Christian fundamentalism. In the foreword, the authors explain their purpose:

> This book is the first of a series which will be published and sent to every pastor, evangelist, missionary, theological professor, theological student, Sunday school superintendent in the English speaking world… Two intelligent, consecrated Christian laymen bear the expense, because they believe that the time has come when a new statement of the fundamentals of Christianity should be made. Their earnest desire is that you will carefully read it and pass its truth on to others.

An important essay, written by the Canadian Canon Dyson Hague, Rector of the Memorial Church, London, Ontario dealt with the history of higher criticism. What follows is a summary of this essay, that starts by explaining the difference between lower and higher criticism. 'The Lower Criticism was employed to designate the study of the text of the Scripture, and included the investigation of the manuscripts, and the different readings in the various versions… The Higher Criticism, on the contrary, was employed to designate the study of the historic origins, the dates, and authorship of the various books of the Bible… But the work of the Higher Critic has not always been pursued in a reverent spirit, nor in the spirit of scientific and Christian scholarship. In the first place, the critics who were the leaders, the men who have given name and force to the whole movement, have been men who have based their theories largely upon their own subjective conclusions.'[7]

Dyson Hague argues that biblical truth is not perceived by philosophical knowledge, but by spiritual insight. 'Any thoughtful man must honestly admit that the Bible is to be treated as unique in literature, and, therefore, that the ordinary rules of critical interpretation must fail to interpret it aright. Some of the most powerful exponents of the modern Higher Critical theories have been Germans, and it is notorious to what length the German fancy can go in the direction of the subjective and of the conjectural. For hypothesis-weaving and speculation, the German theological professor is unsurpassed.'[8]

The dominant men of the movement were men with a strong bias against the supernatural. 'Some of the men who have been most distinguished as the leaders of the Higher Critical movement in Germany and Holland have been men who have no faith in the God of the Bible, and no faith in either the necessity or the possibility of a personal supernatural revelation. The men who have been the voices of the movement, of whom the great majority, less widely known and less influential, have been mere echoes; the men who manufactured the articles the others distributed, have been notoriously opposed to the miraculous.'[9]

German theologian Johann Eichhorn (1753-1827), eminent Oriental Professor at Gottingen, published his work on the Old Testament in 1780. He did not find any religious ideas that were of much importance in the Old Testament. 'Eichhorn's formative influence has been incalculably great. It is through him that the name Higher Criticism has become identified with the movement.' Professor Abraham Kuenen (1828-1891) of Leyden in Holland was one of the most advanced exponents of the rationalistic school. Also extremely important was Julius Wellhausen (1844-1918), 'who at one time was a theological professor in Germany, who published in 1878 the first volume of his history of Israel, and won by his scholarship the attention if not the allegiance of a number of leading theologians'.[10] Wellhausen is particularly notable as the leading proponent of the 'documentary hypothesis' of the Pentateuch. He developed the theory that the first five books of Moses are a composite production of a succession of writers and editors over several centuries. The ideas of the documentary hypothesis provide a rationalistic framework for the understanding of the authorship of the first books of the Bible and are still taught in many Bible seminaries.

The Views of the Continental Critics

Dyson Hague identified three characteristics of the Continental critics. First, they were men who denied the validity of miracles and the validity of any miraculous narrative. 'What Christians consider to be miraculous they considered legendary or mythical.'[11]

Second, they were men who denied the reality of prophecy and the validity of any prophetical statement. 'What Christians have been accustomed to consider prophetical, they called dexterous conjectures, coincidences, fiction, or imposture.'[11]

Third, they were men who denied the reality of revelation. 'They were avowed unbelievers of the supernatural. Their theories were excogitated on pure grounds of human reasoning. Their hypotheses were constructed on the assumption of the falsity of Scripture. As to the inspiration of the Bible, as to the Holy Scriptures from Genesis to Revelation being the Word of God, they had no such belief.'[11]

Rationalism

The formative forces of the higher critical movement were rationalistic forces, by which is meant the presupposition that human reason, not spiritual revelation, provides the only valid basis for religious belief, and that the supernatural is irrational. The men who were its chief authors were rationalists, 'who on account of purely philological criticism have acquired an appalling authority... men who had discarded belief in God and Jesus Christ whom He had sent. The Bible, in their view, was a mere human product. It was a stage in the literary evolution of a religious people.'[12]

'These then were their views and these were the views that have so dominated modern Christianity and permeated modern ministerial thought in the two great languages of the modern world... inasmuch as they refused to recognize the Bible as a direct revelation from God, they were free to form hypotheses *ad libitum*. And as they denied the supernatural, the animus that animated them in the construction of the hypotheses was the desire to construct a theory that would explain away the supernatural. Unbelief was the antecedent, not the consequent, of their criticism. Now there is nothing unkind in this. There is nothing that is uncharitable, or unfair. It is simply a statement of fact which modern authorities most freely admit.'[13]

Here we should note Hague's perceptive insight that the higher critics were not seeking for truth, but were motivated by a presupposition of unbelief. Their worldview was founded on an opposition to biblical Christianity which then found expression in their theories of higher criticism. Their boasted 'scientific' approach was nothing more than unbelief dressed up as 'rational thought'. It was inevitable, therefore, that their conclusions were false.

The British-American Critics

In dealing with British and American proponents of higher criticism, Dyson Hague mentioned five men he considered to be of first importance:

Dr Samuel Davidson (1806-1898), educated at the Royal College of Belfast, in 1842 was appointed to the chair of biblical criticism and literature at the Lancashire Independent College at Manchester. He was obliged to resign in 1857 because of his views on the Old Testament. His *Introduction to the Old Testament*, published in 1862, was largely based on the fallacies of the German rationalists.

Dr William Robertson Smith (1846-1894), a Scot who recast the German theories in an English form in his works on the Pentateuch, including *The Prophets of Israel* and their place in history, to the close of the 8th century B.C. (1882). He combined a professed regard for the Word of God with a critical radicalism that was strangely inconsistent.

George Adam Smith (1856-1942), who studied at the University of Tübingen in 1876 before becoming Professor of Old Testament subjects in the Scottish Free Church College. He was a man of great insight, who in his works on Isaiah and the twelve minor prophets adopted some of the most radical German theories, and in a later work, *Modern Criticism and the Teaching of the Old Testament* (1901), went still farther in the rationalistic direction.[14]

Dr S.R. Driver (1846-1914), the Regius Professor of Hebrew at Oxford, who in his *Introduction to the Literature of the Old Testament* (1891) and his *Book of Genesis* (1909), elaborated with great detail the theories and views of the Continental School. 'Driver's work is able, very able, but it lacks originality and English independence. The hand is the hand of Driver, but the voice is the voice of Kuenen or Wellhausen.'[14]

Dr Charles A. Briggs (1841-1913), for some time Professor of Biblical Theology in the Union Theological Seminary of New York, who was an earnest advocate of the German theories. He was a pro-lific author—important books included, *Biblical Study: Its Principles, Methods and History* (1883); *Whither? A Theological Question for the Times* (1889); *The Bible, the Church and the Reason* (1892) and *Higher Criticism of the Hexateuch* (1893).[15] He is discussed in greater detail in the next chapter.

The School of Compromise

The British-American higher critics represent a school of compromise. Dyson Hague writes: 'On the one hand they practically accept the premises of the Continental school with regard to the antiquity, authorship, authenticity, and origins of the Old Testament books. On the other hand, they refuse to go with the German rationalists in altogether denying their inspiration. They still claim to accept the Scriptures as containing a Revelation from God.'[16]

In their mind, the Bible was not the Word of God in the old orthodox sense of that term. 'It is not the Word of God in the sense that all of it is given by the inspiration of God. It simply contains the Word of God. In many of its parts it is just as uncertain as any other human book. It is not even reliable history. Its records of what it does narrate as ordinary history are full of falsifications and blunders. The origin of Deuteronomy, for example, was "a consciously refined falsification".'[17]

The Real Difficulty

And here we see the deception of the British-American School, for they still claimed to believe that the Bible is inspired, while the Continental School were open and clear in their denial of inspiration. Hague comments that most scholarship in Old Testament criticism had not been in the hands of men who could be described as Christian scholars. 'It has been in the hands of men who disavow belief in God and Jesus Christ… in the hands of Spinoza, and Graf, and Wellhausen, and Kuenen, inspiration is neither presupposed nor possible. Dr Briggs and Dr Smith may avow earnest avowals of belief in the divine character of the Bible, and Dr Driver may assert that critical conclusions do not touch either the authority or the inspiration of the Scriptures of the Old Testament, but from first to last, they treat God's Word with an indifference almost equal to that of the Germans. They certainly handle the Old Testament as if it were ordinary literature.'[18]

The real problem with the British-American School was that it tried to give an appearance of doctrinal orthodoxy, while promoting the ideas of the higher critics. It was mixing truth with error.

No Final Authority

A serious consequence of the higher critical movement, according to Hague, was that it threatened the Christian system of doctrine and the whole fabric of systematic theology. 'For up to the present time any text from any part of the Bible was accepted as a proof-text for the establishment of any truth of Christian teaching, and a statement from the Bible was considered an end of controversy... But now the Higher Critics think they have changed all that.'[19]

'They claim that the science of criticism has dispossessed the science of systematic theology. Canon Hensen [a liberal Anglican priest] tells us that the day has gone by for proof-texts and harmonies. It is not enough now for a theologian to turn to a book in the Bible, and bring out a text in order to establish a doctrine. It might be in a book, or in a portion of the Book that the German critics have proved to be a forgery, or an anachronism. It might be in Deuteronomy, or in Jonah, or in Daniel, and in that case, of course, it would be out of the question to accept it.'[20]

The Scholarship Argument

Hague defends the Faith against the 'superior' scholarship claims of the higher critics. 'There is a widespread idea among younger men that the so-called Higher Critics must be followed because their scholarship settles the questions. This is a great mistake. No expert scholarship can settle questions that require a humble heart, a believing mind and a reverent spirit... and no scholarship can be relied upon as expert which is manifestly characterized by a biased judgment, a curious lack of knowledge of human nature, and a still more curious deference to the views of men with a prejudice against the supernatural.'[21] Scripture teaches that spiritual truth is spiritually discerned. The foolishness of God is wiser that the wisdom of men (1 Corinthians 1.25).

Higher Criticism on the Mission Field

The World Missionary Conference, which convened in Edinburgh in June 1910 (considered in chapter 6), set up a study group to examine the problems involved in the presentation of Christianity to the minds of non-Christian people. To find out what was really happening on the mission field, and to uncover the missionary message that had met with most success, the study group issued a list of questions to a large number of missionaries in all parts of the world. Included in the questionnaire was the issue of higher criticism. Missionaries were asked: 'To what extent do questions of higher criticism and other developments of modern Western thought exert an influence in your part of the mission field.'[22]

What follows are comments from the mission field, published in June 1910 in the report, 'The Missionary Message regarding five non-Christian religions'.

Animistic Religions

The chief feature of animistic religions is a belief in the existence of spirits, which may include a belief in a Great Spirit or Supreme Being. Missionaries working among animistic religions agreed that higher criticism and modern theology exerted no influence on animistic people. But some claimed that 'higher criticism has been and is to the missionary himself a help of the highest value in aiding him towards the elucidation of difficulties, and towards the presentation of a more balanced theology, while the people have benefited unconsciously, by being saved at the start from assuming positions which afterwards would only be abandoned with pain and difficultly.'[23] This remark was probably related to the teaching of creation as taught in the first chapters of Genesis.

Chinese Religions

The religious systems of China are Confucianism, Buddhism and Taoism. The higher criticism had not yet much affected the Chinese Church. However, missionaries working in China felt that a time of unrest was approaching and higher criticism was making itself felt among the younger preachers, the theological students, and in some places among church members. One writer says: 'We cannot teach the Scriptures as our predecessors did. Chinese students are aware of the modern attitude towards the Scriptures… Our theological students, with a smattering of science are in difficulties over Genesis, and one has a suspicion that there is a doubt in their minds that we are keeping something back.' Bishop Frederick Graves writes: 'With the advance in education, and the opening of China… it would be useless to attempt to keep the Chinese in ignorance of the higher criticism. More than this, they ought to be able to avail themselves of its ascertained results, of all that is true in it. For a missionary to teach the Bible just as it was taught a hundred years ago is folly, in the light of all that has been learned about the Bible since. He ought to be able to give his converts, and especially to the ordained men, the very best that scholars have gained by their investigation of the Bible, and not to be afraid of the truth.'[24]

Japanese Religions

The main religions of Japan are Shinto and Buddhism. According to Bishop Yoichi Honda of the Methodist Church of Japan, up to about 1888 Christianity had made wonderful progress. But from about 1884 there entered a strong Unitarian influence. 'In 1887 Mr Otto Schmiedal of the Mission Society of the Tübingen School came to Japan. In 1890 the magazine, The Unitarian, was started as an organ for propagating the higher criticism. This movement shook the Japanese Church to its foundations. For at the same time a movement took place within the Church in the same direction, questioning the inspiration of the Bible and asking for a revision of the Creed. Some doubted the doctrine of the Trinity, others objected to that of Redemption, and still others jeered at the dogma of the Virgin Birth.' The Rev S.L. Gulick writes: 'For over ten years (1890-1900) these higher critical problems so absorbed the thought of the pastors and also shook their confidence in the Gospel that little aggressive work was accomplished.' One effect of this movement was an impression that the missionary is behind the times with his reading and studies, and that the Christianity which he teaches is no longer believed in the West.[25]

Islam

Missionaries working in the Islamic world commented: 'At home the higher criticism has divided Christian opinion. On the one hand are genuine evangelical believers, who have heartily welcomed what their studies have compelled them to regard as assured results of a legitimate method of study as confirming their belief in a real progressive revelation of God to man. On the other hand, there are earnest Christian men who dread this whole movement as an assault not only on the outworks but even the citadel of their faith… There is, however, an opposition of educated Moslems to Christianity, which freely uses the weapon thus put into its hands. In Persia an apostate Christian, writing books against Christianity, makes the most of the discrepancies of the Gospels and the difficulties of the biblical genealogies… In India the higher criticism is welcomed as a sign of the retreat of Christianity; and the argument is advanced that it is absurd to lose home and friends by conversion to a religion, which even cultured Protestants have proved to be false… The attitude of the missionaries themselves on this question is divided. Some of the older missionaries are hostile, and seem even to resent the acceptance of any of the critical views by the younger men.'[26]

Hinduism

The report from missionaries working among Hindus commented: 'The majority, which includes all who are at work among the student class, are disposed to welcome the higher criticism as removing difficulties of Christian apologetic and as leading to a deeper understanding of the nature of revelation. On the other hand, there is a minority which looks upon the higher criticism with much suspicion, and predicts evil from the advance of its methods, primarily among the missionaries themselves, and secondarily among Indian Christians.' One missionary, Mr Fraser, working among Hindu and Buddhist students in Ceylon writes: 'The higher criticism is, I believe, doing a great deal of good in paving the way for the evangelisation of the world… The conception, which is growing in the missionary body, of the Bible as a history of revelation is of tremendous value in meeting these new faiths out here.'[27]

_____

These opinions of missionaries from across the world leave little doubt that the ideas of higher criticism, even at the beginning of the twentieth century, were affecting the way the Bible was being taught. Many of the younger missionaries were influenced by the higher criticism, which meant that they would have been teaching a modified liberal version of the gospel. It was painfully clear that the so-called 'assured results' of the higher critics had won over Christian intellectuals and pastors at home and abroad.

Confessions of a Theologian

Professor J.J. Reeve of South-western Baptist Theological Seminary, in a word of personal testimony in *The Fundamentals*, explains how he came to reject the higher critical movement. He described his experience at one of the great American universities, where the higher critical views were ably and attractively presented. He writes: 'I saw that the whole movement with its conclusion was the result of the hypothesis of evolution.'[28] He found the evolutionary worldview of his professors 'wonderfully fascinating and almost compelling... That this theory of evolution underlies and is the inspiration of the Higher Criticism goes without saying... I discovered that the Critical Movement was essentially and fundamentally anti-supernatural and anti-miraculous'.[29]

Faced with this reality, Reeve concluded that the presuppositions and beliefs of the Bible writers and the critics were absolutely contradictory. As he considered the spirit of the movement, he wrote: 'It became more and more obvious to me that the movement was entirely intellectual, an attempt in reality to intellectualise all religious phenomena. I saw also that it was a partial and one-sided intellectualism with a strong bias against the fundamental tenets of Biblical Christianity. Such a movement is responsible for a vast amount of intellectual pride, an aristocracy of intellect with all the snobbery which usually accompanies that term... They have a splendid scorn for all opinions which do not agree with theirs. Under the spell of this sublime contempt they think they can ignore anything that does not square with their evolutionary hypothesis... Supremely satisfied with its self-constituted authority, the mind thinks itself competent to criticise the Bible, the thinking of all the centuries, and even Jesus Christ himself.'[30]

Reeve says that a preacher who has thoroughly imbibed these beliefs has no proper place in an evangelical Christian pulpit. 'Christianity is beginning to see that its very existence is at stake in this subtle attempt to do away with the supernatural. I have seen the Unitarian, the Jew, the free-thinker and the Christian who has imbibed critical views, in thorough agreement on the Old Testament and its teaching. They can readily hobnob together, for the religious element becomes a lost quantity; the Bible itself becomes a plaything for the intellect, a merry-go-round for the mind partially intoxicated with its theory.'[31]

The Dethronement of God

Sir Robert Anderson was the second Assistant Commissioner (Crime) of the London Metropolitan Police, from 1888 to 1901. He was also an intelligence officer, theologian and author of many Christian articles. His essay 'Christ and Criticism', published in *The Fundamentals*, carefully describes the blunders and errors of the higher criticism. He concludes that the 'effects of this Higher Criticism are extremely grave. For it has dethroned the Bible in the home, and the good old practice of family worship is rapidly dying out. And great national issues are also involved. For who can doubt that the prosperity and power of the Protestant world are due to the influence of the Bible upon character and conduct? ... no one who is trained in the fear of God will fail in his duty to his neighbour, but will prove himself a good citizen. But the dethronement of the Bible leads practically to the dethronement of God; and in Germany and America, and now in England, the effects of this are declaring themselves in ways, and to an extent, well fitted to cause anxiety for the future.'[32]

The higher critical movement, which began in Europe as a rejection of biblical Christianity, is rooted in a desire to dethrone God and destroy the Protestant faith from within the Church. The higher critics were scholars who attempted to use their intellectual ability to argue that the Bible contained many errors, and therefore was not infallible. While it might contain the Word of God, it was not the Word of God. This was the thrust of the higher critics, and although they often pretended to be the friends of the Church, they were in fact wolves in sheep's clothing.

Our brief survey shows that higher criticism was founded on unbelief. Most of the leaders were highly intelligent men who did not believe the Bible to be God's Word. The great majority of higher critics were not true believers, but men given over to rationalism. Yet they achieved high and influential places in the Church, and were widely accepted as Christians. Most were professors of theology who spent their lives studying the Scriptures and teaching students in Bible seminaries, preparing them for ministry in the Church. Many saw it as their calling to inculcate higher criticism in the minds of theological students, for this they believed was the most effective way of getting their ideas into the churches. Even when their apostasy was exposed, they were still eagerly accepted by the Church. Early in the twentieth century, men who were opposed to God's Word and actively seeking to undermine belief in the Bible were leading members of the Church and professors of theology, training men for ministry. The contention of this book is that there are many such men in the Church today.

We need to understand that the ideas and philosophy of the higher critics, which are still with us today, opened the Church to all manner of false teaching. It became acceptable for theologians to question the accuracy and truth of Scripture. The foundation of the social gospel, the antecedent of the holistic movement, was set in place by the higher criticism.

The next chapter explores the effects of the higher critics in the Bible-believing churches of Britain and America.

(Endnotes)

1 New World Encyclopedia, Higher criticism, http://www.newworldencyclopedia.org/entry/ Higher_criticism
2 Larry Walker, 'Some Results and Reversals of the Higher Criticism of the Old Testament', Criswell Theological Review 1.2 (1987) 281-294
3 *Introduction to Reading the Pentateuch*, by Jean Louis Ska, Eisenbrauns , 2006, p104
Ernestine van der Wall, *The Enemy within: Religion, Science, and Modernism,* Netherlands Institute for Advanced Study in the Humanities and Social Sciences, Uhlenbeck Lecture 25, 2007, p35
5 George Harris, A Century's Change in Religion (Boston: Houghton Mifflin, 1914), p78, cited from Archaeology, Bible and Interpretation: 1900-1930, a dissertation by Mark Elliott, p106
6 The Bible and Interpretation website, article 'The Fundamentals, Higher Criticism and Archaeology', by Mark Elliott, July 2005 http://www.bibleinterp.com/articles/Elliott_ Fundamentals.shtml

7 *The Fundamentals – a testimony to the truth*, 90 essays published from 1910 to 1915 by the Bible Institute of Los Angeles, edited by A.C. Dixon and later by Reuben Archer Torrey, pp88-89

8   Ibid. p90

9   Ibid. p91

10 Ibid. pp94-95

11 Ibid. p97

12 Ibid. p98

13 Ibid. p99

14 Ibid. p96

15 Ibid. p96

16 Ibid. pp99-100

17 Ibid. p106

18   Ibid. p106

19   Ibid. pp110-111

20   Ibid. p111

21   Ibid. p116

22 The Missionary Message in relation to Non-Christian Religions, Report of Commission IV, Presentation on 18th June 1910, http://www.archive.org/stream/reportofcommissi04worluoft#page/n23/mode/2up

23 World Missionary Conference 1910, Report of Commission IV, The Missionary Message in relation to Non-Christian Religions, p34

24 Report of Commission IV, p67

25 Report of Commission IV, pp113-114

26 Report of Commission IV, pp151-152

27 Report of Commission IV, p200

28 J. J. Reeve, "My Personal Experience with the Higher Criticism," cited from *The Fundamentals*, Volume 3, p99

29 *The Fundamentals*, volume 3, p100

30 Ibid. p111

31 Ibid. p114

32 *The Fundamentals,* volume 2, Christ and Criticism, p84

Chapter 4

Higher Criticism in the UK and USA

During the 1850s the ideas of higher criticism were imported into England by Samuel Taylor Coleridge, the poet, philosopher and opium addict, who helped introduce German idealist philosophy to the English-speaking world. The female Victorian novelist George Eliot, a radical freethinker with a brilliant intellect, who rejected the Christian Faith, and whose private life shocked decent society, translated David Strauss's *The Life of Jesus* (1835) and Ludwig Feuerbach's *The Essence of Christianity* (1841) into English. As we have seen, both of these German intellectuals were opposed to biblical Christianity.

In 1860 seven liberal Anglican theologians published a volume entitled, *Essays and Reviews*, which dealt with seven controversial Christian issues. These seven essays, largely sympathetic to the higher critical movement, caused a furious storm of controversy between conservatives and liberals that even overshadowed the arguments over Darwin's newly published, *On the Origin of Species* (1859).

The essay, 'On the Study of the Evidences of Christianity', by Professor Baden Powell, Professor of Geometry at Oxford, flatly denied the possibility of miracles. Rev Benjamin Jowett, Professor of Greek at Oxford University, in his essay, 'On the Interpretation of Scripture', urged that the Bible should be read like any other book and made an impassioned plea for freedom of scholarship. Having spent the summers of 1845 and 1846 in Germany, Jowett had become an eager student of German criticism and speculation. The implication of his essay was that divine revelation was progressive and that Scripture was always subject to reinterpretation by succeeding generations.

The *Essays* were described by their opponents as heretical, and the essayists became known as 'The Seven against Christ'.[1] Orthodox

Christians expressed their opposition to *Essays* in a letter to *The Times*, signed by the Archbishop of Canterbury and 25 bishops, even threatening the liberal theologians with the ecclesiastical courts.[2] On the other side of the argument were Charles Darwin and the evolutionary geologist Charles Lyell. A number of liberal churchmen also came out in wholehearted support of *Essays*. Such was the passion generated by the controversy that over twenty thousand copies were sold in two years. Despite the popularity of *Essays* among liberals, two of the authors were indicted for heresy and had lost their jobs by 1862; but the judgement was later overturned on appeal.[3] The Bishop of Oxford, Samuel Wilberforce, however, was not pleased with this turn of events; he went to the Convocation of Canterbury and by 1864 had obtained a 'synodical condemnation' of *Essays and Reviews*.

In 1862, Dr Samuel Davidson (mentioned in chapter 3) published *Introduction to the Old Testament*, a book largely based on the ideas of the German rationalists. Its liberal tendencies caused him to be accused of unsound views; a critical report prepared by the Lancashire Independent College (a project of the Lancashire Congregational Union to provide higher education for Non-Conformists, who were excluded from the Universities of Oxford and Cambridge until 1871) was followed by numerous pamphlets for and against.

William Robertson Smith (1846-1894)

The one man who probably did more than any other to propagate the ideas of the higher criticism in Great Britain was Scotsman William Robertson Smith, a minister of the Free Church of Scotland, professor, theologian, and Old Testament scholar. He was a great intellectual and a man of letters, who in later life was appointed an editor of the *Encyclopædia Britannica*.

At the age of 20 Smith entered the Free Church College at Edinburgh as a student of theology. In 1870 he was appointed to the Chair in Oriental languages and Old Testament exegesis at the Aberdeen Free Church College. According to *Encyclopaedia Britannica* (1963): 'He was the pupil and personal friend of many leaders of the higher criticism in Germany, and from the first he advocated views which, though now widely accepted, were then regarded with apprehension.'[4] In 1875, Smith wrote an article for the ninth edition of the *Encyclopaedia Britannica* entitled, 'Bible', in which 'he stated with complete frankness, that certain claims made in the scriptures could not be considered accurate. The Book of Deuteronomy, for example, obviously could not have been written by Moses himself and had been composed by writers of a much later date.'[5]

Then, in April 1876, an anonymous review appeared in the *Edinburgh Courant*. The reviewer said in his concluding sentences that the *Britannica* article 'is objectionable in itself; but our chief objection to it is that it should be sent far and wide as an impartial account of the present state of our knowledge of the Bible'.[6] The writer, generally acknowledged to be Dr Archibald Charteris, Professor of Church History at Edinburgh University, was a highly respected and orthodox member of the Church of Scotland. The review explained: 'Here an able and scholarly professor had adopted, as his own, theories associated up to that time with advanced and rationalistic criticism, and had set forth views regarding the origin of the Mosaic Law and the scope of the teaching of the Prophets, which seemed to many excellent and not uninformed members of the Church inconsistent with the generally received doctrine of inspiration, and even subversive of Holy Scripture.'[7]

In a letter referring to the *Courant* review, Professor Smith responded to the article. He wrote of the reviewer's malevolence that 'was probably dictated by ecclesiastical jealousy of the Free Church,' and that 'he expressed himself with so little knowledge and so great an air of authority that one seemed to hear the voice of a raw preacher thrust for party ends into a Professor's Chair.'[8]

But Smith's article on the Bible, as it was more widely read, caused a furore in the Free Church of Scotland, attracting much adverse comment. As a consequence of the controversy, Smith demanded a formal heresy trial in order to defend himself. The chief indictment against him concerned the authorship of Deuteronomy, which Smith, true to the beliefs of higher criticism, claimed was not Moses. The trial started in 1878 and dragged on for three years. With public opinion strongly on his side, Smith ably defended himself. Although the formal heresy indictment was dismissed, the Assembly agreed that he should be cautioned to abstain in future from expressing 'incautious or incomplete public statements'.[9]

But Smith was on a campaign to promote the ideas of higher criticism, and had already written another article, 'Hebrew Language and Literature', which again challenged the origins of the Old Testament. This article, which appeared in the 1881 edition of *Encyclopaedia Britannica*, 'was a landmark in the history of biblical criticism in Britain, in particular because it laid before the general public the critical view to which Wellhausen had given classical expression in his *Geschichte Israels* which had appeared less than three years earlier, in 1878'.[10] Yet 'Smith did not merely repeat the arguments of Wellhausen, or anyone else; he approached the subject in a quite original way.'[11] Members of the Free Church of Scotland were intensely displeased with Smith, accusing the young professor of dishonesty. After an Assembly debate in 1881, he was dismissed from his professorial chair at the Free Church College of Aberdeen.[12]

The publicity generated by the heresy trial engendered great sympathy for Smith and his cause. 'Four days after Smith had been deprived of his chair, some three hundreds ministers, elders and other friends and supporters, gathered at the Masonic Hall in Edinburgh's George Street, in a meeting of protest.'[13]

Smith's published works include, *The Old Testament in the Jewish Church* (1881); *The Prophets of Israel* (1882) and *The Religion of the Semites* (1894). 'All three books were initially presented in the form of lecture series addressed to lay audiences in Scotland. The first two disseminated public awareness of the higher criticism, hitherto the province of Continental theology, which cast new light on the composition and history of the Hebrew Bible. His best-known book, *The Religion of the Semites*, became a foundation text for all later studies in comparative religion and anthropology, influencing amongst others Emile Durkheim and Sigmund Freud.'[14] Durkheim helped to establish sociology as a science, and is cited as the father of sociology.

In *The Religion of the Semites*, Smith used sociology to analyse the religious life of the Semitic peoples. In a chapter entitled, 'The nature of the religious community, and the relation between the gods and their worshippers', he wrote: 'Religion did not exist for the saving of souls but for the preservation and welfare of society, and in all that was necessary to this end every man had to take his part, or break with the domestic and political community to which he belonged.'[15] Smith's writings profoundly influenced the direction and development of the young Sigmund Freud, helping him to develop ideas which were later to form the basic tenets of psychoanalysis. Freud read *The Religion of the Semites* just after embarking upon the writing of *Totem and Taboo* (1913).

Smith can rightfully be viewed as the pioneering sociologist of religion.[16] The comments of The William Robertson Website are significant: 'By the end of the century, the principles of biblical "higher criticism" were fully accepted by virtually all British theologians and their findings freely communicated. Even within the Free Church itself there came a more liberal view of such matters. Greater freedom of expression was allowed in both pulpit and college lecture rooms, without detriment to religious faith. And, one might add, the Scots people felt rather proud of their young, brilliant fellow-countryman whose sharp mind and polished argument had enabled him to stand firm against the weight of the clerical establishment.'[17]

The Downgrade Controversy

Such was the influence of higher criticism in Great Britain that it even contaminated the Reformed Baptist churches, which adhered to the 1689 Baptist Confession of Faith. During the 1880s, Charles Haddon Spurgeon, Pastor of the Metropolitan Tabernacle in London and one of the greatest preachers of his day, became increasingly concerned about the influence of higher criticism and the so-called 'new theology' in the Baptist Union. In the spring of 1887, Spurgeon's magazine, *The Sword & Trowel*, drew attention to these matters, which became known as the Downgrade Controversy.

The August 1887 edition of *The Sword & Trowel* carried an article entitled, 'Another Word Concerning the Down-Grade', in which Spurgeon wrote:

> A new religion has been initiated, which is no more Christianity than chalk is cheese; and this religion, being destitute of moral honesty, palms itself off as the old faith with slight improvements, and on this plea usurps pulpits which were erected for gospel preaching. The atonement is scouted, the inspiration of Scripture is derided, the Holy Spirit is degraded into an

influence, the punishment of sin is turned into fiction, and the resurrection into a myth, and yet these enemies of our faith once delivered to the saints expect us to call them brethren, and maintain a confederacy with them ... It now becomes a serious question that those who abide by the faith once delivered to the saints should fraternize with those who have turned aside to another gospel. Christian love has its claims, and divisions are to be shunned as grievous evils; but how far are we justi-fied in being in a confederacy with those who are departing from the truth? ... It is one thing to overleap all boundaries of denominational restriction for the truth's sake ... It is quite another policy to subordinate the maintenance of truth to de-nominational prosperity and unity.[18]

Spurgeon expressed his gratitude to the editor of *Word and Work* for speaking out against doctrinal error and quoted from the editor's article in the September 1887 edition of *The Sword & Trowel*.

In The Sword & the Trowel for the present month Mr. Spur-geon gives no uncertain sound concerning departures from the faith. His exposure of the dishonesty which, under the cover of orthodoxy, assails the very foundations of faith is opportune in the interests of truth. No doubt, like a faithful prophet in like evil times, he will be called a 'troubler of Israel'... The preachers of false doctrine dislike nothing more than the pre-mature detection of their doings. Only give them time enough to prepare men's minds for the reception of their 'new views', and they are confident of success. They have had too much time already, and any who refuse to speak out now must be held to be 'partakers of their evil deeds'. As Mr. Spurgeon says, 'A little plain-speaking would do a world of good just now. These gentlemen desire to be let alone. They want no noise raised...' Only those who have given some attention to the progress of error during recent years can form any just idea of the rapid strides with which it is now advancing. Un-der the plea of liberalism, unscriptural doctrines are allowed to pass current in sermons and periodicals, which, only a few years ago, would have been faithfully resisted unto the death. When anyone even mildly protests, preachers and journalists are almost unanimous in drowning the feeble testimony either by sneers or shouts.[19]

Spurgeon concluded his September 1887 article:

A chasm is opening between the men who believe their Bibles and the men who are prepared for an advance upon Scripture. Inspiration and speculation cannot long abide in peace. Compromise there can be none. We cannot hold the inspiration of the Word, and yet reject it; we cannot believe in the atonement and deny it; we cannot hold the doctrine of the fall and yet talk of the evolution of spiritual life from human nature; we cannot recognize the punishment of the impenitent and yet indulge the 'larger hope'. One way or another we must go.[20]

The 'new theology' attacked the doctrine of penal atonement as immoral and unnecessary. *The Christian World*, a liberal paper that was no friend to biblical truth, supported the ideas of the new theology:

We are now at the parting of the ways, and the younger ministers especially must decide whether or not they will embrace and undisguisedly proclaim that modern thought; which in Mr Spurgeon's eyes is a 'deadly cobra', while in ours it is the glory of the century. It discards many of the doctrines dear to Mr Spurgeon and his school, not only as untrue and unscriptural, but as in the strictest sense immoral; for it cannot recognize the moral possibility of imputing either guilt or goodness, or the justice of inflicting everlasting punishment for temporary sin. It is not so irrational as to pin its faith to verbal inspiration...[21]

An elder in Ebenezer Baptist Church, Swansea, David Boorman, explained the context of the Downgrade Controversy in an article entitled, 'The Big Man must Go!'. 'The nineteenth century was a time of spectacular advances in many spheres of knowledge, when, in the name of progress and in an attempt to harmonise the teaching of Scripture within the alleged findings of science, the Higher Criticism movement called into question the interpretation and inspiration of the Word of

God. Along with attacks on the inspiration of the Scriptures went another attack on other central doctrines.'[22]

David Boorman discussed the reason for Spurgeon's resignation from the Baptist Union. 'Despite Spurgeon's warnings, as delegates travelled to Sheffield for the autumn meetings of the Baptist Union, "the great joke was the Downgrade. It did not seem to be treated very seriously". [23] Whatever his fellow ministers might think, to Spurgeon the matter was no joke, a fact which was brought home when, on 28th October 1887, Spurgeon sent to Booth his letter of resignation from the Baptist Union.'[24]

Spurgeon's resignation from the Baptist Union forced its Council into action. The *Unitarian Herald* commented on the problem facing the Union. 'The authorities of the Baptist denomination are perfectly well aware of what is taking place; and powerful as the name of Mr Spurgeon has always been among them, they know that they must not take his side against the younger men who have the spirit of the age with them ... The big man must go; the big man is nothing before the march of the spirit of the age.'[25]

His argument with the Union arose from the fact that nothing was being done about the minority who were departing openly from the faith. Spurgeon wrote in *The Sword & Trowel*, 'It is our solemn conviction that where there can be no real spiritual communion there should be no pretence of fellowship. *Fellowship with known and vital error is participation in sin*' [26] (Emphasis Spurgeon).

Spurgeon's withdrawal compelled a response from the officials of the Baptist Union. They needed to explain why one of the world's greatest preachers had withdrawn from his own denomination. A meeting called by the Union to discuss Spurgeon's action recognised the gravity of the charges and that their public nature reflected on the whole Union. As Spurgeon declined to give the names of those to whom his charges applied, those charges, in the opinion of the Council, ought not to have been made. The full Baptist Union Council voted to accept Spurgeon's withdrawal and then voted to censure him. Only five of the nearly one hundred members supported Spurgeon in the vote.

Even after their censure of Spurgeon, the Union Council knew it would have to deal with the issue of a statement of faith. Spurgeon advised the Union to adopt a clear evangelical creed. In a letter to the editor of *The Baptist* he pleaded for clarity. He wrote: 'Whatever the Council does let it above all things avoid the use of language which could legitimately have two meanings contrary to each other. Let us be plain and outspoken. There are grave differences—let them be avowed honestly.'[27]

The response of the Baptist Council was to prepare a brief, somewhat vague, doctrinal statement for the April 1888 Assembly meeting, with the caveat that the Union had no authority to enforce doctrinal standards on its members. A proponent of the new theology, Charles Williams, moved that the Assembly adopt the compromised statement, taking the opportunity to deliver a passionate plea in favour of liberal ideas. It is sad to relate that it was Spurgeon's brother James who seconded Charles Williams' resolution.

Rev Henry Oakley recalls the events of the day: 'I was present at the City Temple when the motion was moved, seconded, and carried. Possibly the City Temple was as full as it could be. I was there very early, but found only a "standing seat" in the aisle of the back gallery. I listened to the speeches. The only one of which I have any distinct remembrance was that of Mr Charles Williams. He quoted Tennyson in favour of a liberal theology and justification of doubt... When the motion of censure was put, a forest of hands went up. "Against," called the chairman, Dr Clifford. I did not see any hands, but history records that there were seven. Without any announcement of numbers the vast assembly broke into tumultuous cheering, and cheering and cheering yet. From some of the older men their pent-up hostility found vent; from many of the younger men wild resistance of "any obscurantist trammels," as they said, broke loose. It was a strange scene. I viewed it almost with tears. I stood near a "Spurgeon's [College] man," whom I knew very well. Mr Spurgeon had welcomed him from a very lowly position. He went wild almost with delight at this censure of his great and generous master. I say it was a strange scene, that that vast assembly should be so outrageously delighted at the condemnation of the greatest, noblest, and grandest leader of their faith.'[28]

The vote and the bitterness of the controversy caused great sadness to Spurgeon and no doubt hastened his death a few years later in 1892.[29]

Spurgeon's warnings would prove to be well founded as the Baptist Union turned more and more to higher criticism and gradually abandoned its adherence to God's Word as the sole authority for life and faith.[30] The Downgrade Controversy did not arrest the apostasy in the Baptist Union or the other Nonconformist denominations. In *Spurgeon: Heir of the Puritans* (1996), Ernest Bacon makes the point: 'What is very clear is that the tide of advanced liberal theology and unscriptural teaching which Spurgeon sought in vain to stem, has swept on steadily and increased in momentum since his day; and few in any denomination, now hold to doctrine associated with the name of Spurgeon.'[31]

Higher Criticism in the USA

The ideas of the higher criticism arrived in the USA during the last decades of the nineteenth century. Its effect was devastating, for within a few years all the major denominations had been infected, and this led to the theological battle of the 1920s between the fundamentalist and modernists. Its effect can be likened to the spread of a highly contagious disease.

Charles Augustus Briggs (1841-1913), a Presbyterian theologian, who studied higher criticism in Germany, was the first major proponent of higher criticism in the USA. Pastor David Sproul, senior consultant with International Baptist Missions, comments: 'Within a few years the shock waves could be found in all the major denominations. The rise of rationalism led to a battle in numerous religious bodies during the 1920s. This battle became known as the Fundamentalist/Modernist Controversy. The conflict was between those who believed the Bible and those who did not. Sadly, every battle (with one exception) was won by modernists who took over the denominational bodies, including the Northern Baptist Convention (now known as the American Baptist Convention).'[32]

The young Charles Briggs studied biblical criticism at Berlin University during the 1860s, working under Professor Isaac August Dorner, Briggs acquired a 'scientific' approach to biblical scholarship. After three years' study in Germany, he returned home, convinced of the legitimacy of higher critical theories, and committed to propagating these new ideas in the USA.

After a short period as a Presbyterian pastor, in 1874 he joined the faculty at Union Theological Seminary, New York, and two years later was made Professor of Hebrew. A great opportunity came his way in 1880, when he was appointed co-editor, together with Archibald Alexander Hodge of Princeton Theological Seminary, of a new scholarly journal, *The Presbyterian Review*. Briggs now had a platform for his views and soon published an article in defence of the Scottish proponent of higher criticism, William Robertson Smith, which led to an exchange of articles between Briggs and the Princeton theologians.

In 1891 Briggs was appointed as Union Theological Seminary's first ever Professor of Biblical Theology. In his address inaugurating the new department, Briggs delivered a highly provocative sermon entitled, 'The Authority of Holy Scripture'. He attacked the conservative forces within the Presbyterian Church of the USA, focusing on the doctrine of biblical inspiration advocated by the conservative theologians of Princeton Seminary. In total support of the higher criticism, Briggs boldly declared that it was a *proven fact* that Moses did not write the Pentateuch; that Ezra did not write Ezra, Chronicles or Nehemiah; Jeremiah did not write the books of Kings or the Lamentations; David only wrote a few of the Psalms; Solomon did not write the Song of Solomon or Ecclesiastes and only a few Proverbs; and Isaiah did not write half of the book of Isaiah. The Old Testament was merely a historical record, and one which showed man in a lower state of moral development, with modern man having progressed morally far beyond Noah, Abraham, Jacob, Judah, David, and Solomon. The Scriptures are full of errors and the doctrine of scriptural inerrancy taught at Princeton Theological Seminary 'is a ghost of modern evangelicalism to frighten children'.[33] Not only is the Westminster Confession wrong, but the very foundation of the Confession, the Bible, could not be used to create theological absolutes. Briggs now called on other rationalists in the denomination to join him in sweeping away the dead orthodoxy of the past and work for the unity of the entire Church. The arrogance is almost palpable, the unbelief profound. Yet many supported him.

David Pultz, First Presbyterian Church archivist, comments on the reaction to Brigg's provocative talk: 'The speech cheered Briggs's students – they enthusiastically applauded him at points – but it angered the invited conservative guests and clergy. The speech is very much a polemic, attacking beliefs about the Bible in particular that the Victorians held as eternal and inviolable. Briggs began by asserting that there were three, not one, great sources of divine authority. The first was the institutional Church, the second reason, and the third the Bible.'[34]

There is no doubt that the students' reaction to Briggs's speech and his theological position was overwhelmingly positive. This meant that future leaders of the Presbyterian Church were being indoctrinated with the ideas of higher criticism.

In response to this address, the Presbyterian General Assembly refused to approve Briggs's professorial appointment at Union, and conservatives demanded that he be tried for heresy. He was acquitted by the Presbytery of New York in 1892, but the acquittal was reversed by the Presbyterian General Assembly, which suspended Briggs from the ministry in 1893.[35]

The Union Faculty, most of whom favoured the German higher criticism, stood solidly behind Briggs and fully supported his stand. David Pultz comments: 'Union alumni were also invited to join in the defense of Briggs. A solid majority of them did. One thing this showed was how much the higher criticism had penetrated into certain circles of American religious thought, despite an era generally marked by conservatism.'[36]

In 1889 Briggs published his opus magnum, *Whither? A theological question for our times*, in which he sets out to provide a correct interpretation of the doctrines of the Westminster Confession of Faith. In his treatise he asserts that the doctrine of the inerrancy of Scripture is a modern development of orthodox opinion. His concern is that, 'All Christian denominations have drifted from their standards, and are drifting at the present time… The question that troubles us most is—Whither?'

He explains that 'God himself, speaking in His holy Word to the believer, is the infallible guide in all questions of religion, doctrine and morals. But the sacred Scriptures do not decide for us all questions of orthodoxy. They do not answer the problems of science, of philosophy, or of history. They do not cover the whole ground of theology… The sacred Scriptures are not the only source of Christian theology; they were given in the midst of other sources of knowledge to enlighten us in the fields where these were insufficient... The Bible does not decide all questions of doctrine. It does not give us the mode of creation, the origin of sin and evil, the psychological construction of human nature... The Bible does not decide all questions of morals... It is probable that the reason why the Scriptures have not been more completely mastered in our time is that the divine truth revealed in other spheres has not been brought into proper relation with the Scriptures.'[37]

A great problem, in his opinion, is that some conservative Presbyterian theologians (perhaps he was thinking of A.A. Hodge and B.B. Warfield), 'have assumed an unfriendly attitude to science, philosophy, and history, and even the scientific study of the Scriptures. They have refused to taste the fruits of modern methods and modern learning... They have stoutly resisted everything that was antagonistic to their traditional system... They have been the true successors of the Pharisees... They have wrought serious damage to the science of Christian theology.'[38]

Briggs plea is for the battle against science, philosophy, exegesis, and history to come to an end. 'All truth should be welcomed, from whatever source, and built into the structure of Christian doctrine.'[39] He passionately promoted the 'science' of higher criticism. He writes:

'In the department of the Higher Criticism recent criticisms have shown that the traditional theories that David wrote all the Psalter, Solomon all the Wisdom Literature, and Moses all the Pentateuch, are untenable. These theories are without sufficient historical support, and are against the internal evidence of the writing themselves.'[40] Here Briggs demonstrates his ignorance. Scripture is clear that David was not the sole author of the Psalms; other named authors include, Moses, Asaph, the Sons of Korah and Solomon. Furthermore, Solomon was not the sole author of Proverbs; other authors, Agur son of Jakeh and possibly King Lemuel, contributed to the book.

Briggs is equally passionate in his support for the Church of Rome. In response to the question: Is Rome an Ally? he writes, 'Protestants and Roman Catholics are agreed as to the essentials of Christianity. Our common faith is based on the so-called Apostles' Creed, our worship on the Lord's Prayer, our morals upon the Ten Commandments and the Sermon on the Mount. Who will venture to say that the Roman Catholic Church is not as faithful to these foundations of our common religion as

Protestants?' He asserts that 'on all these great doctrines of our religion Romanism and Protestantism are one. Here we are allies, and it is our common task to proclaim these doctrines to the heathen world…'[41]

Briggs tells his reader that he has 'heard sermons in Roman Catholic churches in Europe which were more evangelical and less objectionable than many sermons I have heard in leading Protestant Churches in Berlin, London and New York… In all matters of worship we are in essential accord with Roman Catholics, and we ought not to hesitate to make an alliance with them…'[42]

He is adamant that the Bible contains errors.

> As I have said elsewhere, it seems to me that it is vain to deny that there are errors and inconsistencies in the best texts of our Bible. There are chronological, geographical, and other circumstantial inconsistencies and errors, which we should not hesitate to acknowledge… But whatever interpretation we may give to these errors, however much we may reduce them in number, the awkward fact stares us in the face, that these Princeton divines risk the inspiration and authority of the Bible upon a single proved error… They cannot escape the evidence of errors in the Scriptures. This evidence will be thrust upon them whether they will or not… What an awful doctrine to teach in our days when Biblical criticism has the field… No more dangerous doctrine has ever come from the pen of men. It has cost the Church the loss of thousands.[43]

Charles Briggs left the Presbyterian Church in 1898, and was ordained as an Episcopal priest. His attention shifted to the cause of ecumenism. Briggs is a significant figure, for he aggressively promoted the ideas of higher criticism in the USA with great vigour. Theological battles over the nature and authority of the Bible would spill over into the twentieth century as many liberals took up the cause. The fact that Briggs taught seminary students meant that many who were training for Christian ministry were indoctrinated in the theories of higher criticism and consequently had a low view of Scripture. Thus a man-made hypothesis, the product of intellectual arrogance and unbelief, was elevated to the status of 'scientific', and then disseminated widely within the Christian Church.

Carl E. Hatch, in his 1969 book, *The Charles A. Briggs Heresy Trial*, lists three main factors that stand out as transforming American Protestant theology—Darwin's theory of biological evolution, higher criticism, and the study of comparative religion. Hatch further makes the point that the impact of Darwin's theory of evolution on American theology is well known, but that of higher criticism and comparative religion, much less so.[44]

Crawford Toy

Crawford Toy, Professor of Theology at Southern Baptist Theological Seminary, was another pioneer of higher criticism in the USA. Shortly after graduating from the University of Virginia in 1856, he began studying at the Southern Baptist Theological Seminary in Greenville, South Carolina. But the American Civil War interrupted his studies; serving in the infantry, he was captured and held at Fort McHenry. After his release he taught Greek at the University of Virginia for a year, and then travelled to Germany and spent two years studying theology under Professor Isaac Dorner. He returned to the USA in 1869 and was offered a post at Southern Baptist Theological Seminary, the school at which he had studied ten years earlier.[45]

Toy had undoubtedly been heavily influenced by German higher criticism and by advances in science, which allowed him to see Darwin's theories as truth revealed by God. He accepted Julius Wellhausen's documentary approach to the Old Testament,[46] and this convinced him that the writers of the New Testament had actually misunderstood the original meaning of several Old Testament passages, such as Psalm 16:10 and Isaiah 53, by placing a Christological emphasis on them.[47]

For ten years Toy taught Old Testament interpretation and Semitic languages at the Southern Baptist Seminary. But he taught ideas that were reckoned to be at variance with Baptist views on the inspiration of the Scriptures. He explored various alternatives to a literal interpretation of Genesis 1, plus Darwinian evolution and the Graf-Keunen-Wellhausen documentary hypothesis concerning the Pentateuch.[48]

Matters came to a head in 1879 when Toy wrote a series of articles for the *Sunday School Times* on the subject of the Suffering Servant in

Isaiah. The essays revealed that he adopted many higher-critical conclusions about interpreting the Old Testament. To Toy's surprise the articles caused controversy, and so he sent a commentary on his views to the Seminary Board, in which he defended his position. He offered to resign his professorship if his defence was not adequate, while admitting that his position, which he believed conformed to the Seminary's confessional statements, was not held by many contemporary Baptists.[49] The committee agreed that Toy's views were not those of most Baptists and accepted his offer of resignation.

Dr Toy lapsed into Unitarianism around 1888, surely evidence that his higher criticism did not provide him with a sound Christian faith.

Comment

Our brief survey of this movement shows that higher criticism was founded on unbelief. Most of the leaders were highly intelligent men, who, although they professed faith in Christ, were not believers and therefore did not believe the Bible to be God's Word. Most higher critics were given over to rationalism and evolutionary theories. It became acceptable for theologians to question the accuracy and truth of Scripture. Yet many higher critics achieved high and influential places in the visible Church, and were widely accepted as Christian academics. Many became professors of theology who spent their lives studying the Scriptures and teaching theological students, preparing them for ministry in the Church. Their calling was to inculcate the doctrines of higher criticism into the minds of theological students, for this they believed was the most effective way of getting their ideas into the churches. Even when their apostasy was exposed, some were still accepted by the Church, and public opinion often backed them.

And so we see the alarming spectre of men who were opposed to God's Word and actively seeking to undermine belief in the Bible, becoming leading members of the Church and professors of theology, training young men for ministry in the Christian Church, thereby corrupting the beliefs of the ordinary churchgoer. We need to understand that the ideas and philosophy of the higher critics, which are still with us today, opened the Church to all manner of false teaching. The foundation of the holistic movement, which would misuse Scripture to reinterpret the mission of the Church, was firmly set in place by higher criticism. But first, on the back of higher criticism came the precursor of holistic mission – the social gospel of Walter Rauschenbusch – the subject of our next chapter.

(Endnotes)

1 *Essays and Reviews – Repercussion, http://www.liquisearch.com/essays_and_ reviews/repercussion*
2 *Essays and Reviews*, from Wikipedia, https://en.wikipedia.org/wiki/Essays_and_ Reviews
3 Higher criticism from New World Encylopedia, February 2014, http://www. newworldencyclopedia.org/entry/Higher_criticism
4 Encyclopaedia Britannica, 1963, vol 20, p836
5 The William Robertson Smith Website, Professorship in Aberdeen and Encyclopaedia Britannica, http://www.william-robertson-smith.net/en/e050profabeEBEN.htm
6 The life of Archibald Hamilton Charteris by Rev the Arthur Gordon, Published 1912 by Hodder and Stoughton in London, New York, p191
7 Ibid. pp190-191
8 Ibid. p191
9 The William Robertson Smith Website, The Heresy Trial, http://www.william-robertson-smith.net/en/e060heresytrialEN.htm
10 John W. Rogerson, "W. R. Smith's The Old Testament in the Jewish Church: Its antecedents, its influence, and its abiding value" in Johnstone, editor, William Robertson Smith. Essays in reassessment (Sheffield Academic 1995), 132-147, cited from Wikipedia article
11 Ibid. pp 132-147
12 Website of William Robertson Smith, The Heresy Trial
13 *William Robertson Smith: His Life, His Work and His Times*, By Bernhard Maier, publisher Mohr Siebeck, 2009, p200
14 GKB Enterprises website, article on William Robertson Smith http://www. gkbenterprises.fsnet.co.uk/wrs.htm
15 William Robertson Smith, *Religion of the Semites*, originally published 1894, Adam and Charles Black, p29
16 Religion of the Semites (Paper), by William Robertson Smith, Google books, p39 of introduction
17 Website of William Robertson Smith, The Heresy Trial
18 Charles Spurgeon, *The Sword & Trowel*, August 1887
19 *The Sword & Trowel*, September 1887, Our Reply to Sundry Critics and Enquirers by C.H. Spurgeon
20 *The Sword & Trowel*, September 1887
21 *The Sword & Trowel*, October 1887, quoted by Spurgeon
22 David Boorman, article 'The Big Man Must Go!' (part 1), published in *Foundations*, journal of the British Evangelical Council, issue 29, November 1992
23 The Freeman, 7 October 1887, cited from 'The Big Man must Go!',

24 Ibid. 'The Big Man must Go!'

25 *Unitarian Herald*, 11 November 1887, cited from David Boorman's article, 'The Big Man Must Go!'

26 *The Sword & Trowel*, November 1887, A Fragment Upon the Down-Grade Controversy by C.H. Spurgeon

27 *The Sword & Trowel*, March 1888

28 Iain Murray, *The Forgotten Spurgeon* (Edinburgh: Banner of Truth, 1966), pp149-50

29 Proclaim & Defend website, From Downgrade to Downfall, http://www.proclaimanddefend.org/2012/07/24/from-downgrade-to-downfall/

30 Website 'Theology thru technology', John M. Fritzius, http://www.tlogical.net/biospurgeon.htm

31 *Spurgeon: Heir of the Puritans*, by Ernest Bacon, Christian Liberty Press, 1996, p144

32 Proclaim & Defend website, Dr David Sproul, From Downgrade to Downfall http://www.proclaimanddefend.org/2012/07/24/from-downgrade-to-downfall/

33 Gary J. Dorrien, *The Making of American Liberal Theology: Imagining Progressive Religion, 1805 – 1900*, Westminster John Knox Press; October 1, 2001, p358

34 David Pultz, 'The Fundamentalist / Modernist Conflict', cited from website of First Presbyterian Church, New York, http://www.fpcnyc.org/about-us/history/harry-emerson-fosdick/the-fundamentalistmodernist-conflict.html#sthash.I9yVHpRp.dpbs

35 Encyclopedia.Com website, http://www.encyclopedia.com/topic/Charles_Augustus_Briggs.aspx

36 David Pultz, 'The Fundamentalist / Modernist Conflict'

37 Charles A. Briggs, *Whither?- a theological question for the times*, published 1889, New York: Charles Scribner's Sons, p9-11

38 Ibid. p14-15

39 Ibid. p18

40 Ibid. p283

41 Ibid. p269

42 Ibid. pp270-271

43 Ibid. p72-73

44 David Pultz, 'The Fundamentalist / Modernist Conflict', cited from website of First Presbyterian Church, New York

45 Harvard Divinity School website; article on 'Crawford Howell Toy', http://library.hds.harvard.edu/exhibits/hds-20th-century/toy

46 World Heritage Encyclopedia, 'Crawford Howell Toy', http://community.worldheritage.org/

47 Crawford Howell Toy, from Wikepedia, https://en.wikipedia.org/wiki/Crawford_Howell_Toy

48 *Baptist Theology: A Four-century Study* by James Leo Garrett, Mercer University Press, (January 1, 2009), p260

49 *Piety and Profession: American Protestant Theological Education, 1870-1970*, by Glenn T. Miller, Eerdmans Publishing Co. (June 11, 2007), p96

Chapter 5

The Social Gospel of Walter Rauschenbusch

Walter Rauschenbusch was an early convert to the cause of higher criticism. Steeped in socialist ideology, he taught a social gospel that in the eyes of many was a more relevant and compassionate gospel.[1] His aim was to replace the true gospel of salvation from sin with a social gospel that transforms the whole of society. Rauschenbusch has been called one of the most influential religious leaders of the twentieth century; *Christianity Today* listing him among the 131 Christians everyone should know. According to *Who's Who in Christian History*, Walter Rauschenbusch 'was undoubtedly the most influential American Christian thinker in the first third of the twentieth century'.[2]

Born in 1861 in Rochester, New York State, he was the son of the Professor of Theology at Rochester Theological Seminary. His parents had an unhappy marriage, and so it was no surprise that the young Walter went through a stage of teenage rebellion. But at the age of 17 he claimed he turned to Jesus. He explains that as he felt the stirring of manhood and worldly ambition, he said to himself: 'I want to become a man; I want to be respected; and if I go on like this, I cannot have the respect of men… And so I came to my Father, and I began to pray for help and got it. And I got my own religious experience.'[3]

Walter's father sent him to Germany for a classical education, where he was influenced by the ideas of higher criticism. Returning to the USA he studied theology at Rochester Seminary, where one of his teachers convinced him that Darwinian evolution could be harmonised with Christianity. In a paper he argued that 'Christ's death is not a sacrifice to appease the wrath of an angry God against sinful men, but a sacrifice to reconcile the heart of sinful men to their loving God'.[4] Rauschenbusch held the view 'that biblical statements are not true merely because they appear in the Bible. Like any other statements, he maintained, biblical statements are true only if they appeal to us as true in their own right'.[5] He dispensed with the belief that Christ's righteousness is imputed to believers. Walter's parents were concerned about his liberal ideas, but he reassured them: 'I believe in the gospel of Jesus Christ with all my heart. What this gospel is, everyone has to decide for himself in the face of his God.'[6]

In 1885 he became Pastor of the Second German Baptist Church in New York City. As a young Baptist pastor he was exposed to the poverty of the notorious Hell's Kitchen district of New York City, which profoundly disturbed him. He served as pastor for eleven years, ministering to a poor immigrant congregation that suffered intense social deprivation, with high infant and childhood mortality rates. He observed human suffering at close quarters and the funerals that he performed for children convinced him of the need for a social gospel. To further his understanding of socialism, in 1889 he made contact with the Society of Christian Socialists, founded by an Episcopal priest, W.D.P. Bliss, who favoured the English Fabian School of socialism.[7] The British Fabian Society existed to promote the spread of democratic socialism throughout society. (Famous members included George Bernard Shaw and Sidney and Beatrice Webb.)

In 1891 Rauschenbusch planned to resign from the pastorate because of his failing hearing, but the church refused to accept his resignation and offered to support him during a sabbatical in Germany, where he found the key to his theology and his life—the coming of the kingdom of God on earth. Rauschenbusch believed that the kingdom was not merely a major part of Jesus' teaching; it was the controlling centre. Christianity is revolutionary because the ethic and example of Jesus are revolutionary. He reasoned that 'because Jesus proclaimed and initiated the kingdom, the church is supposed to be a new kind of community that transforms the world by the power of Christ's kingdom-bringing Spirit'.[8]

During his sabbatical, he found the time to visit England to learn about Anglican socialism and other forms of British social Christianity. He lived with the prominent English socialists, Sidney and Beatrice Webb. He was deeply impressed by Birmingham's municipal socialism.

On his return to the USA, Rauschenbusch established the Brotherhood of the Kingdom, an informal network of pastors and others committed to the social transformation of American society. His plan was to join the Christian and socialist movements in order that they, working together, might transform the social conditions of society. He keenly defended the higher criticism advocates. In a letter to Baptist leaders, he wrote: 'We assert that the critical investigation of the Bible is the proper function for a theological professor, if exercised with wisdom and spiritual insight...'[9] He sought to combine his evangelical passion, which he never abandoned, with his new social awareness. For him complete salvation was both individual and social.

Rauschenbusch was offered a teaching position at Rochester Theological Seminary, but doubted that teaching would work any better than ministry for a deaf person. Gary Dorrien, an Episcopal priest and theologian, who has taught at Union Theological Seminary as the Reinhold Niebuhr Professor of Social Ethics, and at Columbia University as Professor of Religion (both in New York City), in an article published in *The Christian Century*, explains: 'His idea was to resign his position, go abroad for a year, write the dangerous book and launch a literary career. His congregation insisted, instead, that he take a paid sabbatical which he gratefully did, in Germany. There he labored on a book titled *Revolutionary Christianity*, which argued that Christianity should be essentially revolutionary, in the manner of Jesus.'[10] There is no doubt that Rauschenbusch's experiences as a pastor in New York had a profound effect on the way he came to understand the Christian religion.

In an article in the Boston Collaborative Encyclopaedia of Western Theology, author Julian Gotobed explains how Rauschenbusch travelled 'the length and breadth of America by railroad to advocate the cause of the Social Gospel. He was committed to the necessity of vital religious experience to transform individual personalities and political activism to make social structures in society equitable. More than any other person Walter Rauschenbusch captured the spirit of the Social Gospel Movement, alerting his contemporaries to a perceived social crisis unfolding in America during the opening decades of the twentieth century and exhorting them to seize a unique opportunity for social progress.'[11] In 1897 Rauschenbusch was offered a position at Rochester Theological Seminary, where he became Professor of Church History.

The Writings of Walter Rauschenbusch

Walter Rauschenbusch had become a towering figure in the social gospel movement. He consistently argued that the chief aim of the Church should be to transform society. His three most influential books were: *Christianity and the Social Crisis* (1907), *Christianizing the Social Order* (1912), and *A Theology for the Social Gospel* (1917). In these books Rauschenbusch offers a critique of social conditions in the USA and attempts to develop a theological foundation for the social gospel.

Christianity and the Social Crisis was written to discharge a debt to the poor on the West Side of New York, where he had served as a Baptist pastor for eleven years. It became a best-seller, outselling every other religious volume for three years, and making Rauschenbusch the leader of the social gospel movement. This book was immensely important for Christians and others interested in promoting the cause of the social gospel. Rauschenbusch's central thesis was that the essential purpose of Christianity was to transform human society into the kingdom of God, which he believed was a society built on the principles of socialism. The impact of the book was such that the social gospel soon became the dominant theological viewpoint among most Protestant denominations in the USA. In *The Making of American Liberal Theology: Idealism, Realism, and Modernity* (2001), Gary J. Dorrien explains that Rauschenbusch's book was 'short on socioeconomic specifics but long on the need for an alternative to capitalist civilization. While paying little attention to the problems and varieties of socialism, it urged the church to fuse an alliance with the socialist movement... He accepted most of the Marxist critique of capitalism.'[12]

A Theology for the Social Gospel, lays great stress on the theme of the kingdom of God. During his pastorate in New York, Rauschenbusch had helped found an informal Brotherhood of the Kingdom in which the ideas of the social gospel were developed in discussion with other like-minded men. An Amazon customer review of *A Theology for the Social Gospel* entitled, 'A Good Example of Liberal Heresy', says it 'gives the reader a very well written and in depth view of the workings of early twentieth century liberalism operating under the guise of orthodox Christianity. Walter Rauschenbusch dedicated his original version to his professor, the eminent reformed Baptist Theologian,

A.H. Strong, and then presented a work which would have caused his esteemed professor to roll in his grave. Using orthodox Christian language with the meanings changed, Rauschenbusch presents a religion which bears no semblance to Christianity but, instead, presents mankind as god. This book is a good read if you want to see and understand the subterfuge of liberalism.'[13]

It is worth pausing here to reflect that human suffering is capable of profoundly affecting us all, but should never be made the reason for abandoning the true gospel of salvation. We should be zealous to do good works that alleviate human suffering, but we must not adulterate the message of salvation from sin. To politicise the gospel is always disastrous; the gospel of salvation from sin is above politics and culture.

Higher Criticism

To understand Rauschenbusch's theology we need to know that he was committed to the higher criticism. Following the ideas of German higher critics, in *Christianity and the Social Crisis*, Rauschenbusch informs his readers: 'According to the modern critical interpretation only a small part of the Law was of very ancient origin. The Book of Deuteronomy was the outgrowth of prophetic ideas and agitation in the seventh century before Christ. The other portions of the Law did not originate till the Exile or after it, when the life of Judah had been long and deeply saturated with the teaching of the prophets.'[14] He saw what he considered a real danger for the Church if it followed sound doctrine and simply taught biblical truth. He warned that 'If the Church tries to confine itself to theology and the Bible, and refuses its larger mission to humanity, its theology will gradually become mythology and its Bible a closed book.'[15]

As a result of his low view of Scripture, he had little time for what he labelled individualistic Christianity. He writes: 'Individualistic Christianity has almost lost sight of the great idea of the kingdom of God, which was the inspiration and centre of the thought of Jesus. Social Christianity would once more enable us to understand the purpose and thought of Jesus and take the veil from our eyes when we read the synoptic gospels... When the broader social outlook widens the purpose of a Christian man beyond the increase of his church, he lifts up his eyes and sees that there are others who are at work for humanity besides his denomination.'[16]

Committed Socialist

Rauschenbusch was open about his deep commitment to the socialist cause, which he makes clear in both *Christianity and the Social Crisis* and *A Theology for the Social Gospel*. As an ideological socialist, he was vehemently opposed to capitalism. He writes: 'Capitalism necessarily divides industrial society into two classes, those who own the instruments and materials of production, and those who furnish the labor for it… The persistent tendency with capital necessarily is to get labour as cheaply as possible and to force as much work from it as possible. Moreover, labor is always in an inferior position in the struggle… Is this unequal struggle between two conflicting interests to go on forever?'

He continues: 'Here enters socialism. It proposed to abolish the division of industrial society into two classes and to close the fatal chasm which has separated the employing class from the working class since the introduction of power machinery. It proposes to restore the independence of the working man by making him once more the owner of his tools and to give him the full proceeds of his production instead of a wage determined by his poverty… Socialism is the ultimate and logical outcome of the labor movement. When the entire working class throughout the industrial nations is viewed in a large way, the progress of socialism gives an impression of resistless and elemental power.'[17] He concluded 'that one of the greatest services which Christianity could render to humanity in the throes of the present transition would be to aid those social forces which are making for the increase of communism'.[18]

He said that capitalistic control of economic power 'tempts to exploitation and oppression; it directs the productive process of society primarily toward the creation of private profit rather than the service of human needs'.[19] He asserted that Ireland 'had long been drained and ruined by capitalism… Whenever capitalism has invaded a new country or industry, there has been a speeding up in labor and in the production of wealth, but always with a trail of human misery, discontent, bitterness and demoralization.'[20] Rauschenbusch believed that capitalism was the cause of all that was wrong in society. In his eyes, the greatest sin was the creation of private profit.

As referred to above, when he was in England, he stayed with the prominent English Fabians, Sidney and Beatrice Webb, and took time to learn about the socialist programme of Birmingham Council. He was also an admirer of the French Revolution. He wrote: 'In the French Revolution the ideal of democracy won a great victory, not simply because the ideal was so fair, but because it represented the concrete interests of the strong, wealthy and intelligent business class, and that class was able to wrest political control from the king, the aristocracy, and the clergy.'[21]

Rauschenbusch believed that socialism was the answer to the problems of the working class. 'To most thoughtful men today the social question is the absorbing intellectual problem of our time. To the working class it is more. Socialism is their class movement. The great forward movement inaugurated by the French Revolution was the movement of the business men who wrested political control from the feudal nobility and clergy.'[22] He was disappointed that 'The churches in Europe were almost universally hostile to the French Revolution. When the people find their aspirations opposed and repudiated by their churches, they turn away chilled or angry... For a long time the German state Church took no sympathetic interest in the socialist movement... A socialist was a heathen and a publican. It was generally denied that a man could be both a socialist and a Christian... The clergy are now thoroughly awake to social questions. Many of them are more or less socialistic in their thought.'[23]

Theology of the Social Gospel

A Theology for the Social Gospel, is an attempt by Rauschenbusch to develop a systematic theology to support the concept of a social gospel. In the first sentence of the book he boldly asserts: 'We have a social gospel. We need a systematic theology large enough to match it and vital enough to back it. This is the main proposition of this book... The social gospel needs a theology to make it effective; but theology needs the social gospel to vitalize it... We need not waste words to prove that the social gospel is being preached. It is no longer a prophetic and occasional note. It is a novelty only in backward social or religious communities. The social gospel has become orthodox.'[24] With confidence Rauschenbusch asserted that 'conservative denominations have formally committed themselves to the fundamental ideas of the social gospel and their practical application. The plans of great interdenominational organizations are inspired by it. It has become a constructive force in American politics.'[25] He rejoiced that 'The social movement is the most important ethical and spiritual movement, and the social gospel is the response of the Christian consciousness to it. Therefore it had to be. The social gospel registers the fact that for the first time in history the spirit of Christianity has had a chance to form a working partnership with real social and psychological science.'[26]

He believed that what he called the 'old theology' had been a dismal failure, for it failed to grasp the real nature of sin. 'If the exponents of the old theology have taught humanity an adequate consciousness of sin, how is it that they themselves have been blind and dumb on the master iniquities of human history? During all the ages while they were the theological keepers of the conscience of Christendom, the peasants in the country and the working class in the cities were being sucked dry by the parasitic classes of society, and war was damning poor humanity… How is it that only in the modern era, since the moral insight of mankind has to some extent escaped from the tuition of the old theology, has a world-wide social movement arisen to put a stop to the exploitation of the poor, and that only in the last three years has war been realized as the supreme moral evil?[27]

Liberal Definition of Sin

As a good liberal he did not accept the orthodox view of sin and the Fall. 'The traditional doctrine of the fall is the product of speculative interest mainly… the doctrine of the fall does not seem to have as great an authority as it has long exercised.'[28] Having dismissed the doctrine of the Fall, he said 'it is not easy to define sin, for sin is as elastic and complicated as life itself… The definition of sin as selfishness furnishes an excellent theological basis for a social conception of sin and salvation.'[29]

He writes: 'We must democratize the conception of God; then the definition of sin will become more realistic… Sin is essentially selfishness. That definition is more in harmony with the social gospel than with any individualistic type of religion. The sinful mind, then, is the unsocial and anti-social mind. To find the climax of sin we must not linger over a man who swears, or sneers at religion, or denies the mystery of the trinity, but put our hands on social groups who have turned the patrimony of a nation into the private property of a small class, or have left the peasant labourers cowed, degraded, demoralized, and without rights in the land. When we find such in history, or in present-day life, we shall know we have struck real rebellion against God on the higher levels of sin.'[30] It is not difficult to see that Rauschenbusch held to a Marxist analysis and consequently to an unbiblical, social view of sin. He therefore rejected the substitutionary, atoning death of the Lord Jesus; instead he saw Christ only as an example of total unselfishness.

Kingdom of God

Central to Rauschenbusch's theology is the concept of the kingdom of God, which 'is the ideal human society to be established. Instead of a society resting on coercion, exploitation, and inequality, Jesus desired to found a society resting on love, service and equality… God is a father; men are neighbours and brothers… The kingdom of God is the true human society; the ethics of Jesus taught the true social conduct which would create the true society.'[31]

He interpreted the teachings of Jesus as radical and revolutionary. Like the Old Testament prophets, 'the fundamental sympathies of Jesus were with the poor and oppressed…There was a revolutionary consciousness in Jesus; not, of course, in the common use of the word "revolutionary", which connects it with violence and bloodshed.'[32] Indeed, Jesus 'has been called the first socialist. He was more; he was the first real man, the inaugurator of a new humanity. But as such he bore within him the germs of a new social and political order.'[33]

Behind this characterisation of Christ is the liberal heresy that 'Jesus' is not God Incarnate, but only the forerunner of a renewed humanity living in social harmony.

At the centre of Rauschenbusch's social gospel was the kingdom of God, understood in earth-bound social terms. He said that the kingdom of God is not a matter of individuals getting to heaven, but of transforming the life on earth into the harmony of heaven.

Personality of Jesus

Rauschenbusch had his own unbiblical view of the personality and life of Jesus. He wrote: 'Jesus lived out his own life. Like every other Ego he existed for himself as well as for others. He was asserting and defending his right to be himself when he stood up for others. The problems of human life were not simply official problems to him, but personal problems. But unlike others, he did not fall into the sin of selfishness, because he succeeded in uniting the service of the common good with the affirmation of this selfhood. The personality which he achieved was a new type in humanity.'[34] He asserted that Jesus experienced God in a new way. 'Jesus set love into the centre of the spiritual universe, and all life is illuminated from that centre. … So we have in Jesus a perfect religious personality, a spiritual life completely filled by the realization of a God who is love.'[35]

We have a Social Gospel

Rauschenbusch commenced his book on theology with the statement: 'We have a social gospel.' It would have been more accurate for him to have said, 'I have socialism.' For what he had done was to skilfully dress up socialism in Christian garb, and then label it the 'social gospel'. But it is a false gospel, which stands in direct opposition to the true gospel of grace. He openly rejected the 'old theology' and declared that the Church had failed to understand the revolutionary nature of Jesus' mission. In Rauschenbusch's eyes the problem with the apostle Paul was that he saw everything in *spiritual* terms and completely failed to understand the social agenda of Jesus.

Rauschenbusch saw the gospel of individual salvation as half a gospel, for to him the real gospel had social dimensions as well. He claimed that Jesus Christ was a social reformer, even a social revolutionary, who came to transform society into a socialist utopia – the true human society – which he called the kingdom of God. Having accepted the false teachings of higher criticism, he treated the Bible as largely irrelevant and warned the Church that it should not base its theology on the Bible alone. This allowed him to reject the Fall of man and the biblical view that all human beings are sinners. He propagated the concept of 'social sin', teaching that the greatest sin is the selfish capitalist practice of making a profit. He portrayed capitalism as a great social evil that must be opposed and eradicated before his social kingdom of God could be established.

While he did not entirely rule out personal salvation, he was adamant that social salvation was the really important aspect of the gospel—it is *society* that needs to be transformed and saved from the clutches of the capitalists. He presented the liberal heresy of God as the father of humanity and the consequent brotherhood of all men. He made no distinction between believers and unbelievers. His hope was to convince the Christian Church that his socialism was the real gospel.

Student Volunteer Movement

The Student Volunteer Movement for Foreign Missions was an organisation founded in 1886 that sought to recruit college and university students in the United States for missionary service abroad. Early in the twentieth century Walter Rauschenbusch's social gospel began to influence the thinking of the Student Volunteer Movement, undermining its evangelical principles. As a result its leaders began promoting a social gospel approach. The aim was the 'Christianization' of society.

This was to have a particularly important effect on the Student Movement's leader, John Mott, who would later chair the First World Missionary Conference in Edinburgh in 1910 (discussed in the next chapter). He eagerly embraced the social gospel, with far-reaching consequences for the world missionary movement. His 1914 book, *The Present World Situation*, was deeply critical of the West; he wrote, 'We may seriously question whether we have a Christianity worth propagating over the world.'[36]

In *The Search for Social Salvation: Social Christianity and America, 1880-1925* (2000), history professor Gary Scott Smith of Grove City College, Pennsylvania, sums up the influence of Walter Rauschenbusch on Christianity in the USA. 'The publication of Rauschenbusch's *Christianity and the Social Crisis* in 1907, which was widely read, discussed and quoted, quickly made the Baptist professor of church history at Rochester Theological Seminary the chief apostle of social Christianity. ...the hundreds of sermons and speeches he delivered throughout the nation during the early twentieth century helped solidify Rauschenbusch's reputation as the leading interpreter of the movement during the Progressive era. With a host of other prophets of social religion, Rauschenbusch sought to interpret the biblical message in such a way that it could stimulate social change. More powerfully and persuasively than any of them, he explained the roots, nature, and extent of America's economic and social problems, and he masterfully elucidated the principal factors that promoted and thwarted social reform. In addition, he proposed strategies and tactics for alleviating America's social ills and painted an attractive picture of the new cooperative commonwealth he believed Christians could create. Many Protestants fully endorsed, selectively supported, or at least carefully considered his proposals for reconstructing the social order.'[37]

We shall see in this study that the influence of Rauschenbusch is very much alive and well in our day in the guise of the holistic movement. As we turn to the First World Missionary Conference of 1910 we need to remember that John Mott, the man who chaired the Conference, was also the man who had eagerly embraced Walter Rauschenbusch's social gospel as a student leader.

(Endnotes)

1 Dr A.W. Beaven, former president of the Federal Council of Churches. Quoted by Edgar C. Bundy in *Collectivism in the Churches: A documented account of the political activities of the Federal, National, and World Councils of Churches* (Wheaton, Illinois: Church League of America, 1957), page 99, cited from http://www.crossroad.to/articles2/006/conspiracy2.htm

2 Cited from website of First Baptist Church of Toulon, Marks of Apostasy, *Who's Who in Christian History*, 1992, Tyndale House Publishers, http://toulonbaptist.com/sermons/000116.htm

3 Gary Dorrien, The Making of American Liberal Theology: Idealism, Realism, and Modernity 1900-1950, Westminster John Knox Press, 2003, p76

4 Ibid. p78

5 Ibid. p78

6 Ibid. p79

7 Ibid. p86

8 Ibid. p89

9 Ibid. p94

10 'Rauschenbusch's Christianity and the Social Crisis' by Gary Dorrien. This article appeared in *The Christian Century*, November 27, 2007, pp. 29
http://www.religion-online.org/showarticle.asp?title=3501

11 Walter Rauschenbusch (1861-1918), Author: Julian Gotobed, incorporating material submitted by Michelle Charles, published in The Boston Collaborative Encyclopedia of Western Theology, http://people.bu.edu/wwildman/bce,

12 *The Making of American Liberal Theology: Idealism, Realism, and Modernity* (2001), Gary J. Dorrien, p102

13 Amazon review, http://www.amazon.com/review/R1VYGZKZLZ81ZS

14 Walter Rauschenbusch, *Christianity and the Social Crisis*, 1907. Reprint. London: Forgotten Books, 2013, p18

15 *Christianity and the Social Crisis*, p339

16 *Christianity and the Social Crisis*, pp340-1

17 *Christianity and the Social Crisis*, pp406-408

18 *Christianity and the Social Crisis*, p398

19 Walter Rauschenbusch, *A Theology for the Social Gospel*, The Macmillan Company, 1917, p111

20 *A Theology for the Social Gospel*, pp112-113

21 *Christianity and the Social Crisis*, p402

22 *Christianity and the Social Crisis*, pp318-319

23 *Christianity and the Social Crisis*, pp320-321

24 *A Theology for the Social Gospel*, p1

25 *A theology for the Social Gospel*, pp2-3

26 *A Theology for the Social Gospel*, pp4-5

27 *A Theology for the Social Gospel*, pp34-35

28 *A Theology for the Social Gospel*, pp42-43

29 *A Theology for the Social Gospel*, pp45-47

30 *A Theology for the Social Gospel*, pp48-50

31 *Christianity and the Social Crisis*, pp70-71

32 *Christianity and the Social Crisis*, p82, p85

33 *Christianity and the Social Crisis*, p91

34 *A Theology for the Social Gospel*, pp152

35 *A Theology for the Social Gospel*, pp154

36 Embracing another gospel, 16 December, 2009 by Steve Addison. http://www.movements.net/2009/12/16/another-gospel.html

37 Gary Scott Smith, *The Search for Social Salvation: Social Christianity and America, 1880-1925*, p39

Chapter 6

Edinburgh 1910

The World Missionary Conference held in Edinburgh in 1910 was a watershed event – for the first time Protestant missionaries from across the world met together to plan for world evangelization. The influence of the missionary movement was now worldwide, as the gospel had been taken by Western missionaries to China, India and Africa and beyond. Many delegates looked forward to completing the task of evangelising the world. As they gathered in Edinburgh, the question of Church unity was on the minds of some delegates. An ecumenical vision was beginning to be seen as a goal for the future.

Yet the 1900s were filled with theological uncertainty. The theories of higher criticism had gained entrance to the evangelical church through their theological colleges; even on the mission field many had been influenced by its teachings, as we saw in chapter 3. Another disturbing factor was that the ideas of Walter Rauschenbusch's social gospel had become very popular in mainline Protestant denominations. Many believed that the Church should play an active role in addressing the social evils of the day. The social gospel was already having a powerful influence in much of Protestant America. In 1910 the Presbyterian Book of Order expressed what it believed were the 'great ends' of the Church in these words:

> The great ends of the church are the proclamation of the gospel for the salvation of humankind; the shelter, nurture, and spiritual fellowship of the children of God; the maintenance of divine worship; the preservation of truth; the promotion of social righteousness; and the exhibition of the Kingdom of Heaven to the world.

It was in this atmosphere that the World Missionary Conference gathered in Edinburgh in 1910. The records of the Conference describe how Edinburgh 1910 was preceded by interdenominational gatherings convened by foreign mission societies in both Great Britain and the United States. The first was held in 1888 in London to study information regarding missionary work throughout the world. This was followed in 1900 by a gathering in New York City at Carnegie Hall, with over 50,000 attending. Delegates came from mission societies based in the United States, Canada, Great Britain and Europe. The intention was to represent the work of Protestant missionaries worldwide. The New York gathering resolved that another conference should be held in ten years on the other side of the Atlantic, composed of delegates from foreign mission societies actively supporting missionaries in the field. Three points regarding the subject matter to be addressed during the proposed Conference of 1910 were agreed upon—1) The Conference would deal only with missionary work among non-Christian peoples (this meant that Roman Catholic and Orthodox countries were assumed to be Christian and therefore did not need to be evangelised); 2) it would address only the most urgent and immediate problems facing the Church; 3) no opinion on ecclesiastical or doctrinal questions would be expressed by the Conference (this meant that the issues of higher criticism and the social gospel were *not* for discussion).[1]

The 1910 Conference was held in the Assembly Hall of the United Free Church of Scotland, Edinburgh, under the banner, 'The Evangelization of the World in This Generation'. American John R. Mott (whom we met in the previous chapter), a Methodist layperson and leader of the Student Volunteer Movement for Foreign Missions, chaired the Conference. The main organiser was Joseph Oldham, a leader in the Student Christian Movement. The majority of the participants were from Europe and North America. Out of the 1,200 delegates, only 17 were from the 'younger' churches. They came, not as representatives of their churches, but as special delegates appointed by the missionary societies. Edinburgh 1910 can be viewed as an ecumenical gathering of evangelicals, for both evangelicals and liberals were attracted to the continuation committees that followed on from the Conference, and this led eventually to the formation of the World Council of Churches.

Roman Catholics were not invited, but liberals and modernists were. Indeed John Mott, who many consider the architect of the ecumenical movement, invited notable modernists and liberals as speakers. To make a proper assessment of the Edinburgh Conference we need to understand something of John Mott's background and theological views.

John R. Mott (1865 – 1955)

John Mott was a long-serving leader of the Young Men's Christian Association (YMCA). As a young man he became a leader in the Student Volunteer Movement for Foreign Missions, and between 1888 and 1920 he was the chairman of the World Student Christian Federation. Mott was greatly attracted to the ideas of the social gospel and had undoubtedly studied Walter Rauschenbusch's *Christianity and the Social Crisis*. In his book, *The Future Leadership of the Church* (1908), Mott wrote: 'Never before has the Church had such need in ministry of men able to deal wisely with social questions… Not only are social questions an imperative concern of the Church, but it is essential to the Church that it should give itself whole-heartedly to their solution… Moreover, these social problems present to the Church a great opportunity. If she loses herself in helping to solve them, she will find herself in added growth and power and vitality. This is the day above all others when the Church needs to be heard on social questions.'[2] To emphasise his commitment to the social gospel, Mott quoted from Walter Rauschenbusch's book, *Christianity and the Social Crisis*.

Elsewhere, Mott endorsed the social gospel when he affirmed: 'There are not two gospels, one social and one individual. There is but one Christ who lived, died, and rose again, and relates Himself to the lives of men.'[3] Such was Mott's interest in the social gospel that at a conference on social needs in April 1914, he gathered together social gospel leaders, including Walter Rauschenbusch, to address the relationship between students and social action.[4]

Arthur Pierson, Presbyterian pastor, Christian leader and contributor to *The Fundamentals*, in his book, *The Crisis of Missions* (1886), warned about the danger of liberalism in the student movement. By the 1930s his warning had proved to be accurate, as by then Mott's evangelism 'embraced the concerns of the Social Gospel and the practical piety of Methodism, believing a life devoted to Christ would lead people to become morally just individuals'.[5] In the acrimonious debate between liberals and fundamentalists, he was able to steer a middle course. He is reported as saying: 'Evangelism without social work is deficient; social work without evangelism is impotent.'[6] As a skilful diplomat, Mott was able to keep both constituencies happy, and succeeded in persuading evangelicals to tolerate the beliefs of liberals for the sake of unity.

We learn more about Mott's approach to Christian mission from his book, *The Present World Situation* (1915). He argues that the evils of Western civilisation have placed the gospel in a bad light. He asserts: 'The startlingly rapid spread of the corrupt influences of our so-called Western civilization among non-Christian peoples constitutes another reason for prompt and urgent action on the part of the Christian Church.'[7] He claims that the World Missionary Conference in Edinburgh in 1910 'ushered in a better day, for the missionary problem must henceforth be treated more largely than heretofore as a problem in applied science'.[8] He says the Church needs missionary statesmen 'who exhibit conspicuous wisdom and ability in the direction or management of missionary affairs'.[9]

Mott devotes a chapter to 'The Unchristian Aspects of the Impact of our Western Civilization'. He writes: 'More commonly these evil practices are exhibited in the form of dishonest and unscrupulous commercial transactions... Far too often the white man has cajoled, bullied, threatened and bribed the Asiatic and the African, has reaped enormous profits, and when he has fallen into entanglements has called upon his Government to help him out.'[10] He is concerned about the influence of Western tourists: 'The letting down of standards by many Western tourists likewise tends to undermine much of the good influence of the Christian propaganda.'[11] He stresses the importance of Christianizing Western nations: 'Enough has already been stated to make it evident that by far the greatest obstacle to the world-wide spread of the Christian religion is the unchristian impact of our Western civilization. That impact must be Christianized... We must Christianize our impact as Western nations, in order to make amends for the evil which we have done... The ultimate triumph of pure Christianity in non-Christian lands depends absolutely upon Christianizing this impact.'[12] He says that expanding the missionary movement 'is by far the greatest single influence to counteract the bad influences of our civilization'.[13] He goes on: 'It is of transcendent importance that all the Christian forces be brought to bear on Christianizing our own civilization at home.'[14] He makes the point that 'the work of Christian missions is to impart divine vitality to decaying civilizations or to those characterized by low vitality. In doing so forces are liberated whose influence and outreach no one can foretell or estimate.'[15] What is apparent from Mott's writings is that he does not appear to understand that the West is composed of both believers, who seek to live godly lives, and unbelievers, who are slaves to sin and who need the gospel just as much as any unbeliever in a non-Christian nation. For his lifelong ecumenical efforts Mott was awarded the Nobel Peace Prize in 1946.

Joseph Houldsworth Oldham (1874-1969)

J.H. Oldham, the organising secretary of Edinburgh 1910, played an important role in shaping the Conference agenda, and later became a significant figure in the ecumenical movement. He was born in India of Scottish parents, returning to Scotland at the age of 7. He studied at Trinity College, Oxford, graduating in 1894, and then served with the Young Men's Christian Association as a missionary in India for three years, before studying theology in Edinburgh and Germany. In 1908 he was appointed organising secretary for the Edinburgh World Missionary Conference. In 1912 he founded the *International Review of Missions*, a journal that commented on research into missionary practice and theology. Oldham successfully proposed the formation of the International Missionary Council and became its secretary in 1921. At the first assembly of the World Council of Churches (WCC) in 1948, Oldham was made an honorary president of the Council.[16]

———————

In *Roots of the Great Debate in Mission* (1981), Roger E. Hedlund argues that Edinburgh 1910 was both a culmination and a beginning. 'As culmination it represents the climax of a century of Protestant mission in the traditional sense of world evangelization. Edinburgh also began a process with other emphases and goals and which eventually led to a different conception of mission. The traditional conception was questioned in the decades after Edinburgh.'[17] Under the guiding hand of Mott and Oldham, the roots of ecumenical evangelism that would flourish during the twentieth century were firmly established.

Edinburgh 1910 Conference

The Edinburgh Missionary Conference did not place great emphasis on local churches because, it was argued, they only have an indirect connection to the mechanisms of mission. As a consequence the Conference consisted solely and exclusively of delegates sent by mission agencies. In other words, only invited delegates were welcome to attend. Many were delegated by a mission agency, not by a church or denomination. So a major shortcoming of Edinburgh was that the local church was not seen as relevant to the task of mission. Rather, the task of world evangelism was to be accomplished by missionary organisations—the so-called experts. But Scripture emphasises the responsibility of the local church, guided by godly elders, for the ministry of the gospel. A great weakness of Edinburgh was that the chosen delegates were not under the authority of church elders, and therefore free to follow their own ideas and doctrines. Ecumenical thinking, of course, does not necessarily see the local New Testament church as important. The wisdom of man is higher than God's wisdom, at least in ecumenical thinking.

The Edinburgh organisers, including chairman Mott and secretary Oldham, confined the Conference agenda to strategy and policy issues such as missionary training, missions and governance, the message in mission contexts, the Church on the mission field, and so on. As most of the mission agencies were thought to be evangelical, no signing of any theological agreement was required. Following the decision of the New York gathering of 1900, Conference leaders insisted that the divisive issue of doctrine should not intrude into the proceedings.[18] In order to foster unity among delegates, therefore, it was agreed that doctrinal issues would not be discussed, for doctrine was held to be divisive.

As a consequence of this decision, the doctrinal position of the Conference was unclear on the two great issues of the day—the higher criticism and the social gospel. And this was disastrous, for the false doctrines of liberalism and socialism were growing apace, and the ideas of higher criticism were popular in many quarters. The disturbing reality was that Edinburgh had called together genuine doctrinally sound Christians with a group of delegates who were given over to liberalism and ecumenism. This meant that *pragmatic* agreement was central to the thinking of the Conference, and profound doctrinal differences were simply kept under wraps. In other words, worldly diplomacy was elevated at the cost of sound doctrine.

Arthur Johnston argues that the World Missionary Conference at Edinburgh marked a serious departure from historic evangelical evangelism and initiated a trajectory which culminated not long after in the loss of the gospel itself. Johnston asserts that those who led Edinburgh 1910 had adopted a looser, more modern view of biblical inspiration, a more inclusive theological platform, and an openness 'to progressive theology and syncretism'.[19] And according to Johnston, over the next several decades, in various institutional manifestations, this ecumenical movement pursued a theological trajectory of 'larger evangelism' and 'holistic evangelism', which eventually led to a wholesale loss of the gospel. 'At the formation of the International Missionary Council in 1921, it was decided to adopt a non-theological position, which left the movement in a measure defenceless against any theological error or even heresy.'[20]

The modern liberal church establishment criticised the Conference for different reasons. Theologian Kenneth Ross, Secretary of the Church of Scotland World Mission Council, in his book, *Edinburgh 2010: Springboard for Mission* (2009), draws attention to what he regards as the mistakes and limitations of the 1910 Conference. He writes: 'As a child of its time, it had limitations and blind-spots which have been exposed with the passing of the years.' In particular, complicity with imperialism and colonialism were seen as major problems. 'As a century of critique has made plain, the conference did not acquire sufficient distance from the Western imperialism which was at its height at that time. The fact that the Western "Christian" powers dominated world affairs underlay a great deal of the optimism of the conference regarding the missionary enterprise… Much too easily the conference bought into the colonial assumption of the inferiority of the colonised. Much too easily, for example they accepted a colonial caricature of Africa as a savage, barbaric and uncultured continent.'[21]

Ross says the Conference, marked by the mood of the Protestant missionary movement, 'was often expressed in the vocabulary of aggression, attack, conquest and crusade... The aggressive and confrontational understanding of Christian mission which characterised Edinburgh 1910 has provoked much resentment and does not serve to commend Christian faith today.'[22]

David Hesselgrave, in his article on the 'Edinburgh Error' writes: 'Unknowingly Edinburgh organizers had set a pattern for the ecumenical movement of the 20th century. Bishop Stephen Neill rightly says that Edinburgh 1910 was "...the starting-point of the modern ecumenical movement *in all its forms*".'[23]

Arthur Johnston sums up the influence of the Conference: 'Edinburgh 1910 was an epoch-making conference, but its inclusive nature sowed the seeds of a progressive theology so evident later on in Life and Work, Faith and Order, and especially in the International Missionary Council. It was the young leadership of Edinburgh 1910 who exerted great influence in these later world movements, which resulted in the World Council of Churches (WCC) and its inclusive doctrinal basis.'[24]

To demonstrate its eagerness to work in harmony with the Church of Rome, the Edinburgh Conference was clear that Roman Catholic and Orthodox countries were *not* considered to be mission fields. Hence the title of the Conference was 'Carrying the Gospel to the Non-Christian World'. The clear inference was that Roman Catholic countries, such as those of South America, were to be regarded as Christian, and so did not need to be evangelised. Indeed, the hope was that each branch of Christianity – Protestant, Roman Catholic and Orthodox – would work together and evangelise the world, and so usher in the Kingdom of God. To accomplish this mighty task the visible unity of the Church was considered to be essential. Ecumenism, therefore, was firmly on the agenda. And here we have the foundation of the ecumenical movement that, over the century, would seriously undermine evangelical Christianity and produce a large counterfeit Church.

A Continuation Committee set up at the end of the Conference formed the foundation for the establishment of the International Missionary Council (IMC), established in 1921. Another achievement that flowed from Edinburgh was the establishment of the World Council of Churches (WCC) in 1948.

The International Missionary Council

A major outcome of the Edinburgh Conference was the setting up of the International Missionary Council (IMC) in London in 1921. The Council would focus on the emerging ecumenical movement and address 'issues such as missionary freedom, general and theological education, opium addiction, labour, slavery, racial discrimination, the church in rural and industrial society, home and family life, and literature, and advise local and regional church bodies'.[25] In other words, the IMC was to be intensely political in its focus, with a deep commitment to social issues. The *Encyclopedia of Protestantism* sums up the philosophy: 'The new IMC agreed not to speak on matters of doctrine or polity, and to focus instead on uniting Christians in a search for justice in international and interracial relationships. This later goal spoke directly to European and North American domination of the missionary enterprise, and to missionary compromises with colonial powers and racist attitudes, which had brought discredit to the church. One early study commissioned by the IMC and written by J.H. Oldham (1874-1969) was published in 1924 as *Christianity and the Race Problem*.'[26]

In addition to the IMC, Edinburgh 1910 gave rise to two committees—the Committee on Life and Work, which concentrated on the practical activities of the churches, and the Committee on Faith and Order, which focused on the beliefs and organisation of the churches and the problems involved in their possible reunion.

Life and Work Committee

Archbishop Nathan Söderblom of Uppsala played a leading role in organising a Life and Work Conference in Stockholm in 1925. Over 600 delegates from Protestant and Orthodox churches met, but without the Roman Catholic Church, which, although invited, declined to attend. The Conference focused on issues of daily living and the life of the Church in society.[27] The slogan of the Conference was: 'Doctrine divides, service unites.' The gathering reflected on economics and industrial relations, social and moral problems, international issues and education. Although the planners of the Conference intentionally sought to avoid doctrinal differences, difficulties arose over the discussion on the Kingdom of God on earth. 'Some participants, rooted in the social gospel perspective, spoke of the role of persons in contributing to the establishment of the Kingdom of God on earth. Others objected and declared that human beings should not be so arrogant in claiming that they can inaugurate the Kingdom.'[28] These theological differences led to continual misunderstandings and tension between delegates.

The message to emerge from the Conference was that the gospel applies to 'all aspects of life, including the industrial, social, political and international'.[29]

A second conference organised by the Life and Work Committee was held in Oxford, England, in 1937. There were about 300 official delegates from 120 churches in 40 countries. Although the Roman Catholic Church did not send an official delegation it did send observers. By the 1930s the optimism of the social gospel movement had faded in the face of political realities. However, the Life and Work movement, inspired by the leadership of Anglican Archbishop of York William Temple and J.H. Oldham, provided the Conference with information on a number of social and moral issues of the day. The delegates approved a motion favouring the establishment of a World Council of Churches (WCC), which would be achieved by bringing together the work of the two committees established by Edinburgh 1910, that is, the Life and Work committee and the Faith and Order committee. These changes, it was hoped, would further the cause of institutional Christian unity.

The Conference claimed there was a call from God directed at three groups. First, to every local congregation, 'to realise at any cost in its own self that unity, transcending all differences and barriers of class, social status, race and nation which we believe the Holy Spirit can and will create in those who are ready to be led by Him'. Second, to different churches in any district, 'to come together for local ecumenical witness in worship and work'. Third, to all Christians, 'to a more passionate and costly concern for the outcast, the underprivileged, the persecuted and the despised in the community and beyond the community...'[30]

Faith and Order Committee

Bishop Charles Brent of the Episcopal Church of United States returned from Edinburgh 1910 determined to create the World Conference of Faith and Order. According to a WCC paper entitled, 'What is Faith and Order?', Brent recognised that the unity of the Church would only be brought about if there was firm agreement in faith. 'He determined to bring together bishops, Church leaders and theologians to begin the task of studying the division of the churches. It took from 1910 to 1927 to set up the first World Conference on Faith and Order held in Lausanne, Switzerland. In those years 70 commissions in 40 countries worked to prepare the meeting. Protestants, Anglicans and Orthodox were in the thick of it together. Although the Pope expressed his personal friendliness towards the venture and gave it his blessing, the Roman Catholic Church declined to be a part of it, which was finally brought into being at Lausanne in 1927.'[31] The Conference of Faith and Order proposed creating a World Council of Churches (WCC). At Utrecht in 1938 the Faith and Order Committee and the Life and Work Committee agreed to unite and set up a preliminary WCC headquarters in Geneva, but World War II intervened, and so the WCC was not formally inaugurated until 1948.

In 1925 a young Willem Visser't Hooft, who was later to become the first General Secretary of the WCC, visited the USA to work with John Mott. Under Mott's influence, Visser't Hooft became interested in the social gospel, which became the subject for his doctoral dissertation for the University of Leiden in 1928.[32]

IMC Conference Jerusalem 1928

The second international missionary gathering of the International Missionary Council (IMC), the Jerusalem Conference of 1928, represented a triumph for modernist thought and liberal theology. It was attended by John Mott and Bishop William Temple, and 1000 delegates from both the West and the East. Liberal ideas focused on the need for social and political reforms. The authority of Scripture had been seriously undermined by the ideas of higher criticism, and many theologians were now largely interested in social action—evangelism was no longer a priority. Evangelical delegates discovered a growing desire on the part of the liberals to approach non-Christian religions with sympathy and understanding. There was even a move towards universalism. Anglican Bishop Stephen Neill, a prominent WCC leader, observed: 'Evangelism was no longer in the centre of the picture.'[33]

Two major questions on mission emerged during the Jerusalem Conference, to which no real consensus was found. First, the relationship between the Christian Faith and other religions. Second, the theological interpretation of Christian social and political involvement. A concentration on personal salvation was seen as an inadequate response to the vast social problems that were present in every nation on earth. Instead, an emphasis on Jesus Christ as the answer to social conflict was seen as consistent with the teachings of the social gospel.

There was a desire among many Conference delegates to play down the evangelistic fervour of Edinburgh 1910 and to focus instead on the positive values inherent in other world religions. Jerusalem 1928 is remembered because of the controversial nature of several of the preparatory papers. For example, the paper by John Leighton Stuart, who trained at Union Theological Seminary, New York, to become a missionary educator in China, and is widely known as the inaugural President of Yenching University, welcomed 'all the spiritual intuition or ethical enthusiasm that may come through any of the world's great seers or sages as part of the light that lighteth every man coming into the world'.[34]

A paper on Buddhism by missionary scholar Kenneth J. Saunders, suggested a mystical core common to all religions: 'Whatever our Christologies or our Buddhologies may be, the great fact remains that behind all religions there is Religion and the religious consciousness of man. The mystics are the experts who experience the truth by which the rest of us live.'[35]

The most controversial paper was the one on secularism by Rufus Jones, an American Quaker historian, theologian and philosopher with a strong interest in mysticism. Following a visit to Mahatma Gandhi and the birthplace of the Buddha, Jones formulated a new approach to missions—that of giving humanitarian aid to people while respecting other religions and not aggressively converting people to one's own religion. Jones produced the report 'Secular Civilization and the Christian Task', in which he argued that an interfaith alliance was necessary to oppose the creeping influence of secularisation. He wrote: 'Go to Jerusalem, then, not as members of a Christian nation to convert other nations which are not Christian, but as Christians within a nation far too largely non-Christian, who face within their own borders the competition of a rival movement as powerful… as any of the great historic religions…' (Jones was alluding to secularism). 'More than this, we go as those who find in the other religions which secularism attacks, as it attacks Christianity, witnesses of man's need of God and allies in our quest for perfection.'[36]

The presentation of Rufus Jones encouraged some missionary delegates to seek for ways to promote collaboration between Christianity and the other great world religions. Stanley H. Skreslet, Dean of Union Theological Seminary, in his book, *Comprehending Mission* (2012), notes that some who found inspiration in the presentation of Rufus Jones at Jerusalem 'began to search for ways to promote collaboration among the adherents of the world's religious traditions as the new form of Christian mission. It was in the service of this latter vision that the Laymen's Foreign Mission Inquiry was organized in 1930 under the direction of Harvard philosophy professor, William Hocking.'[37]

The paper, 'Beginning at Jerusalem', by Samuel McCrea Cavert, an American Presbyterian minister and General Secretary of the ecumenical Federal Council of Churches, makes the point that at the Jerusalem meeting there was manifest a greater desire to understand other religions sympathetically and to appreciate the things that high-minded non-Christians live by. 'Prior to the meeting a series of stimulating papers had been prepared by competent scholars, setting forth the values in Islam, in Hinduism, in Buddhism and in Confucianism. Criticism of some of the papers was heard on the ground that they were too extravagantly favorable in their estimate of non-Christian faiths, but the very fact that such an impression could be made shows how far missionary thinking has advanced since the days when all religions except Christianity were regarded as evil. At one point at least it was agreed at Jerusalem that other religions can be regarded as allies of Christianity quite as truly as rivals; for a new enemy of all religion, Christian or non-Christian alike, was recognized in the materialism now rampant in all lands… in the past the missionary movement had not "sufficiently sought out the good and noble elements in the non-Christian beliefs," and in a generous spirit went on to call attention to some of the worthy things in non-Christian systems.'[38]

William Temple, the future Archbishop of Canterbury, a highly influential figure who helped establish the WCC, was given the task of writing the Conference Message: 'To non-Christians also we make our call. We rejoice to think that just because in Jesus Christ the light that lighteth every man shone forth in its full splendour, we find rays of the same light where He is unknown or even is rejected. We welcome every noble quality in non-Christian persons .'[39]

The great hope of the Jerusalem Conference was that the spiritual greatness and power of the foreign missionary movement would build a Christian world.

But the liberalism, social gospel and implicit syncretism of Jerusalem was profoundly disturbing to many genuine evangelical Christians. They saw that the biblical foundation of the true Faith had been fatally flawed by the modernist ideas that promoted the notion of a fallible Bible. The consequence was that evangelicals lost confidence in the machinations of the IMC. The Conference ended with a bundle of theological uncertainty, for there was no clear understanding of the mission of the Church, and the mission of Christianity to other religions was shrouded in confusion. Proclamation of the true gospel of salvation was not on the agenda.

The Hocking Report of 1932

In the early 1930s William Hocking, Harvard Professor of Natural Religion, Moral Philosophy and Civil Polity, was asked to lead a Commission, funded by John D. Rockefeller, to study the foreign mission work of six Protestant denominations in India, Burma, China, and Japan. The report entitled, *Re-Thinking Missions: A Laymen's Inquiry After One Hundred Years* (1932), became known as the Hocking Report.

The Hocking Report, which focused on the role of Western missionaries in other cultures, immediately raised a storm of controversy among evangelical Christians, who regarded it as an overt and blatant expression of the most extreme form of liberal Christianity. The Report was generally cool toward evangelism and the proclamation of the gospel. The version of Christianity conceived by Hocking was one without dogma that sought to find the good in all religions. The Report stated, 'A Christian will therefore regard himself a co-worker with the forces which are making for righteousness within every religious system.'[40] Christians should accept the fact that 'in respect to its theology and ethics, Christianity has many doctrines in common with other religions…'[41]

Christian missionaries were to work in partnership with Hindus and Hinduism for some sort of religious and social reform. 'Christianity and other religions must join in a common quest for truth and experience which are not offered in any final and absolute way in Christianity. The missionary will look forward not to the destruction of these religions, but to their continued co-existence with Christianity, each stimulating the other in growth toward the ultimate goal, unity in the completest truth.'[42] The Report claimed: '[that] non-Christian religions do contain elements of instruction for us, imperfect exponents as we are of the truth we have, cannot be doubted. We have just illustrated this in what we have said of meditation.'[43]

The Report went so far as to suggest that missionaries did not adequately capture the spirit of liberal Protestantism, which viewed Christianity 'as less a religion of fear and more a religion of beneficence'. It predicted the emergence of a religion that would appeal to modern man. This new spirituality required a great knowledge and understanding of other world religions. The Report affirmed: 'Ministry to the secular needs of men (and women) in the Spirit of Christ, is evangelism, in the right sense of the word.'[44]

J. Gresham Machen, Presbyterian Professor of the New Testament, a great contender for the Faith and founder of Westminster Seminary, was appalled by the *Re-Thinking Missions* Report and felt compelled to respond. In 1933 he wrote a 110-page pamphlet entitled, 'Modernism and the Board of Foreign Missions of the Presbyterian Church in the U.S.A.' and sent it to every minister and elder in the governing presbytery, as well as to every member and secretary of the Board of Foreign Missions.

Edwin H. Rian, in *The Presbyterian Conflict* (1940), explains the drama of the conflict between Machen and Dr Robert E. Speer, who represented the Board of Foreign Missions: 'The drama and meaning of that day will remain long in the memory of those who were present to hear the debate. Before that large audience in the Fourth Presbyterian Church in Trenton, New Jersey, appeared two men, one the outstanding conservative theologian of America and the other the missionary leader of American Presbyterianism.'[45]

'At the very outset Dr Machen made it plain that his sole standard of judgment was the Word of God, and that every missionary, every institution, and every piece of literature supported and endorsed by the board must be tested and judged by adherence to the Bible… With these preliminary remarks he plunged into the main stream of his argument and mentioned briefly the evidences of modernism in the Board of Foreign Missions contained in his pamphlet.'[46]

The main thesis of Dr Machen's charges against the Board of Foreign Missions was that it had become so entangled with modernism that the need for reform was imperative. He proceeded to prove this contention by making six charges against the board, all substantiated by evidence.

His first complaint had to do with the attitude of the Board of Foreign Missions toward the Hocking Report. Another concern was the Board's attitude toward the modernist Auburn Affirmation (discussed in the next chapter), affirmed by liberal Presbyterians clerics, for one of the Board's most important officers was a signer of the Affirmation.

'The moral earnestness, the dignity, and the tender appeal with which Dr Machen closed his argument brought a hushed silence over the audience. He pled with them to return to the Word of God, to forsake the wisdom of man, to turn against the trend of the age, and to be faithful to the Christ of the Bible.'[47]

Despite the overwhelming case, supported by much evidence, the meeting voted by a large majority against Dr Machen. The modernists in the Presbyterian Church won the day, giving their full support to *Re-Thinking Missions*.

Hendrik Kraemer, a Dutch Reformed lay theologian and missiologist, in *Religion and the Christian Faith* (1956), recalled his objection to the Hocking Report in the bluntest of terms. He wrote: 'The point of view advocated by *Re-Thinking Missions* and its chairman [Hocking] is devoid of real theological sense and is, though intended to be the contrary, a total distortion of the Christian message, its content and real meaning. Religion and Christianity are simply reduced to immanent cultural phenomena. Nowhere is that maintained. Nor is the case stated in this way, because none of the writers had that in mind. In fact, however, the whole argument amounts to that. Its consequence is a suicide of missions and an annulment of the Christian faith.'[48]

The Madras Conference 1938

In 1938 the third Conference of the International Missionary Council (IMC) was held in the newly located Madras Christian College campus in Tambaram, India. The Conference was attended by 471 delegates from 69 countries, with almost half of the delegates coming from what were then called the 'younger churches', including a large delegation from India itself. Evangelicals from Western churches, it appeared, had by now largely withdrawn from the IMC. John Mott chaired the Conference and the Catholic Archbishop of Madras delivered the inaugural address. According to Bishop Stephen Neill, the Madras gathering was the most international gathering, up to that point, in the entire history of the Christian Church. Also attending was Lesslie Newbigin, the famous missionary and theologian, who was deeply ecumenical in outlook (see Bangkok in chapter 9).

But the IMC had a big problem, because many true evangelicals had reacted against the social gospel which had been given such prominence at the Jerusalem Conference a decade earlier. According to Arthur Johnston, 'Madras 1938 attempted to return to a more moderate position, one which would include both an evangelical and a modernist synthesis of evangelism.'[49] At the Conference Mott referred to 'The Larger Evangelism', which is now known by the term 'holistic'. In effect, Madras was an attempt 'to end the polarisation between historical evangelicalism and the modernism/liberalism as expressed in the social gospel. Mott, an astute layman, believed that goodwill could reconcile the two, for he did not seem to recognise the basic theological incompatibility between evangelicalism and liberalism.'[50] Mott's Larger Evangelism, which was a compromise that attempted to repair the damage done by the Jerusalem Conference, sought to incorporate the 'best' of traditional evangelism and the liberal social gospel. The Larger Evangelism was uncertain about the authority of Scripture. According to Arthur Johnston, 'The mystical presence of Christ in the world since the incarnation became the foundation of incarnational theology. Christ present in His Church led to Christ present in the world and in all world events.'[51]

Christianity's engagement with world religions and traditions received a lot of attention from the Madras Conference. Hendrik Kraemer, the Dutch Reformed theologian, had been commissioned by the IMC to write a book for the Madras Conference entitled, *Christian Message in a Non-Christian World* (1938). Kraemer's large 400-page book, which in some ways was a response to the liberalism of the Hocking Report, was a central topic at the 1938 Conference.

Kraemer distinguished between the Christian Faith and non-Christian religions, noting that Christianity 'has stood and stands under continuous and direct influence and judgment of the revelation in Christ', which therefore makes it unique from all other religions. He stated that non-Christian religions are sinful man's attempt to find God. He concluded that there is a radical discontinuity between non-Christian religions and the revelation of Jesus Christ. However, a large number of Indian delegates firmly rejected Kraemer's theology. The Christian scholars of Hinduism from Madras Christian College upheld the position of a continuity between non-Christian religions and Christianity.[52] According to Augustine Kanjamala in *The Future of Christian Mission in India* (2014), 'Some of the radicals even wanted to liberate the Indian church from Western captivity... The confrontation was between the Calvinist exclusivism and the Indian inclusivism. This was a radical breakthrough and beginning to the new Indian mission theology.'[53]

Associate Professor of Philosophy at Madras Christian College, Dr Joshua Kalapati, highlighted a clear tension among the Indian theologians at Tambaram regarding the basis of Christian missions. Anglican Bishop, V.S. Azariah, following Mott and Kraemer, took the position that a united Church was indispensable for Christian mission and witness. As a champion of mass conversions, he felt that a centralised Episcopal system was essential in India.

Standing against this view was the Hocking 'Rethinking Christianity' group in Madras, which argued that the Indian Christian community 'could not ignore the common Hindu heritage, its culture and traditions. They felt that in the wider context of fighting colonialism it was imperative that Indian Christians should go with the overwhelming Hindu majority.'[54]

The Madras Conference ended with the following statement: 'As to whether the non-Christian religions as total systems of thought and life, may be regarded as in some sense or to some degree manifesting God's revelation, Christians are not agreed. This is a matter urgently demanding thought and united study.'[55]

The Larger Evangelism

The Madras Conference called for a fresh definition of evangelism. Mott referred to a Larger Evangelism that is concerned with the total needs of man. The term 'Larger Evangelism' was seen to embrace medical service, educational service, social service and every conceivable activity that might be related to evangelism, as well as some that normally would not. According to Arthur Johnston, it was upon the superstructure of an errant, fallible Bible that the message of the Larger Evangelism was built. 'It was neo-orthodoxy, the acceptance of higher critical findings and of modern scientism, that were foundational in this earlier expression of what is now "holistic" evangelism.'[56] Salvation meant a fulfilment in Christ of both society and the individual. Madras believed that world evangelism is the God-given task of the Church, not the individual Christian. And so the entire and united Church should be involved in evangelism. The Church must be a visibly united body to effectively evangelise; doctrinal divisions must be set to one side.

But even the diplomatic skill of Mott was unable to bridge the theological chasm between evangelicalism and liberalism. Following the Madras Conference the International Missionary Council worked towards joining with the two committees (Life and Work, Faith and Order) that had emerged from Edinburgh 1910, and so ultimately to become the World Council of Churches in 1948.

The first World Missionary Conference of 1910 was called with the aim of taking the gospel to the non-Christian nations of the world. But there was a deep flaw in this 'evangelical' Conference, for its ecumenical ambitions were never far from the surface and biblical doctrine was regarded as too divisive to be discussed. This opened the door to every kind of doctrinal error, including liberalism, modernism, ecumenism and the social gospel. Over the following three decades the missionary movement, skilfully manipulated by John Mott and his social gospel agenda, was overtaken by modernism and liberalism. The result was the growth of ecumenism and the holistic gospel, and the formation of the liberal and ecumenical World Council of Churches, which is discussed in chapter 9. But first we need to return to the modernist/fundamentalist controversy.

(Endnotes)

1 The Burke Library Archives, Union Theological Seminary, New York, Missionary Research Library Archives: Section 12. www.columbia.edu/cu/lwe b/img/assets/6398/ MRL12_WMC_FA.pdf

2 John Mott, *The Future Leadership of the Church*, 1908, pp42-43, p45: https://archive. org/stream/futureleadership00mottuoft#page/n5/mode/2up

3 *John R. Mott, 1865–1955: A Biography*, Charles Howard Hopkins, Grand Rapids: Eerdmans, 1979, p417

4 Charles Howard Hopkins, *The Rise of the Social Gospel in American Protestantism, 1865-1915* New Haven, Yale Univ. Press, 1940, p. 300, cited from 'The Legacy of Walter Rauschenbusch: A Life Informed by Mission', Barbara A. Lundsten.

5 John R. Mott, Website of Institute for the Study of American Evangelicals, http:// www.wheaton.edu/isae/hall-of-biography/john-r-mott

6 Article in Christianity Today, 'Missions and Ecumenism: John R. Mott, Evangelist and ecumenist' by Mark Galli: http://www.christianitytoday.com/ch/2000/issue65/9.36.html

7 John Mott, *The Present World Situation*, 1915, originally published by New York: Student Volunteer Movement, p128 Ibid. pp71-72

9 Ibid. p75

10 Ibid. pp106-107

11 Ibid. p109

12 Ibid. pp120, 122, 123

13 Ibid. p127

14 Ibid. p146

15 Ibid. p210

16 Boston University School of Theology, History of Missiology, 'Oldham, Joseph Houldsworth (1874-1969), English pioneer of ecumenical mission and social concern', http://www.bu.edu/missiology/missionary-biography/n-o-p-q/oldham-joseph-houldsworth-1874-1969/

17 Roger Hedlund, *Roots of the Great Debate*, Evangelical Literature Service (1981)

18 David Hesselgrave, 'Will We Correct the "Edinburgh Error"?— Future Mission in Historical Perspective', Southwestern Journal of Theology, Vol49, No. 2, Spring 2007

19 Authur Johnston, *The Battle for World Evangelism*, Tyndale House Publishers, 1978, p46

20 Ibid. p51

21 *Edinburgh 2010: Springboard for Mission*, Kenneth R. Ross, William Carey International University Press, p30

22 Ibid. p31

23 David Hesselgrave, 'Edinburgh Error'

24 Arthur Johnston, *The Battle for World Evangelism*, p36

25 International Missionary Council, Administrative/Biographical history, Reference code(s): GB 0102 IMC, held at School of Oriental and African Studies Library

26 Encyclopedia of Protestantism by J. Gordon Melton, p298, 'Protestantism'. enacademic.com/340/International_Missionary_Council

27 *The Ecumenical Movement: An Introductory History* by Thomas E. FitzGerald, 2004, Praeger, p89

28 Ibid. p89

29 Ibid. p90

30 Ibid. p92

31 WCC paper, What is Faith and Order? by Mary Tanner, moderator, Faith and Order Commission, August 1995.

32 WCC website, About Us, Willem A Visser 't Hooft http://www.oikoumene.org/en/about-us/organizational-structure/general-secretary/since-1948/willem-a-visser-t-hooft

33 'Reformed Reflections, Mission's Focus Shifts Over Eight Decades', J.D. Tangelder, http://www.reformedreflections.ca/missions/missions-focus-shifts.html,

34 J. Leighton Stuart, 'Christianity and Confucianism,' in IMC Part 1, pp. 62 – 63, cited from T.S. Perry, (1996) theses 'The Christian Message in a Postmodern World: a critical re-appropriation of Hendrik Kraemer's theology of religions, Durham University, p91

35 K.J. Saunders, 'Christianity and Buddhism,' IMC Part I, p128, cited from Perry, p92

36 Rufus M, Jones, 'Secular Civilization and the Christian Task,' in IMC Part I, p338, cited from Perry

37 *Comprehending Mission: The Questions, Methods, Themes, Problems, and Prospects of Missiology*, Orbis books, 2012, by Stanley H. Skreslet, p117

38 Beginning at Jerusalem by Samuel McCrea Cavert. Samuel McCrea Cavert as a Presbyterian minister was later to serve as an executive of the Federal, National and World councils of Churches. He reports here on the International Missionary Conference held in Jerusalem in 1928. This article was published in the *Christian Century*, May 10, 1928.

39 Report of the Jerusalem Meeting of the International Missionary Council, March 24-April 8, vol.1, p490. Cited from Arthur Johnston, p62.

40 Hocking Report, Rethinking missions, p40

41 Hocking Report, Rethinking missions, p49

42 John F. Piper, *Robert E. Speer: Prophet of the American Church*, Geneva Press, 2000, p379

43 Hocking Report, Rethinking missions, p46

44 Hocking report, cited from, 'The Re-forming Tradition: Presbyterians and Mainstream Protestantism', edited by Milton J. Coalter, John M. Mulder, Louis Weeks, Westminster John Knox Pres, 1992, pp168-169

45 Edwin H. Rian, *The Presbyterian Conflict*, Chapter 6. The Orthodox Presbyterian Church, the Independent Board, Committee for the Historian of the OPC reissued book in 1992, originally published by Williams Eerdmans in 1940

46 Ibid. *The Presbyterian Conflict*

47 Ibid. *The Presbyterian Conflict*

48 Hendrik Kraemer, *Religion and the Christian Faith*, first published 1956, reprinted 2002, James Clark and Co. p223-224

49 Arthur Johnston, *The Battle for World Evangelism*, p64

50 Ibid. p65

51 Ibid. p70

52 Augustine Kanjamala, *The Future of Christian Mission in India: Toward a New Paradigm for the Third Millennium*, Pickwick Publications, 2014, p291

53 Ibid. p292

54 An article by Joshua Kalapati, 'Edinburgh to Tambaram: A Paradigm Shift in Missions, or the horizon of Missions broadened?' in Dharma Deepika, Chennai, January, 2010

55 Jan van Lin, *Shaking the Fundamentals: Religious Plurality and Ecumenical Movement*, 2002, p2. The Authority of the Faith, The Madras Series, presenting papers based on the meeting of the International Missionary Council at Tambaram, Madras, India, December 12 -29, 1938

56 Arthur Johnston, *The Battle for World Evangelism*, pp69-70

Chapter 7

Gresham Machen Battles the Modernists

The higher critical movement in the USA became the polluted fountainhead that produced a constant flow of modernist doctrinal error in many of the mainline traditional Protestant denominations. Walter Rauschenbusch's influential ministry had turned the minds of many Protestants to the idealistic promises of the social gospel. It was inevitable, therefore, that there would be spiritual conflict between those who earnestly contended for the Gospel of Truth and those who propagated the false social gospel of the modernisers. During the 1920s and 1930s the theological battle between modernists and fundamentalists became a bitter struggle that was to have a massive impact on evangelical Christianity in the USA and worldwide, an impact that would continue for decades into the future. Moreover, we can only really understand the American input to the meetings of the International Missionary Council in Jerusalem (1928) and Madras (1938) when we appreciate the way the Christian Faith in the USA and in other countries was being shaped by the modernist cause.

In the Presbyterian denomination the battle between fundamentalists and liberals proved to be a long-running saga, that at times became divisive and caused great bewilderment among many Christians, who were disturbed by the theological controversy which they felt presented Christianity in a negative light.

The Five Points

To see the modernist/fundamentalist controversy in context, we need to remind ourselves that back in 1893 the General Assembly of the Presbyterian Church had convicted Charles A. Briggs, arch proponent of the higher criticism, of heresy and suspended him from the ministry of the Northern Presbyterian Church for teaching, among other things, that the Scriptures contained error. The infiltration of liberal ideas from the higher critical movement, and the popularity of the teaching of Charles Briggs, was such that as early as 1910 the General Assembly of the Northern Presbyterian Church saw the need to affirm five essential doctrines of the Christian Faith, which became known as 'The Five Points'. It is surely of interest that the conservative Presbyterians wanted to emphasise the importance of doctrine at the very time the leaders of the World Missionary movement meeting in Edinburgh considered doctrine to be divisive and unnecessary. The Five Points were:

1) The full inspiration and inerrancy of the Bible;
2) The virgin birth of Christ;
3) Christ's substitutionary atonement which satisfied divine justice;
4) Christ's bodily resurrection;
5) Christ's miracles.

But matters within Presbyterianism had declined to such a degree that in 1923 the General Assembly saw the need to again affirm The Five Points, which were simply a statement of fundamental Christian doctrines that had been accepted and believed for centuries, and therefore should not have needed to be restated.

Auburn Affirmation

The Five Points, however, were anathema to the modernists, for they did not like doctrinal clarity. And to make their opposition clear and public, 1,293 ordained Presbyterian ministers signed the Auburn Affirmation in 1924. This public Affirmation asserted that not one of the doctrines declared to be 'essential' by the General Assembly was really essential at all. Indeed, all of The Five Points, far from being essential doctrines, were only 'theories'.[1]

J. Gresham Machen, who we met in the previous chapter as he opposed the heretical Hocking Report, was a prominent conservative Presbyterian theologian and selfless champion of sound doctrine. He was straightforward and outspoken in his condemnation of the Auburn Affirmation and wrote: 'It declares that not a single one of the great verities mentioned by the General Assembly of 1923 is essential; and it declares that all of the five verities are merely "theories" (among other possible theories), which some may and some may not hold to be satisfactory explanations of something else. Thus according to the Auburn Affirmation a man may be a minister in the Presbyterian Church and yet deny the full truthfulness of Scripture, the virgin birth, the substitutionary atonement to satisfy divine justice and reconcile us to God, the bodily resurrection, the miracles of our Lord.'[2]

Machen drew attention to the doctrinal confusion that reigned in the Presbyterian denomination. 'What a morass we find ourselves in here! It is a well-known morass, the morass of that destructive Modernism which is engulfing our Presbyterian Church, as it already has engulfed so many other churches, to the ruin of countless souls.'[3]

Presbyterian scholar and veteran defender of the Faith, Dr William M. McPheeters, who taught at Columbia Theological Seminary, commented on the Auburn Affirmation: 'The oftener I read it the more deeply I am convinced that its conception of Christian liberty in connection with subscription to the system of doctrine set forth in the Standards of the Presbyterian Church in the U.S.A. is intellectually absurd, historically false, ethically detestable and pernicious, and religiously blasphemous.'[4]

Jack Rogers, a professor of theology who served as Moderator of the 213th General Assembly of the Presbyterian Church (USA), in his book, *Presbyterian Creeds*, makes the point that by 1925 there were three identifiable political parties within the Presbyterian Church. 'One was composed of theological liberals, who believed in an inclusive church, containing any who wished to belong. Opposed to them were doctrinal fundamentalists, who argued for an exclusivist church composed only of those who agreed with the five fundamental points. The largest group, though least well organized, was made up of moderates, who were theologically conservative but were inclusivists for the sake of the peace, unity, and mission of the church.'[5]

Harry Emerson Fosdick (1878-1969)

A prominent figure in the controversy was Harry Emerson Fosdick, a popular and very influential modernist. Early on in his professed Christian life he decided he wanted nothing to do with the born-again movement known as fundamentalism. Fosdick also rejected Calvinism, which he believed produced, quote, 'a God who is a devil', and instead relied on his own personal spiritual experiences. The Lord was to be found in living experience, he argued, not at the end of some creed.[6] This is a clear example of a false dichotomy. Biblical creeds and statements of faith help Christian believers to test their spiritual experience and their walk with Christ.

Fosdick was trained for the ministry at Colgate Divinity School, New York, where he was influenced by William Newton Clarke, a major proponent of the New Theology and an early advocate of the social gospel.[7] He then trained in theology at Union Theological Seminary, New York, a leading liberal seminary in the United States, graduating in 1903. The time spent at Union had a large impact on Fosdick's view of the Christian Faith. He was greatly influenced by proponents of higher criticism, like Julius Wellhausen, and by radical liberal thinkers, such as Friedrich Schleiermacher and Albrecht Ritschl. Fosdick's commitment to modernist views are clear from his statement: 'I do not believe in the Virgin Birth, or in that old-fashioned substitutionary doctrine of the Atonement; and I do not know any intelligent Christian minister who does'(!)[8] He also gave himself to the study of sociology. Fosdick wrote: 'We could be Christians without being deaf, dumb and blind in the face of modern knowledge. All truth, we said, is God's truth, and Christian theology can take it in, rejoice in it, and incorporate it into the understanding of the gospel.'[9]

The influence of the social gospel was prominent in his studies. Fosdick's thinking was also shaped by the ideology of the Quaker, Rufus Jones, Professor of Philosophy at Haverford College and a minister of the Society of Friends. Rufus Jones, who we met in the previous chapter at the 1928 Jerusalem IMC Conference, had a deep-seated belief in the essential goodness of his fellowman, and became the leading historian of mysticism.[10] Such men helped to mould the young Fosdick into the pattern of radical liberalism that was gathering pace in the USA.

In his autobiography, Fosdick explains his mystical view of God. He wrote: 'I learned to pray, not because I had adequately argued out prayer's rationality, but because I desperately needed help from a Power greater than my own. I learned that God... is an immediately available Resource... around our spirits is a spiritual Presence in living communion with whom we can find sustaining strength.'[11]

It became clear that Fosdick's unorthodox, tolerant brand of the Christian Faith was extremely popular. He was a profuse author and six of his early devotional books (among others, *The Meaning of Faith* and *The Meaning of Prayer*) sold in the millions. J. Gresham Machen asked, 'The question is not whether Mr Fosdick is winning men, but whether the thing to which he is winning them is Christianity.'[12]

Dr Fosdick served as Professor of Practical Theology at Union Theological Seminary from 1915 to 1946. Although he was an ordained Baptist minister, he became a central figure in the battle between conservatives and liberals in the Presbyterian Church. As an eloquent preacher, and despite being an ordained Baptist minister, he was invited to minister at the First Presbyterian Church on West Twelfth Street, Manhattan. In May 1922 he delivered a provocative sermon entitled, 'Shall the Fundamentalists Win?' Fosdick's prime direction in life was to modernise the Christian Faith and to demonstrate what he saw as the fallacies of orthodox Christianity. In this sermon he openly and vehemently repudiated core beliefs of the Christian Faith—belief in the virgin birth was unnecessary; the inerrancy of Scripture, untenable; and the doctrine of the Second Coming, absurd. Though he ended on a note of reconciliation, he castigated fundamentalists as 'bitterly intolerant'. Fosdick writes in his autobiography, 'It was a plea for tolerance, for a church inclusive enough to take in both liberals and conservatives without either trying to drive the other out.'[13]

Baptist oil baron John D. Rockefeller, one of the wealthiest men in the nation, was greatly taken by Fosdick's controversial sermon and paid for some 130,000 copies to be printed and distributed to every Protestant minister in the United States.

What had been up to this time a series of skirmishes between fundamentalists and liberals now exploded into open warfare.[14] Many conservatives saw all this as a clear challenge to the fundamentals of their faith. Clarence E. Macartney, a minister from Philadelphia, responded to Fosdick with a sermon titled, 'Shall Unbelief Win?' In 1923 Dr Fosdick gave a series of lectures on preaching before the Yale Divinity School, which were published under the title, 'The Modern Use of the Bible'. In the lectures and subsequent book he upheld completely the modern higher critical views of the books of the Bible as to date and authorship.[15]

At the Presbyterian General Assembly of 1923, a number of funda-mentalists, led by William Jennings Bryan, called for Fosdick's removal from the pulpit of the First Presbyterian Church. The outcome was a resolution directing the New York Presbytery to instruct First Church to conform to the Westminster Confession of Faith in its preaching and teaching. Fosdick handed in his resignation, but it was rejected by the Session. At the 1924 General Assembly, with Clarence Macartney as Moderator and Bryan as Vice-Moderator, Fosdick's preaching remained an issue. The two warring factions finally reached a compromise by asking Fosdick to regularise his position at First Church by becoming a Presbyterian minister. He refused, and in October of that year the Session accepted his resignation. *The Presbyterian* made the point that Fosdick's teachings not only openly denied the essential doctrines of the Presbyterian Church, but were 'subversive of the truth of Christianity as received, confessed, held and defended by the Christian church of all ages'.[16]

Following his resignation Fosdick became Pastor of Park Avenue Baptist Church in New York, and then with help from John D. Rockefel-ler, moved on to the large and modern Riverside Church, which seated a congregation of over 2,000. Through a popular radio ministry, known as the National Vespers Hour, Fosdick was able to reach vast audiences with his liberal version of Christianity. Such was his popularity that he has been called the Minister of all America. Week by week for 20 years his voice on National Vespers was one of the most familiar on radio. He sought to popularise Christianity and make it more acceptable. The effect was to make the ideas of liberal Christianity popular with the man in the street. In his famous sermon, 'The Church Must Go Beyond Modern-ism', Fosdick optimistically declared: 'We have already largely won the battle we started out to win; we have adjusted the Christian faith to the best intelligence of our day and have won the strongest minds and the best abilities of the churches to our side. Fundamentalism is still with us but mostly in the backwaters. The future of the churches, if we will have it so, is in the hands of modernism.'[17]

In his 50 books, thousands of sermons, articles, and lectures, Fos-dick walked hand-in-hand with American liberal Christianity as it made its way through the theological conflict of the first six decades of the twentieth century.[18] Such was his popularity that on two separate occasions he was on the cover of *Time* magazine.[19]

Dr J. Gresham Machen (1881-1937)

J. Gresham Machen, Professor of New Testament Theology at Princeton Theological Seminary, is another extremely important figure in the modernist/fundamentalist battle. Machen studied at Johns Hopkins University and then Princeton University, before reading theology at Princeton Theological Seminary. He spent a year in Germany, studying at the Universities of Marburg and Goettingen, where he was exposed to the ideas of higher criticism. As a sound believer he soon recognised the dangers—strongly opposing the liberal theology of Fosdick.

In 1906 he joined the faculty of Princeton Theological Seminary and taught New Testament theology in that Seminary until its reorganisation in 1929. From 1929 until his death, Dr. Machen was Professor of New Testament at the newly-formed Westminster Theological Seminary—the product of his stand against modernism at Princeton. Machen was a man possessed of massive learning, with a powerful intellect and the gift of discernment. As a scholar and as an author, he was one of the great figures of Presbyterianism in America.[20] He believed in the full inspiration of the Bible, and followed and taught the doctrines of the Christian Faith as summarised in the Westminster Confession of Faith and in the Larger and Shorter Catechisms.

His book, *Christianity and Liberalism* (1923), proclaimed his deeply held belief that liberal Christianity was, quote, 'a different religion'. He wrote: 'The present time is a time of conflict; the great redemptive religion which has always been known as Christianity is battling against a totally diverse type of religious belief, which is only the more destructive of the Christian faith because it makes use of traditional Christian terminology. This modern non-redemptive religion is called "modernism" or "liberalism". Both names are unsatisfactory...'[21] He argues that modern liberalism in the Church is no longer merely an academic matter. 'It is no longer a matter merely of theological seminaries or universities. On the contrary its attack upon the fundamentals of the Christian faith is being carried on vigorously by Sunday School lesson helps, by the pulpit, and by the religious press.'[22] He is concerned about the religious leader who, in his desire to 'avoid giving offense', is dishonest in not making the radicalism of his views known by speaking his whole mind.[23] He observes that while liberalism is often hostile to doctrine, it is only the doctrines of the historic creeds to which it objects. He writes: 'The doctrine of God and the doctrine of man are the two great presuppositions of the gospel. With regard to these presuppositions, as with regard to the gospel itself, modern liberalism is diametrically opposed to Christianity.'[24]

Machen points out another crucial difference: 'According to the Bible, man is a sinner under the just condemnation of God; according to modern liberalism, there is really no such thing as sin. At the very root of the modern liberal movement is the loss of the consciousness of sin… Characteristic of the modern age, above all else, is a supreme confidence in human goodness; the religious literature of the day is redolent of that confidence.'[25]

Machen points out that when it comes to the doctrine of the Cross, modern liberals are never weary of pouring out the vials of hatred and scorn. 'They speak with disgust of those who believe "that the blood of our Lord, shed in a substitutionary death, placates an alienated Deity and makes possible welcome for the returning sinner." Against the doctrine of the Cross they use every weapon of caricature and vilification. Thus they pour out their scorn upon a thing so holy and so precious that in the presence of it the Christian heart melts in gratitude too deep for words.'[26] Here we should note that Machen's quote regarding 'the blood of our Lord', is from Fosdick's sermon, 'Shall the Fundamentalists Win?'

A major concern of Machen was that the Church has been unfaithful by admitting great companies of non-Christian persons, not only into her membership, but into her teaching positions. He was deeply concerned about enemies within the Church. He argued that it is perfectly clear that liberalism is not Christianity. 'And that being the case, it is highly undesirable that liberalism and Christianity should continue to be propagated within the bounds of the same organization. A separation between the two parties in the Church is the crying need of the hour.'[27] In effect, Machen was calling for true believers to separate themselves from liberal churches.

Dr Clarence E. Macartney, who at one time was the Moderator of the General Assembly of the Northern Presbyterian Church, remarked: 'More than any other man of our generation, Dr Machen tore the mask from the face of unbelief which parades under the name of Modernism in the Christian church.'[28]

So intense was the warfare between fundamentalists and liberals that it led to a split between the theologians of Princeton Seminary and Union Seminary, with Union choosing to support the higher critical teachings of theologian Charles Briggs (already found guilty of heresy, as described chapter 4). Towards the end of the 1920s there was a growing movement that proposed the reorganisation of Princeton Seminary to make it inclusive of both the conservative 'Old School' theology, which had always been taught there, and the liberal 'New School' theology as well.

Chalmers W. Alexander, who was a ruling elder at the First Presbyterian Church in Jackson, Missouri, and editor of *The Southern Presbyterian Journal*, commented: 'Because of the movement to try to reorganize Princeton Seminary, a fierce struggle had taken place for several years behind the scenes in the Northern Presbyterian Church. By this time the Northern Presbyterian Church consisted of three different groups: a strong, outspoken orthodox group, an active Modernist group, and a so-called "middle-of-the-road" group. This so-called "middle-of-the-road" group was trying to hold on to the Holy Bible and to the Westminster Standards, and at the same time not oppose the Modernists. Many of this so-called "middle-of-the-road" group wanted "peace at any price," even if it had to be purchased at the cost of serious compromise with error in Christian belief. Finally, in 1929, in spite of a valiant and courageous fight by many of the orthodox group in the Northern Presbyterian Church, those who wanted to reorganize Princeton Seminary won the struggle.'[29]

Two significant consequences flowed from the reorganisation. The first was that Machen and a group of reformed theologians, who were not prepared to work in a compromised theological institution, resigned from Princeton and established the new Westminster Theological Seminary. The second consequence was that for the first time some of those who had signed the heretical Auburn Affirmation were placed on the

Board of Trustees which controlled Princeton Seminary. In other words, the reorganisation was a victory for the heretical Auburn Affirmation, and Princeton Seminary was now firmly in the hands of the modernists.

But the modernist agenda had also permeated deep into the programme of the Board of Foreign Missions of the Presbyterian denomination under the leadership of Dr Robert E. Speer. The heretical Hocking (*Re-Thinking Missions*) Report, discussed in chapter 6, had brought into the public arena the apostasy within mainline Presbyterianism. To challenge the false teaching of this infamous Report, Dr Machen introduced an 'overture' into the New Brunswick Presbytery, of which he was a member, and which included the Princeton Theological Seminary. His printed brief, 'Modernism and the Board of Foreign Missions of the Presbyterian Church in the USA', was carefully documented. The Presbytery refused to pass his 'overture', but the Philadelphia Presbytery later presented the same 'overture' to the General Assembly of 1933.

The website of the American Presbyterian Church explains: 'Dr. Machen and those associated with him sought by every proper and lawful means within the church to reform the Board of Foreign Missions and to bring its practice and teaching in line with the Westminster Confession of Faith and the Holy Scriptures. When this effort was unsuccessful, in 1933, he and others took the initiative in forming an Independent Board for Presbyterian Foreign Missions outside the control and authority of the General Assembly. This Independent Board was to promote "truly Biblical missions" and to be an agency through which Christians of all churches, as they were led of the Lord, could obey the Great Commission given to us by Jesus Christ.'[30]

The Independent Board for Presbyterian Foreign Missions was incorporated in December of 1933, with Dr Machen as its President and a young missionary named Charles J. Woodbridge as General Secretary. The liberals, fresh from their victories at Princeton, were determined to crush Machen and gain the Presbyterian Church for modernism. Machen was to be disciplined for disobeying an order from the New Brunswick Presbytery!

An article by Chalmers W. Alexander, 'Exploring Avenues of Acquaintance and Co-operation', explains the background to the trial and expulsion of Machen from the Presbyterian Church. The issue was the success of Machen's Independent Missions Board, which infuriated the modernists. The interest in the new Independent Board was so great that some of the ecclesiastical dignitaries of the Northern Presbyterian Church were aroused to action. 'As a result of their efforts, the General Assembly of 1934 directed "that all ministers and laymen affiliated with the Presbyterian Church in the U.S.A. who are officers, trustees or members of the Independent Board for Presbyterian Foreign Missions …sever their connection with this Board," that in case of their refusal so to act, the presbyteries to which they were subject should institute disciplinary proceedings against them. When the Presbytery of New Brunswick called upon Dr Machen to resign his membership in the Independent Board, his reply was a positive and determined refusal. Then the Presbytery preferred charges against Dr Machen for disobeying the order.'[31]

Dr Machen was charged, tried and found guilty of disobeying an order. Immediately following the announcement of the Presbytery's judgement, Dr Machen issued a statement: 'The Special Judicial Commission of the Presbytery of New Brunswick has simply condemned me without giving me a hearing. I am condemned for failing to obey a lawful order; but when my counsel, the Rev H. McAllister Griffiths, offered to prove that the order that I had disobeyed was not lawful but unlawful the court refused to hear a word of argument. I am condemned for making false assertions about the Modernism of the official Board of Foreign Missions, but when my counsel offered to prove that those assertions were not false but true, the court would not hear a word of the evidence that we were perfectly ready to produce. It is not too much to say that a trial conducted in that fashion is nothing but a farce.'[32]

Chalmers W. Alexander expressed his view: 'Thus, in 1936, Dr Machen was kicked out of the ministry of the Northern Presbyterian Church because he had helped establish and run a foreign missions board which would not tolerate Modernism or give it support in the foreign missions work!'[33]

Machen advocated a split within the Presbyterian Church along theological lines. Together with a number of his supporters, in 1936 he left the Presbyterian Church and formed a new denomination, the Orthodox Presbyterian Church. As Princeton Seminary was drifting into liberalism, Machen and several colleagues had already established Westminster Theological Seminary in 1929. Only six months after the new denomination's beginning, Machen died in Bismarck, North Dakota. He was undoubtedly a true man of God and one of the most important conservative Protestant thinkers of the first half of the twentieth century. He was one of those rare men far-sighted enough to see the inevitable consequences of doctrinal error, and the courage to do something about it.

Rev John P. Galbraith, a student of Machen who was ordained in 1937, in an article, 'Man of God', writes: 'It was not Machen the theologian who drew me to Westminster. It was Machen the loving and devoted follower of Jesus his Savior, the one who raised the flag of truth at all costs, who gripped me. His watchword, as it were, was: God's Word is my command. Before I ever entered seminary, what would become a lifelong memory was founded. For Machen, it was not just a Presbyterian conflict in which he had become engaged, but a proclamation of the gospel for the entire world. His positions were, thus, not of his own devising, but the careful exegesis of the Scriptures.'[34]

Dr Maitland Alexander, the President of the Board of Directors of Princeton Theological Seminary, paid tribute to his friend J. Gresham Machen: 'I do not hesitate to say that he was the world's greatest New Testament scholar, and those who attempted to answer him were thrown back like waves that beat against an eternal rock. He was the greatest champion of the Reformed Faith in the world. By the Reformed Faith – I will put it in words that you will understand and I will understand better than that theological phrase – he was the world's greatest champion of the old-fashioned, evangelical religion. He believed in the eternal purposes of God; he believed that God came down to earth to save the world; he believed in the bodily resurrection of the believer; he believed in the inerrant Bible; and he stood for those things through thick and thin, through the storms of persecution and amid the great efforts that were made to stop him… Then, Dr Machen was a humble Christian. I do not know any man that I have ever known that was as truly humble before his God as he was. He was a man of principle; of course he was a man of intense Bible study. He was a man who gave his heart wholly and unreservedly to the Lord Jesus Christ. Dr Machen was the object of great personal attacks by the men in power in his own church, which issue finally in the end refused him communion in the Presbyterian Church.'[35] To paraphrase Hebrews 11.38, Machen was a man 'of whom the Presbyterian Church was not worthy.'

We learn an important lesson from the battles of J. Gresham Machen. He was constrained by God and a love for the Gospel of Truth to defend the Church against the false teaching of the modernists. He did so by an appeal to Scripture and by careful documentation of the doctrinal errors of the modernists. Yet the modernists made no attempt to answer the doctrinal criticisms raised by Machen. Their response was simply to ignore the criticism and engage in personal abuse. And so it is to-day. A tactic of the false teacher is to refuse to engage with those who defend the Faith, and to accuse them of being intolerant, unloving and harsh. Another tactic of false teachers is to accuse opponents of being judgemental.

As mentioned above, Machen believed that the Church of his day had been *unfaithful* by admitting great numbers of unbelievers not only into membership, but into positions of authority and even into teaching positions. He wrote: 'The greatest menace to the Christian Church today comes not from enemies outside, but from the enemies within; it comes from the presence within the Church of a type of faith and practice that is anti-Christian to the core.' To him it was perfectly clear that liberalism was not Christianity, and he argued passionately for a separation between the two.[36]

Machen was undoubtedly a prophet for the times. He is an example of a good soldier of Christ in the defence of the True Gospel. With great powers of discernment and a boldness that comes from a true faith, together with a pastor's heart, he was able to recognise the serious errors of the false teachers who had invaded the Church. He understood that modernism posed a great threat to the life and mission of the Church. With courage and humility he contended for the Faith at enormous personal cost.

But the battle against false teaching in the Church is an ongoing battle. The errors of higher criticism had left a long trail of unbelief in many Protestant denominations, and many seminaries and professors of theology were openly supportive of the new 'scientific' ideas of biblical interpretation. The integration of liberal ideas with orthodox Christian doctrine caused confusion and uncertainty in many churches and among ordinary churchgoers. Another factor that disturbed the Christian mind was the high-profile Scopes monkey trial on evolution, which made the fundamentalist cause appear ignorant and hopelessly out of date in the eyes of the general population. The faith of many Christians was severely tested by the Scopes trial, the subject of our next chapter.

(Endnotes)

1 Cited from: Chalmers W. Alexander 2. Discipline Found Wanting, What Happened to the Signers Of The Auburn Affirmation? "Exploring Avenues Of Acquaintance And Co-operation"
https://continuing.wordpress.com/2011/05/10/discipline-found-wanting/
2 Cited from Chalmers W. Alexander 4. Some Popular Attitudes Toward The Auburn Affirmation Today, https://continuing.wordpress.com/2011/05/16/chalmers-1949-4-popular-attitudes/
3 Ibid.
4 Ibid.
5 Cited from 'The Fundamentalist / Modernist Conflict' article written by David Pultz, First Church Archivist, as part of an Adult Education lecture series sponsored by the Christian Education Committee, 1995-1996. http://www.fpcnyc.org/about-us/history/harry-emerson-fosdick/the-fundamentalistmodernist-conflict.html#sthash.eMrLaSjI.dpbs
6 *Christianity Today*, Christian History, Harry Emerson Fosdick, Liberalism's popularizer, posted 8/08/2008, http://www.christianitytoday.com/ch/131christians/pastorsandpreachers/fosdick.html
7 Tim Challies, 'The False Teachers: Harry Emerson Fosdick', March 26, 2014, http://www.challies.com/articles/the-false-teachers-harry-emerson-fosdick
8 Cited from: Chalmers W. Alexander 2. Discipline Found Wanting, What Happened to the Signers Of The Auburn Affirmation? "Exploring Avenues Of Acquaintance And Co-operation"
9 H. E. Fosdick, *The Living of These Days*, Harper & Brothers, 1956, p245
10 Reformed Reflections website, article 'Harry Emerson Fosdick (1878-1969)' by Rev Johan D. Tangelder, November, 1969, http://www.reformedreflections.ca/biography/harry-e-fosdick.html
11 *The Living of These Days*, p75
12 *Christianity Today*, Christian History, article 'Harry Emerson Fosdick, Liberalism's popularizer' http://www.christianitytoday.com/ch/131christians/pastorsandpreachers/fosdick.html
13 *The Living of These Days*, p145
14 *Christianity Today*, Harry Emerson Fosdick, http://www.christianitytoday.com/ch/131christians/pastorsandpreachers/fosdick.html
15 Edwin H. Rian, *The Presbyterian Conflict*, Chapter 2. The Auburn Affirmation. http://www.opc.org/books/conflict/ch2.html
16 *The Presbyterian Conflict*, cited from *The Presbyterian* 94 (June 5, 1924), 5

17 H. E. Fosdick, *Riverside Sermons*, p362, cited from Reformed Reflections Tangelder's article on Harry Emerson Fosdick, http://www.reformedreflections.ca/biography/harry-e-fosdick.html
18 *Christianity Today* article on Fosdick, http://www.christianitytoday.com/ch/131christians/pastorsandpreachers/fosdick.html
19 Tim Challies, 'The False Teachers'
20 Cited from Chalmers W. Alexander 5. Northern Aggression, https://continuing.wordpress.com/2011/05/21/chalmers-1949-5-northern-aggression/
21 Gresham Machen, *Christianity and Liberalism*, Victory Press, 1923, p2
22 *Christianity and Liberalism*, p17
23 *Christianity and Liberalism*, p17
24 *Christianity and Liberalism*, p54
25 *Christianity and Liberalism*, p64
26 *Christianity and Liberalism*, p120
27 *Christianity and Liberalism*, pp159-169
28 Cited from Chalmers W. Alexander 10. 'Dr. J. Gresham Machen on Christianity and Modernism or Liberalism', https://continuing.wordpress.com/2011/06/06/chalmers-10-modernism-another-religion-entirely/
29 Cited from Chalmers W. Alexander 8,' The Cause of the Doctrinal Trouble in the Northern Presbyterian Church', https://continuing.wordpress.com/2011/06/02/chalmers-8-the-cause-of-doctrinal-troubles/
30 American Presbyterian Church official website, 'The Independent Board Trials', http://www.americanpresbyterianchurch.org/?page_id=1820
31 Cited from Chalmers W. Alexander 7. 'What the Northern Presbyterian Church did to Dr. J. Gresham Machen' , Southern Presbyterian Journal on 02/06/2011, https://continuing.wordpress.com/2011/06/02/chalmers-7-significance-of-machens-dismissal/
32 Ibid.
33 Ibid.
34 *New Horizons*, 'J. Gresham Machen, Man of God', by John P. Galbraith, Orthodox Presbyterian Church website, http://www.opc.org/nh.html?article_id=686
35 Tributes to Dr. J. Gresham Machen, delivered at First Presbyterian Church, Pittsburgh, Pennsylvania, Sunday, January 3, 1937 http://www.pcahistory.org/findingaids/machen/eulogy01.pdf
36 *Christianity and Liberalism*, pp159-169

Chapter 8

Scopes Monkey Trial

During the theological controversies of the 1920s the infamous Scopes Monkey Trial of 1925 was a very public event that had a huge negative impact on the fundamentalist cause. In fact, it was a public relations disaster of the first order, influencing public opinion for decades to come. The court case, which revolved around the teaching of evolution in a small town in Tennessee, attracted massive publicity as conservative Christianity itself appeared to be on trial. Unprecedented press coverage was given to the event, and it was the first trial in USA history to be broadcast over national radio. As a media event, the case represented a dramatic clash between traditional values and modern values in the America of the 1920s, and offered a great opportunity for the enemies of the Faith to ridicule and mock those who believed that God created the world in six days, as described in the book of Genesis. The rhetorical skills of an aggressive defence lawyer made the fundamentalist position appear ridiculous. The impact on the Church was substantial as many Christians now became increasingly reluctant to defend the fundamentals of the Faith.

The trial was deliberately set up as a media event to attract publicity to the town of Dayton, a small town going through hard times. Teacher John Scopes agreed to serve as a means for those wanting to test the legislation that outlawed the teaching of evolution to schoolchildren. Amid the celebrities and legal scholars, he was the least significant person at the trial. The plan was for a provocative show trial that would examine the highly-charged question: Who would dominate American culture—the modernists or the traditionalists? There is no doubt that journalists from around the USA were looking for a showdown in this small Tennessee courtroom in the summer of 1925. A jury, largely composed of farmers, was to decide the fate of the high school biology teacher charged with illegally teaching the theory of evolution to schoolchildren.

William Jennings Bryan (whom we met in the previous chapter), a conservative Presbyterian and three-time Democratic candidate for President, who had in the past led a fundamentalist crusade to banish Darwin's theory of evolution from American classrooms, offered to join the prosecution team despite not having practised law in over three decades. The eminent journalist H.L. Mencken of the *Baltimore Sun*, who covered the trial, described Bryan as a 'sort of Fundamentalist Pope'.[1]

Clarence Darrow, a brilliant layer who was deeply agnostic in his beliefs and a champion of liberal causes, was chosen by the American Civil Liberties Union (ACLU) to lead the defence team. Hundreds of journalists descended on Dayton for the show trial of the century, no doubt anticipating sensational headlines. They were not disappointed!

On the seventh day of trial, the defence called William Jennings Bryan to the stand as an expert witness on the Bible. Bryan it appears was perfectly happy to defend the biblical record as he saw it. What followed the *New York Times* described as 'the most amazing court scene in Anglo-Saxon history'.[2] Having dismissed the concerns of his prosecution colleagues, Bryan confidently took a seat on the witness stand and in the intense heat of summer began fanning himself.

Darrow's cross-examination started quietly, establishing that Bryan had studied the Bible for about fifty years. The clear implication was that Bryan was an expert on the biblical text. Bryan contended that everything in the Bible should be accepted as given. In other words, the Bible was literally true. Darrow challenged Bryan with a series of questions designed to undermine a literalist interpretation of the Bible. Bryan was asked about a whale swallowing Jonah, Joshua making the sun stand still, Noah and the great flood, the temptation of Adam in the Garden of Eden, and the creation according to Genesis. Under this barrage of questions Bryan was forced to concede that the words of the Bible should not always be taken literally. In response to Darrow's relentless questions as to whether the six days of creation, as described in Genesis, were 24-hour days, Bryan said 'My impression is that they were periods.'[3]

Law Professor Douglas O. Linder, an expert on the Scopes trial, comments on the cross-examination: 'Bryan, who began his testimony calmly, stumbled badly under Darrow's persistent prodding. At one point the exasperated Bryan said, "I do not think about things I don't think about." Darrow asked, "Do you think about the things you do think about?" Bryan responded, to the derisive laughter of spectators, "Well, sometimes." Both old warriors grew testy as the examination continued. Bryan accused Darrow of attempting to "slur at the Bible." He said that he would continue to answer Darrow's impertinent questions because "I want the world to know that this man, who does not believe in God, is trying to use a court in Tennessee…" Darrow interrupted his witness by saying, "I object to your statement" and to "your fool ideas that no intelligent Christian on earth believes." After that outburst, Judge Raulston ordered the court adjourned. The next day, Raulston ruled that Bryan could not return to the stand and that his testimony of the previous day should be stricken from evidence.[4] The confrontation between Bryan and Darrow was gleefully reported by the press as a defeat for Bryan. According to one historian, "As a man and as a legend, Bryan was destroyed by his testimony that day". His performance was described as that of "a pitiable, punch-drunk warrior".'[5]

Darrow's searching cross-examination subjected Bryan to severe ridicule and bamboozled him into making contradictory statements to the amusement of the crowd. Fundamentalist Christians were portrayed as ignorant bigots who were withholding the truth of evolution from children. The significance of the Scopes trial is that it fuelled the public debate over creation and evolution, a debate that has continued into the twenty-first century. The trial had a tremendous impact on the Church, for conservative Christians were concerned about being depicted as ignorant people, who, in their blind devotion to the Bible, ignored the latest scientific advances.

In his novel, *Lila: An Inquiry into Morals* (1991), author Robert Pirsig gives his view of the significance of the Scopes trial. He writes: 'It was this issue of intellect versus society that made the Scopes trial of 1925 such a journalistic sensation… Clarence Darrow was just taking easy shots at a toothless tiger. Only religious fanatics and ignorant Tennessee hillbillies opposed the teaching of Evolution. When that trial is seen as a conflict of social and intellectual values its meaning emerges. Scopes and Darrow were defending academic freedom but, more importantly, they were prosecuting the old static religious patterns of the past. They gave intellectuals a warm feeling of arriving somewhere they had been waiting to arrive for a long time. Church bigots, pillars of society who for centuries had viciously attacked and defamed intellectuals who disagreed with them, were now getting some of it back.'[6]

There is no doubt that media attention given to Christian fundamentalists in the USA was often dismissive and inaccurate. Kevin Mungons, managing editor of the *Baptist Bulletin*, writes that after the Scopes trial it became popular to parody fundamentalist leaders as 'not enough fun, too much damn, too little mental'. 'Rather than engaging the ideas of fundamentalists, it was easier to relegate them to playing stock characters in Hollywood double features: the Bible-thumping revivalist, the hayseed preacher, the storefront church on the edge of town that was filled with rubes and yokels.'[7]

Journalist H.L. Mencken of *The Baltimore Sun* was Bryan's most devastating and influential critic. In his reports he denounced fundamentalism as irrational, backward and intolerant. Bryan he described as a fraud and opportunist – 'a power-hungry hypocrite who promised redemption and salvation without effecting real changes and who used people's genuine faith as a fraudulent means to gain popularity and profit.'[8]

After eight days of trial and only nine minutes of deliberation, the jury found John Scopes guilty and he was fined $100, which both Bryan and the ACLU offered to pay. Six days after the trial, William Jennings Bryan, while still in Dayton, died in his sleep. The judgement of the trial was later overturned on a technicality.

But the damage had been done. The prize witness for the prosecution had floundered hopelessly in dealing with basic biblical issues. Hollywood would later compound the humiliation in its film, *Inherit the Wind* (1960). Fundamentalism was well and truly on the back foot for decades to come. The ground for the new evangelicals had been well prepared.

In chapter 10, which deals with the new evangelicals, we see how the public ridicule and discouragement of the Scopes trial affected the evangelical witness in the USA, but first we return to the ecumenical movement as it achieved its aim of establishing a World Council of Churches.

(Endnotes)

1 Article State v. John Scopes ("The Monkey Trial"), by Douglas O. Linder, http://law2.umkc.edu/faculty/projects/ftrials/scopes/evolut.htm

2 Ibid.

3 This is based on a speech by law Professor Doug Linder, given on the 75th Anniversary of the Scopes Trial (July 10, 2000). http://law2.umkc.edu/faculty/projects/ftrials/scopes/evolut.htm

4 Speech on the Occasion of the 75th Anniversary of the Opening of the Scopes Trial Kansas City (July 10, 2000) by Doug Linder, http://law2.umkc.edu/faculty/projects/ftrials/scopes/confspeech.html

5 State v. John Scopes ("The Monkey Trial") by Douglas O. Linder

6 Robert Pirsig, *Lila: An Inquiry into Morals*, Bantam, 1991, p273   http://lists.moqtalk.org/pipermail/moq_discuss-moqtalk.org/2014-February/072759.html

7 Cited from the Baptist Bulletin. This article is the new foreword to *Biblical Separation: The Struggle for a Pure Church* (Second Edition). http://baptistbulletin.org/the-baptist-bulletin-magazine/the-making-of-biblical-separation/

8 Joe Cain, 'Scopes Trial and Fundamentalism in the United States', p5, University College London, London, UK, Encyclopedia of Life Science, 2001

Chapter 9

World Council of Churches

The formation of the World Council of Churches (WCC) in 1948 was a watershed event in the history of the ecumenical movement. Emerging out of the doctrinal embargo of Edinburgh 1910, the WCC was an organisation that aimed to unify all churches across the globe. The guiding spirit behind the creation of the WCC, although unspoken, was that of modernist thinking and liberal theology, disguised beneath a veneer of evangelical jargon. It was inevitable, therefore, that there would be friction between the liberalism of the WCC and conservative evangelicals who for sound doctrinal reasons decided not to become part of the Council.

The inclusive basis adopted by the WCC in 1948 declared: 'The World Council of Churches is a fellowship of churches which accept our Lord Jesus Christ as God and Saviour.'[1] This brief statement, while it says nothing about the authority of Scripture and nothing about the Triune God of the Christian Faith, says much about the uncertain doctrinal position which formed the foundation of the WCC. The result was the re-formulation, adopted by the Third Assembly (New Delhi 1961), which still stands: 'a fellowship of churches which confess the Lord Jesus Christ as God and Saviour according to the scriptures, and therefore seek to fulfill together their common calling to the glory of the one God, Father, Son and Holy Spirit.'[2]

Aim of the WCC

The stated aim of the WCC is 'to pursue the goal of the visible unity of the church. This involves a process of renewal and change in which member churches pray, worship, discuss and work together' (from the official WCC website).[3] The website of the WCC explains its activities: 'All activities of the WCC are rooted in a threefold vision for transformation of the church and world. This vision is to live out Christian unity more fully, live as churches being neighbours to all while addressing threats to the human community and encouraging churches to take greater care of creation through protection of the earth and its people.'[4] It has been and continues to be the major force and voice of what is commonly called ecumenism, a term used to describe the effort to bring all churches into, quote, 'a visible unity in one faith and one Eucharistic fellowship'.[5]

Historically, the WCC has been led by those who hold to liberal theology and who promote 'progressive' social policies and, as this chapter shall demonstrate, a leftist political agenda.[6]

By the beginning of the twenty-first century, the WCC had brought together more than three hundred churches, denominations and church fellowships in over one hundred countries throughout the world, representing around four hundred million professing Christians, and including most of the world's Orthodox Churches, many Protestant denominations, such as Anglican, Baptist, Lutheran, Methodist and Reformed, as well as a number of united and independent churches. In the early days of the WCC, most churches were European and North American. Over time many churches from Africa, Asia, the Caribbean, Latin America, the Middle East and the Pacific have become part of the WCC.[7]

The WCC claims to stand for unity, justice and peace throughout the world's faith communities. A key aspect of its work is the struggle for social justice among the world's poor and marginalised. The WCC is a fellowship of churches committed to visible unity in Christ, and calls for a deeper expression of that unity through worship and common life, witness and service to the world.[8] The WCC magazine, *Current Dialogue*, 'offers a platform for debate to those within the ecumenical movement who want to build bridges across religious divides and to their partners of different faiths… Issue 57 of *Current Dialogue* explores the phenomenon of "multiple religious belonging", in which people participate or identify with the practices and beliefs of more than one religious tradition.'[9] This statement surely reveals the mindset of the WCC.

As we saw in chapter 6, the WCC originated from the ecumenical Edinburgh 1910 World Missionary Conference, as the two committees set up by the Edinburgh Conference began working towards the establishment of a single organisation. In 1937 the Faith and Order committee and the Life and Work committee accepted a plan to create one new Council. A young Willem Visser 't Hooft, who would become the first General Secretary of the WCC in 1948, worked as an assistant to Archbishop William Temple to produce the official message of the second Life and Work Conference at Oxford in 1937. Visser 't Hooft was well qualified for the task of preparing the ground work for the proposed World Council, for a decade earlier, while in the USA, he had made a study of the social gospel and had written, *The Background of the Social Gospel in America* (1928).

In 1938 church leaders met in Utrecht with the aim of preparing a constitution for the new Council. At this meeting the WCC was formed in principle, and Visser 't Hooft was named as General Secretary of the World Council provisional committee despite the reservations of some that a 38-year-old was too young for the position. The start of World War II in 1939 meant that the first assembly of the WCC could not be held until after the War.

In 1948 delegates of 147 churches assembled in Amsterdam to officially appoint Visser 't Hooft as General Secretary of the new and official WCC, a post he was to hold until his retirement in 1966. John Mott, Chairman of Edinburgh 1910, can rightly be considered the father of the WCC, having been a leader in each of the movements that led to its formation. Having chaired the provisional committee of the WCC, Mott was named Honorary President at the Amsterdam Assembly. Billy Graham was present as a student observer.

At Amsterdam, Willem Visser 't Hooft defined the WCC thus: 'We are a council of churches, not the Council of the one undivided Church. Our name indicates our weakness and our shame before God, for there can be and there is finally only one Church of Christ on earth. Our plurality is a deep anomaly. But our name indicates also that we are aware of that situation, that we do not accept it passively, that we would move forward towards the manifestation of the One Holy Church. Our Council represents therefore an emergency solution – a stage on the road – a body living between the time of complete isolation of the churches from each other and the time – on earth or in heaven – when it will be visibly true that there is one shepherd and one flock.'[10]

Right from the start it was clear that the WCC would follow a socio-political agenda. Rev Krickwin Marak, an ordained Indian Baptist minister, theologian and missiologist, draws attention to the fact that the issues of poverty, justice, equality, struggle for liberation (economic, social, and political), pluralism and unity, were at the forefront of the WCC agenda. He notices that new approaches of mission and evangelism through dialogue and participating in the struggle of people for justice and liberation were advocated. 'In some places, mission fields struggled to survive as the attack on the traditional mission work came from within and without, as even "conversion of individual souls" was strongly criticized by the liberal theologians challenging the evangelicals to "re-read" the Bible in the context of the present world. Polarization in old mission understanding started to take place.'[11]

Evanston Assembly (1954)

In 1954 the Second WCC Assembly gathered in Evanston in the USA. A feature of the Assembly was an interest in the issue of racism. The General Assembly declared that 'any form of segregation based on race, colour, or ethnic origin is contrary to the gospel, and incompatible with the Christian doctrine of man and with the nature of the Church of Christ'.[12]

New Delhi Assembly (1961)

The third WCC Assembly met in New Delhi in 1961. Unity of the visible Church was emphasised. Paragraph 2 of the Assembly report provided a seminal statement on the organic nature of Church unity. 'The Lord who is bringing all things into full unity at the last is he who constrains us to seek the unity which he wills for his Church on earth here and now. It is for such unity that we believe we must pray and work.'[13]

The Assembly is also remembered for the incorporation of the International Missionary Council (IMC) into the WCC and the admission of 23 new member churches, including significant sectors of Eastern Orthodoxy and churches from newly independent nations.[14] The New Delhi Assembly marked the beginning of a new phase of Orthodox participation in the WCC with the entry into membership of the Russian Orthodox and Greek Orthodox Churches, and subsequently, of the remaining Eastern

Orthodox Churches in Central and Eastern Europe. The WCC position on proselytism was that evangelicals should not threaten Eastern Orthodox Churches by seeking converts in Orthodox areas of the world. So there would be no evangelism in Orthodox areas.

The IMC, which had become increasingly less interested in evangelism, joined together with the WCC, thereby becoming its Division of World Mission and Evangelism.

Attending the New Delhi Assembly were the Archbishop of Canterbury, Dr Michael Ramsey, as a delegate, and evangelist Billy Graham, as an observer. While the two men were sitting together on the steps of the Assembly Building, Dr Ramsey politely told Billy Graham that he did not agree with his methods. 'And I don't always agree with your theology. And in fact, Billy G, you've strengthened the evangelicals too much.' Graham replied with a plea: 'But Dr Ramsey, could we – you and I – be good personal friends? Do we have to part company because we disagree in methods and theology? Isn't that the purpose of the ecumenical movement, to bring together people of opposing views?'[15] After this encounter the two men became good friends.

After 1961, the WCC's members included most Protestant and Eastern Orthodox bodies. Although the Roman Catholic Church was not a member of the WCC, it worked closely with the Council and sent representatives to all major WCC conferences, as well as to its Central Committee meetings and assemblies. These developments were a great encouragement to those with ecumenical ambitions. Since 1965 a Joint Working Group (JWG), co-sponsored by the WCC and the Roman Catholic Church, has met regularly to discuss issues of common interest and to promote cooperation. Roman Catholics have become full members of the Faith and Order Commission, and thus have considerable influence with the WCC.

Church and Society Conference (1966)

In 1966 the WCC held a Church and Society Conference in Geneva on the theme of 'Christians in the Technical and Social Revolution of Our Time'. This Conference turned out to be a watershed in WCC thinking, for rather than focusing on the power of the gospel to change people, speakers turned their attention to ways in which the Church could work to change society by socio-economic means.[16] American Presbyterian missionary Richard Shaull promoted the vision of a new and more just world born out of solidarity with the poor and the oppressed. He asserted that Christ was a socio-political revolutionary and that 'the Church should no longer support the status quo but involve itself in this revolution. This necessitated the adoption by the Church of an effective analysis of society which, he argued, had to be based on Marxism because, unlike Conservatism or Liberalism, which seeks to change through gradual evolutionary processes, Marxism demands a radical change in society through revolutionary means.'[17] A recommendation from the Conference was for a programme which would focus on 'the elimination of racism, especially white racism which, it said, was firmly embedded in developed Western countries'.[18]

The Conference message to the churches reads: 'As Christians we are committed to working for the transformation of society. In the past, we have usually done this through quiet efforts at social renewal, working in and through established institutions according to their rules. Today, a significant number of those who are dedicated to the service of Christ and their neighbour assume a more radical or revolutionary position.'[19]

Uppsala Assembly (1968)

The fourth WCC Assembly at Uppsala 1968 bore further testimony to the expanding membership of the Council. It was also noticeable that following the modernising process of Vatican II in the early 1960s, the Church of Rome had a keen interest in WCC initiatives. This meant that Catholic observers actively attended meetings and sought opportunities for cooperation.

The Assembly of 1968 was organised under six sessions: The Holy Spirit and the catholicity of the church; renewal in mission; world economic and social development; towards justice and peace in international affairs; worship; and towards new styles of living. The Assembly supported the idea of 'revolutions in the Third World – although it was more cautious and ambiguous than the Church and Society Conference of 1966 as to whether the use of violence was justified or not'.[20]

Martin Luther King, who was to have delivered the opening address to the Assembly, had been assassinated four months earlier and was replaced by James Baldwin, the African-American author and civil rights activist. Baldwin, the only known gay man in the civil rights movement, delivered a powerful speech against racism in the Christian Church. Moved by his address, the Council voted to create a new initiative to combat the evil of racism, and to help the continuing struggle against apartheid in South Africa. The WCC now had a clear mandate to place the issue of racism near the top of its agenda. The Assembly proclaimed 'that racism was a powerful ideology maintained by economic and political structures which function at all levels of society. It further singled out White racism as the primary proponent of discrimination and declared the need for an urgent programme to guide the Council and its member churches on racism.'[21]

With regard to social concerns 'Human development' became a key word, and the concern for freedom was expressed in terms of 'human dignity'. A concrete outcome of this new emphasis was the critique of racism. The Uppsala statement on racism declared: 'Contemporary racism robs all human rights of their meaning, and is an imminent danger to world peace... Racism is a blatant denial of the Christian faith... Racism is linked with economic and political exploitation. The churches must be actively concerned for the economic and political well-being of exploited groups...The churches must make economic and educational resources available to underprivileged groups for their development... They should withdraw investments from institutions that perpetuate racism... Such economic help is an essential compensatory measure to counteract and overcome the present systematic exclusion of victims of racism from the mainstream of economic life.'[22] The direct follow-up to Uppsala was the establishment of the WCC Program to Combat Racism.

Consultation on Racism (1969)

Building on the Uppsala mandate, in May 1969 a workshop on racism was held in Notting Hill, London, that led to the setting up of the WCC's Programme to Combat Racism (PCR). Participants were a diverse group made up of social scientists, trade unionists, advocates of militant black power, student leaders, exiles from southern Africa, Roman Catholic Church observers, and WCC members.[23] Key personalities were Archbishop of Canterbury Michael Ramsey and anti-apartheid activist Anglican Bishop Trevor Huddleston. Also attending the conference were a strong delegation of American Black Power activists; African National Congress (ANC) chairman Oliver Tambo and Joseph Matthews, an ANC activist, lawyer and Communist sympathiser.[24]

Discussions revolved around the simplistic idea that white racism was the corrupt fruit of unjust political structures. 'Using highly simplistic and essentially Marxist economic analysis, it was argued that the relative wealth of Western societies compared with the rest of the world had come about as a result of exploitation and thus Western wealth was proof of extensive white racism.'[25] This line of reasoning entirely ignores the Protestant work ethic that brought great blessing and prosperity in its wake.

A major decision of the consultation was that force could be used to combat racism in situations where non-violent political strategies had failed. The PCR decided to give financial support to Southern African liberation movements, including the Anti-Apartheid Movement. A WCC photograph of the workshop shows the Archbishop of Canterbury and Trevor Huddleston at the centre of proceedings.

The Consultation delivered a final statement: 'The developed Western and so-called Christian countries of the world have obtained their wealth from centuries of exploitation of the newly independent and developing countries.'[26]

Speaking of the people fighting for a worldwide revolution, Oliver Tambo referred to them as 'volunteers who have freely answered the call to rid mankind of the scourge of racism, colonialism and imperialism. He proceeded to demand that WCC member churches should individually and collectively throw their moral and material resources behind those working for such a revolution.'[27]

The Central Committee of the WCC meeting in Canterbury in 1969 established the Programme to Combat Racism (PCR) with the following functions: 1) to mobilise the churches in the worldwide struggle against racism; 2) to express in word and deed solidarity with the racially oppressed; 3) to aid the churches in educating their members for racial justice; 4) to facilitate the transfer of resources, human and material, for projects and programmes in the field of racial justice. The Central

Committee emphasised that *white* racism is by far the most dangerous form of racism.[28]

The PCR was to have far-reaching consequences for the WCC's relations with South Africa. The PCR's main aim was to carry out programmes that contributed to the liberation of the victims of racism. According to the WCC website: 'One of PCR's most effective tools has been a WCC special fund to combat racism, from which annual grants are made to racially oppressed groups and organizations supporting the victims of racism. The fund is supplied by voluntary contributions from churches as well as from local ecumenical and support groups all over the world. In South Africa, the ANC received several hundred thousand dollars from PCR in support of its educational, social and health programmes during the 1970s and '80s.'[29]

First director of the WCC's Programme to Combat Racism, Baldwin Sjollema, a sociologist from the Netherlands, commented on the situation in South Africa: 'The initial five-year programme concentrated on white racism in South Africa. Specific action included the setting up of a special fund, which was largely based on the need to symbolize a redistribution of power… Its main purpose was to strengthen the organizational capability of racially oppressed groups. The PCR's next move was on disinvestment by the WCC and its member churches… The decision by the WCC to sell forthwith existing holdings and to make no further investments in corporations involved in South Africa, and, later, to deposit none of its funds in banks which maintained direct banking relations in South Africa, sparked heated debates at church synods and assemblies.'[30]

The issue of racism permeated the whole WCC, involving all units and sub-units of the organisation. 'Thus, the Faith and Order Commission co-sponsored a consultation on racism and theology, and the Education sub-unit co-sponsored a meeting on racism in school textbooks. The PCR also sponsored a number of important consultations between church and liberation movement leaders, which helped to chart the course of international church support for the struggle against apartheid.'[31]

Rachel Tingle, a British economist, in *Revolution or Reconciliation?* (1992), shows 'how changes in thinking within the World Council of Churches led to an increasing legitimisation of the activities of the South African liberation movements, including their readiness to use violence'.[32] She demonstrates that the WCC's Programme to Combat Racism sided with the liberation movements and legitimised violence.

Greatly influenced by the Notting Hill Consultation, the Central Committee of the WCC conceded that racism takes other forms than white racism, but the 'accumulation of wealth and power in the hands of white people… is the reason for a focus on the various forms of white racism'.[33] The Central Committee proposed the establishment of an ecumenical programme to combat racism which would be worldwide in scope.[34]

Bangkok (1972-1973)

Over the New Year of 1973 a conference sponsored by the Commission on World Mission and Evangelism (CWME) met in Bangkok to deal with the theme 'Salvation Today'.

The conference was a significant event in defining the agenda of the WCC. According to the WCC website: 'The world mission conference in Bangkok, at the turn of the years 1972/1973, became famous for its holistic approach to the theme "Salvation Today", encompassing spiritual as well as socio-political aspects in equal measure. The Bangkok conference acknowledged the need for contextual theologies and the recognition of cultural identity as shaping the voice of those answering and following Christ. The delegates struggled with the situation of exploitation and injustice also in the relations between churches. In order to enable local churches in Africa, Asia, Latin America and the Pacific to set their own priorities in witness, the proposal was made of a temporary "moratorium" on sending money and missionaries from the North.'[35]

Philip Potter, who served as the WCC's General Secretary from 1972 to 1984, set the tone for the conference in his opening statement. He said, 'the political dominance of the superpowers, the economic exploitation of the poor nations by the rich, and the arrogance of white racism are among the realities with which the mission has to deal if it is to be faithful'.[36]

Lesslie Newbigin, Bishop of the Church of South India, who in 1959 became the General Secretary of the International Missionary Council (IMC) and oversaw its integration with the WCC, offered his interpretation of the conference. He wrote: 'The early plenary discussions were marked by very sharp attacks by the representatives of the Third world on the churches and nations which hold the overwhelming economic and political and cultural power. Their arrogant use of power – in the world of missionary relationships as well as in the political and economic spheres – was repeatedly attacked. The few representatives of the churches in the 'Second World' – Eastern Europe and Russia – made occasional complaints that their problems were being ignored. The representatives of the 'First World' – those whose speeches and documents have usually dominated the proceedings of ecumenical conferences, maintained on the whole an embarrassed silence. It was hard for them to know what to say.'[37]

Bishop Stephen Neill, an Anglican who stood between the conservatives and the liberals and preferred to be thought of as evangelical without any prefix, provided a useful insight into the political agenda of the conference.

Commenting on the discussion around violence Neill wrote: 'The World Council of Churches by its decision to support Frelimo and other similar movements has declared open war on the only governments which exist in South Africa, Rhodesia and the Portuguese territories in Africa, though sometimes it confuses the issue by speaking of war as though it was a form of peace… Others regret that the World Council, by taking up its own bitterly racist attitude (anti-west, anti-white, but not apparently anti-Marxist), has undermined its capacity to fulfil its proper function of bringing forcibly to the notice of all the churches all the points of view which are strongly held by Christians anywhere in the Christian world.'[38]

The debate on pluralism suggested the end of Christian and Western superiority. Neill wrote: 'The Christians themselves have abandoned the idea that there is anything special in Christianity, and no longer make the claim that any man should leave the religion in which he was born for any other. The exclusive claim of Jesus Christ has always been the stumbling block to the Hindu; now that this claim has been abandoned by the Christians themselves, Jesus Christ is warmly welcome to a place in the Hindu pantheon as one of the many Saviours of India.'

The conference attempted to define the true meaning of salvation. Its report stated that salvation 'is committed to man's struggle for liberation, unity, justice, peace and the fullness of life'.[39] South African missiologist David Bosch explained: 'The Uppsala Assembly of the WCC (1968), left it to the Bangkok conference of the Commission on World Mission and Evangelism (CWME 1973), to attempt to determine, once and for all, what salvation was.'[40] Bosch continued: 'The "spirit" of the conference, it seems, emerges where salvation is defined exclusively in this-worldly terms. Section II depicts salvation in four dimensions. It manifests itself in the struggle for (1) economic justice against exploitation; (2) for human dignity against oppression; (3) for solidarity against alienation; and (4) for hope against despair in personal life (WCC 1973: 19). In the process of salvation, we must relate (only?) these four dimensions to each other.'[41] However, he believed that 'in a world in which people are dependent on each other and every individual exists within a web of inter-human relationships, it is totally untenable to limit salvation to the individual and his or her personal relationship with God'.[42]

Bangkok demonstrated the overt political direction of the WCC and its extreme anti-Western bias. It defined salvation in political terms. The traditional Christian understanding of salvation had no place in WCC thinking. The delegates acknowledged the role of culture in shaping contextualized theologies, and emphasised that the gospel must be proclaimed in holistic terms, which included spiritual, socio-economic and political aspects.[43]

In *The Study of Evangelism: Exploring a Missional Practice of the Church* (2008), Paul Chilcote (Professor of Historical Theology at Ashland Theological Seminary, Ohio) and Laceye Warner (Associate Professor of the Practice of Evangelism at Duke Divinity School, North Carolina) write that the Bangkok conference 'fanned the flame of controversy into white heat. Concerned about the complicity of the church with regard to the exploitation and injustice of Euro-American colonialism, sensitive to emerging post-colonial contextual theologies and cognizant of the influence of the cultural identity in the shaping of an evangelistic practice, the delegates proposed a temporary "moratorium" of mission activity from the North.'[44]

Nairobi Assembly (1975)

The fifth WCC Assembly in Nairobi in 1975 dealt with a number of political concerns, such as education for liberation and community; structures of injustice; and struggles for liberation and human development. The Assembly focused on the divisive character of unjust economic structures, and felt that biblical faith urges a special concern with regard to the poor. So the Assembly stated: 'The prophetic word of Jaweh's drawing near to the humble, to the powerless, finds an echo in fundamental passages of the Gospel... The Gospel has been brought to the poor, to the powerless, to the oppressed, to the captives, to the sick. In the person of Jesus, Jaweh has put himself decidedly in the place of the poor...'[45] The Assembly urged the member churches 'to plan their participation in development to be primarily in support of the poorest of the poor.'[46]

When Bishop Arias of the Methodist Church, Bolivia, addressed the Assembly, he proposed a holistic approach – *the whole gospel for the whole person for the whole world.* He rejected both a reduction of evangelism to 'saving of souls' and of a reduction of the gospel to a programme of service or social action. 'Social justice, personal salvation, cultural affirmation and church growth are all integral parts of God's saving acts.'[47]

Mission and Evangelism: An Ecumenical Affirmation (1982)

In 1982 the Central Committee of the WCC issued a statement of its 'evangelical credentials', entitled 'Mission and Evangelism: An Ecumenical Affirmation'. 'More than many other documents of the WCC, the Ecumenical Affirmation has a holistic, encompassing approach to mission, highlighting both the call to a clear witness to Jesus Christ and the promised kingdom of God, as well as the mandate to live in solidarity with those exploited and rejected by social and economic systems.'[48]

In their book *Missions in the New Millennium* (2000), Edward Glenny (Professor of New Testament Studies, University of Northwestern) and

William Smallman (Vice President of communications at Baptist Mid-Missions and a former missionary to Brazil) warn that caution is needed in interpreting the declaration, for although it is laden with evangelical terminology and with Scripture references, it does not always mean what it appears to say. 'One needs to know how to read ecumenese, since the interpretation of their own statements is so fluid. Some naive evangelical leaders have casually expressed deep satisfaction at the biblical nature of "Mission and Evangelism, an Ecumenical Affirmation" as a mandate for evangelism. This is a dangerous effort to placate a notably anti-evangelistic body.'[49] General Secretary of the WCC, Emilio Castro (1985-1992), wrote that the WCC statement was clear: 'the spiritual gospel and the material gospel are one and the same gospel of Jesus Christ. Liberation, development, humanisation and evangelism are all integral parts of mission.'[50] He was, in effect, describing the mission of the Church as holistic.

The WCC gives a practical example of what it understands by evangelism. While saying that the Church is called to declare Good News in Jesus Christ, forgiveness, hope and a new heaven and a new earth, it gives a case study of what this means in practice. To quote Glenny and Smallman again: 'The case study is about the wives of Bolivian miners who stage a hunger strike, demanding more humane working conditions for their husbands in the mines. The demonstration is called evangelism because they did this on Christmas day. The Name was named as they evoked the name of Christ in their demands for justice. The case study shows nothing of the kergymatic [preaching Christ] content of the gospel message. The repentance that was sought was for the bad working conditions, not for being sinners before God. The only ones who were deemed in need of repentance were the rich exploitative mine owners, while the poor workers were presumed to be the people of God by virtue of their poverty.'[51] It was clear that by 1975 the WCC had completely jettisoned the gospel of personal salvation.

Vancouver Assembly (1983)

'Jesus Christ - the Life of the World' was the theme of the sixth Assembly in Vancouver in 1983. A high profile publicity opportunity was the erection of a 15-metre-high totem pole (a gift of the WCC's

Canadian member churches) at the Assembly site in honour of the tribal spirits of the Red Indians. At the conclusion of the Assembly the totem pole was lowered and moved by freighter to Europe, then transported to the Ecumenical Institute near Geneva, where it was raised in 1984.[52]

The Assembly encouraged member churches to publicly commit to addressing environmental concerns as part of a common effort to promote Justice, Peace, and the Integrity of Creation, which became known as the JPIC process.

The relationship between peace and justice was spelled out more clearly than ever before. 'Peace is not just the absence of war – Peace cannot be built on foundations of injustice. Peace requires a new international order based on justice for and within all the nations and respect for the God-given humanity and dignity of every person.'[53]

The Forum on Religion and Ecology at Yale University comments: 'Based on the conviction that issues of justice, peace, and environmental protection are inextricably related, the Justice, Peace and Creation team (JPC) of the World Council of Churches seeks to foster the creation of just and sustainable communities around the world. Based on its vision of an ecumenical Earth, the WCC challenges Christian individuals, denominations, and churches around the world to work together to resist social and ecological destruction and to create viable alternatives to corporate globalization.'[54]

The Assembly was committed to pluralism and welcomed dialogue with fifteen representatives of other living faiths to learn from them spiritually; it was recommended that the different religions should take hands to promote peace on earth.

Glenny and Smallman comment: 'Rhetoric about "God's preferential option for the poor" was commonplace, along with demands that Western economic imperialism be curtailed... Roman Catholic participation was highly visible but self-limited. A new action unit was set in motion with the Vancouver Call for justice, peace, and the integrity of the creation. This new major thrust would formalize the treatment of economic, disarmament, and environmental issues as theological issues for church attention, following an essentially leftist orientation. Through this structural unit the New Age advocates have a field day promoting their views with a pantheistic and evolutionary emphasis.'[55]

Canberra Assembly (1991)

The seventh Assembly of the World Council of Churches in Canberra, Australia in 1991 gave further evidence of the Council's apostasy. I use the word advisedly. *The Fig Tree* website describes the opening ceremony: 'The 1991 Canberra Assembly opened with Australian Aborigines welcoming participants to worship, inviting them to walk through smoke of a sacred fire at the entrance of the worship tent. Didgeridoo sounds filled the air. For some, it was a cultural curiosity. Some called it pagan worship and others familiar with native spirituality welcomed the authenticity of a people sharing their worship with visitors to their land. The other issues there included Professor Chung Hyng Kyung of Korea using feminine images of God, blending Korean remembrances of ancestors in worship and speaking of *han* as unresolved resentment against injustices suffered, particularly by women.' WCC Moderator, Marion Best, comments: 'Her presentation was greeted with resounding applause by some and resounding silence by others, with issues raised by the Ecumenical Decade of Churches in Solidarity with Women, her presentation became a flash point and led to tensions in and among member churches.'[56]

Dr Chung, who connected the work of the Holy Spirit and Kwan Yin, the Buddhist goddess of Mercy and Compassion, drew a standing ovation for her performance in invoking the spirits to 'come'. Her first invocation was to the spirit of Hagar: 'Come. The spirit of Hagar, Egyptian, black slave woman exploited and abandoned by Abraham and Sarah, the ancestors of our faith.' An array of spirits were summoned, including the spirits of Mahatma Ghandi, Steve Biko, Martin Luther King, Malcolm X, Victor Jara, Oscar Romero and many unnamed women freedom fighters who died in the struggle for the liberation of their people.[57]

Dr John Douglas, Principal of the Whitefield College of the Bible in Northern Ireland, reported thus on the Assembly. 'How some members felt regarding what went on in Canberra is evidence enough of the galloping pace at which the apostasy is advancing. It is outrunning even its most ardent admirers. It is a monster of uncleanness that is gaining momentum. One woman delegate to the Assembly said, "The politics of the WCC stink to high heaven". Even the Archbishop of Canterbury [the newly-elected George Carey], said of one of the featured speakers, Dr Chung, "She is dangerously near to Christian heresy!" He also called for the break-up of the WCC. The Archbishop of York said, "The Church of England needs to take stock of its membership of the WCC." One female cleric, complaining of the molesting of female delegates by male delegates, said, "Women have fled in tears… it has been a nightmare for some".'[58]

The ungodly nature of the WCC was now plain and obvious to all who had eyes to see and ears to hear. It is the World Council of the Counterfeit Church, and has no part in the ministry of the true Church.

Harare Assembly (1998)

At the eighth Assembly in Harare, WCC delegates heard from two legendary African political leaders—President Nelson Mandela of South Africa and President Robert Mugabe of Zimbabwe; both gave credit to the WCC for helping them to cast off oppressive political regimes.

Addressing the Assembly President Robert Mugabe made a passionate appeal to member churches of the WCC to help end what he termed 'a global conspiracy against poor nations'. The President said that the current global order belonged to the strong and heartless, a world dominated by 'bullies'. Amid applause from Assembly delegates, he asked: 'Is it not the time for churches to call for an end to the onerous debt burden? The Council should use its moral authority to appeal to the powerful nations of the West to agree to write off debts of Third World nations.' President Mugabe paid tribute to the WCC for its 'courageous gesture' in 1969 of throwing its weight behind the struggle against colonialism in Zimbabwe. He said: 'Today, when we look back, we say the WCC helped the local church re-examine its assumptions of social and political relations in the context of true Christian tenets.'[59]

Mandela at Harare

The University of Zimbabwe's Great Hall was filled to capacity for President Mandela's speech. 'When Mandela entered the hall, the room erupted with applause, and the clamour continued as he slowly made his way amid a thick crowd to his seat on the front row… After Mandela was seated, Pauline Webb, a British Methodist and the first female officer of the WCC, recounted the highlights of past assemblies. When she described how the Fourth Assembly, in Uppsala, Sweden, launched the Programme to Combat Racism in 1968, a choir burst into song from the back of the hall. The South African choral group Imilonji Kantu entered, clad in long robes of white, black, gold, green, red and blue. They sang as they proceeded up the aisle, with a drummer pounding out the beat. Mandela rose from his seat and joined them on stage, moving to the music and drawing loud approval from the assembly.'[60]

Mandela said it was a great honour, as an African, to join this august gathering on African soil. 'We have come to celebrate with you fifty years of achievement in activating the conscience of the world for peace and on behalf of the poor, the disadvantaged and the dispossessed... the WCC helped voice the international community's insistence that human rights are the rights of all people everywhere. In doing so you helped vindicate the struggles of the oppressed for their freedom. To us in South and Southern Africa, and indeed the entire continent, the WCC has always been known as a champion of the oppressed and the exploited. On the other hand, the name of the WCC struck fear in the hearts of those who ruled our country and destabilized our region during the inhuman days of apartheid... When, thirty years ago, you initiated the Programme to Combat Racism and the Special Fund to support liberation movements, you showed that yours was not merely the charitable support of distant benefactors, but a joint struggle for shared aspirations. Above all, you respected the judgment of the oppressed as to what were the most appropriate means for attaining their freedom. For that true solidarity, the people of South and Southern Africa will always remember the WCC with gratitude.'

Mandela acknowledged the role of church education. 'Without the missionaries and other religious organizations I would not have been here today... Therefore when I say we are the product of missionary education, I recognize that I will never have sufficient words to thank the missionaries for what they did for us... The WCC's support exemplified in the most concrete way the contribution that religion has made to our liberation.'[61]

The Harare Assembly made it clear that the political agenda of the WCC was the same as that of Mandela and Mugabe. And there is no doubt that the WCC did indeed play a large part in liberating both countries from their colonial rulers.

Brazil Assembly (2006)

The theme of the ninth WCC Assembly in Brazil in 2006 was world transformation. The Assembly's prayer was: 'God in Your Grace, Transform the World.'

An article in *Touchstone* by George Conger, Episcopal priest and accredited journalist for *The Church of England Newspaper*, describes the opening session of the ninth Assembly and makes the point that the WCC, founded in 1948 to foster the reunification of Christian churches, has effectively shed its *religious* calling, and in its place has chosen *social activism* in the pursuit of 'relevance'.

Conger relates how at the opening session of the Assembly the North American delegates offered a litany of repentance, confessing 'to the delegates from more than one hundred countries "the sin of racism", "our compulsion to despoil the earth", "our thirst for violence", "the hunger for revenge", "our lust for empire", our "self-satisfaction and self-adoration", and our "hearts hardened by terror and media manipulation". Latin American delegates joined the chorus agreeing that America was the problem, confessing to having "to breathe air polluted by foreign-owned industries" and to being "subjected unilaterally to the interests of large corporations or the countries reckoned to be great".'[62]

Conger described Archbishop Desmond Tutu's speech, in which he told the WCC that 'God is not a Christian', as the most warmly received speech of the week and one that seemed to express the mind of the majority. 'After first thanking the WCC for its support of the African National Congress, which "was quite critical in saying our cause was just and noble and that those who as a last resort had opted for the armed struggle were not terrorists but freedom fighters," he told the assembly that "God is allowing any and everybody into heaven." The Nobel laureate noted, "I myself have not felt that I needed to convert other people... Black and white, yellow and red, rich and poor, educated and not educated, beautiful and not so beautiful, Christian, Muslim, Buddhist, Hindu, atheist, all belong, all are held in a divine embrace that will not let us go, all, for God has no enemies," he said.

"Bush, Bin Laden all belong, gay, lesbian, so-called straight, all belong and are loved, are precious".' Conger concluded his article by pointing out that the WCC is supported by funding primarily from German, Scandinavian, and American churches. 'But the WCC's search for relevance in social activism, at the expense of Christian witness, will push it further to the margins of Christian life and ultimately to irrelevance.'[63]

An article in *Culture Wars: An Encyclopedia of Issues, Viewpoints, and Voices*, makes the rather obvious point: 'Though the bulk of WCC membership resides in developing nations in the Southern Hemisphere, its primary donors are European Protestant churches. Due in part to its membership constituency and active political advocacy, the WCC often adopts positions counter to those of the United States and other Western developed nations.'[64]

The social activists of the WCC believe that the great human problem is political oppression and poverty. In their mind a major cause of political oppression is the systematic exploitation carried out by Western nations against the poor nations of Africa, Asia, and South America. Most problems in the world were caused by colonialists and now by Americans. Political oppression and exploitation were compounded by white racism. Socially aware Christians cannot stand aside in the face of this grave injustice. The solution is political activism, anti-racism and the establishment of a new world economic order.

The great debate among theologians and church leaders is how to combine social activity and evangelism. The WCC has succeeded in changing the meaning of evangelism. With the passage of time and much debate and many WCC consultations and Assemblies, the overt left-wing political agenda of the WCC has for a long time been obvious to most evangelical Christians. Many Bible-believing Christians are deeply suspicious of the WCC's ecumenical ambitions and its close relationship with the Church of Rome. Many evangelical churches have steadfastly refused to have any connection with the WCC.

In the next chapter we turn to the new evangelicals who longed for Christianity without conflict. They believed that a small amount of compromise was a price worth paying.

(Endnotes)

1 World Council of Churches website, About Us, The basis of the WCC
2 Ibid.
3 WCC website, What to we do?, What is the aim of the WCC?
4 WWC website, What we do, http://www.oikoumene.org/en/what-we-do
5 WCC website, About Us, https://www.oikoumene.org/en/about-us
6 WCC website, What is the WCC? http://www.gotquestions.org/World-Council-of-Churches-WCC.html#ixzz3EVVWQkyc
7 Programme to Combat Racism, 1939-1996, published by IDC Publishers, 2005
8 Ibid. https://www.oikoumene.org/en/about-us/self-understanding-vision/cuv
9 WCC website, What we do, https://www.oikoumene.org/en/what-we-do/current-dialogue-magazine
10 W.A. Vissser't Hooft, *Memoirs*, London, Westminster Press, 1973, p210. Cited from An Ecclesiological Understanding of Councils of Churches, Rev Dr Alan D. Falconer http://www.wcc-coe.org/wcc/who/crete-06-e.html
11 Developing Mission Curriculum in Theological Education to Impact the Local Churches for Missions in India Today, Krickwin C. Marak
12 Rachel Tingle, *Revolution or Reconciliation*? Christian Studies Centre, 1992, p11
13 WCC website, New Delhi Statement on Unity, 31 December 1961, WCC 3rd Assembly, New Delhi, 1961
14 WCC website, about us, timeline, 4th Assembly, Uppsala 1968, http://www.oikoumene.org/en/about-us/organizational-structure/assembly/since-1948
15 Billy Graham, *Just as I am*, HarperCollins. p703
16 *Revolution or Reconciliation*? 1992, p14
17 Ibid. pp14-15
18 Ibid. p20
19 Cited from *Edinburgh to Salvador: Twentieth Century Ecumenical Missiology* by T.V. Philip, p95 http://www.religion-online.org/cgi-bin/relsearchd.dll/showchapter?chapter_id=1521
20 *Revolution or Reconciliation*? 1992, p20
21 ECHOES, World Council of Churches, an occasional publication of the World Council of Churches', Editorial, Yvonne V. Delk, http://www.wcc-coe.org/wcc/what/jpc/echoes/echoes-17-01.html
22 *The UN-OAU Conference on Southern Africa*, Oslo, 9-14 April, 1973: Papers and documents, Scandinavian Institute of African Studies, edited by Olav Stokke, Carl Gösta Widstrand, p26
23 University of South Africa Thesis, 'The World Council of Churches and its Programme to Combat Racism: The Evolution and Development of their Fight against Apartheid, 1969–1994', by Thembeka Doris Mufamadi, p10
24 *Revolution or Reconciliation*? 1992, p21
25 Ibid. p21
26 Statement of the WCC Consultation on Racism, p14, cited from Rachel Tingle, *Revolution or Reconciliation*? 1992, p22
27 *Revolution or Reconciliation*? 1992, p22

28 *The UN-OAU Conference on Southern Africa*, Oslo, 9-14 April, 1973: Papers and documents, Scandinavian Institute of African Studies, edited by Olav Stokke, Carl Gösta Widstrand, p27

29 WCC website, Former director of WCC's Programme to Combat Racism receives highest South African order, 16 June 2004, : http://www.oikoumene.org/en/press-centre/news/former-director-of-wcc-s-programme-to-combat-racism-receives-highest-south-african-order

30 Baldwin Sjollema, First director of the WCC Programme to Combat Racism, http://www.brill.com/programme-combat-racism

31 Ibid.

32 *Revolution or Reconciliation*? 1992, p8

33 Statement from the Central Committee Canterbury, reprinted in World Council of Churches Statements on Racism: 1948-1979, cited from *Revolution or Reconciliation*?, p26

34 *Revolution or Reconciliation*? 1992, p27

35 WCC website, What we do, History

36 Cited from 'A Taste of Salvation at Bangkok', *Indian Journal of Theology* 22(1): 49-53 by J.E. Lesslie Newbigin

37 Ibid.

38 Stephen Neill, 'Salvation Today?' (quotations are from the official report of the Assembly, Bangkok Assembly 1973 World Council of Churches, Publications Office, Geneva, Switzerland.)

39 Ibid.

40 David J. Bosch, *Transforming Mission: Paradigm Shifts in Theology of Mission*, Orbis Books, 1991, p406

41 Ibid.

42 Ibid.

43 Mennonite World Conference website, The church must be about holistic mission, https://www.mwc-cmm.org/content/church-must-be-about-holistic-mission

44 Paul Chilcote, Laceye Warner, *The Study of Evangelism: Exploring a Missional Practice of the Church*, William B Eerdmans Publishing, 2008, pxxii

45 Justice, Peace and Integrity of Creation website, 1.2.9 Nairobi 1975, http://oikoumene.net/hostudies/gerecht.book/one.book/index.html?entry=page.book.1.2.9

46 Paton, David M. (ed.): Breaking Barriers. Nairobi 1975. The Official report of the Fifth assembly of the World Council of Churches. Nairobi, 23 November-10 December, 1975, London, SPCK, Wm. B. Eerdmans, Grand Rapids http://oikoumene.net/hostudies/gerecht.book/one.book/index.html?entry=page.book.1.2.9

47 Progress in Unity?: Fifty Years of Theology Within the World Council of Churches: 1945-1995, A Study Guide, edited by Martien E. Brinkman, p157

48 Statements on Mission by the World Council of Churches: 1980-2005, http://www.mission2005.org/fileadmin/files/mission_statements_web.pdf

49 W. Edward Glenny, William H. Smallman, *Missions in a New Millennium, Change and Challenges in Missions*, Kregel Academic & Professional, 2000, p213

50 *Missions in a New Millennium,* p213

51 *Missions in a New Millennium,* p213

52 *Anglican Journal*, article Transplanted totem pole is returned to 'the good earth of God's creation' by Bruce Myers on November 29, 2007. http://www.anglicanjournal.com/articles/transplanted-totem-pole-is-returned-to-the-good-earth-of-gods-creation-7569#sthash.Z90j3s7o.dpuf-

53   House of Studies website, WCC news, 1.2.10 Vancouver 1983, http://oikoumene. net/hostudies/gerecht.book/one.book/index.html?entry=page.book.1.2.10

54   Forum on Religion and Ecology at Yale, World Council of Churches (WCC) Justice, Peace, and Creation (JPC), http://fore.research.yale.edu/religion/christianity/projects/ wcc_jpc/

55   *Missions in a New Millennium*, p209

56   The Fig Tree website, Global encounters transform perceptions http://www.thefigtree.org/ dec06/120106dialoguebest.html

57   'The shocking apostasy of the World Council of Churches', a report by Rev John Douglas, in the archives of The Burning Bush, http://www.ivanfoster.net/pdf/Articles4. pdf

58   Ibid. 'The shocking apostasy of the World Council of Churches'

59   World Council of Churches Office of Communication, Press Release no 20, WCC Eighth Assembly, Mugabe makes passionate appeal to WCC to help create a fair World

60   News Archives, Mandela affirms WCC's work for human rights, sees challenges ahead, 12/14/1998, by United Methodist News Service http://archives.umc.org/ umns/news_archive1998.asp?ptid=&story=%7BBA5C4C81-63C0-4AEF-AA13-DBAE384C147E%7D&mid=3370

61   Address by President Nelson Mandela at 50th anniversary of World Council of Churches, Harare – Zimbabwe, 13 December 1998, http://www.mandela.gov.za/ mandela_speeches/1998/981213_churches.htm

62   Article in *Touchstone* – A journal of mere Christianity, by George Conger, 'Bottom of the Ninth Assembly: The Recent World Council of Churches Assembly & the End of the Ecumenical Movement', May 2006
http://www.touchstonemag.com/archives/article.php?id=19-04-053-r#ixzz3UYQN11Owhttp://www.touchstonemag.com/archives/article.php?id=19-04-053-r

63   Ibid. Conger

64   *Culture Wars: An Encyclopedia of Issues, Viewpoints, and Voices* by Roger Chapman, Routledge, 2009, p626

Chapter 10

The New Evangelicals

In chapter 7 we saw that the fundamentalist/modernist struggle was in reality a spiritual war between true believers, who were earnestly contending for the Faith once for all delivered to the saints, and the modernist/liberal camp that was propagating another gospel. Exposing false teaching has always been controversial and difficult, and is vulnerable to misunderstanding and even to misrepresentation. The spiritual struggle against unbelief in the 1920s and 1930s was deeply contentious, and some evangelicals simply did not have the stomach or the heart for the battle. Many evangelicals had become dismayed with what they saw as the growing isolationism of the fundamentalist position. To make matters worse, the ridicule that flowed from the Scopes Monkey Trial (chapter 8) caused excruciating embarrassment among many Christians. This contributed to the formation of a powerful new movement within evangelicalism after the Second World War– the self-styled 'new evangelicals'.

The new evangelicals wanted the evangelical faith, but without the spiritual battle that came from defending the true gospel and exposing error. They wanted only the positive, for they did not like dealing with the negative. They longed for peace and tolerance, and accepted that a small amount of compromise was a price worth paying. As a result they were prepared to accept all who profess to be Christians, whatever their doctrine and conduct. And so the new evangelicals were born— a growing group of believers who longed to make their beliefs appear reasonable and acceptable. They wanted their religion to be attractive, not weighed down by strict doctrinal beliefs that most people did not understand. They also wanted to be accepted as intellectually credible, and as people who were open to the advances of science. The argument was that in a changing modern world Christianity needed to adapt and make itself relevant in the eyes of society at large.

New evangelicalism was the response of those Christians who felt threatened and embarrassed by the criticism that came from the fundamentalist/modernist struggle. What concerned such believers was that in the popular mind and in the mass media evangelicals were seen as obscurantists who held old-fashioned and irrelevant views—small-minded bigots who blindly followed the dictates of a largely discredited book. Many evangelicals came to the view that change was necessary to restore the image of the Christian Faith. Some 'enlightened' evangelicals had already adapted their beliefs to take account of the 'scientific' findings of Charles Darwin – so-called theistic evolution, based on the idea that God used evolutionary processes over eons of time to create the world.

Harold John Ockenga (1905-1985)

Dr Harold John Ockenga, Pastor of Park Street Church, Boston, and the first President of Fuller Theological Seminary, is widely regarded as the father of New Evangelicalism, a movement born of compromise. Other important and high-profile new evangelicals were the evangelist Billy Graham and the theologian John Stott. Because Harold Ockenga played such a prominent role in popularising the new evangelicalism, we need to understand his thinking about the Christian Faith and social philosophy. As a young man Ockenga studied theology at Princeton Seminary, but in the heat of the fundamentalist/modernist controversy of the 1920s, he and a number of conservative classmates followed Gresham Machen when he withdrew from Princeton to establish the Westminster Theological Seminary in Philadelphia in 1929. Two years later Ockenga graduated from Westminster Seminary and went into the ministry. By 1936 he had been appointed lead Pastor of the influential Park Street Church in Boston. In an effort to present evangelical Christianity in a more favourable light, in 1942 Harold Ockenga and J. Elwin Wright established the National Association of Evangelicals (NAE), with Ockenga serving as the founding President from 1942-1944.

Ockenga was also one of the founding fathers of Fuller Theological Seminary. When the Fuller Seminary opened in September 1947, Ockenga was appointed the first President. The hope was that Fuller, through its academic excellence, would train a new generation of evangelical scholars and intellectuals who would rigorously engage in critical dialogue with liberal theology and modern secular thought. In his convocation speech to Fuller Theological Seminary in 1948, Harold Ockenga claimed to have originated the term 'New Evangelical'.[1] He writes: 'Neo-evangelicalism was born in 1948 in connection with a convocation address which I gave in the Civic Auditorium in Pasadena. While reaffirming the theological view of fundamentalism, this address repudiated its ecclesiology and its social theory. The ringing call for a re-pudiation of separatism and the summons to social involvement received a hearty response from many Evangelicals. ... It [new evangelicalism] differed from fundamentalism in its repudiation of separatism and its determination to engage itself in the theological dialogue of the day. It had a new emphasis upon the application of the gospel to the sociologi-cal, political, and economic areas of life.'[2]

In a press release, dated 8 December 1957 (ten years after his convocation speech at Fuller), Ockenga explained his understanding of new evangelicalism: 'The New Evangelicalism is the latest dress of orthodoxy, as Neo-Orthodoxy is the latest expression of theological liberalism. The New Evangelicalism differs from Fundamentalism in its willingness to handle the social problems, which Fundamentalism evaded. *There need be no dichotomy between the personal gospel and the social gospel.* The true Christian faith is a supernatural personal experience of salvation and social philosophy. Doctrine and social eth-ics are Christian disciplines. Fundamentalism abdicated leadership and responsibility in the societal realm and thus became impotent to change society or to solve social problems. The New Evangelicalism adheres to all the orthodox teachings of Fundamentalism, but has evolved a social philosophy'[3] (my emphasis).

Ockenga explains that the new evangelicalism has changed its strategy from one of separation to one of infiltration. 'Instead of static front battles, the new theological war is one of movement. Instead of attack upon error, the New Evangelicals proclaim the great historical doctrines of Christianity. The results have been phenomenal... The strat-egy of the New Evangelicalism is the positive proclamation of the truth in distinction from all errors without delving into personalities which embrace the error. The evangelical believes that Christianity is intellectually defensible but the Christian cannot be obscurantist in scientific questions pertaining to the creation, the age of man, the universality of the flood, and other moot Biblical questions. The evangelical attempts to apply Christian truth to every phase of life.'

Ockenga continued his statement: 'Since I first coined the phrase "The New Evangelicalism" at a convocation address at Fuller Theological Seminary ten years ago, the evangelical forces have been welded into an organization front. First, there is the *National Association of Evangelicals*, which provides articulation for the movement on the denominational level. Second, there is the *World Evangelical Fellowship*, which binds together these individual national associations of some twenty-six countries into a world organization. Third, there is the new apologetic literature stating this point of view which is now flowing from the presses of the *great publishers*, including Macmillans and Harpers. Fourth, there is the existence of *Fuller Theological Seminary*, and other evangelical seminaries, which are fully committed to orthodox Christianity and a resultant social philosophy. Fifth, there is the establishment of *Christianity Today*, a bi-weekly publication to articulate the convictions of this movement. Sixth, there is the appearance of an *evangelist, Billy Graham,* who on the mass level is the spokesman of the convictions and ideals of the New Evangelicalism. The strength of this movement is recognized by the *Christian Century*, America's leading theologically liberal magazine, by its expression of fear that this movement may challenge the religious scene and change the religious climate in this nation. The New Evangelical believes that Christ is the answer; that He must be understood in a Biblical framework, and He and His teachings must be applied to every realm of societal existence (my italics).'[4]

We learn much about the new evangelical movement from Ockenga's detailed statement. It is important to understand that the new evangelicals gained control of the some of the leading Christian publishing houses and launched *Christianity Today*. The role of Fuller Seminary in the new evangelical revolution cannot be over emphasised. Billy Graham, the most well known name in Christianity was a leading advocate of the new evangelicalism. The social gospel was to be an important aspect of new evangelicalism.

In 1955 Edward John Carnell, prominent Christian theologian and apologist, replaced Ockenga as the President of Fuller Seminary. He eagerly engaged in the battle against the fundamentalists. As a rising star among new evangelicals, in *The Case for Orthodox Theology* (1959), Carnell sought to separate the neo-evangelicals from the fundamentalists. He argued that a Reformed orthodox theology was considerably differ-ent from fundamentalism, and attacked what he called the legalism and hypocrisy in fundamentalism, which he described as 'orthodoxy gone cultic'. He launched a vitriolic attack on J. Gresham Machen, whom he accused of causing anarchy in the Church. 'While Machen was a foe of the fundamentalist movement [which he was not], he was a friend of the fundamentalist mentality, for he took an absolute stand on a relative issue, and the wrong issue at that… Machen became so fixed on the evil of modernism that he did not see the evil of anarchy.'[5]

Carnell's attack on Machen is highly significant, for it surely rep-resents the attitude of Fuller Seminary towards believers who held to the fundamentals of the Faith. While Carnell was willing to tolerate modernist ideas, he was deeply hostile toward Machen and his defence of the Faith. New evangelicals, it seems, were able to tolerate every compromised version of the Christian Faith, except the one that con-tended for sound doctrine. And fundamentalism soon became a dirty word in new evangelical circles. It was regarded as a totally different thing from evangelicalism.

Rev E.L. Bynum, Pastor of Tabernacle Baptist Church in Lubbock, Texas, for 44 years, was fully convinced of the compromise in the new evangelicalism. He commented: 'I admire the early fundamentalists that stood up against the modernism that was overcoming the denominations and churches… It is clear that the New Evangelicals had rather run than fight. The Fuller Theological Seminary followed this trend and it led them right into liberalism and compromise. Of course Ockenga felt right at home there as their first President… Billy Graham was clearly a New Evangelical and felt comfortable in bringing some of the leading liberals in America to the sponsoring committees of his crusades.'[6]

Fuller Theological Seminary

One of the first initiatives of the new evangelical movement was the creation of Fuller Theological Seminary, in Pasadena, California, in 1947. Dr Harold Ockenga and Dr Carl Henry both played a key role in the founding of Fuller Seminary, which became the intellectual power-house of the new evangelicals. Edward Carnell, the second President of Fuller, passionately supported the cause of the new evangelicalism. He taught that the primary business of Christianity is love.[7] He wrote: 'While doctrine illuminates the plan of salvation, the mark of a true disciple is love, not doctrine... Doctrine puffs up, love edifies.'[8] It is impossible to exaggerate the influence of Fuller in the development of new evangelicalism.

By the middle of the 1960s Fuller Seminary was firmly in the hands of scholars who were clearly and openly opposed to the doctrine of biblical inerrancy. In *The Battle for the Bible* (1976), Harold Lindsell, who served as a professor and vice-president of Fuller, wrote: 'In or about 1962 it became apparent that there were some who no longer believed in the inerrancy of the Bible, among both the faculty and the board members. One of the key board members, who was later to become chairman and whose wealth helped to underwrite the annual operating budget, was C. Davis Weyerhaeuser... He was clear in his own conviction that the Bible had errors in it. Nor did he hesitate to make his position plain.'[9] In 1965 Fuller's School of Psychology was established to run alongside its School of Theology. The new School played a pivotal role in integrating humanistic theories of psychology and psychotherapy with the Christian Faith. The result was a massive growth in the so-called Christian counselling movement— evangelical churches were persuaded to employ counsellors who would provide psychotherapy for depressed church members.

In 1967, Daniel Fuller, Dean of the Seminary, delivered a pa-per before the Evangelical Theological Society wherein he laid the groundwork for what may be called a doctrine of the partial inspiration of Scripture.[10] He argued that there are two kinds of Scripture—rev-elational Scripture that is wholly without error, and non-revelational Scripture that is not.[11] By the end of the 1960s, 'limited inerrancy' was the dominant view of the Seminary. An article in *The Sword & Trowel* by Dr John Whitcomb, Professor of Theology at Grace Theological Seminary, defined the new evangelicalism 'as an attitude or mentality on the part of evangelicals to compromise – to some extent – the doctrines of Holy Scripture in order to be accepted by professing Christians outside the evangelical community. In other words, new evangelicalism begins with the heart'.[12]

Christianity Today

A vital step in promoting the ideas of new evangelicalism was the founding of the magazine *Christianity Today* in 1956. The young evangelist Billy Graham, with the support of his father-in-law, Nelson Bell, proposed the need for a publication that would 'plant the evangelical flag in the middle of the road, taking a conservative theological position but a definite liberal approach to social problems. It would combine the best in liberalism and the best in fundamentalism without compromising theologically.'[13] Billy Graham explained his vision for the magazine: 'The hallmark distinguishing *Christianity Today* was a commitment to the trustworthiness of Scripture as the Word of God, with all of the ramifications of that commitment. Of supreme importance to me also was our editorial strategy. Instead of using the stick of denunciation and criticism, we would present a positive and constructive program. We would attempt to lead and love rather than vilify, criticize and beat. Conservative Christians had failed with the big stick approach; now it was time to take a more gentle and loving direction… We would not compromise the essentials of our faith, but we would use a positive approach to gain the same objectives that conservative Christians had failed to win using other means for twenty years.'[14]

The magazine proved to be invaluable in promoting the crusades of the Billy Graham Evangelistic Association. Professor Carl Henry was editor when *Christianity Today* was first published in the autumn of 1956. Under Henry's guidance, *Christianity Today* became the leading journalistic mouthpiece for new evangelicalism and lent the movement intellectual respectability. The magazine achieved phenomenal growth and became the most widely read Christian journal. Graham said: 'CT is providing the evangelical cause within the church a tremendous sounding board and an intellectual framework for the expression of our faith, and they're making this their tenth anniversary project, this World Congress on Evangelism in Berlin.'

The Billy Graham Evangelistic Association

To understand the Billy Graham Evangelistic Association (BGEA) we turn to the Wheaton College Archives which hold an article entitled, 'Billy Graham and the Billy Graham Evangelistic Association - Historical Background'. What follows is based largely on that article.

By the end of 1949, following an evangelistic campaign in Los Angeles, the young Billy Graham suddenly came to national prominence when newspaper magnate William Randolph Hearst, for reasons unknown, ordered his publications to 'puff Graham' (that is, to give him maximum publicity). The sudden front-page coverage showered on Graham by Hearst's newspapers nationwide was quickly matched by other newspapers and news magazines—literally a media circus descending on his rallies under a big tent.[15]

Graham comments on how the 'puff Graham' instruction affected his ministry: 'When I arrived at the tent for the next meeting, the scene startled me. For the first time, the place was crawling with reporters and photographers. They had taken almost no notice of the meetings up until now, and very little had appeared in the papers. I asked one of the journalists what was happening. "You've just been kissed by William Randolph Hearst," he responded... Next morning's headline story about the Campaign in the *Los Angeles Examiner*, followed by an evening story in the *Los Angeles Herald Express* – both owned by Hearst – stunned me. The story was picked up by the Hearst papers in New York, Chicago, Detroit, and San Francisco, and then by all their competitors. Until then, I doubt if any newspaper editor outside the area had heard of our Los Angeles Campaign.'[16]

Such was the success of his ministry following Hearst's intervention that in order to run it on a business-like basis, Graham, his wife Ruth, Cliff Barrows, Grady Wilson, and George Wilson incorporated the Billy Graham Evangelistic Association (BGEA) in 1950. At the same time, Graham began his weekly radio programme, *The Hour of Decision*.

Graham's evangelistic crusades were now planned by the staff of BGEA. As his evangelistic ministry became international, the Association set up offices around the world, including, at various times, in Sydney, Buenos Aires, Winnipeg, London, Paris, Frankfurt, Hong Kong, Moscow, and Mexico City. The BGEA with its subsidiaries, including Grason Company and World Wide Pictures, published periodicals, books, records, and audio tapes, as well as producing a variety of media programmes, including films, videos, radio and television programmes and in later years,websites.

The Hour of Decision radio programme was one of the first projects of the BGEA. From 1951 to 1954 there was also an *Hour of Decision* television show. In 1957 it broadcast hour-long programmes of the very successful New York crusade. It then became the usual practice for the BGEA to broadcast programmes that covered Graham's evangelistic crusades. After each broadcast, addresses were given to which viewers could write for more information.[17]

Decision magazine was another branch of the BGEA. The first issue came out in November 1960. Eventually, separate editions were prepared in Spanish, French, and German, as well as special Australian and British versions. By 1988 *Decision* was published only in English and Spanish. The circulation in 1988 was approximately two million.[18]

Grason Company was set up by Billy Graham and George Wilson in January 1952. Its purpose was to publish and distribute books, records, music and other materials which the BGEA produced. Any profits from its retail sales were given to the BGEA.[19] Besides evangelism, radio, television, and films, Graham was involved in many literary endeavours and published numerous books.

The BGEA was a major influence on several twentieth-century evangelical events, such as the founding of *Christianity Today* magazine in 1956, the World Congress on Evangelism in Berlin in 1966, the International Congress on World Evangelization in Lausanne in 1974, and the two large international conferences for itinerant evangelists in 1983 and 1986.[20] A third international conference, called Amsterdam 2000, was attended by over ten thousand evangelists mainly from the Third World.

In the 1980s and 90s, television was used to reach increasingly larger world audiences, culminating in the April 1996 Global World Mission broadcast, with an estimated potential audience of 2.5 billion people.[21] The style of the music presented in these broadcasts would not have sounded or looked out of place on MTV.[22]

When Graham heard his son Franklin preach in Albuquerque in 1998 it confirmed in his mind 'that God's hand was on Franklin in an unmistakable way, and that he was uniquely gifted to reach a new generation with the message of the Gospel... In 2000 the board of the Billy Graham Evangelistic Association appointed him chief executive officer, and a year later elected him president, with me assuming the role of chairman'.[23] Franklin has made his mark by promoting Christian rock festivals across the USA and Canada and in other countries. BGEA festivals have become a showpiece for the contemporary Christian music scene. When the music stops, in the emotional atmosphere of a musical rave Franklin invites the young people to 'accept Jesus'.

As President of the BGEA and Samaritan's Purse, Franklin Graham, according to a news report in 2007, received two full-time salaries and two retirement packages. In 2014 his total remuneration from the two Christian ministries was $1.2 million.[24] The Graham public relations spokesman, Mark DeMoss, said 'the (BGEA) compensation committee believes the overall compensation approved for Franklin was appropriate (and did not ask him to alter it), but Franklin believes the impression given by these somewhat unusual reporting procedures is not a good one'.[25]

Young and Worldly Evangelicals

As time passed the term 'new evangelicals' fell into disuse; the ideas of new evangelicalism became so widely accepted that the adjective 'new' could be dispensed with. A new generation of evangelical Christians arose that Ernest Pickering refers to as the 'young and worldly'.[26] They were characterised by a more overt love for the things of the world, and by more liberal beliefs. In an article in *Christianity Today*, Clark Pinnock wrote: 'The militant conservatives among us are not imagining everything when they charge some of us with surrendering too much in our responses to challenges of biblical criticism, evolution, feminism, political theology and the like. There are signs that some evangelicals are on their way to becoming religious liberals, not because they choose to do so in one great step, but because in working out their ideas they have innocently covered most of the ground by smaller shifts.'[27]

The guiding ethos of 'young and worldly' evangelicals was that at all costs the offence of the gospel must be avoided. They sought to be 'nice' people who could accommodate other views; they strove to be culturally adaptable. Francis Schaeffer in *The Great Evangelical Disaster* (1984), writes: 'A significant section of what is called evangelicalism has allowed itself to be infiltrated by the general world view or viewpoint of our day.'[28] He says the great evangelical disaster is 'the failure of the evangelical world to stand for truth as truth. There is only one word for this—namely accommodation: the evangelical church has accommodated to the world spirit of the age.'[29] Schaeffer continues, 'today we must say that in general the evangelical establishment has been accommodating to the forms of the world spirit as it finds expression in our day… in the most basic sense, the evangelical establishment has become deeply worldly'.[30]

Attributes of New Evangelicalism

Modern new evangelicals, now referring to themselves simply as 'evangelicals', exhibit some or all of the following characteristics:

1) A low view of Scripture

Despite their claim to be Bible-affirming Christians, on closer examination it is obvious that new evangelicals have a low view of Scripture. Fuller Seminary, the intellectual powerhouse of the movement, by the 1960s had rejected belief in the inerrancy of Scripture. Most new evangelicals, to demonstrate their acceptance of Darwin's 'scientific' findings, interpret the first chapters of Genesis in a way that permits the doctrine of theistic evolution.

2) No Separation from False Doctrine

New evangelicals compromised on the biblical command to separate from false doctrine. They disliked the idea of opposing false doctrine, unlike the fundamentalists of the past. They have no stomach for theological battles—instead, their motto was: 'Let's be positive and not negative; let's not oppose, let's promote only the positive.' Harold Ockenga said: 'I think that these fundamentalists are doing irreparable harm to our movement by identifying Christianity with "Thou shall not." They have lost all the joy out of Christianity and Christian living. They have made it negative. They are dividing to absurdity and I assure you that I myself will have nothing to do with that kind of movement.'[31]

Ockenga stressed this point in his convocation speech to Fuller Seminary in 1947: 'We do not intend to be ecclesiastically bound. We will be free. But we are ecclesiastically *positive*... We will not be negative. Now there are those who exist in the world simply, it seems, to attack others, and to derogate others, and to drag them down, and to besmirch them. Our men will have no time for that kind of negativism. We want the *positive* presentation of the Christian faith in a critical world. By the grace of God we will have it. That means a *positive* presentation of the gospel.'[32]

So all was crystal clear—new evangelicalism deals only with the positive and not with the negative. It openly repudiates the idea of separating from false doctrine—it does not seek to expose false teaching; it does not warn the flock against false teachers. This is a profoundly unbiblical position. True believers are exhorted to contend earnestly for the Faith once for all delivered to the saints (Jude 3-4). The apostle John warns of many false teachers and deceivers in the world (1 John 4.1; 2 John 7). And Paul warns of many savage wolves entering the Church (Acts 20.29). Christians should not receive them, neither bid them God speed and thereby become a partaker of their evil deeds (2 John 9-11).

3) Separation from the World

New evangelicals have redefined the biblical concept of worldliness. Separation from the world – love not the world, neither the things in the world – is held to be a hopelessly old-fashioned notion, something that makes Christianity appear dull and unattractive. They want an end to the discipline of separation from the world. The result is that immersion in the prevailing secular culture has become the accepted norm, indeed, virtually a Christian duty, on the pretext of 'winning' the world to Christ and redeeming the culture. The consequence is plain for all to see. Today Christians dress and behave like the world, attend worldly forms of entertainment, watch the worldly TV shows, read worldly magazines. Churches have become places of entertainment, where light-hearted fun, with jokes and laughter and applause, denominate worship services. New evangelicalism has made no difference between the holy and the profane. The disaster of new evangelicalism is that it has brought the world into the Church like a flood.

4) Ecumenical Evangelism

New evangelicals tended to become part of the ecumenical movement, for they desperately wanted unity among all who professed to be Christians. At all costs doctrinal disagreements should be avoided. A common sentiment was 'doctrine divides, love unites'. It follows that they are ecumenical in outlook, eager to form spiritual alliances with all who profess to be Christian, whatever their beliefs. Billy Graham, the world-famous evangelist, was the man who popularised the ideas and beliefs of new evangelicalism. In *The Tragedy of Compromise* (1994), Ernest Pickering observes: 'Through the efforts of Billy Graham, many feel that religious liberalism is no longer the monstrous foe that our forefathers thought it to be… Today we are told that these liberals really are not so bad. From where did this idea arise among those who claim to follow the Bible? It arose from Billy Graham's crusades, where liberals and fundamentalists mixed readily.'[33] *Christianity Today* makes the point: 'For evangelicalism, Billy Graham has meant the reconstruction of a Christian fellowship transcending confessional lines—a grassroots ecumenism that regards denominational divisions as irrelevant rather than pernicious.'[34]

Billy Graham has played a huge part in the ecumenical movement over five decades. And his fellow new evangelical John Stott openly promoted an ecumenical agenda, and sought reunion with the Church of Rome. Under the leadership of John Stott, the second National Evangelical Anglican Congress (NEAC2) in 1977 in Nottingham, England, asserted that: 'Seeing ourselves and Roman Catholics as fellow-Christians, we repent of attitudes that have seemed to deny it.'[35] In a statement of monumental significance, Stott defined the Church as the community of those baptized, a view of the Church that is wholly consistent with the post-Vatican II teachings of Rome.

5) Intellectual Respectability

New evangelicalism strives for intellectual respectability in the hope of being accepted by the world. Harold Ockenga explains the vision: 'The philosophers say we have reached the eventide of the West… There's a task to be done and that task is not going to be done by the ordinary Christian alone. It's going to be done by those who are prepared to do it… We need men who can in an intellectually respectable way present an apology for God, and for the world, and for the soul… And for that reason, my friends, we are launching a theological seminary. We are gathering together professors who are scholars and students who are spiritually and intellectually alert, that they may be ready to enter this critical time in which we live.'[36]

New evangelicals dread the accusation of being anti-intellectual. They want professors and scholars who are keen intellectuals, who will impress the philosophers of the age with their clever arguments. They want intellectuals, who having studied in Bible seminaries, are prepared to help ordinary Christians understand the latest 'scientific' findings of evolution, psychology, sociology and climate change. However, Scripture makes it clear that God has chosen the foolish and weak things of this world to confound the wise and mighty (1 Corinthians 1.27-29).

6) Social Activism

New evangelicals were stung by the accusation of liberals that they do not care for the poor and needy. As a result, new evangelicalism is sympathetic to the ideas of the social gospel, and they have *added* a social component to the mission of the Church. In *The Uneasy Conscience of Modern Fundamentalism* (1947), Carl Henry explains how combating social injustice and poverty must be done, and challenges evangelical Christians to not just speak of change but to be the agents of it as well.[37] John Stott taught that the mission of the Church has two wings, evangelism and socio-political action. Following the lead of the Lausanne Congress of 1974, new evangelicals redefined the gospel as inherently a double mandate—socio-political action and evangelism.

7) Contemporary Worship

New evangelicals are reluctant to separate from the ways of the world. They have eagerly embraced the contemporary Christian worship scene, with its worldly music forms. It is not surprising, therefore, that young and worldly evangelicals disliked the old ways of worship, especially the traditional hymns, which were regarded as boring and stultifying. The organ had to go, for the young and worldly evangelicals wanted music that was more lively, upbeat and entertaining.

The doctrinal shallowness and worldly attitude of the new evangelical movement has manifested itself in its desire for the contemporary music scene that has now swept through the Church. Ernest Pickering writes: 'The contemporary Christian Music so loved by large numbers of evangelicals today is witness to the theological deterioration of the church. Spiritual Christians are aghast at the frothy, wild, undisciplined and earthly music sung and played by so-called Christian rock groups.'[38]

8) The Psychologising of the Church

The doctrinal shallowness of new evangelicalism meant that the Church was wide open to the ideas of psychology. The Christian counselling movement was welcomed with open arms by most new evangelical churches; Christians suffering with stress or depression were offered the benefit of psychological counselling, usually by Christian counsellors, and normally for a fee. Antidepressants were accepted as the answer for many depressed Christians. The spiritual wisdom of the Scriptures, sufficient for the saint of the past, has been superseded by the wisdom of the world, in the guise of secular psychology. (For an in-depth study of the subject see my book, *The Dark Side of Christian Counselling* (2009), Wakeman.)

Evangelising the World

The new evangelical movement was to have a great influence on the mission of the Christian Church. Evangelist Billy Graham, the man who has preached to more people than any other man in history, was the great star in the firmament of new evangelicalism. And Graham's ambition was to evangelise the whole world with his brand of Christianity. To achieve this ambition Billy Graham convened The World Congress on Evangelism in Berlin in October/November 1966, which is the subject of our next chapter.

(Endnotes)

1   Ernest Pickering, *The Tragedy of Compromise, The Origin and Impact of the New Evangelicalism*, Bob Jones University Press, 1994, p8
2   Cited in, Harold Lindsell, *The Battle for the Bible*, Zondervan, 1976, foreword

3   'Evangelicalism, The New Neutralism' by Ashbrook, cited from 'Some had rather run than fight', (Part 2), by E.L. Bynum, Published November & December 2009 as PDF article www.tbaptist.com/clientimages/48350/challengerarticles/runnotfight.pdf
4   Ibid.
5   Edward J. Carnell, *The Case for Orthodox Theology*, Westminster Press, 1959, p115
6   'Some had rather run than fight' by E.L. Bynum (cf ref 3)
7   *The Case for Orthodox Theology*, p121
8   Ibid, p128
9   *The Battle for the Bible*, p108
10   Website of Evangelical Reformed Fellowship, 'The Necessary Consonance of the Doctrines of Scripture: Inspiration, Inerrancy, and Authority' by Steve Curtis, http://www.erfm.org/biblical-inerrancy.html
11   *The Battle for the Bible*, p113
12   John Whitcomb, 'The new evangelicals burst into view', *The Sword & Trowel*, 1987, No.3, p34, Metropolitan Tabernacle, London,
13   Letter from Billy Graham to Harold Lindsell, cited from *Reforming Fundamentalism – Fuller Seminary and the New Evangelicalism* by George M. Marsden, William B. Eerdmans, paperback edition 1995, p158
14   Billy Graham, *Just As I Am*, Harper One-Zondervan, April 2007 edition, p291
15   *Los Angles Times*, Billy Graham Recalls Help from Hearst, June 07, 1997, John Dart. http://articles.latimes.com/1997-06-07/local/me-1034_1_billy-graham-recalls
16   Billy Graham, *Just As I Am*, p149
17   Billy Graham Center Archives at Wheaton College, Billy Graham and the Billy Graham Evangelistic Association - Historical Background http://www2.wheaton.edu/bgc/archives/bio.html
18   Ibid.
19   Ibid.
20   Ibid.
21   Ibid.
22   Mark Green, The Billy Graham Global Mission Sermons: The Power of Belief, p45 http://biblicalstudies.org.uk/pdf/vox/vol26/graham_greene.pdf
23   Billy Graham, *Just As I Am*, p727
24   Franklin Graham moves to address concerns about his $1.2 million pay packages, by McClatchy-Tribune News Service, October 07, 2009 http://www.cleveland.com/nation/index.ssf/2009/10/franklin_graham_moves_to_addre.html
25   Ibid.
26   *The Tragedy of Compromise*, p74
27   Clark Pinnock, *Christianity Today*, Making Theology Relevant, 29 May, 1981, p49, cited from Ernest Pickering in *The Tragedy of Compromise*, p94
28   Francis Schaeffer, *The Great Evangelical Disaster*, 1984, p51, cited from http://sydneyanglicanheretics.blogspot.co.uk/2010/12/fight-of-faith-part-2.html
29   Francis Schaeffer, *The Great Evangelical Disaster*, Crossway, 1984, p37
30   Ibid. p142
31   Cited from The Way of Life website, review of the book *The Surprising Work of God: Harold John Ockenga, Billy Graham, and the Rebirth of Evangelicalism* by Garth M. Rosell (Grand Rapids: Baker Academic, 2008), p184
32   Fuller Seminary, Opening Convocation Address, October 1, 1947, http://fuller.edu/about/history-and-facts/harold-john-ockenga/
33   *The Tragedy of Compromise*, pp63-64

34 *Christianity Today*, 'Can Evangelicalism Survive Its Success?' Oct. 5, 1992, cited from *Billy Graham and Rome* by David Cloud, Way of Life Literature, second edition 2009, p4

35 The Nottingham Statement (1977), the Official Statement of the second National Evangelical Anglican Congress held in April 1977

36 Fuller Theological Seminary, Ockenga's opening convocation address, 1 October 1947, The Challenge to the Christian Culture of the West, http://fuller.edu/about/history-and-facts/harold-john-ockenga/

37 Mark Powell review, http://www.goodreads.com/review/show/390548873?book_show_action=true&page=1

38 *The Tragedy of Compromise*, p114

Chapter 11

Berlin 1966

When the International Missionary Council was officially integrated into the World Council of Churches at New Delhi in 1961, conservative Christians were already deeply concerned about the WCC's clear trajectory into theological liberalism. To counter the errors of the WCC's overt liberalism and socio-political approach to world mission, Billy Graham and his new-evangelical friends saw the need for a conference that would refocus on preaching the gospel of salvation. After several years of planning, the World Congress on Evangelism was held in Berlin in October/November 1966. The Congress aimed to present a unified evangelical vision of missions in explicit contrast to the ecumenical agenda of the WCC.

The Berlin Congress on Evangelism was the brainchild of Billy Graham. He believed that the vision of worldwide evangelism, so evident at the time of the World Missionary Conference in Edinburgh in 1910, had faded: 'I respected the attempts of the original architects of the World Council of Churches (founded in 1948) to bring many segments of the Church into a harmonious relationship. A cornerstone of the ecumenical movement's concern was expressed in Jesus' prayer for his disciples in John 17.21—"that all of them may be one, Father" …I feared that in some circles, however, the preoccupation with unity was overshadowing a commandment to evangelism and biblical theology.'[1]

Graham believed that God wanted to use his ministry to 'reaffirm the priority of biblical evangelism for the Church and to call Christians of different backgrounds to commit themselves to the cause of evangelism. In fact, we had discovered that the only word that would bring some of them together was *evangelism*'[2] (Graham's italics). In 1958 Graham wrote to his friend Rev Tom Allan, a member of the Department of Evangelism of the WCC, setting out several goals for a gathering of evangelicals. Graham wrote: 'I believe there is a desperate need for such a conference at this time of confusion and the necessary readjustment of evangelism and missions in the face of changing conditions. Perhaps out of this conference could come... a new unity among the Lord's people to get the job of world evangelization done in our generation.'[3]

Having received advice from a number of people, Graham sensed the need to work toward an international conference on evangelism.[4] Rome was considered as a possible venue, but it was rejected as 'the conference might be perceived as anti-Catholic'.[5] The divided city of Berlin was decided upon: 'there we would be meeting at a symbolic crossroads of clashing ideologies, expounding Christ as the only answer to the universal desire for hope and peace'.[6]

Graham decided to ask *Christianity Today* to sponsor the conference because 'the magazine had already gained worldwide prestige among both Protestants and Catholics... In the end, Billy Graham Evangelistic Association (BGEA) organized it and raised the money. We formally titled the event the World Congress on Evangelism, but we generally referred to it simply as the Berlin Congress or Berlin '66'.[7] The policy was that participation should be by individuals, 'on the basis of their own unique ministry, not as official representatives of their denominations'.[8] Graham wanted Oral Roberts, a leader of the growing charismatic movement, who was world-renowned for his preaching and healing ministry, to be among the delegates.[9] Graham said of Roberts: 'Oral Roberts was a man of God and a great friend in ministry. I loved him as a brother. We had many quiet conversations over the years. I invited Oral to speak at one of our early international conferences on evangelism held in Berlin in the 1960s.'[10]

The Berlin Congress was coordinated by Dr Carl Henry, editor of *Christianity Today*, assisted Dr Victor B. Nelson and Rev Stanley Mooneyham of the BGEA. Henry was considered by many to be the leading theologian of the new evangelical movement and a pioneer of a new interest in social responsibility. According to Sherwood Eliot Wirt, editor of Graham's *Decision* magazine, Berlin '66 was the first congress 'for Bible-believing evangelicals ever to be held in 2,000 years of church history. Billy suggested that it might be compared in some ways with the Jerusalem Council, which was presided over by James, the brother of the Lord...'[11]

A key objective of the Congress was to provide a worldwide forum for the growing new-evangelical Protestant movement. It was intended as a spiritual successor to the 1910 World Missionary Conference in Edinburgh. The International Congress on World Evangelization held in Lausanne, Switzerland, in 1974 can be viewed as the successor to Berlin '66.

At an opening press conference, Billy Graham said: 'I think this is one of the great, truly great, ecumenical conferences that has been held, because great sections of the world church do not belong to the WCC, and here we have all different groups, including leaders of the World Council and leaders of various movements throughout the world that are not connected with the World Council, all together here. And I think that we are developing a spirit of unity and oneness and agreement that I believe God is going to greatly use to give a dynamic to the whole world church in the years ahead.' Graham went on to mention that Roman Catholics had been invited as observers. He said the purpose of the Conference was discussion and dialogue. In response to a question Graham said that he worked closely with the WCC. He affirmed that the BGEA worked with all groups and all persuasions, 'and I don't give them a theological examination before they come. And I might say that I was at Amsterdam, I was in New Delhi, I was invited to be a speaker at Evanston, (I had a virus), and I hope to be at Uppsala in 68.'[12] Graham was carefully reassuring the Christian world that he was in close fellowship with the World Council of Churches.

Delegates from 104 countries attended the Congress—including 30 countries from Africa and 20 from Latin America. Also attending were delegates from Korea, Japan, and many other countries of the Far East, together with Australia, New Zealand, Europe, the Middle East, Southern and Southeast Asia, the West Indies, Canada, and, of course, the United States.[13]

Also invited to the Congress was the editor of *Ministry* magazine, a Seventh Day Adventist publication with a worldwide distribution. The editor informed his readers: 'An invitation has been extended to your editor to attend this World Congress on Evangelism... This is not an ecumenical council but an evangelistic council. And it surely must appeal to all our *Ministry* readers around the world. We naturally carry the burden of our own denominational program on our hearts, and we thank God for its world outreach.'[14]

The theme of the Congress was 'One Race, One Gospel, One Task'. About 1,200 delegates came together for the opening ceremony on 26 October 1966. The opening address was given by the Emperor of Ethiopia, Haile Selassie, Protector of the Ethiopian Orthodox Church. In his opening address Graham referred to the 1910 Edinburgh conference. 'In many circles today the Church has an energetic passion for unity, but it has all but forgotten our Lord's commission to evangelize. One of the purposes of this World Congress on Evangelism is to make an urgent appeal to the world Church to return to the dynamic zeal for world evangelization that characterized Edinburgh 56 years ago.'[15]

John Stott

John Stott played an important part at Berlin '66, for he was given the task of presenting the biblical understanding of the Great Commission. In three addresses, from Matthew 28, Luke 24 and John 20, Stott emphasised the need for compassionate identification in proclaiming the gospel. 'By his birth, by his life and his death, God's Son identified himself with us. He did not stay apart from us or aloof from us. He made himself one with us... Now he says to us "As the Father sent me into the world, so send I you." I personally believe that our failure to obey the implications of this command is the greatest weakness of evangelical Christians in the field of evangelism today.'[16] In his talk from Luke 24 he said the commission of the Church is '*not to reform society, but to preach the gospel*', and 'the commission of the church is not to heal the sick, but to preach the gospel'.

John Stott's message to Berlin '66 was clear: 'the commission of the Church is not to reform society, but to preach the Gospel. Certainly Christ's disciples who have embraced the Gospel, and who themselves are being transformed by the Gospel, are intended to be salt of the earth and light of the world. That is, they are to influence the society in which they live and work by helping arrest its corruption and illumine its darkness. *But the primary task of the members of Christ's Church is to be Gospel heralds, not social reformers*'[17] (my emphasis).

Stott exhorted evangelicals to love, serve, and identify with those whom they sought to evangelise. He argued that the cumulative emphasis of the Great Commission texts was on preaching, witnessing, and making disciples; the conclusion of Stott's exposition was that the mission of the Church is *'exclusively a preaching, converting and teaching mission'*.[18] Stott's talks were extremely well received and established him as a world figure in the evangelical movement (above italics my emphasis).

Remarkably Stott was to change his mind about the Great Commission, as we saw in chapter 1 and shall explore further in the next chapter. Stott later confessed: 'I now consider that I was unbalanced to assert that the risen Lord's commission was entirely evangelistic, not social... I later argued that at least the Johannine version of the Commission (with its words "as the Father sent me, so I send you") implies in us as in Christ a ministry of compassionate service that is wider than evangelism.'[19]

Oral Roberts

An issue that needed to be addressed by the Congress was the place of the rapidly growing charismatic movement, of which Oral Roberts was a leading representative. Graham was keen to make it clear that he wanted to work with the charismatic movement. He was convinced that Roberts' presence at Berlin '66 would mark the beginning of a new era in evangelical cooperation.[20]

During the Wednesday evening plenary session, Graham invited Oral Roberts to the platform to greet the Congress and lead in prayer. Introducing Roberts to the Congress Graham said: 'Our prayer is going to be led by a man that I have come to love and appreciate in the ministry of evangelism... He is known throughout the world through his radio and television work, and millions of people listen to him. They read what he writes and they thank God for his ministry. I am speaking of Dr Oral Roberts, and I'm going to ask him to say a word of greeting to us before he leads the prayer.' When Roberts rose to his feet he was warmly applauded by the large contingent of South American Pentecostals.[21]

Roberts' greeting to the Congress was received with great enthusiasm. He said: 'If there is a phrase that characterises this Congress to me, it is, "We have been conquered by love". I could not conceive in advance what God would do in my heart as I found that men of diverse backgrounds, religious persuasions and beliefs could not only sit together, but could learn to understand each other… I shall always be glad that I came… I thank you, Billy, and Dr Henry, for helping to open my eyes to the mainstream of Christianity, and to bring me a little closer to my Lord.'[22]

In his book, *Oral Roberts: An American Life* (1985), David Edwin Harrell describes the scene. 'It was an electric moment. When the applause began, "pandemonium broke loose. They jumped up from every angle and applauded and applauded." But it was the prayer that followed that fired the audience.'[23] Many delegates felt that Roberts' prayer moved the entire Congress.

Christianity Today reported: 'Evangelist Oral Roberts won a significant measure of new respect through the Congress. He made a host of friends among delegates who were openly impressed with his candour and humility. When a panel got around to discussing over-emphasis on healing, Roberts readily acknowledged that he made "some mistakes" in the past. He indicated to a plenary session that he wanted to be identified more with mainstream Christianity.'[24]

Graham's very public support for Oral Roberts undoubtedly helped to give the charismatic movement credibility in the eyes of the new evangelicals. The symbolism was clear—speaking in tongues and other charismatic experiences were now regarded as acceptable by evangelicals.

We should remember that Oral Roberts was the man who popularised the 'seed faith' concept, whereby a gift of money to a ministry acts as a kind of 'seed' to bring a future 'harvest' of prosperity. Here is the message from Oral Roberts Ministries: 'When we put our faith in God's hands like a seed we plant, we are giving God something to work with, and He will send the miracle we need… No matter how little you think you have, sow it in joy and faith, knowing in your heart that you are sowing seed so you may reap miracles. Then start expecting all kinds of miracles!'[25]

While the issue of social action was not on the Berlin '66 agenda, numerous speakers unequivocally condemned liberal Protestant attempts to define salvation as social redemption. Yet Graham acknowledged that 'evangelism has a social responsibility', and specifically highlighted the need to bring an end to racism.[26]

The Congress issued a final statement: 'Our goal is nothing short of the evangelization of the human race in this generation'. The statement condemned as sin the divisions caused by racism. 'In the name of Scripture and of Jesus Christ we condemn racialism wherever it appears. We ask forgiveness for our past sins in refusing to recognize the clear command of God to love our fellowmen with a love that transcends every human barrier and prejudice.' Speaking of evangelism the statement concluded: 'Our responsibility is to see that everyone is given the opportunity to decide for Christ in our time.'[27]

In a closing press conference (3 November 1966), Graham was rather pleased about the sympathetic press coverage the Congress received in the USA. He mentioned the spirit of oneness and unity that developed and said the Congress had reached the heart of the delegates. Carl Henry mentioned the brokenness of the evangelical movement, and said the Congress welcomed theological plurality and diverse definitions of evangelism. It had been a historic Congress that would affect the Church worldwide. Graham said he would like to see the papers of the Congress studied by the entire world Church—Catholic, Protestant and Orthodox.

Sherwood Eliot Wirt, founding editor of *Decision* magazine, in his book, *Billy: A Personal Look at Billy Graham* (1997), expressed the view that what Graham did at the World Congress in Berlin was to start a networking of Christian leaders and organisations. 'Then came Lausanne in Switzerland, and plans were laid to reach the world with evangelism. The Lausanne Committee was formed, and thirty years later Lausanne committees are still at work around the world in evangelism.'[28]

Evaluating Berlin

Reactions have been mixed. Melvin Tinker believed that the ideas of social action were already in the minds of some delegates. 'However, it would seem that already at this conference seeds were sown which were later to germinate into an approach to socio-political involvement which would mark a significant change of direction for Evangelicals.'[29]

Carl Henry in his book, *Confessions of a Theologian* (1986), says the Berlin Congress of 1966, 'exposed the speculative philosophy that underlay pluralistic ecumenism', but, simultaneously, stated that the

Graham Crusades were committed to such ecumenism… Berlin ex-hibited additionally the fact that despite ecumenical redefinition of the Christian mission a global vanguard remained fully dedicated to New Testament evangelism as the early Christians had been.'[30]

David Aikman, a former *Time* magazine correspondent, in *Billy Graham: His Life and Influence* (2007), perceptively notes that 'In the view of some church historians, the Congress helped to create a new worldwide ecumenical movement which was evangelical and distinct from the liberal World Council of Churches and the Catholic Church.'[31] The implication is that those evangelical Christians who had rejected the WCC's political ecumenical movement were now being corralled into Billy Graham's evangelical ecumenical movement.

David Allan Hubbard, a long-standing president of Fuller Seminary, expressed his opinion thus: 'Our ecumenical experiment was enriched by the chemistry of two great international conclaves in the mid-sixties. The World Congress of Evangelicals in Berlin, 1966, was jointly sponsored by the Billy Graham Evangelistic Association and *Christianity Today*. Seventy-eight-year old Charles E. Fuller, the American radio evangelist who founded Fuller Theological Seminary in Pasadena, California, in 1947, attended and was celebrated as the Dean of American evangelists. Fuller alumni, active in the world mission of the church, were there in substantial numbers—evidence that Ockenga's vision for mission had been caught even before the School of World Mission was founded… Yet the call to justice, to relief of hunger and oppression, to the conquest of racism was a sighing footnote on the agenda, a passing entry in the list of errata and addenda compiled by the critics in the corridors.'[32]

The Orlando Bible Church of Central Florida, pastored by Rev Hayes Minnick, was the most forthright critic of Berlin '66. The Or-lando Church bulletin dated November 1966 provided the following evaluation: 'Within the past month a World Congress on Evangelism was held in Berlin. It was called by leaders of the New Evangelical movement, headed by Dr Carl F.H. Henry, editor of *Christianity Today*, and promoted by the Billy Graham organization. It might better have been called the "World Conglomeration of Evangelism". The word "conglomeration" according to the dictionary means a "mixed mass". And that it was! World Council officials were there. The chairman of the WCC's department on Missions and Evangelism was a member and a featured speaker. Outright Modernist denominational spokesmen were present. Virtually every denomination was represented, the report said. Ecumenical representatives were there. Churchmen representing the Eastern Orthodox Communion (Greek Catholic) were there. Representatives of the Communist-controlled churches from Iron Curtain countries were there (anti-Communist spokesmen were arbitrarily excluded). Roman Catholic observers were present…Verily, verily – it was a mixed mass!'[33]

Berlin '66 succeeded in making the concept of evangelical ecumenism a reality, with few people understanding the implications. It was now acceptable for evangelicals to work together with charismatics, liberals, modernists, Seventh Day Adventists, under the watchful eye of observers from the WCC and the Church of Rome. Within a decade Billy Graham and his friends were persuaded of the need for another international congress, which would further their ecumenical agenda of social activism. At the right time, *evangelical ecumenism* and the *political ecumenism* of the WCC could merge. The Lausanne Congress of 1974 was the event that brought this to pass, as our next chapter reveals.

(Endnotes)

1   Billy Graham, *Just as I am*, HarperOne – Zondervan, first published 1997, later edition 2007, p559
2   Ibid. p560
3   Ibid. p560
4   Ibid. pp560-561
5   Ibid. p561
6   Ibid. p562
7   Ibid. p562
8   Ibid. p563
9   Ibid. p563
10   Oklahoma's News on 6 website, 'Remembering Tulsa Evangelist Oral Roberts', Posted, Dec 15, 2009, http://www.newson6.com/story/11681586/remembering-tulsa-evangelist-oral-roberts
11   Sherwood Eliot Wirt, *Billy: A Personal Look at Billy Graham*, Crossway Books, 1997, page 219.   http://www.ccel.us/billy.ch25.html,

12 Billy Graham Center Archives, Records of News Conferences - Collection 24, press conference on 27 October 1966, audiotape, 'World Congress on Evangelism press conference in Berlin, Germany, with Billy Graham and Carl Henry'

13 *Ministry Magazine*, Roy Allan Anderson, 'Editorial: Coming—World Congress on Evangelism', May 1966, https://www.ministrymagazine.org/archive/1966/05/coming-world-congress-on-evangelism

14 Ibid.

15 Abstracted from text of Billy Graham's 'Why the Berlin Congress?' in 1966, paper held by the Wheaton Archives of the Billy Graham Center, (prepared text as printed for the Congress, from Collection 14, box 2, folder 2).

16 Cited from Exploring Christianity website, The Mission of the Church, http://www.christianity.co.nz/church11.htm

17 John Stott, 'The Great Commission' in Henry and Mooneyham One Race, One Gospel, One Task, World Congress on Evangelism, Berlin, 1966 (World Wide Publications 1967) vol. 1, pp50-51

18 Arthur Johnston, *The Battle for World Evangelism*, Tyndale House Publishers, 1978, pp301-302

19 Timothy Dudley-Smith, *John Stott: A Global Ministry*, 2001, cited from p123, Stott memorandum to Dudley-Smith, 12 May 1997

20 Hanspeter Nuesch, *Ruth and Billy Graham: The legacy of a couple*, Baker Books, 2014, p231

21 *Oral Roberts: An American Life*, by David Edwin Harrell, John Wiley & Sons; 1st Edition 1985, p203

22 Ibid. p204

23 Ibid. p204

24 Ibid. p205

25 Oral Roberts Ministries website, Seed-Faith, http://oralroberts.com/teaching/seed-faith/

26 Cited from, 'An Alternative Soul of Politics: The Rise of Contemporary Progressive Evangelicalism', p63, by Brantley W. Gasaway, 2008, University of North Carolina dissertation

27 *Just as I Am*, p566

28 *Billy*: A Personal Look at Billy Graham, pp 218-219.

29 Melvin Tinker in *Churchman*, 'Reversal or Betrayal? Evangelicals and Socio - political Involvement in the Twentieth Century', 1999, (The substance of this paper formed the 1999 Evangelical Library Lecture).

30 Carl Henry, *Confessions of a Theologian*, 1986, Word Books, p261

31 David Aikman, *Billy Graham; his life and influence*, Thomas Nelson, 2007, p109

32 David Allan Hubbard, An Ecumenical Experiment, Lecture delivered at Drew University, October 1979, http://fuller.edu/about/history-and-facts/david-allan-hubbard(1)/

33 Orlando Bible Church, 'Dr. Billy Graham: Champion of Compromise and Confusion', November 1966, http://www.orlandobiblechurch.com/index.php/issues-and-answers/dr-billy-graham-champion-compromise/

Chapter 12

Lausanne Congress on World Evangelization

By the 1960s the World Council of Churches, which brought together mainline modernists and liberals, had proved to be a great disappointment to many evangelicals. John Stott echoed the thinking of many when he said: 'We all know that during the last few years, especially between Uppsala and Bangkok, ecumenical-evangelical relations hardened into something like a confrontation.'[1] It was widely believed that the WCC was more interested in a socio-political agenda than in proclaiming the gospel of salvation from sin—social ministry was emphasised over the saving of souls. The WCC's holistic approach to mission was feared in some quarters to mean the subordination of mission to the social agenda of liberal ecumenism.[2] Stott acknowledged that 'the convening by evangelicals of the Berlin Congress on World Evangelization at Berlin in 1966, and the International Congress on World Evangelism at Lausanne in 1974, must unfortunately be understood, at least in part, as a loss of confidence in the World Council of Churches'.[3]

Billy Graham pointed out that the WCC's Commission on World Mission and Evangelism meeting in Bangkok in 1973 (see page 131) focused 'even more strongly on social and political justice to the exclusion of the redemptive heart of the Gospel to a lost world'.[4] *Time* magazine summed up the feelings of many Christians: 'For many in the World Council, the Christian's mission has become more of a campaign to achieve a sort of secular salvation, a human liberation in the political and social sense. To oppose that trend, the Evangelicals at Lausanne laid the groundwork for a post-congress fellowship that could eventually develop into a rival international body.'[5]

The 1966 Berlin Congress was the reaction of evangelical Christians to the perceived need for a new worldwide focus on the Great

Commission. Despite its evangelical ecumenism, it created a fresh vision for the idea of world evangelism. In 1967 Carl Henry commented that the Berlin Congress had brought the evangelical movement to a brink of decision over three major concerns that impinge upon its evangelistic task in the world—theological, socio-political and ecumenical.[6] Evangelical leaders at the Congress were aware that these concerns needed to be dealt with in order for the evangelical movement to take on the challenging task of world evangelism. Some people were so encouraged by the Congress that they urged Billy Graham to consider a second international conference. There was a feeling that the momentum generated by Berlin '66 should not be lost.

Despite his initial reluctance, Graham became convinced that there was a compelling reason to convene another conference. He writes: 'One reason lay in the debate raging in some religious circles within the World Council of Churches (WCC) over the precise meaning of evangelism… For example, in contrast to Berlin, the 1968 Fourth Assembly of the World Council of Churches, held in the Swedish university city of Uppsala—an assembly that I attended as an observer—tended to redefine the good news of the Gospel in terms of restructuring society instead of calling individuals to repentance and faith in Christ.'[7]

In 1971 Graham wrote to 150 influential evangelical leaders throughout the world, asking for their counsel regarding an international conference. The consensus was that the time was right. According to Graham, 'We felt that the Holy Spirit was now directing us to sponsor another conference.'[8]

Billy Graham convened the International Congress on World Evangelization in Lausanne, Switzerland, in July 1974. The theme was 'Let the Earth Hear His Voice'. The Congress, largely American planned, led and financed, was sponsored by *Christianity Today*, with a large amount of financial support from the Billy Graham Evangelistic Association (BGEA). The Lausanne Congress (widely known as Lausanne I) was a unique gathering, for never before had so many Christians from across the world met together in one place. Indeed, almost half of the delegates were from Third World countries. It was a global ground-breaking event and *Time* magazine called it 'possibly the widest-ranging meeting of Christians ever held'.[9]

In his opening address, Billy Graham boldly declared: 'I believe this could be one of the most significant gatherings not only in this century but in the history of the Christian Church... never before have so many representatives of so many evangelical Christian churches in so many nations and from so many tribal and language groups gathered to worship and pray and plan together for world evangelization.'[10] He concluded with the exhortation, 'We are gathered together to hear His voice.' Alongside Graham were John Stott, Francis Schaeffer, Malcolm Muggeridge (who later converted to Roman Catholicism), Ralph D. Winter and other notable church leaders.

The Term 'Evangelization'

The Congress adopted the term *evangelization*, in place of the more traditional term *evangelism*. According to paragraph 10 of the *Lausanne Covenant*: 'The development of strategies for world *evangelization* calls for imaginative pioneering methods. Under God, the result will be the rise of churches deeply rooted in Christ and closely related to their culture' (my italics).

The significance of *evangelization* is that it calls for a renewed mission to the world with a more *holistic* approach to evangelism. Rather than just preaching the gospel of salvation from sin and of new life in Christ, of living a life of obedience to God's commandments, and of daily striving for holiness, *evangelization* encouraged Christians to commit themselves to the cause of social justice, with a special interest in the needs of the poor and oppressed.

Here we should note that the term *evangelization* was within a year to be popularised in the encyclical of Pope Paul VI, entitled *Evangelization in the Modern World* (1975). According to the encyclical, *evangelization* in its totality 'consists in the implantation of the Church, which does not exist without the driving force which is the sacramental life culminating in the Eucharist'.[11] The Roman Catholic Church 'strives always to insert the Christian struggle for liberation into the universal plan of salvation which she herself proclaims... The necessity of ensuring fundamental human rights cannot be separated from this just liberation which is bound up with evangelization and which endeavours to secure structures safeguarding human freedoms.'[12] But

174

how many Protestant evangelicals understand that the term *evangeliza-tion* is widely used by the Church of Rome in a holistic sense to explain what it regards as the real meaning of the gospel?

The Great Commission of the Christian Church is to 'Go ye into all the world, and preach the gospel to every creature.' (Mark 16.15). *Evangelism* means preaching the gospel of salvation from sin in order that souls might be saved. The essential message is 'Christ Jesus came into the world to save sinners' (1 Timothy 1.15). All true Christians know that they cannot earn salvation. 'For by grace are ye saved through faith; and that not of yourselves: it is the gift of God: Not of works, lest any man should boast' (Ephesians 2.8-9). *Evangelization*, on the other hand, means the saving of whole nations or 'people groups' spiritually and temporally through political and social action. It appears that the Lausanne view of evangelization, which combines social and political action with the message of salvation, is remarkably similar to the Vatican version of evangelization, which strives for fundamental human rights and for structures that safeguard human freedoms.

Billy Graham, Honorary Chairman of the Lausanne Committee for World Evangelization, in his opening address boldly declared: 'Evangelism has taken on a new meaning. It is a time of great opportunity, but also a time of great responsibility. We are stewards of our Christian heritage. We must evangelize at all costs while there is yet time. World problems of poverty, overpopulation and the threat of nuclear war mount by the hour. The world is in desperate need of the gospel, now!' And so the Lausanne Congress introduced a new way of evangelism that placed the message of personal salvation from sin alongside the message of social justice.

It was clear from the beginning that Lausanne's new method of evangelism, now referred to as evangelization, was committed to combining evangelism with social action. This new way had little time for the 'niceties' of sound doctrine grounded on biblical truth.

John Stott

John Stott was invited to give an opening address on the nature of biblical evangelism. As we saw in chapter 1, Stott explained that his view of the Great Commission was different from what he had taught at Berlin:

'Today, however, I would express myself differently. It is not just that the commission includes a duty to teach converts everything Jesus had previously commanded (Matthew 28), and that social responsibility is among the things which Jesus commanded. I now see more clearly that not only the consequences of the commission but *the actual commission itself* must be understood to include social as well as evangelistic responsibility, unless we are to be guilty of distorting the words of Jesus'[13] (My emphasis).

In his address Stott emphasised what has become known as the 'incarnational model' of mission, discussed in chapter 1. The guiding text is from John's gospel, 'As the Father has sent me, even so I send you' (John 20.21, RSV). Stott argued that the earthly ministry of Jesus is to be the model for the mission of the Church. As Jesus gave himself in selfless service for others, so the mission of the Church is to do the same, for it is not possible to separate Jesus' words and deeds. Stott maintains that the Johannine version of the Great Commission includes words and deeds. But this model ignores the mission model of the apostle Paul, also discussed in chapter 1.

Having substantially changed his mind about the biblical understanding of evangelism since Berlin 1966, Stott called for 'a note of evangelical repentance... We have some important lessons to learn from our ecumenical critics [He means the WCC]. Some of their rejection of our position is not a repudiation of biblical truth, but rather of our evangelical caricatures of it.'[14]

Stott's address set the tone of the Congress. He said Christians are called to serve— 'Is it not in a servant role that we can find the right synthesis of evangelism and social action? For both should be authentic expressions of the service we are sent into the world to give... If we truly love our neighbour we shall without doubt tell him the Good News of Jesus. But equally if we truly love our neighbour we shall not stop there... True, the Gospel lacks credibility if we who preach it are interested only in souls, and have no concern about the welfare of people's bodies, situations, and community.'[15] In Stott's eyes those who only preached the gospel of salvation from sin were propagating an incomplete gospel. Stott's holistic gospel included a socio-political component. He acknowledged that the redefinition of mission to include evangelism and service was a new 'development' brought about by the WCC movement, yet he saw 'no reason why we should resist this development'.[16]

Stott argued that evangelicals needed to face up to their past mistakes of not paying enough attention to the social needs of the world, and repent of their wrong view of over-emphasising the salvation of souls, while ignoring social action to help those in need. He said it is vital for Christians to distinguish between Scripture and culture. In effect, Stott was preparing the ground for the more radical voices that would come from Latin America.

John Capon, editor of *Crusade* magazine, describes the effect of Stott's speech: 'His address paved the way right at the start of the congress for the spirit of evangelical repentance and openness to greater social consciousness and cultural integrity to come to the surface – not initially from the lips of a Third World "rebel" but from someone who spoke from within the Western tradition.'[17]

Latin American Theologians

Especially prominent was a contingent of Latin American theologians that included Rene Padilla, Simon Escobar and Orlando Costas. A feature of these theologians was that they had been influenced by Latin American liberation theology (which was an unofficial Roman Catholic response to poverty and oppression), and saw it as their responsibility to champion the needs of the poor and oppressed by promoting the cause of social justice. Of great significance was John Stott's support of the Latin American theologians whom he had got to know during a recent trip to South America. Together with several like-minded supporters, Stott and his Latin American friends succeeded in securing in the *Lausanne Covenant* the affirmation that 'evangelism and socio-political involvement are both part of our Christian duty'.[18]

With Stott's backing the Congress offered the Latin American contingent an unprecedented opportunity to speak to North American evangelicals. David R. Swartz in *Left Behind: The Evangelical Left and the Limits of Evangelical Politics 1965-1988* (Doctoral Dissertation 2008), comments: 'The trio [Padilla, Escobar, Costas] held prominent roles at Lausanne, delivering plenary addresses that sharply criticised what they saw as a truncated North American concept of evangelization… Instead of evangelism concerned primarily with numerical growth that turned the Gospel into a cheap product, Padilla urged evangelical activity in the political arena that would ameliorate social injustices.'[19]

The paper delivered by Rene Padilla caused a stir among delegates. Largely in support of Stott's position, Padilla argued against both the universalistic and individualistic versions of the gospel. He argued against an 'individualistic Jesus' who is concerned with the salvation of individuals. He asserted that the gospel had been adapted to the spirit of the times. He objected to what he saw as the imperialism of North American evangelism. He defined 'cultural Christianity' as the identification of Christianity with a culture; and the dominant contemporary form of cultural Christianity, in his eyes, was the American Way of Life.[20] He said: 'The Gospel of culture-Christianity today is a message of conformism, a message that, if not accepted, can at least be easily tolerated because it doesn't disturb anybody. The racist can continue to be a racist, the exploiter can continue to be an exploiter.' He argued: 'A truncated Gospel is utterly insufficient… it can only be the basis for unfaithful churches, for strongholds of racial and class discrimination.' He said he had dealt with American culture-Christianity because of its wide influence.[21]

Padilla answered the charge that he was confusing evangelism with political action by insisting that 'the imperative of the evangelical ethic forms an indissoluble whole with the indicative of the Gospel'.[22] Which probably means social action is an absolute necessity for the true and full gospel.

Dr Vinay K. Samuel, the founding Director of the Oxford Centre for Mission Studies, in his essay, 'Mission as Transformation and the Church', comments on Padilla's paper presented to Congress: 'In this seminal and influential study he drew out the biblical perspective of the "world" and asserted that "the world is claimed by the gospel", not abandoned by it. In my view this identified the "turn to the world" that began among evangelicals concerned about relating the gospel to addressing poverty and bringing social change. The key leaders of this turn were Latin American evangelical leaders like Rene Padilla, Samuel Escobar and Orlando Costas.'[23]

Samuel Escobar's paper, 'Evangelism and man's search for freedom, justice and fulfilment', had a political dimension that attracted a great deal of comment. Professor Brian Stanley in *The Global Diffusion of Evangelicalism: The Age of Billy Graham and John Stott* (2013) comments, 'In his Congress address Escobar boldly took the text dear to liberation theologians, the Nazareth Manifesto of Luke 4.18-19, and insisted that it could not be spiritualised in a world where millions were poor, broken hearted, captive, blind and bruised.' Escobar argued that 'the heart which has been made free with the freedom of Christ, cannot be indifferent to the human longings for deliverance from economic, political or social oppression'.[24] Harold Lindsell, writing in *Christianity Today*, interpreted Escobar's address as claiming that 'socialism is preferable to capitalism'.[25]

Orlando Costa, in his Congress paper argued that to evangelise in depth meant bringing the gospel to bear not simply on individuals but on the socio-economic structures of the present age.[26]

The relationship between evangelism and social action was a theme that ran through the whole Congress and caused an underlying feeling of discomfort among conservative evangelicals, many of whom felt they were under attack. They found it difficult to listen to the radical Latin America voices that were so deeply critical of Western evangelism. Especially hard to take was what American conservatives saw as the hypocrisy of their opponents who were perfectly willing to take American handouts with one hand, while slamming American imperialistic Christianity with the other. But John Stott was thrilled by the debate around social involvement. He wrote: 'the indispensable necessity of socio-political involvement, alongside evangelism, as part of our Christian doctrine and duty were emphasized more clearly, strongly and positively than at Berlin or indeed (I think) ever before in an international gathering'.[27]

The Radical Discipleship Group

But a number of delegates felt that the Congress had not gone far enough in its embrace of social action. In order to publicise their radical views, they formed an ad hoc group of around 500 mainly young delegates, with the aim of producing an alternative Congress statement.

The group was made up of theologians from Latin America, including Padilla, Escobar and Costas. Also prominent in the group were left-wing theologians from the USA, including Jim Wallis, Ronald Sider and John Yoder.

After an impassioned debate, this ad hoc group created a document, which Padilla called 'the strongest statement on the basis for holistic mission ever formulated by an evangelical conference up to that date'. It defined the gospel as 'Good News of liberation, of restoration, of wholeness, and of salvation that is personal, social, global and cosmic'. This initiative undoubtedly influenced the final form of the *Lausanne Covenant* to include not just one sentence on social concerns, as some of the more conservative conveners had originally intended, but an entire section on Christian Social Responsibility.[28]

John Stott met with the radical group leaders in private, and then publicly declared that he was prepared to sign both the *Lausanne Covenant* and the alternative statement of the radicals, which became known as the Theological Implications of Radical Discipleship.

An abstract from this alternative statement reveals the radical political convictions of the group:

> **We affirm that:** the evangel is God's Good News in Jesus Christ... it is Good News of a new creation of a new humanity... of the charismatic community empowered to embody his reign of shalom here and now before the whole creation to make his Good News seen and known. It is Good News of liberation, of restoration, of wholeness and of salvation that is personal, social, global and cosmic...
>
> Methods in evangelization must centre in Jesus Christ... he sends his community into the world, as the Father sent him, to identify and agonise with men, to renounce status and demonic power, and to give itself in selfless service of others for God. **We confess that:** Our testimony has often been marred by triumphalism and arrogance, by lack of faith in God and by diminished love for his people.
>
> We have often been in bondage to a particular culture and sought to spread it in the name of Jesus...

We have been partisan in our condemnation of totalitarianism and violence and have failed to condemn societal and institutionalized sin, especially that of racism.

We have sometimes so identified ourselves with particular political systems that the Gospel has been compromised and the prophetic voice muted.

We have frequently denied the rights and neglected the cries of the underprivileged and those struggling for freedom and justice…

We must repudiate as demonic the attempt to drive a wedge between evangelism and social action…

We resolve… to submit to his Lordship, to know his salvation, to identify in him with the oppressed and work for the liberation of all men and women in his name.

The significance of this report is that it reveals the political mindset of the radical group that, in reality, drove the Lausanne agenda in full view of Billy Graham, and, no doubt, with the full blessing of John Stott.

The Lausanne Covenant

The historic *Lausanne Covenant*, largely drafted by John Stott, was the major achievement of the Congress and of Stott himself. Stott presented the *Covenant*, which had been greatly influenced by the radicals, to a final meeting of the delegates. His task was to persuade Congress to accept what was a fundamental change in the understanding of the Great Commission, and to do so in the face of deeply sceptical conservative American evangelicals. But the diplomatic John Stott proved equal to the task. Editor of *Crusade* magazine, John Capon, described Stott's performance as masterly, establishing him as 'the key figure in contemporary world evangelicalism'.[29] It was Stott's persuasive manner that convinced many conservative Christians, fearful that the new radical agenda was a reincarnation of the old social gospel, to accept the new understanding of evangelization that included socio-political action. But not everybody was convinced and about 500 of the 2,473 delegates did not sign the *Covenant*.

The *Covenant* commented on the authority and power of the Bible: 'We affirm the divine inspiration, truthfulness and authority of both Old and New Testament Scriptures in their entirety as the only written word of God, without error in all that it affirms, and the only infallible rule of faith and practice.'

Francis Schaeffer comments: 'Upon first reading, this seems to make a strong statement in support of the full authority of the Bible. But a problem has come up concerning the phrase "in all that it affirms." For many this is being used as a loophole. I ought to say that this little phrase was not a part of my own contribution to the Lausanne Congress. I did not know that this phrase was going to be included in the *Covenant* until I saw it in printed form, and I was not completely happy with it. Nevertheless, it is a proper statement if the words are dealt with fairly... So that statement, as it appeared in the *Lausanne Covenant*, is a perfectly proper statement in itself. However, as soon as I saw it in printed form I knew it was going to be abused. Unhappily, this statement, "in all that it affirms," has indeed been made a loophole by many... But on the basis of the existential methodology, these men and women say in the back of their minds, even as they sign the *Covenant*, "But the Bible does not affirm without error that which it teaches in the area of history and the cosmos".'[30] In other words, the Lausanne statement on the Bible permits a belief in theistic evolution, as well as doubt about the historical statements of the Bible. In practice, Fuller Seminary's view of partial inspiration is compatible with the *Covenant*.

Paragraph 5 of the *Lausanne Covenant* asserted the need to liberate men from every kind of oppression: 'We affirm that God is both the Creator and Judge of all men. We therefore should share his concern for justice and reconciliation throughout human society and for the liberation of men from every kind of oppression. Because mankind is made in the image of God, every person, regardless of race, religion, colour, culture, class, sex or age, has an intrinsic dignity because of which he should be respected and served, not exploited. Here too we express penitence both for our neglect and for having sometimes regarded evangelism and social concern as mutually exclusive. Although reconciliation with man is not reconciliation with God, nor is social action evangelism, nor is political liberation salvation, nevertheless we affirm that evangelism

182

and socio-political involvement are both part of our Christian duty.'

Paragraph 6 affirmed that 'in the church's mission of sacrificial service, evangelism is primary'. This affirmation would later become a bone of contention between Billy Graham and John Stott, as discussed in the next chapter.

The *Lausanne Covenant* stands as one of the most significant evangelical documents of the twentieth century—a document that has had a massive impact on the way the Church understands its mission to the world. Stott's achievement in making socio-political action a part of the mission of the Church was a triumph for the holistic mission movement. According to Athol Gill, a controversial Baptist theologian who was involved with the radical discipleship movement in Australia, 'the *Lausanne Covenant* marked a turning point in evangelical thinking, a turning point which may well have significant consequences for all Christians'.[31]

René Padilla offers an interpretation of the Lausanne Congress in his paper, 'Integral Mission and its Historical Development'. He writes: 'No one should have been surprised that the International Congress on World Evangelization (Lausanne 1974) would turn out to be a definitive step in affirming integral mission as the mission of the church. In view of the deep mark that it left in the life and mission of the evangelical movement around the world, the *Lausanne Congress* may be regarded as the most important worldwide evangelical gathering of the twentieth century.' Commenting on paragraph 5 of the *Covenant*, Padilla writes: 'This is not merely an affirmation of the Christian duty towards social sin in terms of injustice, alienation, oppression and discrimination... Christian social action is thus regarded as having a theological basis, as an expression of definite convictions with regard to God and humankind, salvation and the kingdom. The importance of this statement coming out of a conference in which a high number of participants had all too often regarded evangelism and social concern as "mutually exclusive" can hardly be exaggerated. The *Lausanne Covenant* not only expressed penitence for the neglect of social action, but it also acknowledged that socio-political involvement was, together with evangelism, an essential aspect of the Christian mission. In so doing it gave a death blow on attempts to reduce mission to the multiplication of Christians and churches through evangelism. The following years, however, showed that, far from settling the matter, the Lausanne Congress had done little more than point to the need to deal with the role of social involvement for the sake of the integrity of the church and its mission.'[32]

Padilla again: 'The *Lausanne Covenant* was received all over the world with great interest and even exhilaration by Christians of different theological persuasions. By contrast, others interpreted Lausanne as a dangerous departure from biblical truth and a tragic compromise with so-called ecumenical theology. John Stott in particular came under fire for defining social action as a "partner of evangelism", thus dethroning evangelism as "the only historic aim of mission".'[33]

Padilla continues: 'In spite of its opponents, most of them identified with the North American missionary establishment, integral mission continued to find support among evangelicals, especially in the Two-Thirds World. The issues it raised became the motivating force for several world-wide consultations that took place in the late 1970s and early 1980s, which explicitly dealt with, or at least touched on, the question of justice.'[34]

Daniel Salinas in *Latin American Evangelical Theology in the 1970's: The Golden Decade* (2009), sums up the influence of the Latin Americans. He writes: 'Even though there were at Lausanne several voices and positions, the Latin American participation was particularly influential in breaking the hegemony of North American agendas. Latin Americans were evaluating and criticising, positively and negatively the theological dependence of North American and European theologies.'[35] Both Padilla and Escobar disagreed with the path the Lausanne Committee for World Evangelization (LCWE) was taking regarding the issues of evangelism and social responsibility. 'They were not opposing evangelism per se, rather a narrow definition of evangelism that left social participation as optional or dispensable... We could say, without exaggeration, that the Latin Americans gave the Lausanne movement an agenda for the decade following Lausanne 74. Such an agenda found support in other parts of the world...'[36]

According to *Christianity Today*: 'In the end, the *Lausanne Covenant* spoke to the moment, expressing a common mission that most delegates could enthusiastically endorse; and it spoke to the future, providing a framework that evangelical groups could use as their basic statement. Lausanne was a defining moment in global evangelicalism. Billy Graham was the indispensable convener, but John Stott was the indispensable uniter.'[37]

What started in Lausanne has ignited a movement that is spread across the globe, serving many thousands of churches and hundreds of the world's missionary organisations. According to Mark Green of the London Institute for Contemporary Christianity: 'The wall that came down was the wall between evangelism and social action. Until then, many evangelicals had regarded social action as a distraction from the primacy of proclaiming the good news. At Lausanne 1974, however, with Billy Graham and John Stott to the fore, the First Congress on World Evangelization agreed that the evangelistic proclamation of the love of God in Christ must be accompanied by the expression of the love of God in Christ by actively engaging with the physical and emotional needs of people – holistic mission. It may seem obvious now, but it wasn't then.'[38] Many evangelical Christians regard the *Covenant* to be one of the most important documents in recent Church history, for they claim that it has brought together Christians from across the theological spectrum, challenging all to work together to make Jesus Christ known throughout the world. The *Covenant* has been translated into more than 20 languages, and adopted by many thousands of churches and para-church agencies as their basis of operations and cooperation.

The *Lausanne Covenant* proved a watershed for the Church. What it achieved, through the diplomatic skills of John Stott, was to change the evangelical understanding of the relationship between evangelism and social action. After Lausanne 74, it was accepted by many evangelical Christians that they should be concerned 'for the liberation of men from every kind of oppression' and that 'evangelism and socio-political action are both part of our Christian duty'. There is no doubt that Lausanne was a massive turning-point in the history of evangelicalism and a great victory for the holistic movement. The concept of social action, also referred to as holistic mission, was now accepted by many, *but not all*, as an equal partner with evangelism in the mission of the Church. However, the battle over the meaning of evangelism continues in our next chapter.

(Endnotes)

1   John Stott quoted at Lausanne: http://www.religion-online.org/showchapter. asp?title=1573&C=1522, 'The Biblical Basis of Evangelism', https://www.lausanne.org/docs/lau1docs/0065.pdf

2   Kenneth R Ross, *Edinburgh 2010: Springboard for Mission*, William Carey International University Press, 2009, p27

3   Lausanne Occasional Paper 21, Evangelism and Social Responsibility, foreword, http://www.lausanne.org/content/lop/lop-21#Appendix A

4   Billy Graham, *Just As I Am*, HarperOne-Zondervan, 1997, p568

5   *Time* magazine, A Challenge from Evangelicals, 5 August 1974

6   Cited from *The Encyclopedia of Christianity*, Volume 3, edited by Erwin Fahlbusch, Geoffrey William Bromiley, published by B Eerdmans, 2003, p205

7   *Just As I Am*, p568

8   Ibid, p568

9   *Time* magazine, cited in *Moral Minority: The Evangelical Left in an Age of Conservatism* by David R. Swartz, University of Pennsylvania Press; reprint edition, March 6, 2014, p123

10   *Just As I Am*, p571

11   Evangelii Nuntiandi, Apostolic Exhortation of His Holiness, Pope Paul VI, 1975, paragraph 28

12   Ibid. paragraphs 38 and 39

13   John Stott, *Christian Mission in the Modern World*, IVP Books, 1975, p25

14   John Stott, 'The Biblical Basis of Evangelism', in Let the Earth Hear His Voice, edited by Douglas, 1975, p65, cited from *John Stott: A Global Ministry*, p211

15   Cited from *Latin American Evangelical Theology in the 1970's: The Golden Decade* by Daniel Salinas, BRILL, 2009, p125

16   Arthur Johnston, *The Battle for World Evangelism*, Tyndale House, 1978, p301, cites Let the Earth Hear His Voice, p66

17   John Capon, 'Lausanne 74', *Crusade*, September 1974, cited from *John Stott: A Global Ministry*, p211

18   *Lausanne Covenant*, paragraph 5. Christian Social Responsibility

19   *Left Behind: The Evangelical Left and the Limits of Evangelical Politics: 1965 - 1988* by David R. Swartz, a Doctor of Philosophy dissertation, 2008, p124

20   *Latin American Evangelical Theology in the 1970*, p129

21   *Left Behind: The Evangelical Left and the Limits of Evangelical Politics*, p124, cites, Padilla, 'Evangelism and the World', p130

22   Cited from *The Global Diffusion of Evangelicalism: The Age of Billy Graham and John Stott*, by Brian Stanley, IVP Academic, 2013, p166

23   *Holistic Mission: God's Plan for God's People*, Regnum Edinburgh Series, 2010, Vinay Samuel, 'Mission as Transformation and the Church', p128

24   Cited from *The Global Diffusion of Evangelicalism: The Age of Billy Graham and John Stott*, by Brian Stanley, p166

25   *Christianity Today*, 13 September 1974, cited in 'Lausanne 1974': The Challenge from the Majority World to Northern-Hemisphere Evangelicalism, by Brian Stanley, University of Edinburgh, 2013, p12

26   Cited from *The Global Diffusion of Evangelicalism: The Age of Billy Graham and John Stott*, by Brian Stanley, p167

27   *John Stott: A Global Ministry*, p212

28   Misión Integral and Progressive Evangelicalism: The Latin American Influence on the North American Emerging Church by Michael Clawson, in *Religions* 2012, 3, 790–807

29   Lausanne 1974: The Challenge from the Majority World to Northern-Hemisphere Evangelicalism, by Brian Stanley, University of Edinburgh, 2013, p19

30   Francis A Schaeffer, cited from chapter 2 of *The Great Evangelical Disaster* Crossway Books, 1984

31   Athol Gill cited in *Crisis and Hope in Latin America: An Evangelical Perspective* by Emilio Antonio Núñez C, William David Taylor, first edition published by Moody Press, 1989, p416

32   Padilla's paper 'Integral Mission and its Historical Development' appears in *Justice, Mercy and Humility: Integral Mission and the Poor*, ed. Tim Chester, (Carlisle: Paternoster, 2003). Also, www.micahnetwork.org/.../integral_mission_and_its_ historical_development

33   Padilla has quoted Arthur P. Johnston, *The Battle for World Evangelism*, p302

34   Integral Mission and its Historical Development, C. René Padilla

35   *Latin American Evangelical Theology in the 1970's: The Golden Decade,* by Daniel Salinas, p159

36   Ibid, pp 159-160

37   *Christianity Today*, 'John Stott Has Died, An architect of 20th-century evangelicalism shaped the faith of a generation', Tim Stafford/ July 27, 2011

38   Mark Greene, 'Mission World – One More Wall To Go?', The London Institute for Contemporary Christianity. www.licc.org.uk/.../EG28%20Mission%20World%20 One%20More%20...

Chapter 13

The Post-Lausanne Battle

While John Stott achieved a great triumph with the *Lausanne Covenant*, making socio-political action part of our Christian duty, a large number of evangelicals were unconvinced by his zeal for political activism. His support for the Latin American radicals made some conservative Americans question his motives. They interpreted the pathway taken by Lausanne as a departure from biblical truth and a compromise with theological liberalism. How was it possible for an evangelical theologian and Bible teacher, who only eight years previously at Berlin '66 had said that the Great Commission of the Church is 'not to reform society but to preach the Gospel', to have so drastically changed his mind? Stott was criticised by conservative Christians for defining social action as a partner of evangelism. According to Arthur Johnston in *The Battle for World Evangelism* (1978), Stott had dethroned evangelism as 'the only historic aim of mission'.[1]

Lausanne Committee for World Evangelization (LCWE)

An outcome of the first Lausanne Congress was the formation of a permanent Continuation Committee to carry on the vision and work of what became known as the Lausanne movement; and in 1976 this became the Lausanne Committee for World Evangelization (LCWE). When the Continuation Committee met for the first time in Mexico City in January 1975, a year before LCWE was officially constituted, there was tension in the air—the two Christian leaders who had created Lausanne were now in open disagreement about the way forward.

At the first meeting of the Continuation Committee it was clearly apparent that many conservative evangelicals were deeply unhappy with Stott's holistic understanding of the mission of the Church. They were also suspicious about his cosy relationship with the Latin American theologians, whom they regarded as socialists.

In his opening address to the Committee, Billy Graham reported that he had received many letters from participants about the direction of Lausanne's ministry. Some advocated a narrow way and others a broad way. 'What I counsel is that we stick strictly to evangelism and missions, while at the same time encouraging others to do the specialised work that God has commissioned the Church to do.'[2] In saying this Graham was directly challenging Stott's two-pronged approach to the mission of the Church—evangelism and socio-political action.

Stott was stunned, for his socio-political initiative, so skilfully advanced at Lausanne, was about to collapse. He was aware that many American conservatives were against what they saw as his social gospel. But Stott's socialist mindset could not accept the narrow way, for he was totally given over to the concept of holistic mission. Stott wrote in his diary: 'The narrow view was that our paramount task was evangelism, that there was no possibility of evangelicals uniting on any other sub-ject… The broad concept was that we should get involved in everything God wants done. Having described the two, Billy made it clear that he favoured the first. If we accepted the second, he added, we'd get "off the mandate given us at Lausanne", as Lausanne had given us in his judge-ment "a rather narrow mandate". So we must "not get bogged down in other peripheral matters". This troubled me very much, and I stayed up several hours thinking about it and preparing a rebuttal.'[3]

The following morning Stott spoke from John 17, outlining his incarnational view of the mission of the Church; he asked the gathering whether Christ's followers were free to adopt a narrower concern than that taught by Jesus. In the following session the first speaker endorsed the narrow view as described by Graham the previous evening. John Stott then took the opportunity to defend his holistic view of the gospel, the so-called 'broad' view. Stott again: 'It was an unenviable task to disagree with Billy Graham in public, but I felt I had to argue for the wider concept (1) from Scripture (Christ calls us to be salt as well as light), (2) from history (the church's constant tendency to unbalanced preoccupations), (3) from the Lausanne Congress (the *Covenant* treat-ing a number of topics besides evangelism), (4) from the Continuation

Committee (we were not all evangelists and some of us ought to go home if that was to be our exclusive concern)... I ended: "if we go back now, and concentrate exclusively on evangelism, it will not be an implementation of the *Covenant* but a betrayal of it". Well, then the fat was in the fire"...'[4]

And as the passionate debate raged on, Stott sensed that things were not going his way. Stott explains: 'I felt so deeply concerned that we were about to betray Lausanne's vision, covenant and spirit that I said I was afraid I would have to resign if the Committee decided to go the way they were indicating. To my surprise Jack Dain from the chair immediately supported me, saying he too would resign... We may well have made a mistake in saying this. The Americans interpreted it as a threat, an illicit form of blackmail, even the behaviour of obstinate children who won't cooperate if they don't get their own way.'[5]

Alastair Chapman, in his book, *Godly Ambition* (2012), offers his view of the drama. 'Stott stayed awake for several hours that night, formulating his response to Graham's proposal. By morning, he had decided to confront Graham, who was bankrolling the meeting and the movement. As business began, Stott stunned everyone by saying that he would resign from the committee if Graham's vision for the movement prevailed. Stott demanded that the *Lausanne Covenant's* emphasis on the social implications of the Gospel be reflected in the organization's ongoing work... The committee was shocked. Many in the room disagreed... But losing Stott would have been a big blow. Some felt he was blackmailing the committee.'[6] Chapman believes that Stott's conscience was troubled, for 'threats were not his normal way of getting things done. Part of the difficulty was that he was used to being in charge... He recognised at the time that his indelicate behaviour could look like "personal power hunger," yet exonerated himself from the charge'.[7]

In *John Stott: A Global Ministry* (2001), Dudley-Smith comments on the drama: 'Over and above the issue under discussion was the shock felt by some delegates at this public disagreement with Billy Graham, in the light of the universal esteem in which Billy was held by the international evangelical community. Some were in tears about it. Others were soon openly accusing John Stott of engaging in a power struggle, challenging Billy Graham for the worldwide evangelical leadership...'[8]

The reality was that the Lausanne movement could not afford to lose John Stott and so a compromise was needed. This was achieved by asking him and Peter Wagner, the charismatic Professor of Church Growth at Fuller Seminary's School of World Missions, to work on a compromised statement that would keep everybody on board. The result was a reference to 'the total biblical mission of the church' in the Committee's statement of purpose. The reality was that Stott had successfully defended the holistic vision of the Lausanne movement, against the wishes of Billy Graham and many conservative American evangelicals. In effect, Stott and his South American radicals now had a free hand to drive the Lausanne agenda into ever more liberal waters.

Church Growth Theory (1977)

Church growth was the subject for the first consultation to be held under Lausanne's sponsorship, in 1977. Hosted by Fuller Seminary, with John Stott acting as moderator, five faculty members of Fuller's School of World Mission, including Donald McGavran, Ralph Winter and Peter Wagner, prepared papers for the meeting.[9] Participants in the consultation included Arthur Glasser, Associate Professor of Theology of Mission, Fuller Seminary; Charles Kraft, Professor of Anthropology, Fuller Seminary; Rene Padilla; Ralph Winter, General Director, United States Center for World Mission; John Yoder, Professor of Theology, University of Notre Dame, Indiana. In addition, 12 of the 27 consultants were from Fuller Seminary—even Seminary President Daniel Fuller was part of the consultation. This gathering spoke volumes about the theological stance of Lausanne. It was now abundantly clear that Fuller Seminary, with its flawed view of Scripture, its theological compromise and charismatic confusion, was the driving force behind the Lausanne movement. It was also clear that theologian John Stott, the architect of Lausanne, was perfectly comfortable working hand in hand with the compromised agenda of Fuller Theological Seminary.

The Willowbank Report: The Gospel and Culture (1978)

The next Lausanne consultation, also under the chairmanship of John Stott, addressed the issue of 'The Gospel and Culture'. According to Stott the process of communicating the gospel cannot be isolated from the human culture from which it comes, or from that in which it is to be proclaimed. The Lausanne Theology and Education Group convened a consultation to meet in January 1978. It brought together from all six continents 33 theologians, anthropologists, linguists, missionaries and pastors to study Gospel and Culture.[10] Included in the working group that met at Willowbank, Bermuda, were two of the well-known Latin American theologians from Lausanne 74, namely Orlando Costas and Rene Padilla, and two professors from Fuller Seminary, William Pannell, Assistant Professor of Evangelism, and missiologist Charles Kraft, Professor of Anthropology and African Studies. This 'expert' group sought to identify the tools that were needed for more adequate communication of the gospel, and then to share the fruits of the consultation with Christian leaders in churches and missionary agencies.

The outcome was a Lausanne Occasional Paper, referred to as the Willowbank Report. Cultural barriers to the communication of the gospel were identified: 'No Christian witness can hope to communicate the gospel if he or she ignores the cultural factor... Two main problems face them. Sometimes people resist the gospel not because they think it false but because they perceive it as a threat to their culture, especially the fabric of their society, and their national or tribal solidarity. To some extent this cannot be avoided. Jesus Christ is a disturber as well as a peacemaker... The other problem is that the gospel is often presented to people in alien cultural forms. Then the missionaries are resented and their message rejected because their work is seen not as an attempt to evangelize but as an attempt to impose their own customs and way of life. Where missionaries bring with them foreign ways of thinking and behaving, or attitudes of racial superiority, paternalism, or preoccupation with material things, effective communication will be precluded. Sometimes these two cultural blunders are committed together, and messengers of the gospel are guilty of a cultural imperialism which both undermines the local culture unnecessarily and seeks to impose an alien culture instead. Some of the missionaries who accompanied the Catholic *conquistadores* of Latin America and the Protestant colonizers of Africa and Asia are historical examples of this double mistake...'[11]

Cultural sensitivity in communicating the gospel was essential. 'Sensitive cross-cultural witnesses will not arrive at their sphere of service with a pre-packaged gospel… It is only by active, loving engagement with the local people, thinking in their thought patterns, understanding their world-view, listening to their questions, and feeling their burdens, that the whole believing community (of which the missionary is a part) will be able to respond to their need. By common prayer, thought and heart searching, in dependence on the Holy Spirit, expatriate and local believers may learn together how to present Christ and contextualize the gospel with an equal degree of faithfulness and relevance.'[12]

Missionary humility meant taking 'the trouble to understand and appreciate the culture of those to whom we go. It is this desire which leads naturally into that true dialogue "whose purpose is to listen sensitively in order to understand" (*Lausanne Covenant*, para. 4). We repent of the ignorance which assumes that we have all the answers and that our only role is to teach. We have very much to learn. We repent also of judgmental attitudes. We know we should never condemn or despise another culture, but rather respect it.'[13]

The working group dealt with the question of conversion. 'Conversion should not be conceived as being invariably and only an individual experience, although that has been the pattern of Western expectation for many years… Much important research has been undertaken in recent years into "people movements" from both theological and sociological perspectives… It is evident that people receive the gospel most readily when it is presented to them in a manner which is appropriate—and not alien—to their culture, and when they can respond to it with and among their own people. Different societies have different procedures for making group decisions, e.g., by consensus, by the head of the family, or by a group of elders. We recognize the validity of the corporate dimension of conversion as part of the total process, as well as the necessity for each member of the group ultimately to share in it personally.'[14]

The Report commented on political power structures: 'We have seen with our own eyes the poverty of the [Third World] masses, we feel for them and with them, and we have some understanding that their plight is due in part to an economic system which is controlled mostly by the North Atlantic countries (although others are now also involved). Those of us who are citizens of North American or European countries cannot avoid some feeling of embarrassment and shame, by reason of the oppression in which our countries in various degrees have been involved... Yet we have to confess that some missionaries themselves reflect a neo-colonial attitude and even defend it, together with outposts of Western power and exploitation such as Southern Africa.'[15]

Padilla Comments on Willowbank Report

René Padilla, in his comments on the Willowbank Report, draws attention to the 'power structures and mission', which he believes is related to the poverty of the masses in the Third World. He claims 'their plight is due in part to an economic system which is controlled mostly by North Atlantic countries'. Padilla writes: 'In the face of this situation, the prophetic document calls for solidarity with the poor and the denunciation of injustice "in the name of the Lord who is the God of justice as well as of justification".'[16]

Comment

In the Willowbank Report we see John Stott in his true colours. The report is a highly political document. It castigates missionaries of the past who took the gospel to Africa and Asia for their cultural insensitivity, racial superiority and paternalism. It repents of the ignorance and judgemental attitudes of the missionaries of the past. It deplores neo-colonialism. It presupposes a cultural equivalence between Western culture, shaped by Christianity, and pagan culture, shaped by superstition and spiritual darkness. It encourages dialogue with unbelievers in order to present a culturally sensitive gospel that does not offend. The basic presupposition is that the gospel of Christ must be adapted so as to make it relevant to each culture. Cultural adaptation is achieved by applying the latest theories of anthropology, and by 'loving engagement with the local people, thinking in their [darkened] thought patterns, understanding their [unbiblical] worldview, listening to their questions, and feeling their burdens'. But such an approach is completely wrong, for the Word of God is above every culture, and every culture must be shaped and modified by God's Word. Gospel presentation must not be modified by the theories of anthropology, but must be faithful to biblical teaching. Adapting the gospel to make it culturally sensitive distorts the message of the gospel, and blunts its spiritual power to transform lives.

The Willowbank Report downplays the biblical concept of the individual conversion of a sinner, and elevates the idea of group conversions. This shows a false understanding of the gospel of salvation, for God deals with individual sinners; each individual soul will stand before the Judgement Throne of God and give account of his or her deeds. There is no biblical mandate and no New Testament model for group conversions.

Christian missionaries are faced with the challenge of preaching God's Word in pagan cultures that are distorted and darkened by sin, ignorance and superstition. Their mission is to bring the light of God's Word to people who are by nature sinners, at enmity with God and living in spiritual darkness. The culture that has shaped their lives is a culture distorted by centuries of sin. Lost sinners living in spiritual darkness desperately need the light of the gospel of Christ. The ministry of Jesus Christ began with these words from Scripture: 'The people which sat in darkness saw great light; and to them which sat in the region and shadow of death light is sprung up. From that time Jesus began to preach, and to say, Repent: for the kingdom of heaven is at hand' (Matthew 4. 16-17).

The Report infers that Third World poverty is due to the oppressive economic system controlled by Western nations. It declares that Western Christians should feel embarrassed and ashamed, by reason of the political oppression they have condoned. The Report presents a serious distortion of the witness of Western missionaries, who gave their lives to take the light of the gospel to many nations ruled by spiritual darkness. Western missionaries spent their lives translating the Bible into many languages, thereby making the light of Scripture available to those living in darkness. Their biographies should not be a cause of embarrassment or shame. Rather we should rejoice in their self-sacrifice, motivated by a love for the Lord Jesus Christ and his glorious gospel of salvation.

The fingerprints of Fuller Seminary and John Stott are all over the Willowbank Report, a Report that encouraged missionaries to propagate a watered-down, culturally sensitive, politically correct, inoffensive gospel.

The Simple Lifestyle Consultation (March 1980)

The radicals were in a hurry to implement the political victory gained in the *Lausanne Covenant*, which included these sentences: 'All of us are shocked by the poverty of millions and disturbed by the injustices which cause it. Those of us who live in affluent circumstances accept our duty to develop a simple life-style in order to contribute more generously to both relief and evangelism.'[17] In order to examine the full implications of these words it was decided to set up a Lifestyle Consultation. And so in 1980 a working group was established under the Lausanne banner, chaired by John Stott and co-ordinated by Ronald Sider, author of *Rich Christians in an Age of Hunger* (1978). It was no surprise that the two men were working closely together, for Stott was attracted by Ronald Sider's left-wing politics and ability to use Scripture in a way that provided support for the socialist cause. The objective of the Consultation was 'to study simple living in relation to evangelism, relief and justice'.[18]

Participants in the working group, under the influence of Sider and Stott, were moved to repentance for their complicity in world injustice. They felt deeply that world evangelism was stifled and compromised by their complacency about social injustice. As Christians they were conscious of their 'own involvement in creating, perpetuating and allowing misery, poverty, destruction and irresponsibility to continue in the world... we can no longer separate ourselves because of distance from the poverty of the world, we must take the only other course – we must repent.'[19]

The social justice theme was writ large. Ronald Sider said that relief and development were not enough. 'One of the most urgent agenda items for the church in the industrialised nations is to help our people begin honestly to explore to what extent our abundance depends on international economic structures that are unjust. To what extent do current patterns of international trade and the operations of the International Monetary Fund contribute to affluence in some nations and poverty in others? Unless we grapple with that systemic question, our discussion of simple life-style has not gone beyond Christmas baskets and superficial charity...'[20]

The working group was convinced that a measure of injustice is built into the current economic system. 'Since it is those who have power who are able to redistribute to the poor, God's call to rulers must be to use their power to defend the poor, not to exploit them. The church of God therefore must stand with God and the poor against injustice.'[21]

The working group agreed that the Church must stand with God and the poor against injustice. 'One quarter of the world's population enjoys unparalleled prosperity, while another quarter endures grinding poverty. This gross disparity is an intolerable injustice—we refuse to acquiesce in it. The call for a New International Economic Order expresses the justified frustration of the Third World.' It was agreed that 'personal and philanthropic endeavours are not enough; political action is essential to achieve fundamental structural change'. John Stott said: 'We become personally culpable when we acquiesce in the status quo by doing nothing.'[22] Thus the working group pointed Christians in two directions – personal commitment and political action – and urged a balance between the two.

Some leaders of the Lausanne Committee for World Evangelization (LCWE) expressed grave concern over the findings of the Simple Lifestyle Report. In March 1981, the Rev Leighton Ford, Chairman of the LCWE, wrote to John Stott to share his initial reaction to a draft of the Report.[23] Ford had a number of profound reservations about the radical nature of the document. He wrote: 'There seems to me to be a pronounced anti-Western bias. On a very quick scan I found over 20 direct or implied references to the West. Most often they appear in the context of a negative judgment. The fewer Third World references are almost uniformly positive. By contrast, I note the omission of any reference to socio-economic problems connected with Marxist countries… I fear the commentary may be thought to have fallen prey to the guilt reaction typical of many Western liberals and to the kind of selective criticism which has distorted the pronouncements of the WCC for years. There appears to me at points to be quite a strong bias against business in the free enterprise system… Western businesses are largely held responsible for the problems of the rest of the world.'

Leighton Ford also expressed his concern that in the Report evangelism was seen as secondary. 'I have noted that throughout the document as a whole references to justice, relief and development outnumber references to evangelism by about three to one… in the section dealing with our responsibility to the poor, there is strangely no reference to the scriptural statements about preaching the gospel to the poor.'

Leighton Ford was concerned about ambiguities of language.

'Several of these have referred to the "call for a new international economic order"... This has been taken to be a call for socialism... it has
left room for those who wish to be critical to suggest that the statement
implies a socialist or Marxist bias...'

These comments of the Rev Leighton Ford, the Chairman of the
LCWE, are remarkable, for they imply that the Simple Lifestyle Report
is seeking to promote, not evangelical Christianity, but Marxist ideology.
Ford's observation that there was 'no reference to the scriptural statements about preaching the gospel to the poor' demonstrates a profound
indifference to the gospel of Christ.

Comment

An Evangelical Commitment to Simple Lifestyle, drafted by Stott
and greatly influenced by Sider, was yet another highly political document—it was simply a regurgitation of the socialist message of Ronald
Sider's *Rich Christians in an Age of Hunger*. The thesis of the Report
is that Christians in the West are responsible for world poverty and
therefore guilty of institutional sin. A Christian's duty is not only to
redistribute resources to those living in poverty, but also to fight for a
New International Economic Order.

Leighton Ford was deeply disturbed by what he read in the draft
Report sent to him by John Stott. He was perceptive enough to realise
it had a serious left-wing bias that promoted an anti-Western agenda,
but was silent on the problems in Communist countries. Ford was concerned that the Report could even be labelled as Marxist by opponents
of the Lausanne agenda. Al Tizon writes: 'For some of the leaders of the
LCWE, the tension actually intensified as they expressed grave concern
over the consultation's findings.'[24] While some of the Lausanne people
were clearly not happy with Stott's highly political Simple Lifestyle
Report, he remained the driving force behind the Lausanne movement.

The Consultation on World Evangelization (June 1980)

By the end of the 1970s the LCWE was deeply concerned by the
political agenda that was being pursued by the radicals in the Lausanne
movement. As a consequence, the first international follow-up meeting,
The Consultation on World Evangelization (COWE), that convened in

Pattaya, Thailand in June 1980, was under the leadership of Leighton Ford who tried to curtail the political activism of the radicals.

Strategic issues pertinent to world evangelization were considered by the 650 delegates and 300 guests. The theme 'How shall they hear?' focused on the concept of unreached people groups. But COWE was again tied up in controversy and tension. Some leaders in Lausanne clearly wanted to downplay the politicisation of the movement, that had become such a prominent feature under the influence of Stott and his friends. While the Lausanne leadership did not want the socio-political aspect of evangelism on the agenda, the radicals had different ideas. The advocates of holistic evangelism considered the limited vision at COWE to be a deplorable step backward. They were critical of the LCWE for not being true to the broad, holistic vision of the *Covenant* and of reducing evangelization to simply the verbal proclamation of the gospel.[25]

Deeply dissatisfied with the 'narrower' direction of the Consultation, the advocates of holistic evangelism drafted a 'Statement of Concerns', signed by around one third of the delegates. In response Leighton Ford called a meeting with the representatives of the 'concerned group', which included Orlando Costas, Vinay Samuel, and Ronald Sider. Tension was in the air as conservative evangelicals met the radicals. But the result, claims Costas, was that the official final version of the Thailand Statement, drafted by Stott, addressed some of the issues raised by the radicals.[26]

Tension between the narrow and broad views of evangelization came to a head at Pattaya, and the narrow view won the official battle.[27] By the end of 1980, the evangelical family was deeply divided. Valdir Steuernagel, a Lutheran pastor in Brazil and a member of the Lausanne Board, made the point that while the Simple Lifestyle Consultation was interpreted as speaking the language of the 'radical evangelicals', COWE was criticised by the radicals because 'social responsibility' had been excluded from its programme, and also because it embraced a definition of evangelization that did not take into account the broader definition of mission as articulated in the *Lausanne Covenant*.[28]

Evangelism and Social Responsibility, Grand Rapids (1982)

John Stott was stung by Dr Arthur Johnston's accusation in *The*

Battle for World Evangelism (1978), that he had 'dethroned evangelism as the only historic aim of mission'.[29] Aware that many in the USA were deeply suspicious of his motives, Stott suggested the need for an international consultation of evangelical leaders to settle the divisive issue of the relationship between evangelism and social action. He made a note in his diary about the suspicions of Christians in the USA. The note makes three points about American concerns. First, 'that the Lausanne Movement was now going the same way as the WCC'. Second, 'that Lausanne was going soft on the Bible and evangelism'. Third, 'that JRWS [Stott's initials] was the villain of the piece, having "dethroned evangelism" as the traditional and primary task of the church.'[30]

Therefore in 1982, 50 evangelical leaders from 27 different countries spent a week together at Grand Rapids, Michigan, in an attempt to settle those questions which had become so divisive among evangelicals. John Stott arrived in Grand Rapids with a considerable degree of apprehension. The outcome of the week was the report Evangelism and Social Responsibility. The drafting Committee was again under Stott's chairmanship, and he was also responsible for the final editing. The Consultation was sponsored by the Lausanne Committee for World Evangelization (LCWE) and the World Evangelical Fellowship (WEF).

The Consultation produced what it considered were three equally valid approaches to the relationship between social concern and evangelism. First, social responsibility is a *consequence* of evangelism. Second, social responsibility is a *bridge* to evangelism. Third, social concern is a *partner* with evangelism. The Consultation helped to unify some of the divergent perspectives in the movement. They were one step closer to a holistic theology of mission, moving beyond the 'primacy of evangelism' view of the 1974 *Covenant*.

Stott was able to write: 'For me it was another and dramatic demonstration of the value of international conferences. When we remain apart from one another, and our only contact with one another is the lobbing of hand grenades across a demilitarized zone, our attitudes inevitably harden and our mental images of each other become stereotyped.'[31]

The context of the Consultation was that the *Lausanne Covenant* of 1974, which dealt with 'The Nature of Evangelism' (paragraph 4) and 'Christian Social Responsibility' (paragraph 5), had left these two duties side by side without spelling out their relationship to each other. However, paragraph 6 of the *Covenant* had affirmed that 'in the church's mission of sacrificial service, evangelism is primary'.[32] The resulting report, Evangelism and Social Responsibility, dealt at length with the relationship between social action and evangelism. The three kinds of relationship mentioned above were discussed.

First, social activity is a consequence of evangelism

'Social responsibility is more than the consequence of evangelism; it is also one of its principal aims… In saying this, we are not claiming that compassionate service is an automatic consequence of evangelism or of conversion, however. Social responsibility, like evangelism, should therefore be included in the teaching ministry of the church.'[33]

Second, social activity can be a bridge to evangelism

'It can break down prejudice and suspicion, open closed doors, and gain a hearing for the Gospel… A recent crusade in an American city was preceded and accompanied by a "Love in Action" programme, with the evangelist's encouragement. Several "social uplift" groups cooperated and were able to extend their ministries to the inner city poor. As a result, we were told, a number of people came under the sound of the Gospel who would not otherwise have come to the crusade. Further, by seeking to serve people, it is possible to move from their "felt needs" to their deeper need concerning their relationship with God.'[34]

Third, social activity accompanies evangelism as its partner

'*They are like the two blades of a pair of scissors or the two wings of a bird.* This partnership is clearly seen in the public ministry of Jesus, who not only preached the Gospel but fed the hungry and healed the sick… His words explained his works, and his works dramatized his words… If we proclaim the Good News of God's love, we must manifest his love in caring for the needy… Thus, evangelism and social responsibility, while distinct from one another, are integrally related in our proclamation of and obedience to the Gospel. The partnership is, in reality, a marriage.'[35] Here we should note the sentence emphasised above is John Stott's phrase that was destined to become the much quoted catch phrase to justify the holistic movement (my italics).

The Question of Primacy

With regard to the question on primacy, the Report explains that in some regards evangelism has a certain priority. 'If social activity is a consequence and aim of evangelism (as we have asserted), then evangelism must precede it... evangelism relates to people's eternal destiny, and in bringing them Good News of salvation, Christians are doing what nobody else can do... Yet this fact must not make us indifferent to the degradations of human poverty and oppression. The choice, we believe, is largely conceptual...'[36]

Call to Social Responsibility

The Report commented on what it called contemporary need. 'We are appalled to know that about 800 million people, or one-fifth of the human race, are destitute, lacking the basic necessities for survival... They can only be described as "oppressed" by the gross economic inequality from which they suffer and the diverse economic systems which cause and perpetuate it. The oppression of others is political. They are denied fundamental human rights by totalitarian regimes of the extreme left or right... And all of us are oppressed by global problems which seem to defy solution... In addition to worldwide evangelization, the people of God should become deeply involved in relief, aid, development and the quest for justice and peace.'[37]

Associate Professor of Holistic Ministry at Palmer Theological Seminary, Al Tizon, offers his interpretation of the Grand Rapids Consultation: 'While conservatives maintained the primacy of evangelism, radicals questioned the very language of prioritization. If any hope existed to find some level of consensus on the social question, it hinged upon the 1982 Consultation on the Relationship between Evangelism and Social Responsibility in Grand Rapids. Steuernagel's description of the CRESR as "the most carefully planned, sensitive, feared, and threatening consultation ever held by the LCWE" underscores what was at stake – namely, unity or another tragic split of the worldwide evangelical family... The strength of the report relied on the fact that it did not arrive at any one conclusion concerning the relationship; instead it offered a range of possibilities that it considered faithful to biblical and historic Christianity.'[38]

Comment

The clever subtlety of the Grand Rapids Report is that it offers something for everyone—for both conservatives and radicals, and even the vague suggestion that in some circumstances evangelism is primary. Stott's phrase, '*They are like the two blades of a pair of scissors or the two wings of a bird*', made evangelism and social action a partnership, and this offered great encouragement to the radicals. Step by step the purpose of the Great Commission was being undermined. Again we note the political undertone that runs through the Report.

The Wheaton Statement (1983)

The Consultation on the Church in Response to Human Need met in Wheaton, Illinois, in June 1983 as the third track of a larger conference sponsored by the World Evangelical Fellowship under the title 'I Will Build My Church'.'[39] The Statement 'Transformation: The Church in Response to Human Need', was produced as an outgrowth of the consultation. It expressed concerns about those Christians who 'have tended to see the task of the church as merely picking up survivors from a shipwreck in a hostile sea. We do not endorse this view either, since it denies the biblical injunctions to defend the cause of the weak, maintain the rights of the poor and oppressed (Ps. 82:3), and practice justice and love (Mic. 6:8). We affirm, moreover, that, even though we may believe that our calling is only to proclaim the Gospel and not get involved in political and other actions, our very non-involvement lends tacit support to the existing order. There is no escape: either we challenge the evil structures of society or we support them.'[40]

The Consultation decided to replace the word 'development' with the word 'transformation', which became the preferred word to describe the mission of the Church. Transformation points to 'a number of changes that have to take place in many societies if poor people are to enjoy their rightful heritage in creation… We have come to see that the goal of *transformation* is best described by the biblical vision of the Kingdom of God... In particular, it means striving to bring peace among individuals, races, and nations by overcoming prejudices, fears, and preconceived ideas about others. It means sharing basic resources like food, water, the means of healing, and knowledge.' Commenting on culture and transformation the Statement says: 'We are called to be a new community that seeks to work with God in the *transformation* of our societies...' [41]

Turning to social justice and mercy the Statement says: 'Our time together enabled us to see that poverty is not a necessary evil but often the result of social, economic, political, and religious systems marked by injustice, exploitation, and oppression... Evil is not only in the human heart but also in social structures... The mission of the church includes both the proclamation of the Gospel and its demonstration. We must therefore evangelize, respond to immediate human needs, and press for social *transformation*. The means we use, however, must be consistent with the end we desire... we must also remember that acts of mercy highlight the injustices of the social, economic, and political structures and relationships; whether we like it or not, they may therefore lead us into confrontation with those who hold power (Acts 4:5-22)... Our involvement with strangers is not only through charity, but also through economic policies toward the poor. Our economic and political action is inseparable from evangelism.' And more: 'Our churches must also address issues of evil and of social injustice in the local community and the wider society' [42] (my emphasis).

The Wheaton document produced 53 statements on the role of the Church in social transformation. Missiologist David Bosch hailed the Wheaton Statement: 'for the first time in an official statement emanating from an international evangelical conference the perennial dichotomy (between evangelism and social responsibility) was overcome'.[43] Rene Padilla, in his 2004 paper on Holistic Mission marked it as a 'historic milestone in the understanding of holistic mission from an evangelical perspective'.

Vinay Samuel expresses the view that the Wheaton Consultation 'popularized evangelical engagement to address poverty, developing responses like emergency relief, community development, enterprise solutions to poverty, advocacy for national debt relief, fair trade and greater flow of aid from rich to poor nations. Relief and development efforts defined engagement with the world in this stream.'[44]

Al Tizon believes that Wheaton '83 'served as a significant marker for the theological maturation of holistic mission thinking among many evangelicals after Lausanne. At this Consultation, the word "transformation" was adopted to convey the large vision of God's redemption, which includes socio-political structures and the human heart and everything in between.'[45]

The word *transformation* rapidly gained credence in explaining the mission of the Church. Vinay Samuel and Chris Sugden offered the following definition: 'Transformation is to enable God's vision of society to be actualized in all relationships, social, economic, and spiritual, so that God's will be reflected in human society and his love be experienced by all communities, especially the poor.'[46]

Al Tizon continues: 'Ever since the holistic missionary movement took on the name transformation, its proponents have steadily advanced their agenda throughout the world, urging churches and mission agencies to refuse to understand evangelization without liberation, a change of heart without a change of social structures, vertical reconciliation (between God and people) without horizontal reconciliation (between people and people), and church planting without community building. Although the degree of integration between these dimensions of mission continues to vary, holistic mission has found its way in the mainstream consciousness and practice of evangelicals around the world.'[47]

The coining of the term *transformation* at Wheaton '83 to describe the mission of the Church was nothing short of a masterstroke. The claim was that the Church should *transform* not only individuals, but also the culture and even the society. The controversial term 'socio-political action' could now be dispensed with; and the post-Lausanne struggle to make holistic evangelism or *transformational development* the mission of the Church had achieved a major breakthrough in the Wheaton Statement of 1983. Yet more was to come as the radicals wanted to go even further, as we see in our next chapter.

(Endnotes)

1   Arthur P. Johnston, *The Battle for World Evangelism*, Tyndale House Publishers, 1978, pp302-303
2   Cited from *Godly Ambition* by Alastair Chapman, Oxford Press, 2012, p142
3   John Stott diary cited from *John Stott: a Global Ministry*, Timothy Dudley-Smith, Inter-Varsity Press, 2001, pp220-221
4   Ibid. p221
5   Ibid. p222
6   *Godly Ambition*, pp142-43
7   Ibid. p143
8   *John Stott: A Global Ministry*, p221
9   Lausanne Occasional Paper 1, Pasadena Consultation - Homogeneous Unit Principle, 1978, Lausanne Committee for World Evangelization
10   'The Willowbank Report: Consultation on Gospel and Culture', 1978, Introduction, Lausanne Committee for World Evangelization
11   Ibid. C, Cultural Barriers to the Communication of the Gospel
12   Ibid. D, Cultural Sensitivity in Communicating the Gospel
13   Ibid. 6, Wanted: Humble Messengers of the Gospel!
14   Ibid. 7, Conversion and Culture
15   Ibid. D, Power Structures and Mission
16   C. René Padilla, 'Integral Mission and its Historical Development', this paper also appears in *Justice, Mercy and Humility*, ed. Tim Chester, (Carlisle: Paternoster, 2003)
17   The Lausanne Covenant, paragraph 9, The Urgency of the Evangelistic Task
18   Lausanne Occasional Paper 20, 'An Evangelical Commitment to Simple Life-style', Introduction, http://www.lausanne.org/en/documents/lops/77-lop-20.html
19   Ibid. Stewardship
20   Ibid.
21   Ibid.
22   Ibid. Justice and Politics
23   Letter from Leighton Ford, Chairman of the Lausanne Committee for World Evangelization to John Stott, dated 10 March 1981, accessed from Wheaton Archive of Stott's papers.
24   Al Tizon in *Transformation After Lausanne: Radical Evangelical Mission in Global-Local Perspective*, Regnum Studies in Mission, 2008, p44
25   Al Tizon in *Holistic Mission: God's Plan for God's People*, Regnum Edinburgh 2010 Series, p71
26   Al Tizon in *Holistic Mission*, p71
27   Al Tizon in *Holistic Mission*, p72
28   'Social Concern and Evangelization: The Journey of the Lausanne Movement', Valdir R. Steuernagel, *International Bulletin of Missionary Research*, April 1991, p54
29   *The Battle for World Evangelism*, 1978, p303
30   John Stott diary, USA, June/July 1982, pp 1a-2, cited from *John Stott: A Global Ministry*, p303
31   Lausanne Occasional Paper 21, 'Evangelism and Social Responsibility: An Evangelical Commitment', foreword by John Stott

206

32   Ibid. A, The Context of the Consultation
33   Ibid. C, Three Kinds of Relationship
34   Ibid. C
35   Ibid. C
36   Ibid. D, The Question of Primacy
37   Ibid, 3, A Call to Social Responsibility, A. Contemporary Need
38   Al Tizon in *Holistic Mission*, pp72-73
39   The Lausanne movement website, 'Transformation: The Church in Response to Human Need', Consultation Statement of Wheaton 1983, https://www.lausanne.org/content/statement/transformation-the-church-in-response-to-human-need
40   Ibid. I, Christian Social Involvement
41   Ibid. II, Not only Development but Transformation
42   Ibid. V, Social Justice and Mercy
43   David J. Bosch, *Transforming Mission: Paradigm Shifts in Theology of Mission*, Orbis Books, 1991, p407
44   Vinay Samuel in *Holistic Mission* , p132
45   Al Tizon, in *Holistic Mission*, p74
46   Vinay Samuel and Chris Sugden in 'Transformational Development: current state of understanding and practice.' *Transformation* (April 2003), p71, cited from Al Tizon in *Holistic Mission*, p75
47   Al Tizon, in *Holistic Mission*, p75

Chapter 14

Radicals Take Up the Fight

Disappointed with the fact that the Lausanne Committee did not appear to be wholehearted in its support for the concept of holistic mission, the radicals who had signed the Statement of Concerns at Pattaya, Thailand in 1980, decided to meet again as a 'two-thirds world' consultation. In other words, the radicals were emboldened to take matters into their own hands. They baulked at the idea of being dependent upon rich American evangelicals, whom they accused of propagating an American cultural version of Christianity. And so in Bangkok in 1982, an international group of radical evangelical theologians resolved to work together to advance holistic mission theology.[1]

Although the International Fellowship of Evangelical Mission Theologians (INFEMIT) was officially formed in 1987, its true beginnings came from the 1980 Lausanne Consultation on World Evangelization (COWE) in Pattaya. Passionate about the need to integrate evangelism and social justice, 'as well as to give voice to churches in the non-Western world, an international group of evangelical theologians resolved to organize together in order to advance holistic, contextual mission theology not only for the worldwide evangelical community, but for the whole church. This holistic, contextual theology did its part to define "Mission as Transformation," as it inspired the development of several structures, including the Oxford Centre for Mission Studies.'[2]

International Fellowship of Evangelical Mission Theologians

The outcome of the 1982 Bangkok meeting was a decision to form an organisation that was independent of Lausanne, and so the idea of the International Fellowship of Evangelical Mission Theologians or INFEMIT was conceived. The radicals, mostly from the Third World, saw the need for a movement that was wholeheartedly committed to the holistic view of the gospel. Early leaders of INFEMIT included Orlando Costas, Vinay Samuel, Rene Padilla, Chris Sugden, Melba Maggay, Ronald Sider, David Gitari, Kwame Bediako, Tito Paredes and Tom Sine. The first three meetings of INFEMIT were in Bangkok, Thailand (1982), Cuernavaca, Mexico (1984) and Kabare, Kenya (1987).[3]

According to its mission statement, INFEMIT is 'a Gospel-centered fellowship of mission theologian-practitioners that serves local churches and other Christian communities so we together embody the Kingdom of God through transformational engagement, both locally and globally'. INFEMIT seeks to live out its identity 'as image bearers of the Community of Love'. It engages in and promotes holistic contextual theologising and integral mission practice. It encourages interdisciplinary research in the service of mission at the Oxford Centre for Mission Studies and other centres.[4] Note the way simple biblical terminology is replaced by complex missional jargon that serves only to confuse.

Through *transformational* engagement (the new word for socio-political action, coined at Wheaton in 1983), INFEMIT challenges 'the people of God to see the realities of their context, particularly the plight and potential of the poor and marginalized, and to be moved to respond in Christ-like fashion'.[5]

Oxford Centre for Mission Studies (OCMS)

The Oxford Centre for Mission Studies (OCMS) is an independent Christian charity based in Oxford, England. The Centre, officially established in 1983, was founded by advocates of holistic mission from Africa, Asia and Latin America. The Centre includes facilities for missiological studies, a publishing group (Regnum Books International), and the journal, *Transformation*.

Its vision is 'To equip leaders, scholars and institutions to bring holistic mission effectively and intelligently to the nations.'[6] The Centre sees its mission as nurturing 'relevant research for leaders on the cutting edge of Christian ministry and mission globally'. According to OCMS its understanding of God's mission goes far beyond evangelism and church planting. 'We engage with issues such as the church's role in poverty, political conflicts, community development, education, women, human trafficking, AIDS/HIV, and many more. This is one of a few places in the world where such cutting-edge mission thinking is further sharpened.'[7]

OCMS received warm praise from John Stott: 'I have been a strong supporter of OCMS and am very appreciative of the partnership between OCMS and the Langham Partnership.'[8] (All Souls, Langham Place, London was Stott's church.) Stott's influence on the OCMS was through the Langham Trust, which was set up to support projects connected with the so-called Majority World (Two-Thirds World). A special Langham bursary fund assists scholars from the Majority World to train in the UK. The first Langham scholar, Vinay Samuel, was involved in founding the Oxford Centre for Mission Studies.[9]

According to its website, being 'truly international in its leadership, fully interdenominational in its reach, and deeply evangelical from its roots to its mission, OCMS brings the world's church together under one roof to research, reflect and respond to challenges faced across cultures and in the varying economic, social and political contexts in which Christians operate. For almost thirty years church leaders, mission and development professionals, and global Christian scholars have met under this roof and have sought to better understand how to bring the transforming nature of their faith to effect change in the lives of those they serve.'[10] The role of OCMS in missiology in the UK is discussed in the next chapter.

Lausanne II Manila (1989)

To keep the Lausanne flame burning, Lausanne's Second International Congress on World Evangelization (Lausanne II) was held in Manila in July 1989. Attended by representatives from 173 countries, for ten days over four thousand participants, guests and media representatives gathered together to further the cause of the Lausanne movement. A prominent presence at Manila was Dr Eugene Stockwell, a leader of the World Council of Churches. Other official observers and special guests came from the Vatican, the Russian Orthodox Church and the Greek Orthodox Church.

A feature of the Congress was a new openness to charismatic influences. Peter Wagner explains: 'In dramatic contrast to Lausanne I, held in Switzerland in 1974, Lausanne II embraced leaders of the

Pentecostal/charismatic movements at all levels from the Lausanne Committee itself through the plenary sessions and workshops to the thousands of participants who regularly worshipped with raised hands. Remarkably, the three most attended workshop tracks (of 48 offered) were on the Holy Spirit, spiritual warfare and prayer.'[11] Charismatic pastor Jack Hayford played a prominent role in plenary sessions, which followed a contemporary style of worship. So-called 'power evangelism' was promoted by the Fuller tandem, Peter Wagner and John Wimber.

Two major plenary sessions dealt with 'Good News for the Poor' and 'Social Concern and Evangelization'. Both subjects were discussed in workshops, and the challenge of poverty and of evangelizing the poor was always on the screen through media presentations. The resulting *Manila Manifesto* referred to social concern for the poor and oppressed: 'We affirm that we must demonstrate God's love visibly by caring for those who are deprived of justice, dignity and food and shelter', and, 'We affirm that the proclamation of God's kingdom of justice and peace demands the denunciation of all injustice and oppression, both personal and structural; we will not shrink from this prophetic witness.'[12] The *Manila Manifesto* declared its concern for the poor, and was distressed about the burden of debt in the two-thirds world.

Valdir R. Steuernagel comments on the way the Congress was used to further the cause of holistic evangelism: 'It should also be recognized that many of those at Lausanne were committed to mission in a holistic perspective and were networking for it at Lausanne II. The *Covenant* had been too big a blessing to be chained and the Lausanne informal network had become too wide and deeply rooted in third-world soil to be restricted to a narrow and ascetic understanding of evangelization.'[13]

In drafting the *Manila Manifesto*, John Stott saw once again the need to repent for a number of misdemeanours among his fellow evangelicals. The Congress publicly repented of its narrow view of the gospel. 'The narrowness of our concerns and vision has often kept us from proclaiming the lordship of Jesus Christ over all of life, private and public, local and global.' Stott wrote: 'We repent of any neglect of God's truth in Scripture and determine to both proclaim and defend it.' He expressed repentance 'where we have been indifferent to the plight of the poor, and where we have shown preference for the rich, and we determine to follow Jesus in preaching good news to all people by both word and deed'. He confessed that 'we have sometimes been guilty of adopting towards adherents of other faiths attitudes of ignorance, arrogance, disrespect and even hostility. We repent of this.' He also repented 'of our share in discouraging the ministry of laity, especially of women and young people'.[14]

The *Manila Manifesto* affirmed the need for cooperation in evangelism. 'Evangelical attitudes to the Roman Catholic and Orthodox Churches differ widely. Some evangelicals are praying, talking, studying Scripture and working with these churches. Others are strongly opposed to any form of dialogue or cooperation with them. All are aware that serious theological differences between us remain. Where appropriate, and so long as biblical truth is not compromised, cooperation may be possible in such areas as Bible translation, the study of contemporary theological and ethical issues, social work and political action. We wish to make it clear, however, that common evangelism demands a common commitment to the biblical gospel.'[15]

This ambiguous statement, typical of John Stott's new evangelicalism, was designed to be all things to all men. It sought to placate those who still followed the doctrines of the Reformation, while at the same time offering encouragement to those of an ecumenical mindset who were keen to work alongside the Roman Catholic Church. Here we should remind ourselves that Stott, at this very time, was working for full reunion with the Church of Rome.

The *Manila Manifesto* did not make clear how in practice there could be 'common evangelism' without a common understanding of the biblical gospel. It was not all that clear whether or not Lausanne accepted the gospel of the Roman Catholic Church as a biblical gospel. Neither was the position of Lausanne's leadership with regard to the doctrines of the Reformation made clear.

Despite the overt politicisation of the WCC, the *Manifesto* saw it as a Christian duty to support the work of the WCC. 'Some of us are members of churches which belong to the World Council of Churches and believe that a positive yet critical participation in its work is our Christian duty.'[16]

John Piper at Lausanne II

Reformed theologian and pastor John Piper expressed his recollections of Lausanne II in Manila. He writes: 'The poor of the world were a strong focus. 800 million people live in absolute poverty… One can generalize and say that vast numbers of the lost are also the poorest. Ways to evangelize the poor must be found. It will imply more identification (incarnation) and simplification. Those who claim to be Christian earn 68 percent of the world's income. They gave 3 percent of it to the church, of which about 5 percent is invested in any international ministry. We must continue to test our inoculation to massive world need.'

Piper attended a workshop in which Robert Schuller, the American televangelist, told his story of how Garden Grove Community Church was born. 'His passion was to start a mission, not a church. Everything, therefore, was calculated to speak to the utterly unchurched.' Piper noted that the focus on 'signs and wonders' in world evangelization was prominent. 'A whole track was devoted to it (where I went most of the time) and Jack Hayford led one plenary session and spoke at another. Clearly one of the major differences between Lausanne '74 and Lausanne '89 was the presence of large numbers of charismatics and the spirit and tone of worship in that direction. It caused quite a lot of complaints behind the scenes I'm told.' [17]

Piper went to a John Wimber workshop. Wimber argued that Matthew 28.19-20 ('teaching them to observe all I command you') 'included the command to heal, and therefore a healing ministry is part of successful world evangelization… He said he sees the next 20 to 30 years as the time when more signs and wonders will be done than ever in history and when the secular media will be overwhelmed and have to report it every day as great revival spreads.' [18]

Stott said the purpose of the *Manila Manifesto* was to clarify the *Lausanne Covenant* and in particular to bring evangelism and social action together, rather than thinking of them as separate topics. [19] Stott wrote in his diary: 'The radicals could see that the *Manifesto* went considerably further than the *Lausanne Covenant* in declaring the indispensability of social action, good works… But conservatives were pleased too…' [20] Here we see the genius of Stott's diplomacy. By his clever use of words

213

he was able to placate two groups who had a fundamentally different understanding of the gospel.

The Iguassu Affirmation (1999)

In October of 1999, a group of missiologists, missionaries, and church leaders gathered in Brazil to reflect together on the challenges and opportunities facing world missions at the dawn of the new millennium, and to review the different streams of twentieth-century evangelical missiology and practice, especially since the 1974 Lausanne Congress. Sponsored by the World Evangelical Fellowship (WEF), participants from 53 countries (half from Latin America, Asia, Africa, the Middle East, and the Pacific Islands: half from North America, Europe, Australia, and New Zealand) gathered in Iguassu, Brazil.

To set the scene for the consultation, participants viewed the 1986 film, *The Mission*, which included scenes of the spectacular Iguassu Falls. The Salvation Army, which is an Associate Member of WEF, comments: 'The film chronicles a tragic incident in Latin America's colonial history in which Christian [Roman Catholic] missionaries were unable to prevent European governments from enslaving the native Guarani, killing many of them and stealing their land. The imperialism portrayed in the film is still part of the memory of Latin Americans and others from less-developed countries.'[21]

The Iguassu Affirmation reversed the traditional idea of a flow of Western missionaries to the Two-Thirds World, and advocated instead the vision of 'doing missiology and mission by people of all nations to people of all nations'.[22]

The Affirmation claimed that in recent years the Church had helped missions shed paternalistic tendencies. 'Today, we continue to explore the relationship between the Gospel and culture, between evangelism and social responsibility and between biblical mandates and the social sciences. We see some international organizations – among them the World Evangelical Fellowship, the Lausanne Committee for World Evangelization, and the AD 2000 and Beyond Movement – that have begun a promising process of partnership and unity.'[23]

The Affirmation affirmed the holistic nature of a gospel that addresses all human needs. 'We emphasize the holistic nature of the Gospel of Jesus Christ…' and commit 'to work for human rights and religious freedom', and express gratitude 'for many helpful insights gained from the social sciences.'[24]

The Affirmation committed to address the realities of world poverty and oppose policies that serve the powerful rather than the powerless, and called on 'all Christians to commit themselves to ecological integrity in practicing responsible stewardship of creation, and we encourage Christians in environmental care and protection initiatives'.[25]

The Affirmation ended with this pledge: 'We, the participants of the Iguassu Missiological Consultation, declare our passion as mission practitioners, missiologists and church leaders for the urgent evangelization of the whole world and the discipling of the nations to the glory of the Father, the Son and the Holy Spirit… As evangelicals, we pledge to sustain our biblical heritage in this ever-changing world. We commit ourselves to participate actively in formulating and practicing evangelical missiology…'[26]

Christopher Little, an experienced missiologist, in his article 'What Makes Mission Christian?' comments: 'Embedded in the Affirmation is a desire to emphasize "the holistic nature of the gospel"; an interest in pursuing appropriate responses "to political and economic systems"; an invitation to study the "operation of the Trinity in the redemption of the human race and the whole of creation"; a pledge to "address the realities of world poverty"; a call "to all Christians to commit themselves to reflect God's concern for justice"; and a challenge to engage "in environmental care and protection initiatives." It must be promptly added, however, that the Affirmation also upholds the commitment to proclaim the gospel of Jesus Christ in faithfulness and loving humility.'[27]

The Iguassu Affirmation reveals how evangelical missiologists, mainly from Third World countries, are committed to promoting the holistic gospel to the whole world. They made their commitment to holistic mission using evangelical-sounding language. Two underlying themes were prominent in the Iguassu Affirmation. First, a commitment to a political agenda; second, a strong anti-Western bias.

Amsterdam 2000 Conference

In 2000 the Billy Graham Evangelistic Association convened the

Amsterdam Conference, which brought together over 10,000 evangelists, pastors, missionaries, theologians and church leaders for this landmark event in the Netherlands. Participants came from across the world, mostly from Third World nations. An estimated 40 percent of the participants were Pentecostals. This was to be the last international gathering for the aging Billy Graham who, even though he was too ill to attend, planned to address the attending evangelists via a videotape recording. At the last minute, however, Graham was forced to cancel the videotape address at the opening session.

Among the speakers were Dr George Carey, Archbishop of Canterbury; Chuck Colson, Chairman of Prison Fellowship; Ravi Zacharias, Christian apologist and President of Ravi Zacharias International Ministries; Bill Bright, founder of Campus Crusade for Christ; Anne Graham-Lotz, founder of AnGel Ministries; Franklin Graham, son of Billy Graham and President of the international relief organisation Samaritans' Purse; evangelist Luis Palau; theologian J.I. Packer; and John Stott. Rev Nicky Gumbel, well-known promoter of the Alpha course, received a personal invitation from Billy Graham to run a workshop. 'Your experience and expertise as a leader will be a great asset to the conference, and participants will gain invaluable knowledge and insight from the content of the workshop.'[28]

The Amsterdam Declaration was studied by hundreds of Christian leaders and evangelists from around the world. 'It is commended to God's people everywhere as an expression of evangelical commitment and as a resource for study, reflection, prayer and evangelistic outreach.' It addressed a variety of issues, including social responsibility and evangelism. Those signing the Declaration affirmed the need 'to stay involved personally in grass-roots evangelism so that our presentations of the biblical gospel are fully relevant and contextualized… When our evangelism is linked with concern to alleviate poverty, uphold justice, oppose abuses of secular and economic power, stand against racism, and advance responsible stewardship of the global environment, it reflects the compassion of Christ and may gain an acceptance it would not otherwise receive. We pledge ourselves to follow the way of justice in our family and social life, and to keep personal, social, and environmental values in view as we evangelize.'[29]

Billy Graham had asked Paul Eshleman, who was running the Jesus Film project, to gather together missionary leaders from across the world to deal with the issue of unreached people groups. During group discussions, Marcus Vegh of Progressive Vision asked missionary leader Avery Willis, 'How do you make disciples of oral learners?' The question made a very strong impression on Willis: 'I heard his voice as if it were the voice of God. I am not sure why it hit me so hard. While serving as Senior Vice-President for Overseas Operations with the International Mission Board of Southern Baptists I had helped lead our 5,000 missionaries to focus on reaching the unreached. I was aware of oral learners and Chronological Bible Storying but never considered they were my responsibility. Now I heard God telling me it was... The goal was to help evangelize and make disciples, and to begin to nurture indigenous church planting movements.'[30]

As a consequence of Amsterdam 2000 plans were made to explore oral methods of communicating the gospel.[31] The issue of orality (or storytelling the gospel) was now firmly on the Lausanne agenda, as an increasing number of mission groups began to think about how to effectively communicate the gospel among so-called 'oral people groups'. Amsterdam 2000 was a significant step towards the creation of the International Orality Network, which is discussed in chapter 20. The next chapter explores the growth of a new academic theological discipline that was to greatly facilitate the acceptance and spread of holistic mission—missiology.

(Endnotes)

1 INFEMIT website, history, http://infemit.org/sample-page/history
2 Ibid.
3 Ibid.
4 Ibid, Vision and mission, http://infemit.org/sample-page/vision-and-mission
5 Ibid.
6 OCMS website, Vision and Mission, http://www.ocms.ac.uk/content/index.php?q=ocms/about/vision_and_mission
7 Global Connections website, Advancing holistic mission through scholarly engagement, http://www.globalconnections.org.uk/organisations/oxford-centre-for-mission-studies

8   OCMS website, Testimonies, http://www.ocms.ac.uk/prospective/index.
php?ccid=437&mid=438

9   Langham Partnership website, Our History, http://uk.langham.org/what-we-do/
langham-scholars/our-history/

10   OCMS website, Welcome to OCMS, http://www.ocms.ac.uk/content/index.
php?q=node/204

11   Peter C Wagner, *Wrestling With Dark Angels: Toward a Deeper Understanding of the
Supernatural Forces in Spiritual Warfare*, Monarch Books, 1990, p6, cited from the
Seeking God website, http://www.seekgod.ca/darkangels.htm

12   The Lausanne movement, *Manila Manifesto*, 1989, affirmations 8 and 9

13   Valdir R. Steuernagel, 'Social Concern and Evangelization: The Journey of the
Lausanne Movement', International Bulletin of Missionary Research, April 1991,
endnote 15

14   *Manila Manifesto*, affirmation 4, The Gospel and Social Responsibility, http://www.
lausanne.org/all-documents/manila-manifesto

15   Ibid, affirmation 9, Cooperating in Evangelism

16   Ibid.

17   Desiring God website, 'Thoughts from Lausanne II in Manila', John Piper 1989,
http://www.desiringgod.org/articles/thoughts-from-lausanne-ii-in-manila

18   Ibid.

19   Timothy Dudley-Smith, *John Stott: A Global Ministry*, Inter-Varsity Press, 2001,
pp304-305

20   John Stott diary, Lausanne II in Manila, 11-21 July 1989, p9, cited from *A Global
Ministry*, p304

21   Salvation Army International News, 'Missiologists Affirm New Models', 4
November 1999, https://www.salvationist.org/intnews.nsf/vw_web_articles/B94B7A81
4D1E99AE80256C000031607E?opendocument

22   Ibid.

23   Iguassu Affirmation, published in *Christianity Today*, 1 November 1999, Wendy
Murray Zoba

24   Ibid.

25   Ibid.

26   Ibid.

27   Christopher Little, 'What Makes Mission Christian?' *International Journal of
Frontier Missiology*, 25:2 Summer 2008

28   Billy Graham Invites Alpha, *Alpha News Online*, No. 3, March-July 2000

29   Amsterdam Declaration underscores 'biblical integrity' in evangelism
by Art Toalston, posted Monday, August 07, 2000, *Baptist Press*, http://www.bpnews.
net/6314

30   Avery T. Willis, Foreword to *Orality Breakouts*, published by International Orality
Network, 2010, pp5-6, http://www.heartstories.info/sites/default/files/Foreword.pdf

31   The International Orality Network, History of ION, http://www.oralbible.com/about/
History

Chapter 15

A Short History of Missiology

Missiology is a new academic branch of theology that has played a prominent role in promoting the cause of holistic mission. As a branch of theology, it has made enormous strides in the last half century, with most theological seminaries and Bible colleges having departments that teach the discipline of missiology. Despite its popularity, few people seem to really understand exactly what missiology is all about. According to J.A. Scherer, Emeritus Professor of Missions and Church History, Lutheran School of Theology at Chicago, 'The quest for an agreed definition of missiology remains elusive.'[1] Even David Bosch, the eminent South African professor of missiology and author of *Transforming Mission* (1991), confesses, 'Ultimately, mission remains indefinable… the most we can hope for is to formulate some approximations of what mission is all about.'[2] Professor of Mission and Anthropology at Trinity Evangelical Divinity School, Deerfield, Illinois, Robert J. Priest, admits that his doctoral students are often at a loss in attempting to define missiology.[3]

Undeterred by this lack of an agreed definition, Professor Priest provides an interesting account of what he understands by the term missiology. He writes: 'I am a missiologist. For twenty-three years I have taught missiology. And for twelve years at Trinity Evangelical Divinity School I have helped mentor the next generation of missiologists pursuing their PhD's. I serve on the boards of the American Society of Missiology and the Evangelical Missiological Society, and publish articles in the journal *Missiology: An International Review*.'[4]

Professor Priest lists five observations to help explain his understanding of missiology. First, missiology constitutes its own discipline and has its own history. 'It has its own professional societies, such as The American Society of Missiology, The Evangelical Missiological

Society, The Association of Professors of Mission, The International Association for Mission Studies…' and the list goes on and on. His second observation is that missiology, at a fundamental level, is interdisciplinary. He points out that historically those teaching missiology have often had doctorates in other disciplines—like anthropology, communications, comparative religions, philosophy of religion, history, linguistics or theology. His third observation emphasises the point that missiology is grounded in research and is not merely reflection. He writes: 'In my definition, missiology requires a research engagement with human realities related to Christian mission, where research is guided by specific research questions, is carried out by formally specified procedures designed to gather, measure, and interpret data, and has as its goal the production and transmission of new knowledge.' Priest's fourth observation is: 'While informed by theology, missiology is also strongly anthropological, on my definition. Some definitions make missiology a purely theological enterprise… But in missiology, it is not merely God's agency that we study, but human agency exercised on behalf of Christian mission in diverse cultural, religious, and linguistic contexts… What differentiates missiology from the rest of the theological curriculum, historically, is its central focus on helping Christians understand diverse human contexts as a basis for wisely carrying out Christian mission in those contexts.' His final observation is that 'missiology, on this definition, is intended to be of value both for what it contributes to the academy, and for how it helps practitioners of Christian mission. Missiologists, at core, hope that the knowledge we produce would be of benefit to those who are deeply committed to carrying out the mission of God in the whole world.'

On the basis of the above observation he offers his definition: 'Missiology is an interdisciplinary discipline which, through research, writing, and teaching, furthers the acquisition, development, and transmission of theologically-informed, contextually-grounded, and ministry-oriented knowledge and understanding, with the goal of helping and correcting Christians, and Christian institutions, involved in the doing of Christian mission.'[5]

What we gather from Priest's attempt to explain the meaning of missiology is that it is an academic discipline that depends much on the fallible wisdom of man coming from anthropology and sociological research. Evidently, missiologists believe that to understand the mission of the Church, Christians need more than Scripture.

Dr Ed Stetzer, who holds a Ph.D in missiology and is the Executive Director of LifeWay Research, offers this explanation in response to the question: What is a missiologist? 'I think it's important to define what a missiologist is. At the most basic level, a missiologist is a specialist who studies and is trained in the science of missions. However, this definition may oversimplify the task of a missiologist. Missiology is accomplished at the intersection of gospel, culture, and the church. It is a multi-disciplinary study that incorporates theology, anthropology/sociology, and ecclesiology. That seems rather complex doesn't it? Well, for this reason missiology constitutes its own discipline. I often talk to churches about their need to join God on His mission by understanding their context and by being faithful to the mission He has given them. I do a lot of research on church planting. I write often on missiological issues. I have written extensively on the subject of missiology and have a book called *MissionShift*, which examines the shifts in missions the past one hundred years, how those shifts shape how we define mission, discussions on contextualization, and the nature of the church's mission… Missiology is not only grounded in theological reflection, it is also grounded in anthropological/sociological research… A missiologist comes alongside the church and helps her think critically about the task of contextualization.'[6]

But here we see a major problem. Scripture is clear that the Church is governed by godly elders who are responsible for maintaining sound doctrine in the Church (Titus 1.5-9, 2.1). But to whom are missiologists, most of whom work in academic institutions, accountable? Perhaps a better definition of missiology would be: An unaccountable academic discipline pursued outside the oversight of the Church, relying on the fallible and ever-shifting opinions of 'experts' to supplement biblical truth as to what the mission of the Church should be.

Missiology in Theological Seminaries

The academic study of missiology gained momentum with the founding in the mid-1960s of the School of World Mission at Fuller Theological Seminary, Pasadena, and Trinity Evangelical Divinity

School's department of Mission and Evangelism, Deerfield, Illinois. Over the following five decades mission studies have become an accepted and established theological and academic discipline. Academic missiologists have led the debate in new concepts of mission, such as liberation theology, contextualization, the holistic gospel, socio-political concerns and globalization.

Fuller Seminary took a special interest in mission studies and played a crucial role developing missiology into an academic 'science'. In 1965 Fuller's President, David Allan Hubbard invited 67-year-old Donald McGavran to be the founding dean of a new School of World Mission and the Director of the Institute of Church Growth. Hubbard's goal was to create a dynamic center for research and the training of missionaries and missiologists.[7] In *History of the American Society of Missiology, 1973 – 2013* (2013), Wilbert R. Shenk, a member of Fuller's School of Intercultural Studies, explains that Hubbard soon realised that the School could only remain part of the Seminary if missiology was developed into a credible academic field of study. But McGavran was not really interested in missiology as an academic discipline, and so Hubbard turned to another member of the faculty, Ralph Winter, to take the lead role in turning missiology into an academic discipline.[8] For the next decade Ralph Winter worked to fulfil Hubbard's vision of Fuller as the world leader in missiology. In laying the foundation of the new academic discipline, Ralph Winter saw the need to invite participation from all Christian traditions, including Roman Catholics.

American Society of Missiology

The American Society of Missiology (ASM) was founded in 1973 for 'the purpose of encouraging and facilitating critical reflection on the nature, purpose, and goals of Christian mission'.[9] The Society established a tripartite pattern of leadership between Roman Catholic, mainline Protestant (churches that belong to the World Council of Churches) and independent/evangelical Protestant. The founding of ASM was a pivotal step in gaining academic recognition for the field of mission studies. Today the ASM describes itself as an inclusive and diverse professional association made up of members from Independent churches (Evangelical, Pentecostal, etc.), Conciliar churches (Anglo-Catholic, Old Catholic and Eastern Orthodox communions), and Roman Catholic communions. 'This unique make up of our membership provides a dynamic and lively exchange of ideas, issues, and scholarship focused on the church's call to participate in God's mission to the world.'[10] As an ecumenical professional association, the ASM includes more than 600 academicians, mission agency executives, and missionaries in a unique fellowship of scholarship and mission. The Society seeks to incorporate the knowledge, skills and techniques provided by the social and behavioural sciences in all of its publications.[11] Roman Catholics are well represented on the Board. The ASM's website provides links to The United States Catholic Mission Association, the World Council of Churches and the Lausanne Committee for World Evangelization, among others.

According to Wilbert Shenk the years 1965 to 1982 were marked by far-reaching developments that shaped and reshaped the world Christian movement. He mentions the major missiological events that took place during this period, including Wheaton 1966, Berlin 1966, Uppsala 1968, Lausanne 1974, Nairobi 1975, Melbourne 1980, Pattaya 1980, Wheaton 1983, and a compelling Apostolic Exhortation by Pope Paul VI, *On Evangelization in the Modern World* (1975). 'The lines of debate kept evolving as new themes emerged, including liberation theology, contextualization, the holistic gospel, the "shifting center of gravity", and globalization.'[12]

Fuller's Professor of Anthropology, Alan Tippet, was secured as the founding editor of the journal *Missiology: An International Review*. 'Fuller Theological Seminary provided an invaluable base for the fledgling society by permitting Winter to manage the journal and granting Tippet a reduced teaching load in order to have time to serve as editor.'[13] In his report to the editorial board, Tippet wrote: 'I have a firm conviction that the symbiosis of theology and anthropology in missiography is turning into syngenesis—something new is being born.'[14] Arthur Glasser of Fuller succeeded Alan Tippet as editor of *Missiology*. According to Shenk, 'It was a boon to *Missiology* to have the help of two Fuller faculty, Winter and Tippet in getting the journal launched.'[15] Over the years the journal has played a prominent role in developing literature in the field of mission studies.

Professor David Hesselgrave of Trinity Evangelical Divinity School's department of Mission and Evangelism, describes the motivation of those who founded the ASM. He writes: 'Those who initiated and led the effort made abundantly clear that their primary goal was to lend credibility and visibility to missiology as a social science discipline by encouraging scholarship, promoting research and writing, and representing mission studies in the academy. At the time, I was among the majority who approved of the ideas.'[16] Hesselgrave, obviously concerned about the direction the ASM was taking, appears to regret the fact that he gave his approval to turning missiology into a social science.

Donald McGavran expressed his concern about the ecumenical and secular drift of the ASM in a letter to David Hesselgrave. 'When the present American Society of Missiology was formed, it took in – against my advice – both Roman Catholic missiologists and conciliar missiologists. Thus, The American Society of Missiology seems to say that missiology is everything done outside the four walls of the church. The net result is that the heart of all missiology, which is the discipling of segment after segment of the world's population, has been gravely neglected.'[17]

Evangelical Missiological Society

By the 1980s a number of missiologists were disturbed by the direction that missiology was taking. The concern was that Christian mission itself was being reviewed and redefined by some scholars in ways that seemed incompatible with Scripture. According to the Evangelical Missiological Society website: 'An increasing number of conservative missiologists came to believe that a scholarly society committed to the Great Commission was becoming more and more necessary. Many felt that an organization composed only of classroom teachers was too restrictive in light of the growing number of mission scholars within the churches and mission organizations.'[18]

In 1988, Donald McGavran wrote to his friend and colleague David Hesselgrave: 'I want to lay before you... a very important item... What is really needed in North America and around the world is a society of missiology that says quite frankly that the purpose of missiology is to carry out the Great Commission.' (Personal letter to David Hesselgrave dated April 7, 1988).[19]

And so in 1990 the Evangelical Missiological Society (EMS) was founded 'to advance the cause of world evangelization through study and evaluation of mission concepts and strategies from a biblical perspective with a view to commending sound mission theory and practice to churches, mission agencies, and the schools of missionary training around the world.' The Society, which claims to be evangelical, is 'committed to the doctrinal foundations that salvation is found in Jesus Christ alone and that the Bible is the inspired Word of God'. It exists 'to promote fellowship and professional stimulation among active and retired professors of missiology, anthropology, and closely allied disciplines, missionaries, mission administrators and pastors with strategic missiological interests, and students of missiology. Emphasis is also given to the preparation and dissemination of information, books, and practical tools designed to assist members in missionary training, missionary service, and mission-related administration.'[20]

EMS has a close working relationship with the International Society for Frontier Missions. All members of the EMS are required to affirm the evangelical tenets of the Christian Faith as set forth in the statement of faith of the Lausanne movement.[21]

Although the EMS is aware of the deep compromise and false teaching of the ASM, it remains tied to the concept of integrating the teachings of anthropology with Scripture, and to the doctrines of the Lausanne movement which, as we saw in chapter 12, fully endorse holistic mission.

International Association of Mission Studies

In the early 1970s a group of European missiologists met in Oslo, Norway, with the purpose of forming the International Association of Mission Studies (IAMS). According to its website, IAMS is an international professional society for the scholarly study of Christian witness and its impact in the world, and of the related field of intercultural theology. It is an international umbrella body that acts as a network of missiological associations; it links individual scholars and missiological associations from Africa, Asia, Latin America and the Pacific together with North America, Germany, the United Kingdom and Ireland, Scandinavia, the Netherlands, South Africa, India and elsewhere. IAMS is a thoroughly ecumenical body that includes Roman Catholics, Orthodox and Conciliars, as well as evangelical Protestants and members of the Pentecostal, charismatic and Independent churches.

The objectives of the association include the promotion of the scholarly study of practical questions relating to mission and intercultural theology; the promotion of fellowship, cooperation and mutual assistance in mission studies; and the organisation of international conferences of missiologists and intercultural theologians.[22]

Wilbert Shenk, in his *History of the American Society of Missiology*, concludes a chapter entitled, 'The roots and emergence of mission studies', with these approving words: 'These initiatives on both sides of the Atlantic boosted morale: mission studies were about to enter a phase of unprecedented development. In North America this would mean that mission studies finally gained academic legitimacy while training a new generation of missiologists and producing *instrumenta studiorum* that included encyclopaedias, dictionaries, bibliographies, monographs, journals and a rich offering of scholarly journal articles. The American Society of Missiology was to play a central role in these developments.'[23]

Missiology in the UK

The missiological flag was hoisted in the UK by the Oxford Centre for Mission Studies (OCMS), founded in 1983 (discussed in chapter 14). The Centre sees its mission as nurturing relevant research for leaders on the cutting edge of Christian ministry and mission globally.

According to the OCMS website, 'For almost thirty years church leaders, mission and development professionals, and global Christian scholars have met under this roof and have sought to better understand how to bring the transforming nature of their faith to effect change in the lives of those they serve.' The Centre 'has been training a new generation of mission scholars and practitioners to become a key resource to the church in mission in contemporary contexts of complexity and diversity for almost thirty years'. It has drawn key people from Asia, Africa, Latin America and Eastern Europe to its research and postgraduate study programmes.

The website claims that through its publications, including the journal *Transformation*, and imprint of Regnum Books, OCMS has been a major influence in shaping mission theology and strategy in the growing churches of the Two-Thirds World, giving voice to those from the South and enabling it to be heard in other parts of the developing world. Truly global through its structures of governance, its staff and its students, OCMS's importance to the world Church has stemmed largely from the sense of ownership of its work by the Christian leaders of the Two-Thirds World. The Centre is now seen as a vital instrument in the development of post-graduate training institutions in the global South. OCMS nurtures relevant and engaged research for leaders on the cutting edge of Christian ministry. By studying in an environment that is culturally sensitive and globally informed, Christian leaders from around the world can engage in ground-breaking scholarship that helps them to understand the nature of the issues they face in their own contexts and ministry, and how better to deal with them.[24]

OCMS programmes claim to 'offer an attractive and affordable alternative for people from the non-western world, and our approach allows scholars to remain active in their ministries throughout their studies, ensuring that their research is culturally relevant and contextually informed with only minimal disruption to families and ministries'.[25]

Rev Richard Harries, former Bishop of Oxford writes: 'The Oxford Centre for Mission Studies does extremely valuable work supporting Christian leaders in the developing world. I particularly appreciate the fact that their programmes are concerned not just with individuals but with the transformation of whole societies.'[26] Here we should note that the word 'transformation', first coined at Wheaton '83, described in chapter 13 (pages 203-5), has found its way into British missiology.

Holistic Mission

The influential book, *Holistic Mission: God's Plan for God's People* (2010), a product of the publishing arm of OCMS, claims that 'prior to the twentieth century the work of the church and the missionary societies had naturally been holistic'. With the striking growth of Christianity in the majority world, 'the centres of thriving Christianity are now found in the south, in the majority world in countries of Africa, South America and Asia. And the paternalist attitudes, even the colonial, imperialistic attitudes, are no longer appropriate, certainly no longer acceptable to the majority world. Even the understanding of the gospel, what is God's good news, has changed for many – though not all – Christians… We would argue that Christians should revert to the traditional and biblical position and see God's good news as being holistic, being concerned with transforming the whole of the creation, the whole person, mind and spirit.'[27] These confident assertions are revisionist in the extreme, presenting a distorted view of the past.

The editors of *Holistic Mission*, Brian Woolnough (research tutor at OCMS) and Wonsuk Ma (CEO of OCMS), assert that the kingdom of God is here on earth and therefore we are to seek, as we pray so often in the Lord's Prayer, that his will be done on earth as it is in heaven. 'And this implies justice, peace, health, and wholeness, shalom, on earth as it is in heaven. Hence the term Holistic Mission, which addresses all aspects of human and social life…'[28]

In 2009 OCMS joined in dialogue with the leadership of the Edinburgh 2010 Centenary International Council (see chapter 19) around the need to 'undertake a study process to look at holistic mission'. During the dialogue two outcomes were agreed. The first was to gather together expert practitioners, church leaders and theologians with experience and expertise in the practice of holistic mission, and ask them to write chapters for the book *Holistic Mission*. The second was to hold a conference at OCMS. The editors were thrilled that Ronald Sider, author of *Rich Christians in an Age of Hunger* (1977), contributed a chapter to *Holistic Mission* and also gave a keynote address at the Oxford Conference.[29]

Brian Woolnough writes: 'It is difficult not to recognise that the good news that God wants us to share with the world is holistic… The growth of holistic mission in the twentieth century, especially in the latter half, has arguably been one of the most significant and most heartening in the history of the church's mission to the world.'[30]

Important contributors to *Holistic Mission* include Ronald Sider, Professor of Theology, Holistic Ministry and Public Policy, at Palmer Theological Seminary (USA) and President of Evangelicals for Social Action; Bryant Myers, Professor of Transformational Development at Fuller Seminary; Vinay Samuel, a founding secretary of INFEMIT and Director of the Oxford Centre for Religion and Public Life; Chris Sugden, member of founding board of OCMS, Executive Secretary of

Anglican Mainstream and member of the General Synod of the Church of England; Al Tizon, Associate Professor of Holistic Ministry at Palmer Theological Seminary (USA).

This brief survey shows that missiology is an enterprise based on fallible human wisdom. Its central dogma is that God has now in our day revealed the holistic mission of the Church through anthropology and the social sciences. This means the Church needs to supplement Scripture with the social sciences and anthropology to really understand the mission of God. Missiology is a relatively recent development, and the discipline has no clear doctrinal standard and is deeply ecumenical. Yet virtually all missiologists are agreed that the true mission of the Church is, and always has been, holistic; but only in recent times has this truth been rediscovered.

The discipline of missiology is accountable to no one but its own academic faculty. It works closely with the Church of Rome, with whose mission methods and philosophy it has much in common. Fuller Seminary, the intellectual power house of new evangelicalism, has played a leading role in propagating missiology, and consequently has had a massive influence on the training of missionaries. A common feature of missiologists is an intense dislike of Western civilisation, and even of what they pejoratively label 'Western Christianity'.

In chapter 18 we deal with contextualization, an issue that lies at the very heart of missiology. But in the next chapter we look at the man regarded by many as the missionary statesman of our time—Ralph Winter.

(Endnotes)

1 J.A. Scherer, quoted by Michael Raiter, in R.J. Gibson, *Ripe for Harvest: Christian Mission in the New Testament and in our World* (Carlisle: Paternoster, 2000), p138 cited from the article, 'Mission: A Problem of Definition' by Keith Ferdinando, in *Themelios*, volume 33, issue1
2 David Bosch, *Transforming Mission: Paradigm Shifts in Theology of Mission*, Centre for Contemporary Christianity, 1991, p9
3 Robert J. Priest, What in the world is missiology!? Posted, March 7, 2012 http://www.missiologymatters.com/2012/03/07/what-in-the-world-is-missiology/
4 Ibid.
5 Ibid.

6   What Is a Missiologist? The Theology, Tools, and Team of a Missiologist, Ed Stetser, 10 June 2013, *Christianity Today*: http://www.christianitytoday.com/edstetzer/2013/june/what-is-missiologist.html?paging=off

7   *History of the American Society of Missiology, 1973 - 2013*, by Wilbert R Shenk, Institute of Mennonite Studies, 2014, p9, https://archive.org/stream/HistoryOfTheAmericanSocietyOfMissiology1973-2013/Shenk_asmHistory#page/n9/mode/1up

8   Ibid, p10

9   Ibid, p20

10   Website of American Society of Missiology, http://www.asmweb.org/content/home

11   Ibid.

12   *History of the American Society of Missiology*, pp19-20

13   Ibid. p24

14   Ibid. p25

15   Ibid. p25

16   *Missionshift: Global Mission Issues in the Third Millennium*, edited by David Hesselgrave and Ed Stetzer, Broadman & Holman Publishers, 2010, p268

17   Ibid, p266

18   Evangelical Missiological Society, https://www.emsweb.org/about

19   Ibid.

20   Ibid.

21   Ibid.

22   International Association for Mission Studies website, http://missionstudies.org/

23   *History of the American Society of Missiology*, p11

24   Oxford Centre for Mission Studies website, http://www.ocms.ac.uk/content/index.php?q=ocms/about

25   Ibid.

26   Ibid, Prospective Students, http://www.ocms.ac.uk/prospective/index.php?ccid=437&mid=438

27   *Holistic Mission: God's Plan for God's People*, edited by Brian Woolnough and Wonsuk Ma, Regnum Edinburgh 2010 Series, 2010, preface, pxi

28   Ibid, preface, pxi

29   Ibid, preface, pxii

30   Ibid, p3

Chapter 16

Ralph Winter: The Missionary Statesman

Dr Ralph D. Winter (1924-2009) is recognised as a giant in the field of Christian missions. The term 'missionary statesman' has even been used to describe his ministry. According to Ray Tallman, Professor of Missiology at Golden Gate Baptist Theological Seminary, California, 'Dr Ralph Winter was perhaps the most influential person in missions of the last 50 years and has influenced missions globally more than anyone I can think of.'[1] John Piper said Winter's 'vision of the advance of the gospel was breathtaking'.[2] Some consider him to be the greatest missionary strategist of the twentieth century. In 2005 Dr Winter was named among the top 25 Most Influential Evangelicals in America by *Time* magazine. Winter referred to himself as a 'social engineer', for he prided himself on looking at problems on the mission field in new ways, asking questions that no one else had ever thought of, and proposing solutions that shook up the status quo.

Winter's Education

Ralph Winter received a degree in civil engineering from the California Institute of Technology, a bachelor of divinity from Princeton University, a M.A. from Columbia University in Teaching English as a second language (TESL), and a Ph.D in linguistics, anthropology, and mathematical statistics from Cornell University. Winter explains his thinking: 'When I moved from my Caltech background in engineering to Cornell for a doctorate in linguistics, anthropology and mathematical statistics, people said, "Why are you leaving engineering?" I answered "I am moving from civil engineering to social engineering." When, after that degree, I then completed theological seminary I told people I was moving "from social engineering to Christian social engineering." When I became a missionary I was now in Christian mission engineering.'[3]

In 1973 Winter co-founded the American Society of Missiology (ASM), an ecumenical professional association for mission studies in North America, which would bring together mainline Protestant, Roman Catholic and Conciliar streams of mission scholarship (see page 222). For the first three years he was the secretary and de facto business manager of the society's journal, *Missiology: An International Review*. He successfully negotiated a merger with the secular journal, *Practical Anthropology*.

Winter's vast achievements include founding of The Frontier Mission Fellowship in 1976, and soon afterwards initiating two major projects—The U.S. Center for World Mission (USCWM), Pasadena, and the William Carey International University, Pasadena. Such was Ralph Winter's status in the field of missiology that he was recognised with the Lifetime of Service Award in 2008 at the North American Mission Leaders Conference, during which representatives from nearly 300 mission organisations, Christian colleges and churches paid their sincere homage to him. [4]

In December 2001, to honour his much-loved wife who had recently died from multiple myeloma, he officially established the Roberta Winter Institute with the primary focus on a new theological drive for, quote, 'destroying the works of the devil'. He had a deep personal concern about the way disease and evil seemed to tear down God's creation and tarnish God's reputation, making Christian gospel witness ineffective.[5] The new Institute encouraged Christians to see disease eradication as an essential calling from God. According to the Institute's website: 'While destroying the works of the devil will naturally include the urgent necessity of involvement on the physical level of combating major human problems like apathy, corruption, racism, exploitation and violence, the particular niche we as an organization feel called, empowered and commissioned by God to fill is in the area of disease, specifically the eradication or neutralization of disease pathogens.'[6]

As a young man, Winter was one of the first students to study at Fuller Theological Seminary. After seminary he served as Presbyterian missionary to a Mayan tribal group in Guatemala for ten years, during which time he also served as Professor of Anthropology for Landivar University in Guatemala (1961–1966). In 1967 Donald McGavran, eminent missiologist of Fuller's School of World Mission, invited him to join the faculty, which has subsequently been renamed the School of Intercultural Studies. Under the guidance of McGavran, Winter worked at Fuller as Professor of Missiology for ten years. While at Fuller he taught hundreds of missionaries and gained valuable insights into what was happening on mission fields around the world. He soon came to the realisation that there were many cultural groups, or what he called 'people groups', that were untouched by the gospel.

Ralph Winter at Lausanne

At the first Lausanne Congress in 1974, Ralph Winter's presentation entitled, 'The Highest Priority: Cross-Cultural Evangelism', was widely acclaimed and gave birth to the concept of unreached people groups. Using statistics and graphs, Winter skilfully demonstrated that there were still 2.5 billion people who could not hear the gospel in their own language and cultural setting in a way they could understand. He concluded that cross-cultural evangelism was the highest priority for world evangelization.

Winter's presentation was a watershed moment for the world missionary movement, and many believe it changed the outlook of mission agencies worldwide. An article in *Christian Post*, which described Ralph Winter as a giant in the field of missiology, called his Lausanne presentation ground-breaking. 'It was at this legendary summit, convened by American evangelist Billy Graham, where Winter introduced the term "unreached people groups" that had the profound effect of shifting the entire global mission strategy thereafter.'[7] Billy Graham said: 'Ralph Winter was a man of God who gave a vision to many Christians of a world in need of the gospel. I used to meet with him on many occasions, often in small group prayer. Some of my vision for world evangelization came from my interaction with him, and I am grateful.'[8]

After returning from Lausanne '74, Winter helped to set up the Institute of International Studies, with the purpose of training people for the mission field. Over time the Institute became known as 'Perspectives on the World Christian Movement', or simply *Perspectives* for short. A core doctrine of *Perspectives* is that the task of world evangelization requires strategic holism in which community development is integrated with church planting. Evangelization invariably integrates relief and development endeavours. The integration of evangelism and social endeavors should be strategic. With over 100,000 alumni in North American alone, the *Perspectives* training course is said to be a life-changing experience for many who have taken it. With his oversight of the influential *Perspectives* training course, Winter has redefined the methods and doctrine of evangelization and trained an entire generation of missionaries in these new doctrines. *Perspectives on the World Christian Movement* (2009) is a very large book of 782 pages, containing 136 articles on missiology, published by Winter's William Carey Library, and is now in its fourth edition.

The U.S. Center for World Mission (USCWM)

Ralph Winter saw the need for a place where mission agencies could collaborate in order to complete the unfinished task of world evangelization. He tried to persuade Fuller Theological Seminary to create such a missions think-tank, but when Fuller decided not to do so, Winter took the opportunity to set up his own missionary campus.

Winter writes: 'I was glad for my time at Fuller. A thousand missionaries passed through my classes and through their papers and theses I learned details about strange mission fields all over the world. After ten years, in view of all the new ideas about missions that were being churned up, I came to realize that it was necessary to establish a major base nearby where we could not just teach, but actually put things into practice and promote all these new ideas and important insights. The new Center and University we have established is located on a former Christian college campus in Northeast Pasadena [the college moved to San Diego]. It took us 13 years, with a lot of amazing help from God, to buy that campus plus a hundred homes surrounding it. We now have close to a hundred families in our mission society (the Frontier Mission Fellowship), about half of them working in different places around the country and the world. In addition, 35 other organizations are at work on the campus.'[9]

In 1976 the U.S. Center for World Mission (USCWM), situated on a 35-acre campus in Pasadena, California, was established. The Center, which has now changed its name to Frontier Ventures, is dedicated to the unfinished task of reaching every 'people group' with the gospel. Run by members of The Frontier Mission Fellowship, the Center is a place for missiologists and other mission-minded people to plan together for the great task of evangelizing the world. It is an umbrella organisation which oversees the mission work of much of the global evangelical Church. It follows the aims of the *Lausanne Covenant*—so joint initiatives fall under the Lausanne banner, such as the AD2000 and Beyond Movement, the Global Consultation on World Evangelization (GCOWE) and numerous others. Among the 4,000 plus groups that partner with USCWM are Mission Aviation Fellowship, Wycliffe Bible Translators, Intervarsity Fellowship, Campus Crusade for Christ, the Billy Graham Evangelistic Association, Christian Educators Association and many other organisations and groups of similar outlook.

Ralph Winter's Theology and Philosophy

The book, *Frontiers in Mission: Discovering and Surmounting Barriers to the Missio Dei* (2008), published by William Carey International University Press, provides a large collection of Ralph Winter's articles and papers. The 59 articles that make up this book provide us with a clear view of Winter's doctrines and methods. In the preface he acknowledges that one idea 'looms larger and more significant in my mind than any other. It is the concept of our having to identify with God's concern for defeating evil in order properly to glorify Him. This idea, if valid, would clearly expand hugely our contemporary understanding of mission.' He continues, there 'are two significant barriers to Christian belief: the rampant evil in this world if there is no Satan behind it, and a Bible with the feet of clay beginning with Genesis 1:1'. He concludes that the solution is 'to interpret Genesis in such a way as not to conflict with the very latest scientific views'. This he suggests will help both non-Christians, and those Christians about to lose their faith.[10] What follows is an attempt to outline his thinking.

Age of the Earth

Ralph Winter frequently commented on the age of the earth. In the Donald McClure Lecture to students at Pittsburgh Theological Seminary in 2005, he said: 'By tracing the contents of the universe backwards, scientists came to the remarkable conclusion that the entire universe began suddenly about 13.7 billion years ago, exploding from a tiny speck. Some scientists at first ridiculed this idea, calling it derisively, "The Big Bang" theory. Some warned that religious people would assume that this theory confirmed their Biblical ideas about creation. However, now this Big Bang theory has become widely accepted.'[11] Winter continues: 'As I earlier explained, 11,000 years is an exceedingly short time in the light of a universe which is said to be about 13.7 billion years old, a planet 4.5 billion years old, the conjectured 4-billion-year earliest appearance of life, or even the last half billion years (the last 500 million years since the Cambrian Explosion).'[12] Despite his belief in a universe that is billions of years old, Winter is adamant that he does not believe in evolution as such. Rather he believes in what he calls 'progressive development', which takes place over 13.7 billion years. Yet he says he believes in both the old earth and the young earth theories. He writes, 'For me it is very satisfying to be able to uphold what Genesis says and at the same time to embrace both the young earth and the old earth interpretations of events...'[13] Winter seemed to have no difficulty in holding together contradictory views when it suited his theories.

Winter's Prehistory

A dominant theme that runs through Winter's writings is his idiosyncratic speculation and theologising about 'prehistory'. He attempts to 'explain at least hypothetically the origin and development of life on this planet from the simplest and earliest forms of life to the most complex, whether large or small... Furthermore, I would like for the moment to try to avoid "accepted" religious terminology about a supreme being.' He invites us to 'speculate with as much evidence as possible and be willing to go beyond present evidence where it seems necessary. Thus, we begin with a roughly five-billion-year-old planet and a roughly four-billion-year record of life.'[14]

He asserts that 'a major milestone was achieved when the angels, no doubt following God's blueprints, created the first cell, each one containing in its nucleus an essential coded DNA molecule... Once the cell was achieved, then building larger life out of cells became a new challenge, one which could and did accelerate far more rapidly.'[15]

According to Winter, 'multi-celled or even single-celled life appeared quite late in the [creation] story… It might also be postulated that just as thousands of intelligent engineers and workers were necessary in the development of the automobile, so thousands of non-human beings have been involved in the development of life, and that these intelligent beings could learn as they went, and that a superior being was pleased with their learning progress.'[16]

He speculates that 'hominids appear in the record as long as several million years ago, and manlike creatures such as the Neanderthals very much more recently, like 60 thousand years ago, but DNA studies now indicate that the Neanderthals were neither human nor an antecedent of *homo sapiens*. What seems quite possible is that a smaller asteroid collided with the earth about 10 thousand years ago, and that the events of Genesis record the immediate results as well as what followed as various forms of life appeared and, specifically, *homo sapiens*.

'The immediate result of such a collision would have been formlessness and darkness (due to the immense dust clouds hurled into the air from the impact). Gradually the dust would settle and it would eventually be possible to tell the day from the night but not to see the sun itself. Finally the dust canopy would thin to the point that the sun and the moon would appear as visible bodies (and actual rays of light would enable rainbows). Meanwhile various kinds of animals would be redeveloped. This could have been when a brand new and radically different form of life appeared, *homo sapiens*, but only in a unique garden spot intended to enable a new counterthrust to the previous 500 million years of rampant evil and destruction.' Winter says that Genesis 1.1-2 actually permits this interpretation, namely, 'When God began His work of rehabilitation He had to deal with a battered, formless and darkened earth.'[17]

Intermediate Beings

Throughout his theology Winter speculates about the existence of what he calls 'intermediate beings'. 'The whole story may go like this: God created highly intelligent, but finite, intermediate beings through whom He then, over a lengthy period of time, developed life as we know it. These intermediate beings over time were instructed in the incredibly complex matters of DNA and what we call microbiology.

But at the Cambrian period, where forms of life vastly larger than fairly small animals were achieved, one of the leaders among the intermediate beings not only chose to go on his own but decided to mar and mangle the good creation intended by God. This period of rebellion continues to this day and explains why redeemed humans have a mission that is much larger than just redeeming humans, but requires the identification of all evil with Satan, not with God's "mysterious ways".'[18] Winter explains elsewhere: 'Are some of them [intermediate beings] small enough or smart enough to tamper directly with DNA as modern humans are beginning to do? If there are such beings, it would seem quite reasonable for them to have been involved in a lengthy learning curve. We can then imagine that their final achievement of cellular development and the consequent potential for large animals might have been the occasion of one of the key angelic leaders deciding to turn against God and systematically sabotage His creation.'[19]

Winter's theory of intermediate beings is without biblical foundation and contrary to Scripture. In fact, it reveals a surprising theological ignorance.

Works of the Devil

Winter firmly believed that evangelism should be concerned with defeating the works of the Devil. He says that Jesus went about doing good and curing all who were under the tyranny of the Devil, because God was with him (Acts 10.38). One of the great works of the Devil that needs to be overcome is disease. Winter acknowledges that he is well known 'for believing that disease is probably the greatest killer and producer of suffering in the entire world... But nine out of ten Americans in our wonderfully blessed country die prematurely – and by no means painlessly – because of disease.'[20] He is really pleased that former U.S. President Jimmy Carter aroused world opinion to the need to eradicate disease. 'It is unfortunate that Carter has not been able to get substantial money from Christian sources for this activity.'[21]

Winter writes: 'In my theology, Satanic disruption, distortion, and destruction of God's good creation is so extensive and pervasive that it even extends to what are often called "genetic defects". I have a strong suspicion that these defects are often actually intelligently evil distortions by Satan not just things that went wrong accidentally. Why?

Because, simply, some of these are so cleverly destructive. The same goes for destructive viruses, bacteria and especially parasites. These represent incredibly ingenious evil. They represent, I am thinking, the involvement of intelligence. They are not just unguided evolution or, much less, errors in creation.'[22]

Winter claims that nature was extremely violent long before the Fall of Adam described in Genesis 3. He writes: 'Nature, prior to the appearance of *homo sapiens*, is shot through and through with terrible slaughter, bloodshed, violence, and suffering, as the result of the fall of Satan, long before Adam fell. Man was intended to work with God in destroying the source of that evil. This was once God's good world, but it became severely distorted by the fallen adversary of God long before *homo sapiens* existed. "The Son of God appeared for this purpose, that he might destroy the works of the devil (I John 3.8)".' [23]

Here we must note that Ralph Winter says that death and chaos were in the world before the Fall of man. In other words, death is not the result of sin, as the Bible teaches. This is not simply bad theology, it is obviously completely unbiblical. He does not appear to understand the nature of the Fall and the Curse (Genesis 3).

Winter is concerned that 'Christians are not well known for fighting the viruses, the bacteria, and the tiny parasites that cause illness… We mount no offense against the pathogens themselves. We are willing to fight back at visible human muggers but not invisible bug muggers! That is, our pre-germ theological tradition does not trace disease back to the work of an Evil One. Thus, to my knowledge there is not a single avowedly Christian institution on the face of the earth that is working specifically for the eradication of disease pathogens.'[24] There is nothing in Scripture to support Winter's bizarre ideas about the eradication of disease pathogens.

Winter and the Reformation

Winter is distinctly cool, even dismissive in his attitude towards the Reformation. He claims, 'The first reformation was the shift from Jewish clothing to Greek and Latin clothing. A second happened when our faith went from Latin Christianity to German Christianity. This "second" reformation is THE Reformation that everyone talks about, of course.'[25]

Winter explains his view of the Reformation thus: 'It is hardly necessary to explain in detail the events of the Protestant Reformation/ Rebellion, which broke away from the Greek and Latin Mediterranean cultural vehicle for Biblical faith.'[26] Notice Winter's reference to Roman Catholicism as the 'Latin Mediterranean cultural vehicle' for biblical faith. He wants his readers to accept that the Church of Rome is a vehicle for biblical faith. Winter writes: 'Ironically, in the Reformation for the Protestants to have chosen to emphasize faith and the Catholics to have chosen to emphasize obedience rendered both sides heretically one-sided.'[27] This is not merely a simplistic view of the Reformation, it is a radically distorted presentation of a movement of God that restored the true gospel—salvation by the grace of God alone, through faith in Christ alone.

Winter writes: 'Just as Greek formulations had earlier "replaced" the Jewish carrier vehicle, the Jewish way of life, but not the (Jewish) Biblical faith, so now, in the Reformation, Germanic formulations replaced a Latin way of life but not the Biblical faith within the Latin carrier vehicle.'[28] Winter here is inferring that the Catholic Church is based on the Bible. Nothing, of course, could be further from the truth. Indeed, the Catholic Church at one time actually placed the Bible on its list of forbidden books, the notorious *Index Librorum Prohibitorum*.

Winter says that many pastors and missionaries have continued to replace the biblical agenda with one of the central issues of the Reformation, namely, mission that simply offers (or sells) advice to people on the attractive subject of 'how to get to heaven', or 'how to be assured of eternal salvation'.[29] He has caricatured the Protestant Faith, and reduced it to no more than selling advice on how to get to heaven. He appears to have forgotten those, like Ridley and Latimer, who were burned at the stake for defending the truth of salvation from sin through faith in Christ alone. But Ralph Winter clearly does not think that the Protestant doctrine of salvation by faith alone, in Christ alone, is important, and neither, it appears, does he believe in Christian assurance.

He is decidedly unimpressed with the Western Christian tradition, which says he, 'has often tended to concentrate on the next world, and, for this world, on merely the obligation to maintain good behavior. This has been especially true since the Reformation's massive over-emphasis on simply how to get to heaven.'[30] We must conclude that this much admired man does not accept the doctrines of the Reformation, and does not regard the doctrine of justification by faith as a central doctrine of biblical Christianity.

Mere Evangelism

Throughout his extensive writings, Winter appears to be uninterested in, even dismissive of personal salvation from sin. He writes: 'It may today have become one of the distinctive heresies of the Evangelical as we have become known as specialists in getting people into heaven…'[31]

Winter asks the rhetorical question: 'Does getting people into heaven adequately glorify God? Or, is the destructive plundering of His creation a problem with which we can be involved that will also glorify His Name?'[32]

Winter again: 'There is, evidently, a very great difference between a mission to get people into heaven and a mission to recover the glory of God by defeating the powers of darkness and distortion. In this latter, larger mission evangelism is to be viewed as in part recruitment for war. Mere evangelism, or mere recruitment for the Kingdom is not the single Divine goal.'[33]

And again, 'the saving of souls will no longer be the central strategy of mission, but will in large part be merely a means'.[34]

He dislikes a brand of Christianity that seeks merely to 'recruit' more and more people into the Faith. 'But I see that we are, to too great an extent, producing a self-collapsing Christianity, insofar as our converts are told that the only important thing to do is to win more converts. It's like getting the people into the armed forces, and they ask what they are supposed to do. "Oh, well, you are supposed to recruit." Then they recruit more and more people, and set them also to recruiting still other people.'[35]

Winter it seems found little joy in sinners being saved from their sin. But the Lord Jesus told his disciples there is great joy in heaven over one sinner who repents (Luke 15.7). And the Philippian jailor, deeply convicted of his sin, and in anguish of soul, did not cry out, 'What must I do to save society?' No. The Lord had come to deal with his eternal soul, which faced eternal judgement. Under the convicting power of the Holy Spirit, he cried out, 'What must I do to be saved?' The answer, recorded in Scripture for all future generations was, 'Believe on the Lord Jesus Christ, and thou shalt be saved' (Acts16.30-31).

The Kingdom of God

Winter's *Perspectives* course teaches that 'God accomplishes His purpose by triumphing over evil in order to rescue and bless people and to establish His kingdom rule throughout the earth… As groups of people come to glorify and obey the risen Christ, they find that His kingdom governance brings genuine transformation and substantial measures of God's intended justice to their communities. It is this triumph over evil and the transformation of communities by Christ's effective Lordship that constitutes the blessing of the nations.'[36]

Winter says that if we wish truly to glorify God in all the earth, 'we need to realize that we cannot go on allowing people to believe that our God is not interested in defeating the Evil One… The Biblical mandate is "the Gospel of the Kingdom," not merely a "Gospel of salvation." The Gospel of the Kingdom is the central matter of God's will being done "on earth as it is in heaven." It is a mandate that is distinctly larger than getting along in this life with the help of business, and getting to heaven with the help of missions. God's glory is at stake. His glory is our main business.'[37]

Winter responds to the question: 'What in the world could microbes have to do with the Kingdom of God or global evangelism?' The answer, he says, is simple. 'Distorted microbes war against the Kingdom of God. Distorted genes make animals violent and destructive. Destructive parasites kill off many varieties of plant and animal life, and as well as, by the malarial parasite, 1.2 million people a year, most of them children, four of whom die every minute from malaria alone. All this massive damage to the purposes of the Kingdom of God amounts to noise so loud that people can't hear what we are preaching to them.'[38]

Winter asks: 'What is it that we can all pray for? Well, what did Jesus tell us to pray for? He said that we must pray "Thy Kingdom come, Thy will be done on earth as it is in heaven." What this means is that our concept of God's desire to reach all peoples and persons must somehow be part of His desire for His Kingdom to come on earth.'[39]

Winter says, 'Christ's reference to the coming of the kingdom of God, and the present outworking in this world of the "Your will be done" in the Lord's Prayer (Matt 6.10) are actually echoed by the Great Commission itself.' The problem is that mission theology is not broad enough 'to the point where we would plan to tackle some of the bigger problems such as the wiping out of Guinea worm, problems which have existed for over a century under the very noses of missionaries. *Such extra breadth must not be seen to be a divergence from the preaching of eternal life but rather an empowerment of the message of a gospel of a kingdom, which is both here and hereafter*. This is the gospel of Jesus Christ. It is the gospel of the kingdom, the announcement of a rule and reign of God that must be extended to the whole world and all of creation. We must stand up and be counted as active foes of the world's worst evils'[40] (Winter's italics).

David Hesselgrave, who knew Winter very well, comments on his Kingdom theology: 'Winter himself had a change of mind and began to promote his "kingdom mission"—his "radical new interpretation of the Lord's Prayer and the Great Commission" that even many missiologists find confusing.'[41] Of serious concern to Hesselgrave is that 'Winter has shifted his focus away from gospel proclamation and church development and in the direction of social transformation and kingdom-building.'[42]

Hesselgrave points out that Winter's meta-scientific narrative 'has to do with the struggle between good and evil, with the battle between God and Satan... Building on that struggle as a foundation, Winter constructs his new understanding of mission/missiology out of theological/biblical components, yes, but also out of materials that emanate from both social and physical science. What citizens of our postmodern globalized world will discover here – and perhaps find compelling – is a blending of components emanating from the sciences as well as Scripture—from astronomy, paleontology, anthropology, sociology, psychology, linguistics, history and still other sciences... .'[43]

Winter interprets the verse in the Lord's Prayer 'Your kingdom come, your will be done on earth as it is in heaven' (Matthew 6.10) to mean that the Church should do more than just pray for the coming kingdom—it must also take an active role in advancing the kingdom.[44] Hesselgrave comments thus on Winter's kingdom mission: 'Winter's interpretation of Matthew 28.19-20 highlights the phrase "observe everything that I have commanded", from which he infers that Christian mission includes all that the Great Commandment requires. In obeying it, Christians not only demonstrate kingdom principles and values; they also bring them to earth by, for example, eradicating disease-bearing microbes, overcoming poverty, greening the environment, and establishing peace. Winter does make it clear, however, that in his view we do not establish the kingdom. The final establishment of the kingdom awaits the coming of Christ.'[45]

De-Westernizing the Gospel

In 1996 at the Urbana '96 Students' Missionary Conference in the USA, attended by representatives from over a hundred countries, Ralph Winter put forward the argument for the 'de-Westernization' of the gospel. He told students that Christianity must be taken out of its Western context if the gospel is to reach Hindus, Muslims, and Buddhists effectively. He said that when followers of Islam and Hinduism look at Christianity they see sex obsession, drinking, drugs, and family breakdown.[46] He claimed that the key task of the West should be to allow other cultures to develop their own distinct kind of Christianity.

A constant theme of Winter's teaching has been the critical need to de-Westernize the gospel.[47] He spoke against missionary endeavours that have planted versions of 'Western Christianity' all over the world, but failed to recognise the brutal reality that the Western missionary movement was one of the main barriers to the gospel of the Kingdom.[48]

He asserted that the future is 'bleak for the further extension of our faith into the vast blocs of Chinese, Hindus, Muslims and Buddhists unless we are willing to allow our faith to leave behind the cultural clothing of the Christian movement itself. Do we preach Christ or Christianity? … Our task may well be to allow and encourage Muslims and Hindus and Chinese to follow Christ without identifying themselves with a foreign religion. The Third Reformation is here!'[49]

According to Winter, the Third Reformation is the creation of a 'biblical' faith for Muslims, Hindus and Buddhists that is beyond the Christian Church. It is a religion that pledges allegiance to Christ without involving the Church.

In dealing with the issue of radical contextualization (discussed in chapter 18), it occurred to Winter 'that our own form of Christianity has been unthinkingly assumed to be the main balanced, biblical, total, properly contextualized thing. Think about it. Is it possible that we need to know how to decontextualize our own Christianity before we can ever very successfully contextualize the Bible for somebody else?'[50]

He maintains that the distinctive heresy of evangelicals is that they 'have become specialists in merely getting people happy and getting them into heaven'. According to Ralph Winter, latter day evangelicals have made their 'Gospel of Salvation' a nearly total substitute for the 'Gospel of the Kingdom'. Winter finds the Gospel of Salvation to be sadly lacking because it contributes very little to 'Thy will be done on earth', as Jesus asked us to pray. His concern is that missionaries who preach the Gospel of Salvation 'are not normally trained, nor well-equipped to take on the social, commercial, medical, engineering, and political problems of Africa. Neither are the national pastors. This vast array of problems is not part of our Gospel of Salvation even though it is definitely part of the Gospel of the Kingdom.'[51] The implication is that Winter has two gospels. He promotes a contextualized gospel, which he calls the gospel of the Kingdom, that takes on social, commercial, medical, engineering and political problems, but he appears to have little time for the true gospel of salvation.

Because preaching the 'Gospel of Salvation', in Winter's mind, has failed to provide what people really need, he says that some people around the world will choose to go beyond Christianity. He writes: 'We have already noted the existence of millions of Africans who are eagerly following Christ and the Bible but not identifying with any form of traditional Christianity.' He mentions the Lutheran-Missouri Synod study which 'describes millions of devout followers of Jesus and the Bible in the one city of Chennai (Madras), alone, who have not chosen to call themselves Christians nor to identify with the socio-ecclesiastical tradition of Christianity and who still consider themselves Hindu.'[52]

Winter does not have much time for Western, Protestant evangelical Christianity. He says: 'Today we must understand more clearly that neither Western Christianity nor Protestantism, nor even Evangelicalism is the only substantial cultural tradition stemming from the Bible…

Furthermore, it is now reported for all to know that the incredible impact of the Bible on India, for example, has produced between 14 and 24 million daily Bible-reading believers in Jesus Christ who are still part of their Hindu communities. They do not call themselves Christians. The same is true in more than one movement to Christ within the world's Islamic traditions... Do we preach Christ or Christianity? If the latter, it may be the greatest mistake in missions today.'[53] The question is, of course, what kind of Jesus is being followed by these communities?

The Christian Mission

Winter describes the scope of the Christian mission as devolving on every follower of Christ the duty 'to seek constantly what is the maximum contribution he or she can make to glorifying God and fighting evil. This includes healing the sick, rescuing those who are suffering for any reason, preventing disease and malice, and eliminating or eradicating sources of evil and disease. It requires us to engage meaningfully in the global battle against human slavery, corruption in government and private enterprise, family breakdown and so forth.'[54]

According to Winter, the crucifixion of Christ on the Cross of Calvary exemplifies 'the reality of an unspeakably cruel enemy, not merely a salvation from sin to be greeted with joy and praise. The saving of souls will no longer be the central strategy of mission, but will in large part be merely a means, the means of the recruitment of human beings into the ongoing war against the distorting work of a formidable evil intelligence utterly opposed to the restoration of all creation and the reglorification of God. Glorifying God will become more than a worship exercise. It will require all-out war against all distortion of creation, including the carnivorous state of present-day destructive animal life (that is, all life forms except those like dogs and horses which have been deliberately and intelligently genetically restored). Yes, if wolves have been genetically altered through selective breeding we can begin to understand how that might be done even more efficiently through gene-splicing with animals that are still violent. Feeding man-eating tigers grass won't restore them to a non-carnivorous state, but gene-splicing might. Humans going vegetarian may not change their carnivorous nature. Also, fighting pathogens at the molecular level, if possible, would seem to have to be added to limited understandings of the Christian mission.'[55] While it is tempting to dismiss these ideas as weird nonsense, we must remember that they are the ideas of a leading missiologist who has trained tens of thousands of people for the mission field and whose *Perspectives* training programme is still massively influential.

In Winter's mind, the saving of souls is not central to the mission of the Church. Rather, he wants the Church to be engaged in an all out war against disease pathogens, destructive animal life, all distortions of creation, human slavery, and corruption in government and private enterprise, thus facilitating the growth of his vision of God's kingdom.

The Future of Evangelicals in Mission

Ronald Sider, author of *Rich Christians in an Age of Hunger* (1977), expresses his wholehearted support for Ralph Winter's approach to mission. Responding to Winter's essay, 'The Future of Evangelicals in Mission', published in 2007, Sider writes:'What I want to underline— and celebrate with Ralph Winter—is the historic shift in the modern evangelical world in the last forty or so years. Forty years ago, most evangelical leaders would have agreed that the primary mission of the church is "saving souls"—i.e., evangelism is our primary mission… Ralph Winter rightly celebrates the fact that things have changed dramatically. Today, almost all evangelical leaders agree that we are to do both evangelism and social action. They are both parts of a biblically shaped mission. Many persons, documents and movements have contributed to this significant change. John Stott, Samuel Escobar and René Padilla all contributed to the historic affirmation in the *Lausanne Covenant* (1974) that evangelism and social responsibility are both part of our biblical task as Christians.' Sider says, 'we also need more evangelicals enthusiastically engaged in social and societal transformation. And we need millions of Christians and hundreds of thousands of congregations who understand concretely how to combine evangelism and social action.'[56]

Sider is elated that Ralph Winter (whom he claims has for many decades been powerfully identified with the evangelistic task of sharing the gospel) 'shouts clearly and loudly toward the end of his long fruitful career what he has often said before: word and deed belong together…

This essay is both a significant measure of how much progress the evangelical world has made in embracing holistic mission and a clarion call to the next generation to get on with the biblical task of following Jesus our perfect model in combining evangelism and social action in the power of the Spirit.'[57]

Conclusion

Ralph Winter has proved to be a powerful advocate for the holistic gospel. Through his various organisations and the *Perspectives* training programme, he has undoubtedly had a massive and worldwide influence on the Christian missionary movement. His commitment to anthropology has led him to develop frankly incredible (even risible) theories about the prehistory of the planet and the purposes of the 'Supreme Being' (Winter's term). Our analysis of his writings has shown his doctrines and teachings to be deeply compromised and unbiblical. Many of his theories come from wild speculations, the product of an over-active imagination. His ideas about 'intermediate beings' are pure speculation without a shred of biblical support. He is prepared to go well beyond Scripture in shaping his theories. Indeed, most of his handling of Scripture is superficial; he simply takes biblical verses to support his latest theories.

Of concern is a profound bias that runs through his voluminous writings. He does not support the doctrines of the Reformation, and is dismissive of the doctrine of personal salvation through faith in Christ alone, which he caricatures as getting a ticket to heaven. He has a strong aversion to Western culture in general and Western Christianity in particular, which he regards as a barrier that prevents people from accepting the gospel.

He promotes a false holistic gospel that seeks to create his version of God's kingdom on earth. To him the main ministry of the Church is to fight against Satan's evil empire and to eradicate disease, poverty and injustice. Winter, with his flawed theology and ridiculous speculations, has promoted a false gospel. It is not surprising that Ronald Sider celebrates Winter's ministry, for they are both proponents of the same false holistic gospel.

Our next chapter looks at another vastly influential missiologist, this time from the UK.

(Endnotes)

1 *The Christian Post*, Ralph D. Winter Remembered as 'Giant' in Mission Field, By Michelle A. Vu, Christian Post Reporter, May 22, 2009: http://www.christianpost.com/news/ralph-d-winter-remembered-as-giant-in-mission-field-38739/
2 *The Christian Post*, Preachers, Pastors Pay Tribute to Dr Ralph D. Winter, 2 July 2009
3 Antecedents to the Founding of the U. S. Center for World Mission, cited in 'The Introduction to the Reprint of Mission Frontiers 1979-1981', Ralph Winter, July 2004, p4
4 *The Christian Post*, Ralph D. Winter Remembered as 'Giant' in Mission Field
5 Website of Roberta Winter Institute, http://www.robertawinterinstitute.org/birth-of-an-institute/
6 Ibid, http://www.robertawinterinstitute.org/mission-vision/
7 *The Christian Post*, Ralph D. Winter Remembered as 'Giant' in Mission Field,
8 *The Christian Post*, Preachers, Pastors Pay Tribute to Dr. Ralph D. Winter
9 Ralph Winter, Growing up with the Bible, *International Journal of Fontiers Mission*, 22:2 Summer 2005
10 'The Embarrassingly Delayed Education of Ralph D. Winter', by Ralph D. Winter, http://www.wciu.edu/docs/resources/5_Winter,_Delayed_Education_of_Ralph_Winter.pdf
11 'Planetary Events and the Mission of the Church', Part 1. Planetary Events: Pre-Edenic, Donald McClure Lectureship, Pittsburgh Theological Seminary, Ralph D. Winter, Monday, October 3-4, 2005, cited from *Frontiers in Mission*, chapter 53, p287
12 'Planetary Events and the Mission of the Church', Part 2. Planetary Events: the New Beginning', cited from *Frontiers in Mission*, chapter 53, William Carey International University Press p296
13 'Introduction', Ralph D. Winter, Sunday, August 7, 2005, cited from *Frontiers in Mission*, pxv
14 'A Larger Worldview?' Ralph D. Winter, Missiology Hour USCWM, Tuesday, October 20, 2001, cited from *Frontiers in Mission*, chapter 42, pp197-198
15 'Theologizing Prehistory, Implications for Mission', Part I, Ralph D. Winter, Tuesday, July 31, 2001, cited from *Frontiers in Mission*, chapter 42, p208
16 'A Larger Worldview?' Ralph D. Winter, pp197-198
17 'A Larger Worldview?' Ralph D. Winter, p198
18 'Introduction', Ralph D. Winter, Sunday, August 7, page xv
19 'Planetary Events and the Mission of the Church', Part 1. cited from *Frontiers in Mission*, Chapter 53, p. 293
20 *Missionshift: Global Mission Issues in the Third Millennium*, edited by David Hesselgrave and Ed Stetzer, B&H Publishing Group, 2010, p186
21 *Missionshift*, p186
22 'Evolved or Involved?', Ralph D. Winter, May 2004, cited from *Frontiers in Mission*, chapter 48, p245
23 'Twelve Frontiers of Perspective', Ralph Winter, cited from *Frontiers in Mission*, chapter 10, p36
24 Ibid, p38
25 Ibid, p31
26 'The Significance of Post-Adamic Evil: First the Good News', Seminar, March 1, 2002, cited from *Frontiers in Mission*, chapter 12, p231

27 'The Story of Our Planet', Ralph D. Winter, October 30, 2004, cited from *Frontiers in Mission*, chapter 50, p263
28 'The Story of Our Planet', chapter 50, p267
29 'Beyond Transformation: An Ancient Syncretism as a Handicap to a Public Theology', Ralph D. Winter, American Society of Missiology, June 2005, cited from *Frontiers in Mission*, chapter 52, p281
30 'Planetary Events and the Mission of the Church', cited from *Frontiers in Mission*, chapter 53, p295
31 'Eleven Frontiers of Perspective', Ralph Winter, *International Journal of Frontier Missions*, 20:3 Fall 2003, p81
32 Ralph D. Winter, Mission Frontiers blog, Editorial Comment, July 01, 2005
33 'Planetary Events: the New Beginning', Monday, October 3-4, 2005
34 'Introduction', Ralph D. Winter, August 7, 2005, cited from *Frontiers in Mission*, page xv
35 *International Journal of Frontier Missions*, 'Understanding the Polarization between Fundamentalist and Modernist Mission', by Ralph Winter, 26:1 Spring 2009, page 10
36 Perspectives on the World Christian Movement, Core Ideas, pdf, p2
37 *International Journal of Frontier Missions*, 'When Mission Can Be Business Where Both Business and Mission Fall Short', Ralph D. Winter, May 2005, cited from *Frontiers in Mission*, chapter 11, p47
38 'The Significance of Pre-Adamic Evil', Ralph D. Winter Seminar, February 22, 2002, cited from *Frontiers in Mission*, chapter 42, p227
39 'The Analysis of a Movement', Ralph D. Winter, From the booklet 'Thy Kingdom Come', for the GCOWE '95 in Korea, May 1995.', cited from *Frontiers in Mission*, chapter 26, p135
40 *Missionshift: Global Mission Issues in the Third Millennium*, edited by David Hesselgrave and Ed Stetzer, pp188-189
41 *Missionshift*, p275
42 *Missionshift*, p286
43 *Missionshift*, p287
44 *Missionshift*, p289
45 *Missionshift*, p289
46 *Christianity Today*, 'Urbana 96: Missions Agencies Told to "De-Westernize"' Gospel', by Ted Olsen in Urbana, Illinois/ February 3, 1997, http://www.christianitytoday.com/ct/1997/february3/7t2086.html
47 Catalyzing Kingdom Breakthrough, article from the March-April 2015 issue: Frontier Ventures, http://www.missionfrontiers.org/issue/article/catalyzing-kingdom-breakthrough
48 Ibid. http://www.missionfrontiers.org/issue/article/catalyzing-kingdom-breakthrough
49 'Twelve Frontiers of Perspective', Ralph D. Winter, General Director, Frontier Mission Fellowship, cited from *Frontiers in Mission*, chapter 10, pp32-33
50 'Twelve Frontiers of Perspective', Ralph Winter, p31
51 'Twelve Frontiers of Perspective', Ralph Winter, p32
52 'Twelve Frontiers of Perspective', Ralph Winter, p32
53 'The Greatest Mistake in Missions', Talk at Kabul Reunion, Ralph Winter, August 8, 2004, cited from *Frontiers in Mission*, chapter 31, p166
54 'The Embarrassingly Delayed Education of Ralph D. Winter', cited from *Frontiers in Mission*, chapter 57, p348

55 'Beyond Transformation: An Ancient Syncretism as a Handicap to a "Public Theology",' Ralph D. Winter, American Society of Missiology, June 2005, cited from *Frontiers in Mission*, chapter 52, p284

56 *Mission Frontiers*, January 01, 2008, 'Response to Ralph Winter The Future of Evangelicals in Mission Article' by Ron Sider, http://www.missionfrontiers.org/issue/article/response-to-ralph-winter

57 Ibid.

Chapter 17

Missiology of Christopher Wright

Christopher J.H. Wright (born 1947) is an Anglican clergyman and prominent missiologist who has donned the mantle of his mentor John Stott. He is currently the International Ministries Director of Langham Partnership International, an organisation founded by John Stott to train church leaders from the Third World. Wright is an honorary member of All Souls Church, Langham Place, London. Following in Stott's footsteps, Wright wrote the *Cape Town Commitment* after the Third Lausanne Congress in Cape Town in 2010. In the preface to his book, *The Mission of God*, he readily acknowledges his debt to John Stott, 'who has constantly encouraged and prayed for me in this project, and graciously allowed me the frequent benefit of his writing retreat cottage, the Hookses, on the west coast of Wales.' Through his two books, *The Mission of God* (2006) and *The Mission of God's People* (2010), which have become standard works for aspiring missiologists and widely used by theological seminaries, his influence in the modern missiology movement is profound.

Creation Care

Like Stott, Wright is passionate about the environment. He is on the Council of Reference of A Rocha, a Christian environmental organisation that aims to bring a Christian voice to the climate discussions – and take the climate change agenda to the Church.

In an article in Ralph Winter's *Perspectives on the World Christian Movement*, Fourth Edition (2009) entitled, 'Mission and God's Earth', Wright expresses the view that 'a biblical theology of mission, flowing from the mission of God himself, must include the ecological sphere within its scope and see practical environmental action as a legitimate part of biblical mission'.[1] He asserts that 'creation care embodies justice because environmental action is a form of defending the weak against the strong, the defenceless against the powerful, the violated against the attacker and the voiceless against the stridency of the greedy'.[2] He concludes that 'there is no doubt that a major contributor to contemporary environmental damage is global capitalism's insatiable demand for more'.[3]

In the *Cape Town Commitment*, Wright demonstrates his passion for creation care. He says that creation care is a gospel issue within the Lordship of Christ. 'Such love for God's creation demands that we repent of our part in the destruction, waste and pollution of the earth's resources and our collusion in the toxic idolatry of consumerism. Instead, we commit ourselves to urgent and prophetic ecological responsibility. We support Christians whose particular missional calling is to environmental advocacy and action, as well as those committed to godly fulfilment of the mandate to provide for human welfare and needs by exercising responsible dominion and stewardship.[4]

He is frustrated that many Christians do not support his environmental agenda. He writes: 'It is baffling to me that there are so many Christians, including sadly (and especially) those who claim to be evangelicals, for whom this matter of creation-care, or ecological concern and action, is weak and neglected at best, and even rejected with hostile prejudice at worst. It seems to me that the reason for this is a very defective theology of creation among contemporary evangelicals. To put it bluntly, some people seem to have damaged Bibles, in which the first two and last two pages have got mysteriously torn off. They start at Genesis 3, because they know all about sin. And they end at Revelation 20, because they know all about the day of judgment.'[5] The sarcasm of Wright towards evangelicals who do not share his eco-theology is plain for all to see.

Wright's Common Word

An event that casts more light on Wright's theology occurred in 2007, when a large group of Muslim clerics sent a letter to Christian leaders entitled, *A Common Word between Us and You*. The Muslim letter urged followers of the two faiths to find common ground between Christianity and Islam. The Christian response entitled, *Loving God and Neighbor Together*, claimed that 'The Infinitely Good and All-Merciful One' (i.e. Allah) and the 'God of Scripture' are actually one and the same 'God of Love'.

In other words, Christians and Muslims worship the same God. Because of Christian sins against Islam, the letter declared that 'before we [Christians] "shake your hand" in responding to your letter, we ask forgiveness of the All-Merciful One and of the Muslim community around the world.' This Christian response, which can be viewed online, was a deeply heretical document. Yet both John Stott and Chris Wright signed it. The fact that Wright signed this letter tells us much about his view of the Christian Faith, for he actually affirmed in a public document, published in the *New York Times*, that Christians and Muslims worship the same God. Note the hypocrisy of Wright's position. To the evangelical world, he claims to be committed to taking the whole gospel to the whole world. Yet to the Muslim world he presents himself as a passionate supporter of interfaith dialogue, and has signed a letter affirming Muhammad as a prophet, and that says nothing about taking the gospel to the Muslim world.

Here we must note again that Wright's two books on missiology, referred to above, are massively influential in Bible seminaries around the world. We therefore need to understand what this British missiologist is teaching.

The Mission of God

In T*he Mission of God: Unlocking the Bible's Grand Narrative* (2006), a large book of over 500 pages, Chris Wright boldly claims that the entire Bible is all about 'God's mission'. It is an important book, for it represents a strand of thinking about mission that is now widely accepted across the evangelical world; and it is used by many theological seminaries, being one of the standard evangelical works on missiology. Wright's special contribution to missiology is his assertion, '*the whole Bible is itself a "missional" phenomenon*'[6.] He argues that '*our mission (if it is biblically informed and validated) means our committed participation as God's people, at God's invitation and command, in God's own mission within the history of God's world for the redemption of God's creation*'[7] (his italics).

Despite his emphasis on 'mission', Wright does not like the word 'missionary'. He writes: 'The term *missionary* still evokes images of white, Western expatriates among "natives" in far off countries—and it still does so all the more regrettably in churches that ought to know better... many mission agencies that now build networks and partnerships with majority world churches and agencies prefer to avoid the term missionary because of these unreconstructed mental images, and describe their personnel as "mission partners" instead.' According to Wright the offensive word 'missionary' is out, replaced by the more pleasing term 'mission partners'.[8]

He asserts that to correctly interpret the Bible, we need a 'missional hermeneutic'. He writes: 'Mission is what the Bible is all about; we could as meaningfully talk of the missional basis of the Bible as the biblical basis of mission.'[9] But he would have been more accurate about the way in which he interprets the Bible if he had written, 'Holistic mission is what the Bible is all about', and frankly stated that *The Mission of God* is based on a '*holistic* hermeneutic'.

Wright uses his missional hermeneutical perspective to provide what he regards to be a firm foundation for holistic mission. According to a blurb promoting the book: 'Wright emphasizes throughout a holistic mission as the proper shape of Christian mission. God's mission is to reclaim the world – and that includes the created order – and God's people have a designated role to play in that mission.'[10]

Wright states that a 'missional reading' of Scripture embraces 'liberation', claiming that a broadly missional reading of the whole Bible must necessarily subsume liberationist readings into itself. 'Where else does the passion for justice and liberation that breathes in these various theologies come from if not from the biblical revelation of the God who battles with injustice, oppression and bondage throughout history right to the eschaton?'[11]

He deals with the question of the primacy of evangelism: 'Even if we agree that biblical mission is intrinsically holistic and that Christians should be involved in the whole wide range of biblical imperatives— seeking justice, working for the poor and needy, preaching the gospel of Christ, teaching, healing, feeding, educating, and so forth—isn't it still the case that evangelism has primacy in all of this? Evangelism may not be the only thing we should do in mission, but isn't it the most important? Shouldn't it have priority over all else?'[12]

His answer is no! He takes a firm stand against those who see evangelism as primary: 'We are back to so exalting the New Testament evangelistic mandate that we think it absolves us from all other dimensions of God's mission that the rest of the Bible clearly requires of God's people. However, it is one thing to say (rightly) that we must engage in evangelism. It is another thing altogether to say (wrongly, as I have tried to argue) that evangelism is the only thing that constitutes engaging in mission.'[13]

He continues: 'The language of the "priority of evangelism" implies that the only proper starting point must always be evangelistic proclamation. Priority means it is the most important, most urgent, thing to be done first, and everything else must take second, third or fourth place.' Instead, 'we can enter the circle of missional response at any point on the circle of human need'.[14] In other words, Wright is content in practice for evangelism to be in fourth place.

Indeed: 'Mission may not always begin with evangelism. But mission that does not ultimately include declaring the Word and the name of Christ, the call to repentance, and faith and obedience has not completed its task. It is defective mission, not holistic mission.'[15] Here Wright is completely wrong. Mission that does not include declaring the Word and name of Christ is not defective, it is not mission at all—it has nothing to do with the Christian Faith.

Wright dismisses the argument that the best way to achieve social change is to evangelise. 'Then those who become Christians will do the social action part. I have often heard this as an argument for prioritizing evangelism over social action, and it sounds very plausible, but it has some serious flaws'. He boldly affirms: 'The logic is flawed because all those new Christians will, following the same advice, give time to evangelism, so who is going to be engaging in the social engagement side of mission?'

He asserts that simply preaching the gospel of salvation in Christ does not achieve social change. He mentions examples of 'where rapid conversion of whole communities to a pietistic gospel that sings the songs of Zion to come but demands no radical concern for the social, political, ethnic and cultural implications of the whole biblical faith here and now has led to massive and embarrassing dissonance between statistics and reality.'[16]

He gives the appalling Rwandan genocide of 1994 as an example. He refers to the tragic irony of Rwanda, which he sees as one of the most Christianized nations on earth and the birthplace of the East African Revival. 'And yet whatever form of Christian piety was taken to be the fruit of evangelism they could not stand against the tide of intertribal hatred and violence that engulfed the region in 1994. The blood of tribalism, it was said, was thicker than the water of baptism. Again, successful evangelism, flourishing revivalist spirituality and a majority Christian population did not result in a society where God's biblical values of equality, justice, love and nonviolence had taken root and flourished likewise.' This interpretation of the Rwandan genocide tells us much about Wright. He refers to Rwanda (a country I have visited on five occasion), as an example of a Christian country, although Roman Catholicism was the dominant religion, and biblical preaching was almost non-existent. Moreover, he fails to notice that the Catholic Church was implicated in the genocide. And so Wright begs 'to dissent from the notion that evangelism by itself will result in social change...'[17] What Rwanda needed was the Gospel of Truth and sound biblical teaching, not Wright's social, political, ethnic and environmental concerns.

Wright claims that the apostles in the early Church 'appointed people who would have as their priority the practical administration of food distribution to the needy'.[18] The implication is that the early Church organised a feeding programme for the world. But this is a wrong interpretation of the apostles' action in Acts. They appointed men to take care of food distribution among the *believers* so that they could devote their time and energy to preaching the gospel. Clearly the New Testament Church, unlike Wright, saw evangelism as primary and food distribution as secondary (Acts 6.1-6).

Contextual Theology

Wright draws a contrast between two approaches to reading the Bible text. The first approach is to read the Bible with the interests of particular groups of people in mind, like the poor and oppressed. This approach is supposed to help develop contextualized theologies that address the real needs of people. The second approach, which developed in the West, is one that claims to be objective and free from ideological interest. Wright refers to this approach pejoratively as 'the rather blinkered view of theology that developed in the West'. He says that theologies have emerged (he has liberal theologies in mind) 'that declare such disinterested objectivity to be a myth—and a dangerous one in that it concealed hegemonic claims. These theologies argue that contexts do matter, that the act of interpreting the Bible, the questions of who you are, where you are, and whom you live among as a reader make a difference. The Bible is to be read precisely in and for the context in which its message must be heard and appropriated. So these approaches to the Bible and theology came to be called "contextual theologies" within the Western academy. This term in itself betrayed the arrogant ethnocentricity of the West.' Wright says the West must be seen for what it is—'a particular context of human culture, not necessarily any better or any worse than any other context for reading the Bible and doing theology'.[19] At a stroke Wright has dismissed Western theology, such as the Westminster Confession of Faith (1647), the Baptist Confession of Faith (1689), the vast Puritan literature, the commentary of Matthew Henry and the sermons and writings of Charles Spurgeon, which have brought a deep understanding of the true Faith and great blessing to the life of the Church and individual believers far beyond the Western world.

He comments that many of the new contextual theologies 'arise from the conviction that it is fundamental to biblical faith to take a stand alongside the victims of injustice in any form. Thus the Bible is to be read with a liberationist hermeneutic—that is, with a concern to liberate people from oppression and exploitation... Theology was not to be done in the study and then applied in the world. Rather, action for and on behalf of the poor and oppressed was to be undertaken as a *first priority*, and then out of that commitment and praxis, theological reflection would follow' (my emphasis).

He mentions a number of contextual theologies that present a radical paradigm challenge to the standard Western way of doing theology. The aim of these contextual theologies is to intentionally 'read in interests of those they speak on behalf of—the poor, the outcasts, Blacks, women and so forth'.[20]

Wright continues his polemical argument by raising the missionary stereotype. Half in jest he writes: 'Given that missionaries in popular mythology are seen as the compromise adjuncts of colonialism and almost synonymous with Western arrogance and cultural totalitarianism, it might be more natural to propose a liberation theology from missionaries (which is what some radical forms of non-Western theology have in fact advocated).'[21]

Two aspects of Wright's missiology deserve to be highlighted. First, his deep commitment to contextualization. He is adamant that theology should not start in the Bible (the study), but with problems in the world. Clearly, he does not believe in the sufficiency of Scripture; he believes the Bible must be interpreted according to the priority needs of the people among whom we live. In his thinking it is fundamental to biblical faith to take a stand alongside victims of injustice and oppression, for their greatest need is political liberation. The second aspect of Wright's missiology that needs to be highlighted is his deep hostility to Western Christianity. He speaks easily of 'the arrogant ethnocentricity of the West'. He wants us to see the ministry of Western missionaries, supposedly with their roots in colonialism, as something of which the West should be ashamed. In his eyes the term *missionary* still evokes disparaging images of white, Western expatriates among 'natives' in far-off countries.

A Review by Pastor Mike Gilbart-Smith

Mike Gilbart-Smith, the Pastor of Twynholm Baptist Church in Fulham, London, has written a critique of Wright's book, published on the 9Marks website. 'Wright employs polemical language to dismiss those who see the "physical" model of the Exodus in the Old Testament fulfilled "spiritually" in the New. Within two pages they are accused of "press[ing] a spiritualized application of the exodus" and "airbrush[ing] the *socioeconomic* and political dimensions of the original historical event" (ital. his)... The Exodus is clearly picked up in the New Testament as a paradigm of our salvation from slavery to sin. Yet it is nowhere picked up as a mandate for Christian political and socioeconomic activism. On the contrary, Jesus insists that his disciples refuse political resistance because his kingdom is not of this world.'

He also makes the point that Wright 'insists on giving equal primacy to the political, economic, and social aspects of the Exodus, even though the Jesus of the Gospel records does not' – for the Lord Jesus came to preach (Mark 1.38), to call sinners to repentance, and to save his people from sin in a new exodus. 'Strangely, Wright describes this very emphasis on salvation from sin as a "spiritualizing" of the Old Testament (p276). In so doing, does he unwittingly end up choosing his own interpretation over Jesus?'

Gilbart-Smith perceptively notes that while Wright 'uses the Exodus as a central model for the mission of God, I fear that he has overlooked the central event in the Exodus, namely, the sacrifice of the Passover lamb and the sharing of the Passover meal. For Wright, Passover is seen purely as a reminder that God's redemption is social: God judges the genocidal Egyptians by destroying their own firstborn (p267). But the Passover lamb is strikingly absent from this description. Once we see the centrality of the lamb, we recognize that the Passover is a reminder first and foremost that those who are redeemed would fall under the same judgment as the enemies of God was it not for a substitutionary sacrifice. Yet Wright sees the Exodus as "decidedly not deliverance from their own sin" (p277)… The Exodus is a great model of New Testament redemption precisely because in it we see how God's people, though deserving of the same judgment as God's enemies, are redeemed through the sacrifice of a perfect substitute. This is why the New Testament presents Jesus as the Passover Lamb. Yet Wright seems to miss, or at best ignore, all this.'

He observes that Wright is reluctant to mention the dangers of hell. While heaven is mentioned frequently, hell is mentioned but once. 'And the one reference to hell says nothing about the importance of evangelism, but, ironically, simply warns those who do not care for the poor (p306).'

He concludes: 'Wright's conception of the gospel is as inclusive as his definition of mission. So, according to Wright, mission is not merely preaching the gospel, but also social, political and environmental action. And, according to Wright, the gospel itself is not merely the good news of salvation for sinners from the consequences of their sin: "Bluntly, we need a holistic gospel because the world is in a holistic mess." (p315).'[22]

Critique by Pastor Gary Millar

Gary Millar, Principal of Queensland Theological College in Brisbane, Australia, in a talk to The Gospel Coalition in 2013, declared, 'I think that *The Mission of God* contains key flaws; which if left unchallenged will lead to the dilution of the missionary efforts of the evangelical church across the world.'

Millar is concerned about Wright's reluctance to allow the New Testament to shape the way the Old Testament is read and interpreted. He is also concerned about Wright's contention that evangelism is ultimate but not primary. He is dismayed by Wright's weak doctrine of sin and judgement and the fact that the gospel is never clearly defined.

Millar concluded his talk with this devastating evaluation: 'If this book dominates evangelical and reformed thinking on mission for the next twenty or thirty years then where will we be? Very simple, my fear is that we will be in a place where there is no hell, no judgment, not really any hope for a cross. My fear is that no one will go anywhere, that no one will preach to anyone, that no one will actually care... I think it would be disastrous if we took our theology of mission from *The Mission of God*. That's why, however reluctantly, I agreed to do this critique. It's not so much what's in the book, as what's left out. And my fear is that if we leave out what's left out of *The Mission of God* then there will be no going, there will be no preaching because who would stand up and preach a gospel that may get us persecuted if there is an option, there will be no evangelism, there will be no hell, there will be no judgment, there will ultimately be no need for a cross. I do not want to overstate it but ultimately there would be no mission.'[23]

The Mission of God's People

Wright's second book on missiology entitled, *The Mission of God's People: A Biblical Theology of the Church's Mission* (2010), seeks to answer the question: 'What does the Bible as a whole in both testaments have to tell us about why the people of God exist and what it is they are supposed to be and do in the world? What is the mission of God's people?'[24] To explain the meaning of mission, Wright quotes John Stott: 'Mission arises from the heart of God himself, and is communicated from his heart to ours. Mission is the global outreach of the global people of a global God.'[25] Wright is clear that when he speaks of missions, he is thinking 'of the multitude of activities that God's people can engage in, by means of which they participate in God's mission… God's mission, we are told from the Bible, includes the whole of creation.'[26]

How does the mission of the Church in the New Testament relate to the identity of Old Testament Israel? Wright says that while most of us can relate to 'the so-called Great Commission and vaguely recall that it comes at the end of a gospel',[27] it was the Scriptures of the Old Testament that provided the motivation for the missional practices of the early Church. But Wright takes no account of the fact that the risen Christ appeared to the apostle Paul and said to him: 'But rise, and stand upon thy feet: for I have appeared unto thee for this purpose, to make thee a minister and a witness both of these things which thou hast seen, and of those things in the which I will appear unto thee; Delivering thee from the people, and from the Gentiles, unto whom now I send thee, to open their eyes, and to turn them from darkness to light, and from the power of Satan unto God, that they may receive forgiveness of sins, and inheritance among them which are sanctified by faith that is in me' (Acts 26.16-18). And the apostle was obedient to the commission he received from Christ, engaging in three missionary journeys. So the motivation for Paul's 'missional practices' came directly from his obedience to Christ's command, rather than a missional reading of the Old Testament.

Here we should notice Wright's dismissive attitude towards the, quote, 'so-called Great Commission'. His comment that his readers 'vaguely recall that it comes at the end of a gospel' infers that it is not really all that important. Wright even denies that the Great Commission was the major reason why the early Church was so missionary-minded. He says that the written record of Jesus' words was not in the hands of the early Church. 'I am not suggesting for a moment the Great Commission never happened, only that it is not referred to as an explicit driver for the missionary expansion of the church in the New Testament after Acts 1.'[28] But according to Scripture, the apostles had heard the following words of the Lord spoken in the Upper Room on the first Resurrection Sunday: 'that repentance and remission of sins should be preached in his name among all nations, beginning at Jerusalem' (Luke 24.47). The Lord promised that the Holy Spirit would lead them into all truth, and the apostle Paul was God's chosen vessel to preach Christ from Jerusalem to Rome. All these events simply confirmed the continuity between Old and New Testaments. For Wright to suggest that the Great Commission was unknown to the early Church because the words of the Lord Jesus were not yet written down is specious reasoning. The apostles and other evangelists of the period spread abroad in oral form all the words of the Lord and the events of his life, death and resurrection. They most definitely proclaimed the gospel and the Great Commission to all. But Wright does not like the attitude of those who believe 'that all you need is the Great Commission and the power of the Holy Spirit'.[29]

Wright explicitly critiques the idea that we should 'put individual salvation and personal evangelism at the centre of all our efforts'. He asserts that Paul's order of the gospel message in Ephesians and Colossians is creation, then Church, and then individual Gentile believers.[30] In dealing with the issue of the perceived division between evangelism and social action, Wright raises the question, 'Is the church's mission primarily the delivery of the message of the gospel—in which case the verbal element is all that really matters?'[31] To help us understand the gospel, he writes: 'One of the dangers with a word like "gospel" is that we all love it so much (rightly), and want to share it so passionately (rightly again) that we don't take time to explore its full biblical content... What did Jesus and Paul mean when they used it – particularly since, as I've already said, they had no New Testament to read to tell them.'[32] Wright says that if we go back to the Old Testament, 'Once again, we will find that the Bible itself will correct our tendency to reduce the gospel to a solution to our individual sin problem and a swipe card for heaven's door...'[33] This is amazing theology. Wright actually says that the Lord Jesus and Paul did not know the content of the New Testament Scriptures. But the Lord Jesus is the author of all Scripture and the apostle Paul wrote much of the New Testament! Again we must take note of Wright's dismissive approach to what he refers to as the problem of individual sin, and his sarcastic reference to a believer's eternal inheritance in Christ as 'a swipe card to heaven's door'. Does Wright actually understand or care about the Gospel of Truth?

According to Wright the text of Exodus portrays 'at least four dimensions of the bondage that Israel suffered in Egypt – political, economic, social and spiritual – and goes on to show how God redeemed them in every one of these dimensions… The exodus, then, as a model of redemption is part of the biblical foundation for the holistic understanding of mission that seems to me to be demanded from a holistic reading of the Bible.' So Wright uses the Exodus as a model to justify his holistic approach to mission; saying we should avoid the temptation 'to spiritualize its meaning into merely an Old Testament "picture" of personal deliverance from the power of sin.'[34]

His reasoning is that just as the Exodus had political, economic, social, and spiritual dimensions, so too God's act of redemption in the Cross of Christ has the exact same breadth. He asserts: 'The exodus has been seen as the biblical foundation par excellence for theologies of mission that emphasize the importance of social, political, and economic concern alongside the spiritual dimensions of personal forgiveness. Or rather, and with greater biblical faithfulness, it is the biblical basis for the integration of all these dimensions within the comprehensive good news of the biblical gospel. Such holistic, or integral, understandings of mission point to the totality of what God accomplished for Israel in the paradigmatic redemptive event—the exodus. And I believe they are right to do so.'[35]

Author Bobby Jamieson, a Ph.D. student in New Testament at the University of Cambridge, has posted a review of *The Mission of God's People* on the 9Marks website.[36] He concludes: 'Wright's application of his "holistic" understanding of the exodus to the New Testament obscures the New Testament's emphasis on redemption as forgiveness of sins and reconciliation to God… That Wright articulates a view of the exodus which doesn't align with the New Testament's use of exodus imagery betrays a basic methodological error. That is, Wright fails to allow the New Testament authors' interpretations of the Old Testament to properly influence his.'

Jamieson's critique hits the mark. Wright has adopted a holistic hermeneutic to support his flawed missiology. It is not difficult to see that he does all he can to downplay the importance of the Great Commission. His indifference to the doctrine of salvation from sin is a feature of his writings.

Conclusion

Wright's mission is to develop and promote the holistic agenda of his mentor John Stott. His missiology is characterised by a great commitment to saving the earth from what he sees as an impending environmental disaster. He believes that capitalism is a major cause of climate change, and yet he has little to say about the enormous benefits that have come from the market economy. His environmental agenda is virtually the same as that of the present Pope, Francis 1. Throughout his writings he downplays the importance of preaching the gospel of salvation from sin, while promoting a wide spectrum of socio-political action. He is adamant that evangelism should not be a primary ministry of the Church, for that would mean that all other good works are secondary. He is strangely dismissive of Western Christianity, despite the fact that Western missionaries took the gospel to China, India, the Far East in general, the Pacific Islands, South America and Africa, at enormous personal cost and because the love of Christ constrained them, willingly enduring great suffering for the sake of the gospel.

Wright's two most influential books on missiology, widely studied in seminaries at home and abroad, present a distorted model for mission. The critique of Gary Millar hit the mark: 'I think it would be *disastrous* if we took our theology of mission from *The Mission of God*… there will be no evangelism, there will be no hell, there will be no judgment, there will ultimately be no need for a cross' (my italics). Wright's contention that the Bible is to be read always with the intention of addressing cultural, social and political problems, and that theology must always start with the context of human problems, robs God's Word of its power to act as the unchanging, authoritative and sufficient pattern and mandate for mission in all centuries and in all cultures. Without this bedrock understanding, we are left only with men's ever-shifting opinions, in this case Wright's holistic, socio-political substitute for the true gospel.

In the next chapter we explore the full-blown concept of contextualization.

(Endnotes)

1 Christopher Wright, 'Mission and God's Earth', from *Perspectives on the World Christian Movement*, fourth edition, edited by Ralph Winter and Steven Hawthorne, William Carey Library, p30

2 Ibid. p32

3 Ibid. p32

4 The *Cape Town Commitment*, The Third Lausanne Congress on World Evangelization 16-25 October 2010, p181

5 Integral Mission and the Great Commission, 'The Five Marks of Mission', Chris Wright International Ministries Director Langham Partnership, p17, http://www.loimission.net/wp-content/uploads/2014/03/Chris-Wright-IntegralMissionandtheGreatCommission.pdf

6 Christopher Wright, *The Mission of God: Unlocking the Bible's Grand Narrative*, (Downers Grove: IVP Academic, 2006), introduction, p22

7 *The Mission of God*, pp22-23,

8 *The Mission of God*, p24

9 *The Mission of God*, p29

10 *The Mission of God,* promotional blurb, http://www.amazon.com/Mission-God-Unlocking-Bibles-Narrative/dp/0830825711

11 *The Mission of God*, p44

12 *The Mission of God*, p316

13 *The Mission of God*, p317

14 *The Mission of God*, p318

15 *The Mission of God*, p319

16 *The Mission of God*, p320

17 *The Mission of God*, p321

18 *The Mission of God*, p322

19 *The Mission of God*. p42

20 *The Mission of God*, p43

21 *The Mission of God*, p43

22 Book Review: *The Mission of God*, by Christopher Wright, 9Marks website: review by Mike Gilbart-Smith, http://9marks.org/review/mission-god/

23 Missio Dei website, Gary Millar's Evaluation of Christopher J. H. Wright – Outline, http://keithwalters.org/2013/07/02/gary-millars-evaluation-of-christopher-j-h-wright-outline/

24 Christopher Wright, *The Mission of God's People*: A Biblical Theology of the

Church's Mission, Zondervan, 2010, Preface, p24

25 *The Mission of God's People*, p24, citing John Stott in *The Contemporary Christian* p335

26 *The Mission of God's People*, pp25, 27

27 *The Mission of God's People,* p29

28 *The Mission of God's People*, p36

29 *The Mission of God's People*, p39

30 *The Mission of God's People*, p273

31 *The Mission of God's People*, p30

32 *The Mission of God's People*, p31

33 *The Mission of God's People*, p31

34 *The Mission of God's People*, pp101, 102

35 *The Mission of God's People*, p109

36 Book Review of *The Mission of God's People*, posted on the 9Marks website by Bobby Jamieson, a Ph.D. student in New Testament at the University of Cambridge, posted October 2010, http://9marks.org/review/mission-gods-people/

Chapter 18

Contextualizing the Gospel

The term 'contextualization' was introduced into missiological thinking by Shoki Coe, General Director of the Theological Education
Fund of the World Council of Churches (WCC), when he coined the
term in the 1972 annual report of the Education Fund. Since then the
term has increasingly become part of missiological thinking. After
the Uppsala Assembly of 1968, the mandate of the WCC was transformed so that nearly all WCC projects were in some way concerned
with developing 'contextual theologies'. By the mid-1970s, the idea
of contextualization was closely associated with the development of
liberation theology. Such was the interest in the opportunities generated by this new way of doing theology that the January 1978 issue
of *Evangelical Missions Quarterly*, published by the Billy Graham
Center for Evangelism at Wheaton College, was devoted entirely to
the issue of contextualization.

Prominent missiologist Dr Ed Stetzer, visiting Professor of Missiology at Trinity Evangelical Divinity School, seeks to explain the
importance of contextualization. In *Christianity Today* he writes:
'Contextualization involves an attempt to present the Gospel in a
culturally relevant way. For this reason, discussions about contextualization are connected to discussions about the nature of human
culture; we cannot separate the two.' He says that discussions about
culture are unavoidable, for all people live in a culture of some sort.
'A failure to understand this point can actually lead to a form of cultural imperialism. A person might begin to believe that his culture's
way of practicing Christianity is the only way to practice Christianity.
Should such a person begin to minister in a different culture, he will
inadvertently share not only the Gospel but also his cultural traditions.

This action would be unhelpful; it would try to force a distant culture onto potential converts.'[1]

There is no doubt that 'contextualization' is a fluid word that means different things to different people. South African missiologist, David Bosch, author of *Transforming Mission: Paradigm Shifts in Theology of Mission* (1991), refers to contextualization as a 'blanket term for a variety of theological models'.[2] Baptist theologian Richard W. Engle, in his paper 'Contextualization in Missions', points out that liberals apparently gave birth to the word and associated it with socio-economic unrest. 'They may use the terms basic to classic fundamentalism in connection with "contextualization", but they empty those terms of their biblical and orthodox meanings and infuse them with new meanings.'[3]

Dr. Richard J. Gehman, who was Principle of Scott Theological College in Kenya for eight years, writes in *Guidelines in Contextualization*: 'But what often passes for a contextualized theology falls short of biblical theology. It is beyond dispute that contextualization, as defined by many, is not rooted in Scripture. You begin with the context, understand the particular revolutionary situation where you are, and then later connect this with some "theological motif". What we have is a political ideology in the garb of Christianity with no vital relationship with the heart of Scripture.'[4]

The WCC was active in spreading contextual theology to many countries in the Third World. In *Revolution or Reconciliation?* (1992), Rachel Tingle, a British economist, documents how the WCC, in order to develop a theological justification for its Programme to Combat Racism, enthusiastically encouraged work on the contextualization of theology (see chapter 9).

Tingle explains: 'The contextualisation of theology is a term used to describe a general approach to theology which is fundamentally different from that of orthodox Christian theology. Traditionally, theology has as its starting point the Bible... Orthodox theology seeks to discover and present truths about God and about God's dealing with the human race. These truths are eternal and universal... By contrast, contextual theology is deeply relativistic; it is also essentially humanistic, focusing on man rather than God... Contextual theology's starting point, both in terms of its chronological development and in terms of its general methodology, is not the Bible or the historic teaching of the Church, but is, rather, an active commitment to "liberation" from some oppression.'[5]

Tingle continues: 'The first act of theology is thus a historical praxis – that is, some experience of political oppression and a political action, often of a revolutionary nature, designed to liberate the oppressed. The second act, in the contextual approach to theology, is a *critical reflection* on this action in the light of the Bible or Catholic faith. The result of this is a highly selective reading of the Bible, which make use only of those passages (typically the Exodus of the Israelites from their slavery in Egypt, the Magnificat and Luke 4: 18-19) which might be interpreted in such a way as to show God's support for "liberating" political action' (Tingle's italics).[6]

In the 1980s the Central Committee of the WCC called for more contextualization of theology in order to produce a theology that would help to transform society. Discussions tended to focus on socio-political issues and were often careless in the use of Scripture. A particular feature of the dialogue was the notion that Western Christianity and its theology is problematic because of its association with colonialism and imperialism.

Contextualization plays an important part in the thinking of most missiologists. Although the term means different things to different people, and although there is no clear definition of the term, it forms an important building block for the discipline of missiology. A key point is that contextualization always starts with a political problem, usually some form of oppression (that is the context), and then seeks biblical texts to justify the proposed solution to the problem.

Charles Kraft

Dr. Charles H. Kraft, Professor of Anthropology and Intercultural Communication at Fuller Seminary School of Intercultural Studies, has been one of the most influential voices in missiology. His book, *Christianity in Culture* (1979), suggested 'dynamic equivalence' (a method of biblical and general translation which tends to employ a more colloquial rendering but with less literal accuracy) to New Testament models as the appropriate approach to contextualisation. He believes revelation to be subjective and continuing.[7] To Kraft the Bible is only potentially the Word of God: 'The Scriptures are like the ocean and supra-cultural truth like the icebergs that float in it.'[8] He is author of a number of articles in the fourth edition of the standard missiology text book, *Perspectives on the World Christian Movement* (2009). In 1979 Charles Kraft and Harvie Conn, Professor of Missions at Westminster Theological Seminary, published important articles on the nature of Muslim culture and new ways to follow Christ. In 1982 Kraft became an early proponent of the 'power evangelism' ministry model of John Wimber and helped popularise the 'Third Wave of the Holy Spirit' movement. He is deeply involved with the charismatic movement and was the Founder and President of Deep Healing Ministries. He has conducted seminars around the world on what he calls Deep Level Healing, Deliverance and Spiritual Warfare.

Mission to Muslims

Charles Kraft, who had been teaching at Fuller Seminary since 1971, is one of the architects of the so-called Insider Movement (IM), that teaches that a Muslim can come to saving faith in God while remaining within the culture of Islam. David Garner, Associate Professor of Systematic Theology at Westminster Seminary, has traced 'one important strand of Insider Movement back to the laboratories of Fuller Seminary, specifically to the work of Donald McGavran and Charles Kraft, who brought together the emerging field of cultural anthropology on the one hand with a renewed call for world evangelization on the other. They thus redefined the task of missions using the categories of social science. From this starting point, Insider Movement advocates "have found ways to affirm a broader range of religious and cultural neutrality".' Garner comments on how this social-science orientation is shaping how the Scriptures are being read and interpreted—with, quote, 'devastating consequences'.[9]

Philip Mark, who has spent most of his life among missionaries and institutions dedicated to reaching Muslims with the gospel writes: 'Whether we follow this IM hermeneutic downstream as Garner does, or whether we start with the monstrosities that I have observed down-river and work our way upstream, the conclusion is the same.' Here he quotes Garner: 'In bequeathing ultimate authority to cultural analysis,

Insider Movement advocacy has redefined the content and the conduct of the gospel, as well as the means to advance this "gospel." And in it all, this redefinition has made such a "gospel" biblically unrecognizable.'[10]

One of the first evangelical proponents of radical ideas of contextualization in the Muslim world was Charles Kraft. In 1974 he spoke to a group of mission leaders gathered in Marseille, France for a consultation concerning the best approach to reaching Muslims for Christ. He told the missionaries that a Muslim doesn't have to be convinced of the death of Christ. 'He simply has to pledge allegiance and faith to the God who worked out the details to make it possible for his faith response to take the place of a righteousness requirement. He may not, in fact, be able to believe in the death of Christ, especially if he knowingly places his faith in God through Christ, for within his frame of reference, if Christ died, God was defeated by men, and this, of course, is unthinkable... He simply has to pledge in faith as much of himself as he can to as much of God as he understands, even the Muslim "Allah"... The principle here is that a fraction of the truth well communicated is preferable to the antagonism engendered when a whole truth is totally rejected...'[11]

Commenting on Kraft's speech, Robertson McQuilkin, President of Columbia Bible College, wrote: 'Kraft goes on to quote several scholars, who are considered evangelical, to the effect that people can be saved without a knowledge of Christ... He clearly indicated that a Muslim can be saved without a conviction of sin and without accepting the death of Christ as historically true. It would seem that for a Muslim to be saved all he would need was a consciousness of inadequacy and a sincere calling upon Allah to save him.'[12]

Kraft said to the mission leaders at Marseille that they needed to redouble their efforts in order 'to assist in the raising up of a people of God who are genuinely saved by faith but who remain culturally Arab or North African'.[13] To remain fully culturally Arab, however, means remaining within the confines of Islamic culture, which is an expression of the teaching of the Qur'an—culture and mosque are largely synonymous. Kraft said, 'I would press hard for a faith relationship with God and for a faith renewal movement starting within Islam as a culture, based on the faith of Abraham... pointing to the Qur'an, the Old Testament and the New Testament as sources of our information concerning this faith, and issuing in a renewal and a distinct People of God, who retain their Muslim cultural allegiance, worship forms and self-respect. I would press further for this faith renewal movement to use *all three books* as its basis' (my emphasis).[14]

Kraft defended the right for converts from Islam to create their own theology: 'The more he accommodates his theology to the cultural expectations of Western churches, the less likely he is to be able to effectively witness to his own people… It raises the spectre that he may have to be theologically heretical to communicate to his own people.'[15]

Christianity in Culture

First published in 1979, Charles Kraft's *Christianity in Culture* celebrated its twenty-fifth anniversary in 2004 with a new edition that includes updated themes. According to the book's blurb, 'Long a staple in evangelical seminaries, Kraft's work has a deep understanding of anthropology and its impact on Christian witness. This book helps you identify cultural baggage that stifles the gospel and interpret any culture you're in – in order to mold others into disciples.' In the preface, Kraft reminds readers that he has been teaching a course on the relationship between Christianity and culture at Fuller Seminary since 1971. 'These have been advanced courses in the contextualization of Christianity, presupposing at least an elementary exposure to both theology and anthropology… The year 1979 is a long time ago. But people are still buying and using this book. *Christianity in Culture* is now in its eighteenth reprinting. When I wrote the book, I never anticipated such longevity.'

Missiologist Paul Hiebert wrote the foreword to the twenty-fifth anniversary edition: 'Charles Kraft's *Christianity in Culture* marks one such paradigm shift in missiology. Drawing widely on his expertise in linguistics and on his extensive field experience in Africa, Kraft raised new questions, and reframed the debate on the cross-cultural communication and contextualization of the gospel. He introduced new methods of analysis that have altered the debate in the field of missiology.'

Kraft's book was severely criticised by Edward Gross in *Is Charles Kraft an Evangelical?* (1985). Gross questioned whether Kraft could still be considered an evangelical since 'he, evidently, does not appreciate the irreconcilable differences between Christianity and anthropology'.[16]

Carl Henry's Critique

In 1980, Carl Henry wrote the article, 'The Cultural Relativizing of Revelation' in the *Trinity Journal*, which offered a devastating critique of Kraft's *Christianity in Culture*. He is concerned with Kraft's insistence that our ideas of the Christian Faith must change as society changes. Henry's article included the following: 'Kraft indicates that no universal criteria are applicable to all cultures and that each culture is valid only for its own participants. None can be regarded as final, and no transcendently absolute criterion is allowed to judge any. Kraft declares this belief in the validity of other cultures to be the equivalent in anthropology of the Golden Rule in theology.'[17]

Henry continues: 'Kraft's assumptions provide no basis for regarding any culture as either superior or inferior to any other.' And 'Scriptural teachings are devalued as culturally conditioned, while modern communication theories are assimilated to the revelation of the Spirit.' Rev Ralph Allan Smith, who has served as a missionary in Japan since 1981 and pastors Mitaka Evangelical Church, offers this evaluation: 'The radical cultural relativism of Kraft's approach is apparent. Henry's trenchant evaluation of Kraft should have been more than enough of a warning to evangelical theologians and missionaries to beware the quicksand of cultural relativism.'[18]

The real concern about *Christianity in Culture* is that it has placed man-made culture, which changes over time, above Scripture, which is God's eternal and unchanging truth. Kraft's idea of a moral equivalence between all cultures is wildly wide of the mark. Scripture does not teach a moral equivalence between the pagan culture of Canaanite tribes that worship Molech and practise child sacrifice and temple prostitution, and God's people, Israel, who were given God's moral law on Mount Sinai. Cultures based on ancestor and spirit worship place enormous spiritual power in the hands of the witch doctor or shaman, and are clearly not morally equivalent to Western culture, that over many centuries has been influenced and shaped by the teaching of the Bible and the Christian Faith.

Kraft's essay entitled, 'Culture, Worldview and Contextualization', published in *Perspectives on the World Christian Movement* (2009), (Ralph Winter's 700-page manual on missiology that contains writings from more than 100 mission scholars), expresses concern that we have 'continually reverted to the assumption that becoming Christian means becoming like us culturally'. The result is that 'missionaries may be tempted to replace traditional religion with the religious forms of Western Christianity'.[19] He says that 'the contextualization of Christianity is not simply to be the passing on of a product that has been developed once for all in Europe or America... Though many non-Western churches today are dominated by Western approaches to doctrine and worship, it is not scriptural that they remain so.' Kraft concludes that the quest 'for a vital, dynamic, biblical, contextualized Christianity will require experimenting with new culturally and biblically appropriate ways of understanding... To this end the insights of anthropologists into culture and world worldview can be harnessed to enable us to advocate a Christianity that is truly contextualized, truly relevant and truly meaningful.'[20]

Paul Hiebert

Paul Hiebert served as a missionary in India, and then taught anthropology at Fuller Theological Seminary. He later became Chairman of the Department of Mission and Evangelism and Professor of Mission and Anthropology at Trinity Evangelical Divinity School. He is one of the most influential and most eloquent advocates of contextualization, and has four articles in the fourth edition of *Perspectives*.

In the 1980s Dr Paul Hiebert wrote his first article on the subject of 'Critical Contextualization'. The article was regarded as such an important contribution to the discipline of missiology that it was later published by *Christianity Today* in its 'Best in Theology series'. In the article Hiebert argued that Protestant missionaries from roughly the 1850s to the 1950s rejected all the old cultural practices as pagan, and did not understand the need for contextualizing the gospel message. This missionary rejection of the old primitive cultures resulted in the widespread idea that Christianity was a Western religion. Hiebert also criticises what he describes as 'uncritical contextualization', namely a new way of thinking among anthropologists, that affirmed the good in all cultures, and claimed that no culture was superior to any other. This anthropological 'wisdom' opened the pathway to what Hiebert calls 'critical contextualization', which requires a study of the old culture that is then evaluated against Scripture.

Hiebert ends his article with these words: 'Critical contextualization… seeks to find meta-cultural and meta-theological frameworks that enable people in one culture to understand messages and ritual practices from another culture with a minimum of distortion. It… sees all human knowledge as a combination of objective and subjective elements, and as partial but increasingly closer approximations of truth… Finally, it sees contextualization as an ongoing process in which the church must constantly engage itself, a process that can lead us to a better understanding of what the Lordship of Christ and the kingdom of God on earth are about.'[21]

Trinity Journal sums up Hiebert's contribution. 'Critical contextualization has served as a tool for missionaries and national leaders as they have sought to express biblical meanings in cultural forms… Hiebert integrated anthropology, theology and missiology into a contextual methodology. His experiences as a missionary in India enabled him to combine anthropological principles with missionary practice in the service of the church… His "critical contextualization" has become a basic framework for doing theology and mission in a globalizing world.'[22]

Hiebert outlines his approach in the essay, 'The Gospel in Human Contexts: Changing Perceptions of Contextualization', published in *Missionshift* (2010). He is concerned that many Americans 'fail to recognize that many of the assumptions and values that underlie our culture are not biblical… As Christians, we are often unaware that we are shaped more by our contexts than the gospel.' Missionaries he says, 'are forced to deal with socio-cultural differences and, therefore, with social and cultural contexts'.[23] He argues that a 'full analysis of missions must take social, historical, personal and other contexts into account'. He describes a model 'to help us understand ourselves, to understand the history of the modern mission movement in which missionaries from Europe and North America went to the ends of the earth, and to learn from past experiences'.[24]

When missionaries enter another culture they encounter deep differences and experience religious shock. 'We meet Muslims and Hindus who are good people, often better than some of the Christians we know…

How can we say they are lost? Why are we Christians? Was it a matter of conviction or of birth and upbringing?'[25] Missionaries are forced to deal with cultural differences. 'The more we live with and study the people we serve, the more we become aware of the depth and power of the people's culture and the need to contextualize both the messenger and the message for them to understand and live the gospel; but we are afraid that this can distort the gospel, so it must be done minimally... We see other cultures as primitive or evil, with little to contribute to our understanding of reality.'[26]

Hiebert emphasises the important role of anthropology in understanding primitive cultures. 'After the 1930s anthropologists began to realize the importance of understanding the world as the people they studied see it, seeking to understand culture like an insider. This change in perspective led to a profound shift in the nature of anthropological and missiological theories... The growing awareness of anthropological insights into human contexts leads in missions to a growing awareness of the importance of radically contextualizing the gospel in other contexts so that the people can understand the gospel and become followers of Jesus Christ.'[27]

Hiebert is clear that 'the gospel must be put in specific socio-cultural contexts for people to understand it. To do so we must study Scripture and humans and build a bridge between them. This process is doing missional theology.'[28] To study humans in their context, church leaders and missionaries 'can draw on human studies, such as anthropology, sociology, psychology, history, and the humanities'. He says, 'anthropology can help because it has sought to develop trans-cultural frameworks...'[29]

It helps us to understand Hiebert's model when we realise that he saw Western cultural arrogance as a problem. In *Missiology* (1991), he wrote: 'The anti-colonial reaction was a necessary corrective. It called into question Western cultural arrogance, and it forced Western Christians to differentiate between the gospel and their culture.'[30] Hiebert's critical contextualization model is based on an anthropological understanding of cultures. The claim is that the gospel needs to be radically contextualised to each culture to make it understandable. But the great danger is that in doing so the gospel message is changed to make it culturally relevant. But God's Word and the Cross of Calvary stand above culture, as they make an appeal to the heart and mind of sinful man. We do well to remember that God's Word not only stands above culture, but also stands in judgement over culture. The real effect of contextualization is to distort the message of salvation by removing the offence of the Cross.

The Lausanne Committee for World Evangelization

In January 1978 the Lausanne working group on 'Gospel and Culture' brought together a group of theologians, anthropologists, linguists, missionaries and pastors from all six continents. The group aimed to identify the tools required for more adequate communication of the gospel.

As John Stott later said, cross-cultural messengers of the gospel needed to address the question: 'How can I, having been born and raised in one culture, take the gospel from Scripture which was written in other cultures, and communicate it to people in a third culture, without either distorting the message or rendering it unintelligible?'[31]

The outcome was a Lausanne Occasional Paper, referred to as the Willowbank Report (discussed in chapter 13). Cultural barriers to the communication of the gospel were identified: 'No Christian witness can hope to communicate the gospel if he or she ignores the cultural factor... the gospel is often presented to people in alien cultural forms. Then the missionaries are resented and their message rejected because their work is seen not as an attempt to evangelize but as an attempt to impose their own customs and way of life. Where missionaries bring with them foreign ways of thinking and behaving, or attitudes of racial superiority, paternalism, or preoccupation with material things, effective communication will be precluded.'

Behind the Willowbank report was a strong anti-Western bias. Missionaries from Western countries were labelled as imperialists with attitudes of racial superiority. The Report was deeply concerned that some missions, having accepted the need for indigenous leadership, recruited and trained 'local leaders, indoctrinating them (the word is harsh but not unfair) in Western ways of thought and procedure'.[32]

David Bosch

David Bosch, Professor of Missiology at the University of South Africa, Pretoria, published in 1991, *Transforming Mission: Paradigm Shifts in Theology of Mission*. This large book, which was received with great enthusiasm by the American Society of Missiology, has transformed the thinking of many about the Church's mission. According to John Roxborogh of the Presbyterian School of Ministry, Dunedin, New Zealand, by the time of Bosch's death a mere year later in 1992, *Transforming Mission* was on its way to becoming the classic text of missiology. 'Bosch had succeeded in providing a comprehensive theoretical framework for missiology that rose above the polarities of his generation. Ten years later *Transforming Mission* has been translated into 11 languages and continues to sell at a significant rate. Practically everywhere missiology is taught, *Transforming Mission* is the standard working document.'[33]

In *Transforming Mission*, Bosch claims he has identified a major twentieth-century crisis in the mission of the Church. He argues that the association between mission, colonialism and Western superiority produced unsatisfactory missionary practices. He says that because of complicity in the subjugation and exploitation of, quote, 'people of colour', Western Christians tend to suffer from an acute sense of guilt. Because the world is divided into rich and poor, and because, by and large, the rich are those who consider themselves Christian, this has created anger and frustration among the poor and 'reluctance among affluent Christians to share their faith'. For centuries Western theology and practices were normative in the mission fields. But today 'the younger churches refuse to be dictated to'. In addition, Western theology is today suspect in many parts of the world and being replaced by Third-World theologies, such as, liberation theology, black theology, contextual theology, African theology and Asian theology.[34] He appeared to have a low view of Western missionaries, for he wrote: 'British missionaries, let me reiterate, were as racist as Germans, not least because of the influence of "social Darwinism". And those from other Western countries were hardly any better.'[35]

The thesis of Bosch's book is that these changes are 'the result of a fundamental paradigm shift, not only in mission and theology, but in the experience and thinking of the whole world'.[36] Bosch argued that the paradigm of mission which prevailed in the nineteenth and twentieth centuries, that is, the ministry of Western missionaries, had run its course. What was needed was no longer a missionary movement 'from the West to the rest', but rather 'from everywhere to everyone'. Bosch attempted to define mission: 'Mission is not primarily the mission of the church... but an attribute of God. God is a missionary God ... Mission is thereby seen as a movement from God to the world; the church is viewed as an instrument for that mission... To participate in mission is to participate in the movement of God's love toward people, since God is a fountain of sending love... The *missio Dei* is God's activity, which embraces both the church and the world, and in which the church may be privileged to participate.'[37]

He concludes his large book with comments on what he calls the 'Emerging Ecumenical Missionary Paradigm', and focuses on topics such as the *missio Dei*, justice, evangelism, contextualization and liberation. He inclined to the view that mission includes much more than evangelism and salvation. He believed that God's mission in the world includes social and other aspects of Christian witness. He wrote: 'We do need a more radical and comprehensive hermeneutic of mission... Mission is a multifaceted ministry, in respect of witness, service, justice, healing, reconciliation, liberation, peace, evangelism, fellowship, church planting, contextualization, and much more.'[38]

In a discussion on the meaning of the Cross of Christ, Bosch writes: 'The scars of the risen Lord not only prove Jesus' identity, however, they also constitute a model to be emulated by those whom he commissions: "As the Father has sent me, even so I send you" (Jn 20.21). It's a mission of self-emptying, of humble service... The cross also stands for reconciliation between estranged individuals and groups, between oppressor and oppressed. Reconciliation does not mean a mere sentimental harmonizing of conflicting groups. It demands sacrifice, in very different but also in very real ways, from oppressor and oppressed. It demands the end to oppression and injustice and commitment to a new life of mutuality, justice and peace.'[39]

Bosch comments: 'Mission is, quite simply, the participation of Christians in the liberating mission of Jesus, wagering on a future that verifiable experience seems to believe. It is the good news of God's love, incarnated in the witness of a community, for the sake of the world.'[40] Professor Pieter Verster, Head of the Department of Missiology at the University of the Free State, Bloemfontein, South Africa, comments on *Transforming Mission*.[41] He says that important aspects discussed by Bosch are inculturation and contextualization. Although Bosch emphasises respect for culture and the meaning of contextualization, 'he tends to lean towards the premises of liberation theology. The way in which the gospel is brought to people must therefore be seen against the background of liberation. Bosch carefully steers away from a one-sided approach, but nevertheless he is of the opinion that liberation is the way in which God's salvation surfaces in inculturation and contextualization... Salvation must therefore be seen in a total light. Salvation is "comprehensive", "total" and "universal". He sees the role of the church as a comprehensive role to change the situation in which people are exploited and undermined to a situation in which they can experience true life with and of Christ... However, it is not clear from Bosch's use of the term that he specifically emphasises redemption from sin in Jesus Christ as *focus of salvation*' (Verster's italics).[42]

Verster quotes the work of Dutch theologian C.J. Haak on Bosch's use of Scripture. Verster writes that Haak shows that Bosch 'tends to delete the important way of salvation, atonement and reconciliation through the cross. He even accuses Bosch of postulating his own view of Jesus. Concerning the poor, Haak issues a strong warning against Bosch's interpretation of the poor and the heathen. He [Haak] is of the opinion that even the poor are in need of reconciliation in Christ and that salvation is for both rich and poor... Haak is of the opinion that Bosch uses the wrong starting point in his exegesis and is thus misled into proclaiming a gospel that does not accord with the essence of Scripture. He states that the use of higher criticism misled Bosch. Haak also states that Bosch omitted very important aspects of mission, namely the conversion of the heathen and the planting of the church.'[43]

Conclusion

Christians need to use spiritual discernment to evaluate every new theological idea that emerges. 'Contextualization' never has been, and never should be, considered a true theological word. Indeed, the concept of contextualization is a subtle way of introducing heretical ideas into the Christian Faith. Yet again we see a man-made reconstruction of biblical mission and a reliance on human wisdom. Despite the impressive array of intellectual reasoning and research, the concept of contextualization is fundamentally flawed, because the gospel is the trans-cultural product of divine wisdom.

Our next chapter describes the great celebration of the modern holistic mission movement to mark the centenary of the Edinburgh World Missionary Conference of 1910.

(Endnotes)

1   *Christianity Today*, Ed Stetzer, 'What is Contextualization? Presenting the Gospel in Culturally Relevant Ways', 12 October 2014

2   David J. Bosch, *Transforming Mission: Paradigm Shifts in Theology of Mission* (Maryknoll, New York, 1991), p421.

3   Richard W. Engel, 'Contextualization in Missions: A Biblical and Theological Appraisal, Grace Theological Journal 4.1, 1993, p100

4   Guidelines in Contextualization, Richard J Gehman, biblicalstudies.org.uk/pdf/ ajet/02-1_024.pdf

5   Rachel Tingle, *Revolution or Reconciliation?*, Christian Studies Centre, 1992, p53-4

6   *Revolution or Reconciliation*, p54

7   Charles H Kraft, *Christianity and Culture*, Orbis Books, 1979, p184

8   *Christianity and Culture*, p131

9   Article 'Insider Movements - Gutting the Bible', by Philip Mark, June 2013, in Reformation 21 website, at: http://www.reformation21.org/articles/insider-movements-gutting-the-bible.php#sthash.GQeFm90N.dpuf

10   Ibid

11   C. Kraft, 'Distinctive Religious Barriers to Outside Penetration', Report on Consultation on Islamic Communication Held at Marseille, 1974, p70, cited from *Journal of the Evangelical Theological Society*, The Behavioural Sciences under the Authority of Scripture, J. Robertson McQuilkin, p40,

12   Ibid. Robertson McQuilkin, p40

13   Charles Kraft, 'Guidelines for Developing Message Geared to Horizon of Receptivity' (Marseille, 19 February 1974), pp. 5, 9. (A transcript of a lecture from the Archives of the Billy Graham Center at Wheaton College, Collection 86, Box 27, Folder 28.)

14   Ibid. pp. 10-11.

15   Ibid. p. 6.

16   Edward N. Gross, *Is Charles Kraft an Evangelical?* A Critique of *Christianity in Culture* (published by the author, 1985), p101

17   Cited from essay 'Worldviews and Culture: Interacting with Charles Kraft, N. T. Wright, & Scripture', by Rev Ralph Allan Smith, http://www.berith.org/essays/worldviews_culture/02.html

18   Ibid.

19   Charles H. Kraft, 'Culture, Worldview and Contextualization', *Perspectives* chapter 64, pp402-403

20   Ibid. 'Culture, Worldview and Contextualization', pp404-405

21   Paul G. Hiebert, article 'Critical Contextualization', in International Bulletin of Missionary Research, July 1987

22   'Paul G. Hiebert and Critical Contextualization', Eunhye Chang, Rupert Morgan, Timothy Nyasula, Robert Priest, *Trinity Journal*, 2009, pp199-207, http://hiebertglobalcenter.org/wp-content/uploads/2014/04/199_Chang_Critical-Contextualization.pdf

23   *Missionshift: Global Mission Issues in the Third Millennium*, edited by David Hesselgrave and Ed Stetzer, B&H Publishing Group, 2010, Paul Hiebert essay, 'The Gospel in Human Contexts', p83

24   *Missionshift*, p84

25   *Missionshift*, p87

26   *Missionshift*, p88

27   *Missionshift*, p90

28   *Missionshift*, p95

29   *Missionshift*, pp95-96

30   Hiebert, 'Beyond Anticolonialism', p271, Missiology: An International Review, Vol. XIX, No. 3, July, 1991

31   Stott, John, ed. *Making Christ Known*, Grand Rapids, Michigan: William B. Eerdmans, 1997. (page xvii)

32   The Lausanne Movement, 'Willowbank Report', http://www.lausanne.org/content/lop/lop-2

33   John Roxborogh, After Bosch: The Future of Missiology Princeton Currents in World Christianity Seminar, 2 February 2001, p5

34   David Bosch, *Transforming Mission*, 1991, pp3-4

35   *Transforming Mission*, p565

36   *Transforming Mission*, Introduction, p4

37   *Transforming Mission*, pp390-391

38   *Transforming Mission*, p512

39   *Transforming Mission*, p526

40   *Transforming Mission*, p519

41   'All-inclusive mission – A discussion of *Transforming mission* (1991) by D.J. Bosch', an article by P. Verster, Department of Missiology, University of the Free State published in *Die Skriflig*, 31(3) 1997, p251-266

42   Verster, p254

43   Verster, p257

Chapter 19

Edinburgh Centenary Celebration 2010

The Background

As we have seen, the growth of the holistic mission movement in the second half of the twentieth century has been one of the most significant developments in the history of the Christian Church. At the time of the World Missionary Conference in 1910, the mission of the Church was clearly understood as carrying the gospel of redemption from sin to the non-Christian world. Over the last 100 years, however, the way the gospel is viewed has changed dramatically. It is now widely believed, even in evangelical circles, that the mission of the Church is holistic, comprised of evangelism, socio-political action and environmental care. The need for personal salvation is no longer considered a priority.

In 1974 the Lausanne movement for World Evangelization, inspired by the passion of the Latin American evangelicals who were sympathetic to the ideas of liberation theology, led the charge towards holistic mission. Central to holistic thinking is the idea that poverty and political oppression, not sin, are the greatest human problems. The argument is that a hungry man has no time for spiritual things—he first needs to be fed. As a result of this thinking, the great debate among theologians and church leaders during the twentieth century revolved around the role of social action in evangelism. Some tried to find a compromise by arguing the mission of the Church was both evangelism and social action, and some even conceded the evangelism should have priority. But with the passage of time and much debate and many books and endless conferences, the movement towards socio-political activity has gained an unstoppable momentum. And so by the time of the centenary celebration of the World Missionary Conference 2010 in Edinburgh, the debate had been decided firmly in favour of social and political activism, and the mission of the Church was triumphantly declared to be holistic.

Every true and discerning believer will recognise that this new approach to mission is far removed from the traditional understanding of the Great Commission, which focused on preaching the gospel of Christ in order that souls, that is, individual people, by the grace of God, might be saved from their sins and receive the hope of eternal life through faith in Jesus Christ our Lord. During the nineteenth century mainstream Protestantism was firmly of the conviction that 'the purpose of missions was evangelism; the goal was the conversion of the heathen. Both in scale and results it was the great century of Christian expansion.'[1] The vast missionary endeavours of the nineteenth century had been greatly blessed by God, as the true gospel of Jesus Christ was proclaimed in many countries across the globe. New churches were planted in China, India, elsewhere in the Far East, the Pacific, South America and many African countries. The commitment of missionaries like Hudson Taylor, Henry Martyn, Adoniram Judson, David Livingston, David Brainerd, William Carey, William Burns, John Paton, and many others to the true gospel was a cause for rejoicing; their labours for Christ and their preaching of the gospel were blessed with much fruit.

Proponents of the holistic movement, in an attempt to justify their position, propagate the notion of what they call 'The Great Reversal'. They assert that a more accurate historical understanding of the mission of God's people shows that the true message of nineteenth-century evangelism was in fact holistic, and that in the first half of the twentieth century there was a huge retreat by evangelicals from a holistic understanding of the gospel to an individualised, soul-saving mission that polarised and divided the Church. This so-called retreat from the holism of nineteenth-century evangelicals, discussed in chapter 2, is The Great Reversal.

The Centenary World Missionary Conference

Many in the holistic movement saw the centenary of the World Missionary Conference held in Edinburgh in 1910, as a great opportunity to celebrate the achievements that had furthered the cause of the holistic gospel.

Theologian Kenneth R. Ross, Secretary of the Church of Scotland World Mission Council, who played an important role in convening the Edinburgh 2010 centenary celebration, argued that the history of mission in the twentieth century revealed a serious division between the World Council of Churches and the Lausanne Committee for World Evangelization.[2] Concerned about this division, and keen to rekindle the spirit of Edinburgh 1910, he commented: 'One constructive response to this situation is to re-gather, to listen to each other, to share perspectives and to seek direction from the Holy Spirit in face of contemporary challenges. Could the centenary provide an opportunity for both streams to re-engage with the Edinburgh 1910 heritage and with each other?... A process taking its inspiration from the 1910 Conference but thoroughly contemporary and forward-looking would give an opportunity for connections to be made which will be fruitful in shaping Christian mission for a new century.'[3]

Deliberations for the Edinburgh 2010 celebrations started in the year 2002 with a series of annual lectures on relevant issues. The hope was that the upcoming centenary of Edinburgh 1910 could be used as an occasion for renewing the vision for mission in the new century.

The Edinburgh 2010 project

The initial driving force behind Edinburgh 2010 was the 'Towards 2010 network' under the leadership of Professor Kenneth Ross. In 2005 the network established an international group, the General Council, to work collaboratively to develop an intercontinental and multi-denominational project, now known as Edinburgh 2010.[4]

The General Council was made up of 20 representatives from Orthodox, Roman Catholic, Pentecostal, Evangelical and other Protestant Christian traditions, and had the authority to decide all matters of strategy and policy. It met for the first time in September 2006, again in 2008, and again in April 2009.

Organisations represented on the General Council included: African Independent Churches; the Anglican Communion; the Baptist World Alliance; the Church of Scotland; Churches Together in Britain and Ireland; International Association for Mission Studies; International Fellowship of Evangelical Students; Latin American Theological

Fellowship; Lausanne Committee for World Evangelization; the Orthodox Churches; the Roman Catholic Church; Seventh Day Adventist Church; World Alliance of Reformed Churches; the World Council of Churches; World Evangelical Alliance; the World Methodist Council; World Student Christian Federation.[5]

Executive Committee

The Edinburgh 2010 Executive Committee met in April 2009. Its task was to ensure implementation of the major policy decisions of the General Council. Organisations on the Executive Committee included: the Lausanne Committee for World Evangelisation; World Evangelical Alliance; Asian Pentecostal Society; Anglican Communion; World Council of Churches.[6]

Funding bodies included: Anglican Communion; Asian Pentecostal Society; Baptist World Alliance; Church of Scotland; Churches Together in Britain and Ireland; Council for World Mission; International Association for Mission Studies; International Fellowship of Evangelical Students; Latin American Theological Fellowship; Lausanne Committee for World Evangelization; Lutheran World Federation; Orthodox Churches; Roman Catholic Church; Seventh Day Adventist Church; World Alliance of Reformed Churches; World Council of Churches; World Evangelical Alliance; World Methodist Council; World Student Christian Federation.

Other funding bodies: Areopagos; Church of England; Church of Sweden; Evangelical Lutheran Church in America; Evangelisches Missionswerk Germany; Finnish Evangelical Lutheran Mission; Methodist Church of Great Britain; Norwegian Missionary Society; Presbytery of Denver; Presbyterian Church of Canada; Protestant Church in the Netherlands; Roman Catholic Bishops' Conference of Scotland; Scottish Episcopal Church; Scottish Society for Promoting Christian Knowledge; Yoido Full Gospel Church, South Korea; Young Nak Presbyterian Church, South Korea.[7]

These lists are provided to show how deeply the holistic movement has penertrated the Christian Church. The ecumenical nature of the Edinburgh 2010 planning process was clear to all.

Study Groups

The General Council identified several main study themes, which included: foundations for mission; Christian mission among other faiths; mission and power; mission and unity; mission spirituality; forms of missionary engagement; theological education and formation. Conveners for each of the main study themes were nominated from those who had expressed interest in the process; research was done by a core group for each theme. The study groups were globally diverse—each included people of many different Christian traditions and represented a variety of institutions and organisations. The report of these groups was included in the preparatory material for the Conference.[8]

Dr Kirsteen Kim, Professor of Theology and World Christianity at Leeds Trinity University, England, was appointed as Research Coordinator to liaise with study group conveners. The study process prepared papers for the Conference. According to the website, 'the goal of the study process is to study the Bible and the world in which we live, listen to each other across geographical and ecclesial borders on key issues in mission today in order to bring together insights from academics, mission practitioners and policy makers – with a commitment to produce resources for churches, mission movements, colleges etc. The focal point is that a new vision in terms of God's purposes for creation in Christ and a renewed spirituality and mission ethos be developed in the life of churches worldwide.'[9]

Mission Spirituality

The Conference recognised the large contribution of the charismatic movement to the cause of world Christianity. The study project on mission spirituality aspired to a holistic engagement with spirituality in Christian mission. Charismatic spirituality in the non-Western world was accepted as adding to the richness of Christian spirituality.[10]

Transversals

Issues that ran across the whole Conference were called 'transversals'; they needed to be discussed within each of the themes because of their transverse nature. The General Council recognised seven transversals. Topics covered by transversals included: women and mission;

youth and mission; healing and reconciliation; contextualization; and ecological perspectives on mission.

Women in Mission

Women in mission attracted a lot of interest. A group of women gathered at Bossey Ecumenical Institute of the World Council of Churches in Switzerland in November 2008 for a consultation entitled, 'Towards Edinburgh 2010: Women's Perspectives on Mission and Theological Education in the 21st Century'. The consultation was organised by the Women's Programme of the WCC, together with numerous other organisations. The aim was to bring together different women's perspectives on engagement in mission and theological education, with the hope of making women's voices and perspectives an integral part of the Edinburgh 2010 process.[11]

The consultation identified 'the Church's complicity in the domination over women and nature in the name of mission. We must repent of this and work for the transformation of unjust structures within the Church itself as well as the wider society.' It celebrated the fact that 'the status and role of women in society and in church has advanced in many contexts and in many ways. We have women theologians and women in ordained and lay ministry. More doors of seminaries and theological faculties have opened to women as well as increased opportunities for lay formation. There has been a proliferation of feminist theological literature around the world.'

The consultation recommended to the General Council that there should be 'parity between women and men and between the global south and global north in each aspect of the Edinburgh 2010 process and event, planning and programme, including plenary speakers, persons giving testimonies and workshop leaders'.

Ecological Perspective

The transversal on ecological perspectives on mission, acknowledged that tackling ecological issues of climate change and global warming 'is on the agenda of most mission organisations, and learning to look at mission from the point of view of the earth and its peoples is a vital part of Christian witness in this situation'.[12] For example, The

United Evangelical Mission, a communion of churches in three continents, regards climate protection as a human right. 'Climate change is an issue of justice. This means to choose the option for the poor, to stand up for the victims of the climate change and to help them enforce their rights.'[13]

Rethinking in the ecumenical movement

Professor Kirsteen Kim describes the background to the 2010 Conference: 'By the 1960s the imperial world which formed the context for Edinburgh 1910 was gone, the United States was the new global power and lots of newly independent nations were making their voices heard. As a result there was a great deal of reflection among mission agencies and churches about how to be faithful to the Great Commission in this new world order... This re-thinking in the ecumenical movement led to a new paradigm of mission which has become known by the shorthand *missio Dei*, God's mission. Not only did it become the paradigm of the mainly Protestant and Orthodox churches in the WCC, but by the 1970s Catholics and Evangelicals had also come to use and to own this broad approach.'[14]

Kim explains that the *missio Dei* paradigm affirms that God's concern is with the whole world and all life. 'Therefore mission is holistic and transformative of every area of human existence. In the middle years of the twentieth century the ecumenical and evangelical missionary movements were torn apart by the question of which took priority in mission: evangelism or social action. At Edinburgh 2010 both were able to agree on integral mission encompassing both.'[15]

A key objective of the Edinburgh Centenary was to emphasise that the Church finally understood its mission. After years of struggle and tension in the evangelical world, at last there was a consensus that the mission of the Church was holistic, a true partnership between evangelism, socio-political action and environmental care. While the understanding of the 1910 Conference was heavily influenced by Western imperialism, with a focus on personal salvation at the expense of a holistic gospel, the 2010 Conference had moved a long way from that narrow view of Christianity. The world had changed, and as the Christian Faith spread to the Majority World, so the stifling shackles of colonialism had been thrown off as the holistic nature of the gospel had become fully understood.

The Conference Convenes

The Centenary Conference was held in Edinburgh in June, 2010. It was a landmark occasion, for it had brought together a wide assortment of churches and mission organisations from across the world. It was heralded as a great celebration of world Christianity; it was very different from the Conference of 1910. Rather than being centred in Edinburgh, a 'polycentric' approach was taken, with events around the world. Christians worldwide were invited to gather ecumenically in their locality and hold celebrations of mission. But the biggest celebration was on 2 June 2010, as 300 mission leaders from across the world were welcomed in Edinburgh.

Christian leaders from across the theological spectrum had gathered together to work out a common vision for mission in the twentieth-first century. In the true sense of the word the Conference was *ecumenical*, and the idea of *visible* unity between different strands of the Church was a major theme that ran through the four days of the gathering. To emphasise its ecumenical credentials the final plenary session was organised around a Common Call to mission, which aimed to visibly demonstrate the unity of the churches attending Edinburgh 2010 in the eyes of the world.

The Opening Celebration

The worship services were prepared by the Spiritual Life Committee, led by John Bell of the Iona Community (an ecumenical Christian organisation working for peace and social justice), and coordinated by Douglas Galbraith, both ministers of the Church of Scotland. The common prayers of the Conference moved between three official languages – English, French and Spanish – with the occasional addition of minority languages.

The opening worship celebration had a definite Celtic feel, with bagpipes playing a prominent part. Delegates were invited to hold in their hands the stones they had brought with them from their own countries. The following was spoken by two voices in dialogue: 'What I hold in my hand is older than my name, my language, my culture... What I hold in my hand is as old as the human race ... It is as old as the earth, but younger than God. For this stone is part of God's creation. God made and meant its shape, its colour, its journey from below to above. This stone bears witness to God's intention to make a world which was loved and lovely before humanity ever walked the earth. And to us, who come from all over the world, God has given the care of this planet, to love, admire and preserve it for others. So let us bring these stones from all over the world and lay them together round the cross, because it was for the world and not just humanity that Jesus was born and lived and died and rose again. And any theology, any spirituality, any worship which does not take the world seriously does not bear witness to Christ.'[16]

The worship procession proceeded into the hall. As they entered, they laid their stones upon the cross-shape on the floor. The distinctive circle at the head of this cross was an ancient Celtic symbol for the resurrection and for Christ's supremacy over the world and all things. While moving into the hall, they sang the Caribbean traditional spiritual: 'Halle, halle, hallelujah'.[17]

Welcoming remarks of Cardinal O'Brien

Roman Catholic Cardinal Keith O'Brien drew attention to the tremendous change which had occurred over the past 100 years since the first Edinburgh Missionary Conference. 'Then, there were no Roman Catholics at all present at the Conference; and the thought of a Roman Catholic Cardinal being invited to speak at the Opening Service would have been unthinkable. And, of course, I am not here as the only Roman Catholic... Our Delegation of 20 members represents Catholics from literally all over the world actively involved in the work of promoting Christian Unity. How things have changed!'[18] The Catholic delegation included the Archbishop of Glasgow, Mario Conti, President of the Commission for Doctrine and Christian Unity of the Bishops, and also Bishop Brian Farrell, Secretary of the Congregation for Christian Unity in Rome.

Words of Greeting from WCC

Rev Dr Olav Fykse Tveit, General Secretary of the World Council of Churches, greeted the Conference with these words: 'Today in the

World Council of Churches we give thanks to God for how this hundredth anniversary of the contemporary ecumenical movement brings us back to where we came from and sends us out to where we need to be. Whether you come from churches and mission movements linked to the WCC or not, together we can give thanks to the Holy Spirit for assembling such a wide spectrum of disciples of Jesus Christ in today's world... Among the visits I have received during these first months, I have very much appreciated those of the two leaders of the World Evangelical Alliance and the Lausanne Movement. It has been moving and inspiring for me to realise how deeply we share a holistic understanding of mission.'[19]

Words of Greeting from WEA

Rev Geoff Tunnicliffe of the World Evangelical Alliance (WEA) greeted the Conference: 'It gives me great pleasure today to speak to the Edinburgh 2010 conference on behalf of the World Evangelical Alliance and our close friends in the Lausanne Movement. The WEA brings together some 128 national evangelical alliances, linking together churches of many denominations, and one hundred international organisations, thirteen major global networks, one thousand Bible colleges and seminaries, representing around 420 million evangelicals worldwide... But I hope that we can listen to one another with love and respect, build bridges rather than create chasms, pray together, learn together, establish new friendships. In WEA we have had fruitful long-term discussions in recent years with many of the constituencies you represent: the Pontifical Council of the Roman Catholic Church, the WCC, the Orthodox Churches, and others. We are committed to continue these conversations, to further mutual understanding, and to find ways of standing alongside one another wherever possible.'[20]

Conference Talks

Dana L. Roberts, Professor of World Christianity and the History of Mission at Boston University School of Theology, gave a plenary talk on the first day of the Conference. She referred to the final 'Message' from the groundbreaking WCC mission conference of 1963, 'Witness in Six Continents', which affirmed that the mission movement involves Christians in all six continents. 'This statement in a nutshell, reflected fifty years of missiological developments set in motion by Edinburgh 1910. In retrospect, we see that it marked the symbolic beginning of a post-colonial framework for the liberation of mission from captivity to Western Christendom, and growth into mutuality. The articulation of a united world community – as opposed to Western-dominated Christianity – emerged from struggles for Christian solidarity under the horrific conditions of the Second World War... In 1948, both the founding of the World Council of Churches and the passage of the Universal Declaration of Human Rights resulted from hard work by Christians to frame a global Christian ethic suitable to an interconnected World.'[21]

She said that 'conviction about the mutual necessity of both evangelization and social justice gained momentum at mission conferences sponsored in 1989 by the WCC in San Antonio, and the Lausanne Movement in Manila. Theological convergence increased with the papal encyclical *Redemptoris Missio* appearing the following year.'[22]

She concluded: 'Seen in historical perspective, the multiplicity of 2010 celebrations around the world should be affirmed as signs of hope and opportunities for new forms of mission that must engage each other.'[23]

The Pontifical Council for Christian Unity

Roman Catholic Bishop Brian Farrell, Secretary of the Pontifical Council for Promoting Christian Unity, gave an address entitled, 'Mission in the Catholic Perspective'. He said that Roman Catholics feel strongly that they are in continuity with the Church's mission from the beginning. Since 1910 many things had changed, 'but above all, it is our outlook on "the other" that has changed. The worth and dignity of every human being, human rights, including religious freedom and freedom of opinion, are becoming a shared consciousness of a large part of the human family. Mission must take account that the Gospel cannot be imposed on anyone... for interreligious relations, the *Code of Conduct on Conversion* being drafted in collaboration by the World Council of Churches and the Catholic Church, with the participation of the Evangelical World Alliance deserves keen attention.'[24]

He said that Catholic missiology today is deeply involved in reflection on the precise relationship between evangelization and inculturation of the gospel, as well as on the impact of the gospel on justice, peace and the safeguarding of creation. 'In the Catholic view, the transformation of the world is a constitutive dimension of the preaching of the Gospel; in other words, humanity's liberation from every oppressive situation is an indispensable part of the Church's missionary activity. It has been the proclamation of Christ together with the promotion of the human person through works of charity, justice and peace that has brought the power of the Gospel into the heart of human cultures and societies: building a civilisation of love.'[25]

The Bishop referred to Christ's call for the unity of his disciples. He referred to the remarkable Encyclical Letter of John Paul II (*Redemptoris Missio*), which concluded that the most significant ecumenical achievement has been 'brotherhood rediscovered'.[26]

The Environment

Environmental issues featured prominently in Conference proceedings. Kenneth Ross drew attention to the fact that until recently concern for the natural order was often absent from the prevailing understanding of Christian mission. 'The Western missionary movement was closely allied to a commercial enterprise which sought to make profit from new resources and new markets with little thought for the future of the environment. The ecological crisis now finding expression in rapid global warming has exposed the inadequacy of a vision of the future which failed to take account of the threats to the planet posed by the expansion of the modern industrial economy. The extent of the calamity already taking effect through climate change, water scarcity, rising sea levels and desertification has awoken missionary thinkers and strategists to a challenge ignored for too long. It has provoked a re-reading of the Bible and a rediscovery of the fundamental reality that God loves the whole creation and embraces it in his saving purposes. There has been a move from a personal to a cosmic view of salvation which is far-reaching in its implications for mission.'[27]

The paper, 'Witnessing to Christ in the face of the current ecological crisis', was presented at a parallel session. The Conference was told that human attitudes towards the Earth will determine the future of life on planet Earth. 'The belief that the natural world exists solely for human use is a product of modernity and, in some Third World countries, by

Enlightenment influenced Protestant mission theories… Unfortunately, this Western worldview (which is rooted in the Protestant Reformation, the Enlightenment, and eighteenth-century economic theories) still dominates our mission activities. Yet it is putting the planet in jeopardy. While some effects of this theory are felt in the West, sadly, the poor and millions of nonhuman species suffer the most. For this reason, witnessing for Christ today demands addressing the pending ecological disaster!'[28]

Closing Celebration

On 6 June 2010 the Edinburgh Conference reached its climax as delegates were joined by local and international visitors. The event was streamed live. The prolonged closing celebration, attended by around a thousand people, was a time of singing, dancing and prayers in the Assembly Hall of the Church of Scotland, the venue of Edinburgh 1910. John Bell of the Iona community again led the worship. He explained to the gathered audience that 'in our singing, as distinct from 1910, we have so far sung very few songs from what might have been called the colonial powers… We have recognised that not every culture sounds like British Victorian.'[29]

Prayers were led in several different languages and hymns from each continent were sung. A colourful African choir began the proceedings with music that had delegates on their feet, many swaying to the rhythmic sounds. An Indian dance group performed their interpretation of 'The Woman at the Well'. The performers received generous applause for their efforts. The Anglican Archbishop of York, Dr. John Sentamu preached the sermon, raising the question: 'Where in heaven's name is the Church going?' He called on the audience to 'be, see, think and do mission'.[30]

The Common Call

The Common Call brought the proceedings of Edinburgh 2010 to an end. The Call was read by representatives of world Christianity, from Roman Catholic, Evangelical, Orthodox, Pentecostal, and Protestant churches. The Call consisted of statements read to the Conference by representatives from the study groups. What follows are brief extracts.

'We are called to incarnate and proclaim the good news of salvation, of forgiveness of sin, of life in abundance, and of liberation for all poor and oppressed.'

'We are called to authentic dialogue, respectful engagement and humble witness among people of other faiths – and no faith – to the uniqueness of Christ.'

'We are called to become communities of compassion and healing, where young people are actively participating in mission, and women and men share power and responsibilities fairly, where there is a new zeal for justice, peace and the protection of the environment.'

'Disturbed by the asymmetries and imbalances of power that divide and trouble us in church and world, we are called to repentance, to critical reflection on systems of power, and to accountable use of power structures.'

'We are called to work together in new forms of theological education.'

'Hearing the call of Jesus to make disciples of all people – poor, wealthy, marginalised, ignored, powerful, living with disability, young, and old – we are called as communities of faith to mission from everywhere to everywhere.'

'We are called to ongoing co-operation, to deal with controversial issues and to work towards a common vision. We are challenged to welcome one another in our diversity, affirm our membership through baptism in the One Body of Christ...'

'We invite all to join with us as we participate in God's transforming and reconciling mission of love to the whole creation.'

In a press conference following the ceremony Rev Rose Dowsett, a member of the Edinburgh 2010 General Council and the World Evangelical Alliance, said the Common Call was not a creed, but 'simply an attempt to capture what it is the Lord is asking us to do'. She hoped delegates would consider how they could use the Common Call within their own local settings. The Common Call was welcomed by the Catholic Archbishop of Glasgow, Mario Conti, who said it had been drafted with a view to getting 'as much in as possible'.[31]

Closing Statements

Pentecostal participants in a closing statement expressed their satisfaction at being included in the Conference. 'We have taken our rightful place on the landscape of contemporary Christianity... We appreciate that Pentecostals are recognised in a positive way. At the same time we leave with the challenge to find fuller expressions of global Pentecostalism in an ecumenical context.'[32]

Indigenous Complaints

A statement by Indigenous participants expressed a note of discord: 'While in 1910 there were only twenty non-Europeans present – Bishop Azariah the most notable – in 2010 we were now present but not presented!... In the audible and visual representations of the conference, as in the organisation of the events and activities, the influence appeared to be largely Western.'[33] The statement continued: 'Yet, even while we note the flowering of Indigenous faith, we must note, its contrast: the high profile role that the Western churches played in the misery of colonialism... The churches of the West have yet to comprehend, much less repudiate, the effect on themselves and on others of the destructive aspects of a mission strategy that frankly acknowledged its goal was to make Indigenous peoples disappear while simultaneously gentrifying other peoples to roles of servitude according to Western ideals. Sadly, it must be admitted that this strategy is still active in many parts of the world.'[34]

And more: 'Instead, perhaps representatives of the churches that were, for the most part, complicit in the attempts at eradicating or assimilating us culturally and spiritually, could have stepped aside. Their prominence as presenters, organisers and guides in the conference commemorated, by default, the intentions of the 1910 gathering to assimilate all those who did not belong to a Western cultural framework.'[35]

Holistic Mission: God's Plan for God's People

The book, *Holistic Mission: God's Plan for God's People* (2010), published by the Oxford Centre for Mission Studies (OCMS), reflects the ethos of Edinburgh 2010—it was an unabashed victory celebration of the holistic movement. The editors write: 'Even the understanding of the gospel, what is God's good news, has changed for many – though not all – Christians. There has grown a polarisation within Christendom.

Whereas many still do see the gospel as being essentially about personal salvation, others see the gospel as primarily in terms of a 'social gospel'. We would argue that Christians should revert to the traditional and biblical position and see God's good news as being holistic, being concerned with transforming the whole of creation, the whole person, body, mind and spirit. The kingdom of God is here on earth and we are to seek, as we so often pray in the Lord's prayer, that "His kingdom may come, his will be done, on earth as it is in heaven." And that implies justice, peace, health, and wholeness, shalom on earth as it is in heaven. Hence the term Holistic Mission.'[36]

Comment

The purpose of the 2010 Conference was to show how much the Christian Faith had changed since Edinburgh 1910. The spirit of ecumenism was dominant; every brand of Christianity was acceptable, no matter how false. The call for sound doctrine was absent. The Roman Catholic Church was openly accepted as an essential component of world Christianity. The Reformation was entirely disregarded—by implication, a dreadful mistake, and now a distant memory. Worship was dominated by contemporary and charismatic influences.

Over the last century a new holistic form of Christianity had been developed that freed the Church from what the proponents of the holistic Christianity saw as the tyrannical dominance of Western culture. The great cry was that the poor and oppressed needed liberation from the shackles of Western domination, and the crisis of climate change needed to be addressed. The new mission of the Church was holistic, to save the whole world and establish God's Kingdom of love on earth.

Here we must understand that Edinburgh 2010 was a gathering of the worldwide visible Church. The major players were the World Council of Churches, the Lausanne movement for World Evangelization, the World Evangelical Alliance and the Roman Catholic Church. Yet every true and discerning believer will be deeply disturbed by the view of the Christian Faith on display, a view that had a form of godliness, but that denied the power thereof (2 Timothy 3.5). The Conference was deeply influenced by the 'spirit of the age', and very probably by 'the god of this world' (2 Corinthians 4.4) and the 'spirit of error' (1 John 4.6).

Presenting itself as an 'angel of light', Edinburgh 2010 was driven by a counterfeit spiritual agenda.

Four months after the Edinburgh celebration, the ecumenical evangelicals met in Cape Town to further the cause of holistic mission and their version of world evangelization. The Lausanne movement was actively pursuing its holistic agenda.

(Endnotes)

1 *The Re-forming Tradition: Presbyterians and Mainstream Protestantism*, edited by Milton J. Coalter, John M. Mulder, Louis B. Weeks, Westminster John Knox Press; 1st edition (May 1, 1992), p167
2 *Edinburgh 2010: Springboard for Mission*, Kenneth R. Ross, William Carey International University Press, 2009, p41
3 *Edinburgh 2010: Springboard for Mission*, pp41-42
4 Edinburgh 2010 website, governance, http://www.edinburgh2010.org/en/about-edinburgh-2010/governance/general-council.html
5 Ibid.
6 Edinburgh 2010 website, Executive Committee, http://www.edinburgh2010.org/en/about-edinburgh-2010/governance/executive-committee.html
7 Edinburgh 2010 website, funding bodies, http://www.edinburgh2010.org/en/about-edinburgh-2010/funding-bodies.html
8 Edinburgh 2010 website, Main study themes, http://www.edinburgh2010.org/en/study-themes/main-study-themes.html
9 Edinburgh 2010 website, Study Theme Groups, Guidelines, www.edinburgh2010.org/.../Guidelines%20for%20Edinburgh%202010...
10 *Mission Spirituality and Authentic Discipleship*, edited by Wonsuk Ma and Kenneth R. Ross, Regnum Books International, 2013, foreword, pviii
11 Edinburgh 2010 website, Transversals, Women and mission, http://www.edinburgh2010.org/en/study-themes/transversal-topics/1-women-and-mission.html
12 Edinburgh 2010 website, Transversals, Ecology, http://www.edinburgh2010.org/en/study-themes/transversal-topics/7-ecological-perspectives-in-mission.html
13 Edinburgh 2010 website, Transversals, Climate protection as a human right: United Evangelical Mission (UEM), http://www.edinburgh2010.org/en/study-themes/transversal-topics/7-ecological-perspectives-in-mission.html
14 *Edinburgh 2010, Mission today and tomorrow*, edited by Kirsteen Kim and Andrew Anderson, Regnum Books International, 2011, p352
15 *Mission today and Tomorrow,* p353
16 *Mission Today and Tomorrow*, pp38-39
17 *Mission Today and Tomorrow*, p39
18 *Mission Today and Tomorrow*, pp11-12
19 *Mission Today and Tomorrow*, pp7-8

20   *Mission Today and Tomorrow*, pp10-11

21   Dana Roberts, Mission and Unity in the Long View, 3 June 2010, cited in *Mission Today and Tomorrow,* p62

22   Roberts, p66

23   Roberts, pp66-67

24   Bishop Brian Farrell's speech, 'Mission in the Catholic perspective', to Plenary Session I, on 3rd June 2010, cited in *Edinburgh 2010: Mission Today and Tomorrow*, Regnum Edinburgh Series, pp69-70

25   Bishop Brian Farrell, p71

26   Bishop Brian Farrell, p71

27   *Edinburgh 2010: Springboard for Mission*, 2009, p68

28   Witnessing to Christ in the Face of the Current Ecological Crisis, Kapya John Kaoma, cited from *Mission Today and Tomorrow*, first published 2011, pp296-97

29   Closing celebration at the Assembly Hall, Vimeo video, 36.05 minutes, http://www.edinburgh2010.org/en/resources/videos.html

30   Ibid. Video of Closing ceremony

31   *Christian Today*, Edinburgh 2010 Ends with Call for Cooperation, by Maria MacKay, June 7, 2010, http://www.christianpost.com/news/45455/#lxK0uM5b6H2FMkcX.99

32   *Mission Today and Tomorrow*, p343

33   Ibid. p345

34   Ibid. pp348-349

35   Ibid. p349

36   *Holistic Mission: God's Plan for God's People*, edited by Brian Woolnough and Wonsuk Ma, 2010, preface, p. xi

Chapter 20

Lausanne III: Cape Town 2010

To complete our study of the holistic movement, we need to return to the Lausanne movement. In chapter 1 we saw that the architect of Lausanne, John Stott, actually changed his mind about the meaning of the Great Commission, deciding that the commission of Christ to the Church included socio-political action. Stott wrote: 'I now see more clearly that not only the consequences of the commission but the actual commission itself must be understood to include social as well as evangelistic responsibility, unless we are to be guilty of distorting the words of Jesus.'[1] Stott's change of mind was already clearly evident at the International Congress on World Evangelization of 1974, held in Lausanne. We have seen how Stott spent the three decades after the first Lausanne Congress defending and then promoting his holistic theory of the Great Commission.

After the 1974 Congress, in the face of resistance from Billy Graham and others, Stott continued to press for an *equal* role for social action in Christian missions. In 1982, the triumph of Stott's view was made clear and public, when he was asked to chair a Lausanne committee that examined the role of social action in evangelism. Under Stott's guidance, the committee affirmed that evangelism and social action are a partnership, 'like two blades of a pair of scissors or two wings of a bird'.[2] He passionately defended this position for the rest of his long global ministry, using his vast reputation and every opportunity afforded to him as a highly-regarded evangelical Christian leader to propagate the holistic mission of the Church.

Our Lord, when speaking of false prophets (in the context of teachers), said that we would know them by their fruit. The test is straightforward—a good tree brings forth good fruit, and a bad tree bad fruit: 'Ye shall know them by their fruits' (Matthew 7.16). We are now in a position to examine the fruits of the Lausanne tree, so carefully planted by John Stott in 1974. He used his considerable diplomatic skills to persuade the International Congress to affirm in the *Lausanne Covenant* 'that evangelism and socio-political involvement are both part of our Christian duty'. Three and a half decades later, the Third Lausanne Congress was held in Cape Town. John Stott, Honorary Chairman of the Lausanne movement, gave this word of endorsement: 'I praise God for the Lausanne movement and as chairman of the Africa Host Committee it will be my privilege to welcome the Cape Town 2010 delegates to the continent of Africa. The church in Africa and also around the world needs the fresh stimulation and motivation to evangelism which this Congress will bring. The Congress will also equip us all in tackling the new issues and demanding challenges facing Christianity both here and world-wide.'[3]

My book, *Ecumenism Another Gospel: Lausanne's Road to Rome* (2014), deals with the Third Lausanne Congress in some detail. What follows is a summary of the main points to emerge from the Cape Town Congress, most of which are more fully covered in my book.

Lausanne III

The Third Lausanne Congress in Cape Town in October 2010 brought together around four thousand leaders from across the world. The Congress was heartily endorsed by Rick Warren, author of *The Purpose Driven Life* (2002). He invited 'every Christian leader, church, denomination and believer—anyone who cares about reaching the world for Christ—to join hands and band together backing the 2010 Lausanne Congress.'[4] He begged all Christians to put aside petty differences and be a part of this historic event.[5]

Some of the most influential evangelicals in the world, including Rev Nicky Gumbel, Tim Keller, Os Guinness, Vaughan Roberts (President of the Proclamation Trust) and John Piper attended the Congress. Also attending were a host of African Anglican bishops. Other prominent personalities included Paul Eshleman of Campus Crusade for Christ and Richard Stearns of World Vision.

WCC at Lausanne III

The Lausanne movement publicly demonstrated its ecumenical credentials by inviting the head of the World Council of Churches (WCC) to address the Congress. In his speech on the opening day Rev Olav Fykse Tveit, a Norwegian Lutheran theologian, said Christians of different traditions needed to participate together in God's mission, for they are called to be one. He explained that Dr Birdsall's invitation to greet friends in the Lausanne movement reminded him of what it was all about (Dr Douglas Birdsall being Lausanne's Executive Chairman). 'This historic invitation is a sign that God has called all of us to the ministry of reconciliation and to evangelism. I am honoured to be here with a delegation from the World Council of Churches and to greet you on behalf of this global fellowship of Orthodox, Protestant, Old Catholic, Anglican and Pentecostal member churches. Many of you belong to these churches... I can see how much *we share a common vision of the holistic mission of God*. I am very encouraged by how evangelicals, churches and individuals share our calling as the WCC to address the needs of the whole human being and the whole of creation. *The distance between Lausanne and Geneva is not very far*, and it should not be. Let us keep the road open, and the dialogue going, so that we learn from one another how we can participate in God's mission together with respect to others as one Body of Christ'[6] (my emphasis).

The opening and closing ceremonies, organised by Fuller Theological Seminary, were musical extravaganzas, with a large orchestra, massive choirs, colourful dance scenes, flowing banners, waving flags, a backdrop of projected images, flashing lights, rhythmic drumming, and much, much more. The overwhelming impression was that of the gathered Emerging Church at worship.

Lausanne's Road to Rome

Following the euphoria of the Cape Town Congress, Douglas Birdsall made the ecumenical ambitions of the Lausanne movement plain and obvious. He wrote in a memo published in *Lausanne World Pulse* (December 2010): 'It is my hope in 2020 that the evangelical Church will make progress in its relationships with the historic churches of the Christian faith. It is in this same spirit of humility and integrity that we must extend the hand of fellowship to the Catholic, Orthodox, and Ecumenical Church. We must embrace those in renewal movements, such as the Pentecostal, Charismatic, and Emergent. It is only in community with the churches of the past and of the present and future that the Church as a whole can move forward as a powerful witness in the world.'[7]

So there is no longer any doubt where Lausanne is going. Its long-term aim is to take 'separated' evangelicals back to the Mother Church of Rome. And along the way it will eagerly promote the ideas of the emerging church. In effect, Lausanne has declared war on the Reformation and the Reformed faith, and by implication the true gospel. For all its spectacular choreography and eloquent presentations, Cape Town 2010 was, to the discerning eye, error masquerading as Christian zeal, with even true believers caught up in the excitement.

Lausanne and the Alpha Course

Rev Nicky Gumbel, prominent promoter and main architect of the Alpha Course, was one of the main speakers. A key objective of the Alpha Course is to draw together both Protestants and Catholics, for 'Alpha bids to focus on common ground'.[8] Alpha's approach fitted perfectly with Lausanne's ecumenical vision for the Church. Gumbel said that the gospel is both words and actions. 'We are not just concerned about the conversion of individuals, as important as that is, but we are concerned about the transformation of our society.' He concluded, 'This is an exciting time to be a Christian and my appeal is that we as Christians, we as the Church of Jesus Christ entrusted with the gospel of Jesus Christ, should stop fighting one another and unite together to take this message to the world.'[9]

Gumbel's call for unity between Protestants and Catholics lies at the very centre of the Alpha message. But there are three major problems with the Alpha course. First, it presents a flawed, shallow and compromised view of the gospel and of conversion. Second, it is deeply ecumenical in approach, claiming that there are only minor differences between evangelical Christianity and the Church of Rome. Third, the actual course material leads into charismatic experiences at its culmination.

Promoting the Visual Arts

The Cape Town Congress was characterised by visual images and a large number of dramas were performed by the Lausanne arts team. The stated aim of the Congress was 'to celebrate the arts across a wide spectrum of culture diversity'.[10]

Lausanne's paper entitled, *Redeeming the Arts*, draws attention to a fundamental difference in the position between the Church of Rome and the Reformation. Roman Catholicism has always promoted the use of images, statues, pictures and other works of art in the 'worship' of God. The Reformed faith, in obedience to the Second Commandment, removed images, statues and works of art from the churches in order to focus on preaching, teaching, and understanding the Word of God. What is significant is that Lausanne's position on the arts is entirely consistent with that of the Roman Catholic Church, and entirely at odds with that of the Reformation.

To help us interpret Lausanne's enthusiasm for the arts we need to turn to the so-called 'Emerging Church' movement. The Lausanne movement, which was founded on the compromised principles of new evangelicalism, is currently on the same theological path that the Emerging Church has been following for the last few decades with respect to not only the arts in worship, but also to ecumenism, the social gospel, the threat of global warming, the global conversation, and the importance of 'storytelling' the gospel.

Following the pattern of the Emerging Church, the Lausanne movement made sure that the arts, drama and visual images had a significant presence at the Cape Town Congress. 'Art in all of its forms serves as a means of communication, opening us to fresh perspectives and allowing us to make discoveries about ourselves, our world and the God who has created all things... Our desire is that the presence of the arts at the historic Cape Town 2010 gathering will be seen as expressions of praise to the God that we serve.'[11] The *Cape Town Commitment* made the remarkable statement: 'Artists at their best are truth-tellers and so the arts constitute one important way in which we can speak the truth of the gospel. Drama, dance, story, music and visual image can be expressions both of the reality of our brokenness, and of the hope that is centred in the gospel that all things will be made new.'[12]

The above statement about the 'truth of the gospel' is completely false, and deeply heretical, for spiritual truth is found in Scripture alone, and not in drama, dance or music. It is God's Word, recorded in Scripture, that declares God's truth. Our Lord said, 'Sanctify them through thy truth: thy word is truth' (John 17.17).

A bizarre pantomime was used to illustrate the theme of Ephesians chapter 2, at a plenary gathering of the Congress. The performance comprised four dancers prancing around the Lausanne stage, performing a series of moves—jumping, shaking, rolling, flinging their arms about, to the beat of 'Dirty Pool', composed by AudioSparx. This demonstration of the visual arts speaks volumes about the Lausanne movement. The leaders of Lausanne apparently believe that the dark music of 'Dirty Pool' is helpful in worshipping God. But of one thing we can be sure, the holy God of heaven is not worshipped by the sounds of 'Dirty Pool'. Lausanne's commitment to the visual arts is a clear indication that it is following the ways and methods of the Eemerging Church movement.

Yet it is difficult to understand how four thousand intelligent Christian men and women could witness this trite performance and actually believe that the Body of Christ was being edified. And here we see the tragedy of compromise—while Lausanne uses drama, visual images and music to cultivate the imagination, it has little place for biblical truth.[13]

Storytelling the Gospel

The high point of the Third Lausanne gathering was the plenary session on storytelling the gospel. The Congress was told that there are over four billion oral learners in the world—one billion out of necessity because they are illiterate, and three billion from choice, for they prefer not to read, and therefore are known as 'preferenced' oral learners. The Church needed to recognise that the traditional way of taking the gospel to unreached people had been a failure. Therefore Christians needed to develop new appropriate methods of communication, such as storytelling, drama, songs, visual arts, poetry, chants and music, for they are the most effective methods for reaching the four billion oral learners of this world with the gospel of Christ.[14]

In 2004 the Lausanne Committee for World Evangelization claimed to have been led by the Holy Spirit to hold a conference to deal with the most significant issues in the task of taking the gospel to the world. The theme of the conference, held in Thailand was, 'A new vision, a new heart, a renewed call'. However, even before the conference Lausanne's global research programme had identified oral methods of communication as an important issue facing the Church. And so the Orality Issue Group was given the task of answering the question: 'How do you make disciples of oral learners?' The Group concluded that missionary initiatives of previous centuries had failed to engage with 'people groups' made up of oral learners, and therefore a new approach was needed. They believed that storytelling was the most effective method for taking the gospel to oral learners.

The work of the Orality Group resulted in this affirmation: 'We acknowledge the reality that much of the world is made up of oral learners who understand best when information comes to them by means of stories. A large proportion of the world's populations are either unable to or unwilling to absorb information through written communications. Therefore, a need exists to share the "Good News" and to disciple new Christians in story form and parables.'[15] The Orality Group produced the booklet *Making Disciples of Oral Learners* (2005). A theme that runs through this booklet is that a literate approach to communicating the gospel is ineffective among those who live in an oral culture.

It is vital to understand that orality is something utterly different to hearing the Bible read out loud. Even that is claimed to be a literate approach which oral learners cannot understand. Orality is a paradigm-shift away from the Bible to a novel and man-made model of communication.

The Orality Group claimed that to make disciples of oral learners it was necessary to use 'communication forms that are familiar within the culture: stories, proverbs, drama, songs, chants, and poetry. Literate approaches rely on lists, outlines, word studies, apologetics, and theological jargon. These literate methods are largely ineffective among two-thirds of the world's peoples.'[16] The assertion that a literate approach, which makes use of the written Word to preach the gospel of Christ, is ineffective among two-thirds of the world's people is contrary to Scripture, for God has promised that his Word will not return to him void (Isaiah 55.11). Faith comes by hearing the Word of God (Romans 10.17). Telling stories does not engender faith, God's Word does.

308

The Oral Bible

The orality movement claims to have developed what it has chosen to call an oral Bible that, quote, 'allows God's Word to be produced accurately from memory for the purpose of re-telling. The "oral Bible" is the singular key to unlocking church-planting movements among unreached people groups.'[17] There is no definitive oral Bible. This means that each teacher and each disciple has their own version of an oral Bible. Moreover, an individual's oral Bible will change over time as their memory fades. Clearly, an oral Bible does not endure forever, as God's Word does, but only as long as an individual's unreliable memory endures. The deep irony of the oral Bible is that it is the product of highly literate intellectuals, who promote their concept of 'orality' through literate means, such as books, journal articles, theological papers and PowerPoint presentations.

At the heart of the orality movement is the concept of crafting Bible stories to make them culturally acceptable. Lausanne's booklet, *Making Disciples of Oral Learners* explains: 'Crafting Bible stories is shaping the stories from a literature format to an oral format, and *making such changes as needed…* and *to make necessary changes needed for accommodating certain worldview issues* and story continuity'[18] (emphasis mine).

According to the orality movement, the reasons for crafting Bible stories are to make them understandable, culturally appropriate, worldview sensitive, interesting and appealing, and to avoid words that may confuse oral learners, like *sinner* and *repent*.

The orality movement aims to present a 'gospel' that is neither confrontational nor offensive to oral learners. The reason there is no offence is because the crafted stories do not challenge the sin in the heart of oral learners. Crafted stories are not 'sharper than any two edged sword, piercing even to the dividing asunder of soul and spirit' (Hebrews 4.12), for they are not the Word of God but the futile, culturally-sensitive words of men.

There is now such confidence in oral methods that organisations such as the International Mission Board (IMB) of the Southern Baptist Convention are heavily engaged in this approach. Hundreds of field teams are using storytelling as a primary strategy in dozens of countries.[19]

The orality movement makes a tragic nonsense of the heroic labours and sufferings of past generations of missionaries who gave up all and risked their lives to take the gospel to the uttermost parts of the world. Their great mission was to give indigenous people the Word of God in their own language. To this end they toiled, reducing many languages to a written script for the first time, thereby enriching and purifying cultures with the soul-saving doctrines of the Bible. The flawed wisdom of the orality movement is gleaned not from Scripture but from the minds of men. From its roots in new evangelicalism and the Lausanne movement, storytelling the gospel represents, in theory and practice, a sustained attack on Scripture and the Gospel of Truth.

The International Orality Network (ION)

This Network is a loose association of hundreds of ministries, both Western and non-Western, whose sole purpose is to spread the concept of storytelling to mission organisations and churches around the world. The Network subscribes to the *Lausanne Covenant* and promotes training resources for implementing orality programmes.

The Director of the International Orality Network (ION), Rev Avery Willis, said that past methods of using literature and the written word had been a failure among people living in oral cultures. 'The fact that literate, print-oriented missionaries from the West have missed this oral storying method for so long may be one of the single most serious tactical mistakes we have made in the last two hundred years. I grieve over all the time, energy and funding that I have personally directed toward print evangelism mission endeavours that missed the mark for oral learners.'[20]

The Network now has over a hundred mission organisations in partnership. Membership organisations include: The Lausanne movement, Youth with a Mission (YWAM), Wycliffe Global Alliance (formerly Wycliffe Bible Translators, name changed in 2011), Trans-World Radio (TWR), T4 Global, Story Runners, Summer Institute of Linguistics (SIL), The Seed Company, Scriptures In Use, One Story Partnership, The International Missions Board of the Southern Baptist Convention (IMB), Heart Sounds, Global Recordings Network, The God's Story Project, Faith Comes By Hearing, E3 Partners, Call2All, and Campus Crusade for Christ.

Cape Town Commitment 2011

Following Lausanne III, the *Cape Town Commitment: A Confession of Faith and a Call to Action* 2011,drafted by Chris Wright, expressed its total commitment to the orality agenda. The *Commitment* agreed to the following actions, among others:

1. Make greater use of oral methodologies in discipling programmes, even among literate believers.

2. Make available an oral format Story Bible in the heart languages of unreached people groups as a matter of priority.

3. Encourage seminaries to provide curricula that will train pastors and missionaries in oral methodologies.[21]

The Real Agenda of the Orality Movement

The real agenda of the orality movement is to downgrade Scripture in the eyes of two-thirds of the world's population. The actions of the orality movement represent an insidious and sustained attack on God's Word. Having asserted that the written word is a barrier to the gospel, the orality movement is committed to creating an oral Story Bible as a matter of priority. In this way it is replacing the divine wisdom of Scripture with the trivial messages of the storyteller and the trivial images of the Emerging Church. Visual images, art, dance and drama are actively promoted as effective methods for teaching the truths of the Christian Faith. The result is a distorted, non-biblical version of Christianity that is based on stories—a version of Christianity that is without a doctrinal base, and that feeds its adherents on crafted stories.

Lausanne's Socialist Agenda

The Lausanne movement lays claim to special Christian love for the world's poor and suffering. The *Cape Town Commitment*, declares: 'Such love for the poor demands that we not only love mercy and deeds of compassion, but also that we do justice through exposing and opposing all that oppresses and exploits the poor. We must not be afraid to denounce evil and injustice wherever they exist.'[22]

An advance paper for the Cape Town Congress, entitled 'Poverty and Wealth', insists that 'we urgently need to consider the overwhelming reality of structural sins brought on by the startling inequity present in our world today. The stark reality of wealth and the stark reality of poverty mutually explain each other. One cannot be understood apart from the other... Poverty cannot be understood in isolation without reference to the immoral levels of wealth in the world.'[23]

The paper argues that Third World poverty 'calls us to assume our prophetic role if we understand that one of the fundamental causes of poverty is injustice. Almost a century after the Declaration of Human Rights, an incredible step taken by the states of many nations, we witness the violation of the dignity of the poor on a day-to-day basis as they experience the violation of fundamental rights. The unequal distribution of resources and accumulated wealth is one of the most blatant ways in which injustice manifests itself. The existence of unprecedented levels of concentration and accumulation of wealth by individuals, corporations and nations; all indicate that something is fundamentally wrong with the way humankind has organized the economy, power relationships and society as a whole.'[24]

The underlying assumption of this paper is that poverty is caused by social injustice and the structural sins perpetrated by rich Christians in the West. The assertion that 'the stark reality of wealth and the stark reality of poverty mutually explain each other', is consistent with socialist ideology that entirely ignores the link between wealth and the biblical work ethic. The political message of this paper is similar to that found in Ronald Sider's *Rich Christians in an Age of Hunger* (1977), and accords with John Stott's socialist agenda.

Richard Stearns, one of the keynote speakers at the Cape Town Congress, expressed his frustration with Christians in the USA in his book, *The Hole in Our Gospel* (2009). Stearn's basic premise is that the real gospel entails a public and transforming relationship with the world, resulting in a social revolution to help the poor, express compassion for the sick, and pursue liberation for those who are victims of political, social or economic injustice. He believes that the 'hole' in the gospel is collective neglect of the poor and the marginalised, because Christians in the USA have reduced the good news of Jesus Christ to a 'personal transaction with God, with little power to change anything outside our own hearts'.[25] One critic said Stearn's book 'promotes a false gospel within a socialistic philosophy. It fails miserably in its hermeneutic, is ecumenical in focus, promotes human performance as a method of pleasing God, and believes people on earth can do good to "usher in the Kingdom".'[26]

In his presentation to the Congress, Stearns said he sometimes dreams of what could happen if Christians responded to his call and gave lots of money to the poor. Stearns thinks that if Christians in the West embrace the whole gospel and not the gospel 'with a hole in it', then his dream could come true. The massive redistribution of resources from the Global North to the Global South could start with the four thousand leaders at the Cape Town Congress, who have it within their power to change the world for Christ.[27]

The Lausanne movement asserts that the cause of Third World poverty is economic injustice. We are told that the structural sins of the West have brought on the startling inequality in wealth that is apparent in our world today. At the Cape Town Congress Rene Padilla expressed concern about the globalisation of what he calls an unjust economic system (by which he means capitalism), which he says is 'destroying humankind'.[28] Lausanne is doing all it can to persuade its supporters that a New International Economic Order is the solution to global poverty. Here we should note that Lausanne's support for a new economic order is entirely consistent with the ideology of socialism.[29]

The socialism of the Lausanne movement is a profoundly unbiblical ideology. The focus on Third World poverty is designed to produce guilt among Christians in the West, persuading them that the answer is a socialist economic order that redistributes the world's resources. But the Lausanne model is a recipe for disaster that will not help the world's poor. Indeed, socialism has led to economic decline in many countries around the world.

Lausanne's Feminist Agenda

Lausanne III promoted an overt feminist agenda, advocating female leadership in the Church and mutual submission in marriage. The message to emerge from the Congress is that women should have an equal role in preaching and leading the Church.

Husband and wife team, David Claydon (Senior Adviser to Lausanne) and his wife Robyn Claydon (Vice-Chair of the International Lausanne Committee) dealt with the issue of equal partnership in marriage. David Claydon stressed mutual submission in marriage by quoting Ephesians 5.21 and simply ignoring Ephesians 5.22-24, which teaches that wives must submit themselves to their own husbands. Claydon was adamant that God is the head of his household and that he and his wife practise mutual submission.[30]

One delegate was so upset by the feminist agenda that was being propagated that he made the following comment: 'I was very disappointed in the Lausanne leadership in allowing the extremely one-sided viewpoints related to men and women in Christian ministry. A prime example was the multiplex on men and women. It was totally feminist, spent most of its time preaching feminism, and ignored that there is another viewpoint on the matter. In addition to the total lack of balance and Christian charity toward other viewpoints, how they handled Scripture, twisting it to fit their viewpoints, was sad to see, and a terrible precedent to allow in the Lausanne movement which does not bode well for its future.'[31]

The misuse of Scripture in the presentations on female leadership and mutual submission in marriage, illustrates how the leadership of Lausanne is prepared to select and twist Scripture to drive their ideological agenda. The Lausanne campaign to promote women's leadership in the Church is contrary to Scripture, which teaches an authority principle that is to be upheld in both the home and in the church.

Lausanne's Environmental Agenda

An advance paper entitled, 'The Challenge of Environmental Stewardship', written by Las Newman (President of the Caribbean Graduate School of Theology), and Dr Ken Gnanakan (an Indian theologian), provided an overview for the multiplex session devoted to the environmental crisis. Congress delegates were informed that the biblical mandate to rule and have dominion has caused the environmental disaster. Ken Gnanakan asserted that colonialism, capitalism and our Christian arrogance lay behind the ecological crisis. The authors of the paper went on to say that 'the global environmental crisis is a stark reality that compels us to act. We are threatened with climate change, depletion of land and marine resources, dwindling fresh water reserves, an energy crunch, biodiversity extinction and devastated ecosystems… While the threat is global, sadly the impacts of the crisis are already being felt by some of the world's poorest communities.'[32]

The authors want Christians to become environmental activists, and so they advise all Christians to commit to re-reading the Bible from an environmental perspective. In other words, we are being encouraged to reinterpret Scripture in the light of the claims of the modern-day environmental lobby. The authors advise Christians to join environmental groups and fight for change.[33]

Lausanne's Religious Agenda

Cape Town 2010 provided a vivid picture of ecumenical confusion. It showed that the ever closer unity of evangelicals with every other brand of 'Christianity', no matter how unbiblical, no matter how compromised, is gathering momentum.

There is no doubt that the Lausanne leadership is comfortable with the liberal ideology of the World Council of Churches, the excesses of the charismatic movement, the ecumenical and deficient 'gospel' of the Alpha Course, the false teachings of Roman Catholicism, and the new ideas and methods of the Emerging Church. Evidence from the Cape Town Congress demonstrates that Lausanne has turned its back on the doctrines of the Reformation.

Tragedy of the Lausanne Compromise

The corrupt fruit of the Lausanne movement has been produced by the coming together of the ecumenical movement, the compromise of the new evangelicals (led by Billy Graham and John Stott) and the false teaching of the Emerging Church. Lausanne's compromise, so vividly illustrated at Cape Town 2010, is the true legacy of the worldwide ministries of Billy Graham and John Stott.

When Billy Graham, as a world-famous evangelist, embraced the compromise of new evangelicalism in the 1950s and 60s, he opened the door to a liberal theological agenda. He used his very considerable reputation and influence to enable Fuller Theological Seminary, a deeply compromised institution, to act as a driving force behind the Lausanne agenda. Over the decades, Fuller Seminary has eagerly grasped the opportunity offered by Lausanne to promote its compromised theological ideas to the world. Fuller's church growth strategy has succeeded in changing the focus of the Great Commission of Matthew 28 from preaching the gospel of salvation, to a people's movement that aims primarily to redeem cultures, not to save individual souls.

John Stott, as a world-famous theologian, must have been well aware of the theological corruption within Fuller Seminary, yet he chose to walk the same road. He undoubtedly understood the significance of the orality movement in downgrading Scripture, yet he endorsed the Cape Town Congress, knowing full well that the promotion of the orality movement was presented as a strategic priority. Stott never opposed Lausanne's commitment to an oral story Bible. Over the years he used the Lausanne movement as a vehicle for promoting his holistic mission concept which was entirely consistnent with his socialist ideology. Indeed, Stott's holistic mission and socialism are 'like two blades of a pair of scissors or two wings of a bird'.

The corrupt fruit of Lausanne III stands as a theological disaster perpetrated in the name of new evangelicalism, and driven by the deeply flawed ministries of John Stott and Billy Graham. The tragedy of Lausanne is that it brings together true believers, mainly from developing African, South American and Asian countries, with false teachers, mainly, but not exclusively, from the West. It is deeply disturbing that genuine believers from growing churches in the Third World are being profoundly influenced by the false teachings of the Lausanne movement.

In the light of such evidence, we must conclude that Lausanne is in effect a heretical movement that is perverting the Gospel of Truth. Its oral Bible cannot remotely measure up to God's written Word revealed in Scripture—rather, it perverts the Word of Truth. Its socio-political message is a deceitful utopian gospel based on the ideology of socialism. The Lausanne movement simply does not contend for the Gospel of Truth once for all delivered to the saints.

The year 2010 was highly significant in the history of the holistic movement. At the Centenary Conference in Edinburgh 2010, proponents of the holistic movement took the opportunity of celebrating what they believed was the final victory of the holistic gospel movement. Lausanne III in Cape Town, in the same year, provided clear evidence of the heretical fruits that have flowed from John Stott's original holistic gospel, presented at the First Lausanne Congress in 1974. Our Lord said, 'Wherefore by their fruits ye will know them' (Matthew 7.20). In the final chapter we bring together all the threads of our discussion around the holistic movement and draw our conclusions.

(Endnotes)

1   John Stott, *Christian Mission in the Modern World*, IVP Books, 1975, p25
2   "Evangelism and Social Responsibility: An Evangelical Commitment," Grand Rapids Report No. 21, Consultation on the Relationships between Evangelism and Social responsibility (CRESR) (Wheaton, IL: Lausanne Committee on World Evangelization and the World Evangelical Fellowship, 1982)
3   Lausanne Movement website, Gatherings, Cape Town 2010, Endorsements, 'What Global Leaders Were Saying About Cape Town 2010', John Stott
4   Ibid, Endorsements, 'What Global Leaders Were Saying About Cape Town 2010', Rick Warren
5   Youtube, Rick Warren on Cape Town 2010,
6   World Council of Churches website, Greetings to the 3rd Lausanne Congress for World Evangelization, Cape Town, South Africa, Sunday 17 October 2010, by the Rev Dr Olav Fykse Tveit, general secretary of the World Council of Churches,
7   *Lausanne World Pulse*, December 2010, 'Pressing on towards 2020 in Humility, Reflection, and Hope' by Douglas Birdsall,
8   *Alpha News*, March-June 1998, cited from, 'The Alpha Course – Friend or Foe?' by W.B. Howard, Editor of *Despatch Magazine*. Information gathered from the Alpha Conference in Brisbane, Australia, 1998, p7
9   Alpha website, What people say, Church leaders,
10   The Lausanne Movement website, Cape Town 2010, Arts at Cape Town 2010
11   Cape Town 2010 website, Arts at Cape Town 2010
12   Lausanne Movement website, The Cape Town Commitment, Part 2, Section IIA, 'Truth and the arts in mission'
13   Cape Town 2010 website, video drama, Bible Exposition: Dance Reach, Choreography by the Cape Town 2010 Performing Arts Team; Music credit, "Dirty Pool" by AudioSparx
14   Cape Town 2010 website, Video, Quote from 'Communicating to Oral Learners - Introduction and Transitions', http://conversation.lausanne.org/en/conversations/detail/11520
15   Lausanne Occasional Paper No. 30, 'Globalization and the Gospel: Rethinking Mission in the Contemporary World', produced by the Issue Group on this topic at the 2004 Forum for World Evangelization hosted by the Lausanne Committee for World Evangelization in Pattaya, Thailand, September 29 to October 5, 2004
16   *Making Disciples of Oral Learners*, Lausanne Committee for World Evangelization and International Orality Network, 2005, p74

17 Ibid, p117

18 Ibid, p117

19 Ibid, pp67-68

20 *Lausanne World Plus*, 'What Do You Think, Mr. Guttenberg? The Challenges Print Evangelism Ministries Face in Meeting the Needs of Oral Cultures' by Avery Willis and James Greenelsh, October 2006

21 The Lausanne Movement, The *Cape Town Commitment: A Confession of Faith and a Call to Action* (2011), paragraph 2 D, Discerning the will of Christ for world evangelization, Oral cultures http://www.lausanne.org/ctcommitment

22 The *Cape Town Commitment*, We love God's world, paragraph 7c

23 Cape Town 2010 advance paper, 'Poverty And Wealth', authors Corina Villacorta and Harold Segura, date: 20.07.2010, category: Poverty & Wealth

24 Ibid.

25 A review of *The Hole in our Gospel* (2009), Richard Stearns, by Ryan Dueck, http://rynomi.wordpress.com/2010/06/08/the-hole-in-our-gospel-review/

26 A review of *The Hole in our Gospel* (2009) by Pastor Paul D. Van Noy, Candlelight Fellowship, Idaho. cited from The Lighthouse website

27 Cape Town 2010 Congress video, 'Wealth, Poverty and Power - The Hole in our Gospel', author Richard Stearns, date: 24.10.2010, category Poverty & Wealth

28 Cape Town 2010 website, Plenary 3: session on 'World Faiths – Lausanne and Latin America - Samuel Escobar and Rene Padilla', cited from *Ecumenism: Another Gospel*, E.S. Williams, Belmont House publishing, 2014, p40

29 Socialist Party Manifesto 2010, Capitalism's limits, http://www.socialistparty.org.uk/partydoc/Socialist_Party_manifesto_2010/4

30 Cape Town 2010 Congress, videos, 'Men and Women: Husband and Wife Partnership', authors David and Robyn Claydon

31 Comment by William Lauesen, http://conversation.lausanne.org/en/conversations/detail/10557

32 The Lausanne Global Conversation, Cape Town 2010 advance paper, 'The Challenge of Environmental Stewardship', authors Las Newman and Ken Gnanakan, 2010, p1

33 Ibid. p2

Chapter 21

Concluding Remarks

Machen on Social Reform

In our concluding remarks we turn to the biblical wisdom of J. Gresham Machen, the man who in the face of the modernisers, courageously contended for the true gospel in the 1920s and 1930s (described in chapter 7). In his *Introduction to the New Testament* (Banner of Truth, 1976), he provides a biblical account of the relationship between the gospel and social reform, which has great relevance to the holistic mission debate of our day. Machen saw social reform as *secondary* to the gospel, but also as something that would develop normally under Christian influence.

He writes: 'Apostolic Christianity was not a reform movement. Social conditions in the apostolic age were exceedingly bad.' He mentions the great distraction of slavery that produced a thousand miseries. 'Under such conditions the Church might have been expected to come forward with a social programme... As a matter of fact, however, Christianity seemed to exhibit a remarkable patience in its attitude toward the evil institutions of the time.'[1]

He says that Christianity is independent of earthly conditions. The apostolic Church promised, not the improvement of earthly conditions, but an abundant entrance into heaven. 'A gospel which proposes merely improvement in the world is dependent on worldly conditions... Christianity is a life in communion with God... that can be maintained in poverty and in plenty, in slavery and in freedom, in life and in death.'[2]

Touching on social action, Machen clearly distinguishes it from the gospel itself, whilst commending its proper use: 'The consecration of human relationships to God does not involve any depreciation of what is known as "social service". On the contrary it gives to the social services its necessary basis and motive power… The improvement of social conditions… is seen by him who believes in a future life and a final judgement and heaven and hell, to have value not only for time, but also for eternity, not only for man, but also for the Infinite God.'[3]

But this understanding of social justice does not obscure the soul-saving doctrines of the gospel as applied to individual men and women: 'It is sometimes regarded as a reproach that old-fashioned, evangelical Christianity makes its first appeal to the individual… Everyone knows, it is said, the "social gospel" is the really effective modern agency; yet some evangelists with only the very crudest possible social pro-gramme are accomplishing important and beneficent results!' Machen concludes: 'Despite the importance of social reforms, the first purpose of true Christian evangelism is to bring the individual man directly and consciously into the presence of his God. Without that, all else is of but short temporary value…'[4]

Deception in the Church

Despite the clear biblical teaching of Machen, a majority of the Christian Church now accepts that holistic mission is the true mission of the Church. But the Church has been deceived, for Scripture teaches that the true mission of the Church is to preach Christ and salvation from sin in his name. The deception has arisen from *within* the Church. As forewarned by Scripture, certain men have crept into the church *un-noticed* to teach their error and even heresy (Acts 20.17-31: Jude 3-4). We must remember that the people of God are engaged in a perpetual spiritual war against the forces of darkness. As we have seen in this study, the war on the gospel – the pearl of great price – is relentless and constant. Today the principal field of that battle is missions.

Those who would be faithful to Christ our Lord, need to understand that we are involved in spiritual warfare against the principalities and powers of wickedness in high places (Ephesians 6.10-18). The battle is not only personal, but also corporate—for the defence of the gospel. Those who would be true to Christ are to earnestly contend for the Faith once for all delivered to the saints (Jude 3). As Spurgeon wrote, 'compromise there can be none, *fellowship with known and vital error is participation in sin*'.[5] Whether we like it or not, true believers are engaged in an ongoing spiritual war over the very meaning of Christ's Great Commission to his Church. In these days of confusion and deception, the faithful remnant of God's people need to boldly challenge the apostasy behind the holistic movement.

Having documented the downgrade of the Christian gospel since the nineteenth century, we must now draw together our conclusions, taking into account the teachings of Scripture and the evidence before our eyes. In this final chapter we are seeking to learn from the lessons of history. And as we do so, we must use the gift of discernment that God gives to all his children to help us divide truth from error. We must understand the deceptive nature of the assault on the Gospel of Truth. Our task is to defend the Faith once for all delivered to the saints.

Undermining the Bible

Our thinking about the holistic movement must begin by acknowledging that the true Faith is based on Scripture. True Christianity is *biblical* Christianity. The enemies of God understand this fundamental relationship. For this reason they seek to undermine the Bible, God's revealed Word, thereby perverting the Christian Faith. Therefore a major strategy of the enemy of souls, Satan, is to cast doubt on the *truth*, *reliability* and *sufficiency* of the Bible. We started our study by looking at a long-forgotten subject, higher criticism of the Bible. Such was the deceptive influence of the higher critics that even godly missionaries in the early 1900s were seduced by these teachings. This meant that the false views of higher criticism were taught on the mission field. To really understand the times in which we are living, we need to recognise that progressively through the nineteenth and twentieth centuries, the ideas of higher criticism have succeeded in downgrading the authority of the Bible in the eyes of large numbers of professing Christians, as well as the general public. We must understand that the influence of higher criticism is still present in the Church today. Over the past century the Bible has increasingly been treated just like any other book, subject to an increasingly postmodern hermeneutic in which the reader, not the text, is the source of its meaning.

A significant principle that emerged from our study of higher criticism was the failure of the Church to fully engage in the battle.

While a few courageous men did so, like Charles Spurgeon, Gresham Machen, and the authors of *The Fundamentals* in the early 1900s, the overwhelming response of the professing Church was to form an accommodation with the higher critics, and thereby avoid controversy and conflict. The catastrophic consequence of this accommodation was that prominent higher critics were accepted into theological colleges and Bible seminaries, where they were allowed to corrupt and contaminate generations of students with their false view of Scripture. This contamination of seminaries and Bible colleges meant that, within a generation, many theological colleges were producing Christian preachers and theologians who were sympathetic to the 'new theology' called *liberalism* (see chapter3). It was both a compromise and sin for the Church not to deal firmly with the higher critics and to expose them as the false teachers that most of them undoubtedly were. Instead, the Church accepted the viper into its bosom, and the poison was spread widely through its vitals.

But God was not without his witnesses. In the 1920s and 30s, with J. Gresham Machen in the vanguard, a courageous battle was waged against this new theology by those who came to be pejoratively labelled as 'fundamentalists'. Machen was bold enough to declare that liberalism was a different religion that had no part in the Christian Faith. He argued that modern liberalism in the Church was not merely an academic matter among theological seminaries, 'On the contrary its attack upon the fundamentals of the Christian faith is being carried on vigorously by Sunday School lesson helps, by the pulpit, and by the religious press.'[6]

The new evangelicals who emerged in the 1940s and 50s, were determined to *compromise* with the liberals. They wanted the evangelical faith, but without the spiritual battle that came from defending the true gospel and exposing error. They longed for peace and tolerance, and were willing to accept a small amount of compromise as a price worth paying.

New evangelicalism fostered a low view of Scripture and even questioned its infallibility. Fuller Seminary was able to deny the inerrancy of Scripture with the tacit support of important new evangelicals, such as John Stott and Billy Graham. By the middle of the 1960s the Seminary was firmly in the hands of scholars who were clearly and openly opposed to the doctrine of biblical inerrancy. Harold Lindsell's book, *The Battle for the Bible* (1976), carefully documents the way in which the theological leaders of Fuller rejected the inerrancy of Scripture and promoted the idea that what they called 'non-revelatory' Scripture contained errors (see chapter 10). One important example of this compromise is the claim that the first chapters of Genesis are a poem and therefore must not be taken literally. This view of Scripture has led to the widespread acceptance of theistic evolution.

The next major assault on Scripture was the advent of the orality movement, cultivated by Lausanne, which developed the concept that the most effective way to communicate the message of the Bible was by crafting and adapting Bible stories to make them culturally appropriate. Storytelling thus became the new way of communicating the gospel to so-called oral learners. In this way many millions of people have been denied access to God's written Word.

The Fruit of Compromise

An important principle that we learn from this story is that compromise never stands still; it always leads on to the next downgrade. Despite the obvious apostasy of the higher critics, the Church was reluctant to obey the biblical injunction to condemn their error and separate from them. The inevitable result was that many higher critics ended up as professors of theology teaching in famous Bible seminaries, polluting the minds of tens of thousands of young men studying for the ministry with their false views of Scripture. Fuller is surely the outstanding example of a theological Seminary that misuses Scripture. Today, the evil fruit of the higher critics is ubiquitous throughout the visible Church.

Compromise within American Presbyterianism was such that in the early 1900s liberal ideas from the higher critical movement had infiltrated to the point where the 1910 General Assembly of the Northern Presbyterian Church saw the need to affirm five essential doctrines of the Christian Faith, which became known as 'The Five Points'. The Five Points, however, were anathema to the modernists, for they did not like doctrinal clarity. And to make their opposition clear and public, in 1924 over 1,200 ordained Presbyterian ministers signed a public Affirmation asserting that not one of the doctrines declared to be 'essential' by the

General Assembly was really essential at all. Indeed, all of 'The Five Points' were only 'theories'[7] (see chapter 7).

The new evangelicals, who rose to prominence in the post-war period, became skilled in the art of compromise—and we now bear the consequences. They did not stand against doctrinal error, and they were not prepared to defend sound doctrine, for they feared that to do so would cause controversy and exclude some who professed to be evangelicals. Such was the compromise and theological confusion of the new evangelicals that they opposed the fundamentalists (who were true believers), and separated themselves from them! They promoted tolerance of all shades of doctrine on the pretext of promoting unity. The influence of the new evangelicals has made compromise an article of faith for a large section of the evangelical Church.

Confidence in the Social Gospel

The misuse of Scripture and the elevation of the social sciences led to the development of the social gospel in the latter part of the nineteenth century and on into the first decades of the twentieth century. Theologian Walter Rauschenbusch, who was a supporter of the higher criticism, was able to declare that 'we have a social gospel'. He claimed that Jesus Christ was a social reformer, even a social revolutionary, who came to transform society into a socialist utopia – the true human society – which he called the Kingdom of God. His book, *A Theology of the Social Gospel* (1917), misused Scripture to support his false theology. Despite Rauschenbusch's distortion of Scripture, his writings became extremely popular among the Christian community. His social gospel was 'holistic', in that it combined good works with salvation. His central idea was that the purpose of the gospel was to establish God's Kingdom on earth.

This idea was extremely popular with liberals like Harry Emerson Fosdick, who fought a vehement campaign against the fundamentalists who defended the true gospel. There is no doubt that the social gospel of good works has a great appeal to the carnal mind. And so through the twentieth century there have been repeated attempts to elevate the social gospel in the mind of Christians. Most notable was the First Lausanne Congress in 1974, when John Stott succeeded in writing socio-political action into the *Lausanne Covenant*. At the time few people seemed to grasp the fact that what Stott had succeeded in doing was to legitimise the old social gospel of Rauschenbusch.

The Great Controversy

The great controversy that runs through this study concerns the nature of the mission of the Church. How should the Church interpret the Great Commission? As we saw in chapters 1 and 2, John Stott, regarded as one of the greatest Christian thinkers of the twentieth century, actually changed his mind about this matter. In 1966, speaking to the Berlin Congress on World Evangelism, the thrust of Stott's message was clear and biblical: 'the specification of the risen Lord is exclusively a preaching, converting and teaching mission' (see chapter 11).

However, by 1974 Stott had radically changed his mind: 'I now see more clearly that not only the consequences of the commission but the actual commission itself must be understood to include social as well as evangelistic responsibility, unless we are to be guilty of distorting the words of Jesus.' Stott was emphasising what has become known as the holistic model of the Great Commission. The *Lausanne Covenant*, largely written by Stott, expressed 'penitence both for our neglect of our Christian social responsibility and for our naive polarization in having sometimes regarded evangelism and social concern as mutually exclusive... we affirm that evangelism and socio-political involvement are both part of our Christian duty.'[8]

In this study we have seen that Stott's view of the Great Commission is deeply flawed. To understand the Great Commission we need to turn to Scripture. Stott is insistent that what he calls the Johannine Commission, from the words of Jesus in John 20.21, is the most profound expression of our Lord's commission to the Church. Stott explains: 'deliberately and precisely he made his mission the *model* of ours, saying "*as* the Father has sent me, even *so* I send you"' (Stott's emphasis). Here we should note that Stott's entire theological edifice is built on one verse of Scripture, and completely ignores the writings and ministry of the apostle Paul. Moreover, it does not take a theologian to see that Stott's interpretation of this verse of Scripture, namely, that missionaries are sent *as* Jesus was sent, is deeply flawed. The similarity is in the *sending*, not in the *as*. No man can be *as* the Lord Jesus is. Yet, there has been very little opposition to his false interpretation of the Great Commission. Many in the Christian community have eagerly accepted Stott's flawed incarnational model of the Great Commission, and propagated it widely through Bible seminaries and missionary organisations. It has become the theological backbone of the holistic gospel.

Missiology

The new discipline of missiology, which came into prominence in the 1970s and 80s, has been a major force behind the holistic movement. An essential characteristic of missiology is that it is built on the foundations of anthropology and social research. It is an enterprise based on human wisdom. It propagates the view that the Church needs to supplement Scripture with the social sciences and anthropology to really understand the mission of God. But combining Scripture with anthropological and sociological theories is a blatant denial of the sufficiency of God's Word. The ideas of man have been elevated above Scripture. But Scripture warns that we should not to be deceived by human knowledge: 'Beware lest any man spoil you through philosophy and vain deceit, after the tradition of men, after the rudiments of the world, and not after Christ' (Colossians 2.8).

Missiology claims that all cultures have an equal moral standing. Therefore it is morally repugnant to assert the superiority of Western culture over the pagan cultures of the Third World. Missiology spends a great deal of time and effort studying different cultures, in order to present the gospel message in a way that they hope is culturally relevant. This is called 'contextualization'. Missionaries are exhorted not to undermine traditional cultures; and so the tendency is to overlook the evil aspects inherent in some cultures. But the Bible does not teach the equivalence of all cultures. Indeed, Scripture is clear that Canaanite culture, which included the worship of Molech, child sacrifice and temple prostitution is *evil*. So there was no moral equivalence between Canaanite culture and the culture of Israel, which was based on God's moral law. The Bible stands above culture, and all cultures are to be judged by the moral law of God. Ancestor worship, for example, is wrong because it breaks the First Commandment. Cultures must conform to the Bible, not the other way round. It is wrong to attempt to make the message of Scripture conform to any culture.

A major error of missiology is its drive to contextualize the gospel. Missiologists identify culture as being a significant obstacle to communicating the gospel. They claim that the gospel needs to be contextualized to make the message culturally relevant and worldview sensitive. Contextualizing has gone so far as to teach that Muslims can accept Christ even without believing that he was crucified.

Contextualization results in different kinds of Christianity and a different theology for each culture. Missiology has helped to produce an Asian theology, a Latino theology, an African theology, a Pacific Islander theology, a liberation theology and so on.

There is no doubt that missiology is having a huge impact on the mission field. Joel James and Brian Biedebach, from their long experience of the mission field in Africa comment: 'Today churches and missionaries are being told that to imitate the ministry of Jesus they must add social justice to their understanding of the church's mission.' They make the point that influential 'missional' voices currently dominating the evangelical conversation about missions, are promoting a new kind of mission: shalom, social justice, or the gospel of good deeds and human flourishing. 'As a result, the evangelical church in the West is commissioning and sending a generation of missionaries to Africa and elsewhere whose primary enthusiasm is for orphan care, distributing medicine, combating poverty, and other social action projects. For the most part, these new missionaries value the church, but in many cases they seem to view the church primarily as a platform from which to run and fund their relief projects.'[9]

The result of all this is a generation of missionaries who focus on social needs and transforming society, building schools and digging wells. By this the gospel of salvation is being seriously undermined (see chapter 1).

Mere Evangelism

There is no doubt that missiologists and holistic gospel practitioners are remarkably indifferent to true evangelism. Ralph Winter (discussed in chapter 16), held by many to be the greatest modern missiologist, frequently used the phrase 'mere evangelism' to denigrate the true mission of the Church. Throughout this study we have seen a dismissive attitude towards those who preach the authentic gospel of salvation— they are portrayed as selfish, unloving conservative Christians who have no social conscience and are only interested in increasing the numbers in their 'own tribe'.

John Stott uncritically quotes Moberg's social research in *Issues Facing Christians Today* (1984), claiming to show that Christians who place a high value on salvation are *conservative, anxious to maintain the status quo*, and *unsympathetic or indifferent* to the plight of the black and the poor. Research data, we are told, suggest a portrait of the religious-minded as a person having a *self-centred preoccupation* with saving his own soul.[10] The evangelical Christian is caricatured as having but one task – the winning of souls to Christ. The only important goal in his life is to be a 'fisher of men'. 'Trophies for Christ are sought in somewhat the same way a big-game hunter in Africa stalks his exotic prey.'[11] It is not difficult to detect Moberg's dislike of evangelicals who focus on winning souls to Christ; in his eyes, they behave like cruel big-game hunters. Yet Stott approvingly cites him to buttress his holistic agenda.

The vitally important point is that the holistic movement has redefined the meaning of evangelism. We must understand that although holistic practitioners still use the word 'evangelism', they do not always mean preaching the gospel of salvation from sin.

Anti-Western Ideology

A theme identified throughout our study is the anti-Western agenda of the holistic movement. The World Council of Churches early on made it obvious that it was driven by a political agenda committed to liberating Third World countries from exploitation and oppression. Colonialism, imperialism and Western culture were identified as enemies that needed to be overcome. Liberation theology, which emerged from Marxist thinking in South America, was recognised to be a key weapon in the struggle against Western imperialism. The concept of white racism was developed by the WCC as a means of discrediting Western nations that were seen to be the oppressors. Many Western missionaries were accused of delivering a culturally-conditioned and westernised brand of Christianity that disparaged and damaged the traditional cultures of Third World nations.

There is also a deep disdain for Western culture and white people. David Bosch referred to British and German missionaries as racists.[12] The Christianity that has come from the West is portrayed as arrogant, exploitative, and the cause of much oppression and even poverty in the Third World. Colonialism and imperialism are hotly condemned as making the Christian message unacceptable to people in the Third World. Indeed, Western Christians are exhorted to contextualize their 'oppressive' Western brand of Christianity, in order to make it more acceptable to indigenous cultures. Missiology discredits sound biblical theology by calling it 'Western theology'. But there is no doubt that God has used Western theology to preserve the true gospel. We should thank God for his grace in sending the missionaries from the West, who, with courage and Christ-like compassion, went out and witnessed to the truth of God's saving grace through the Cross of Christ and engaged in Bible translation. Many were martyred in obeying the call of God.

Missiology developed in an ethos that was profoundly anti-Western. Ralph Winter, the so-called missionary statesman, preached the need to de-Westernise the Christian message. He insisted that the gospel needed to be contextualized and made acceptable to each foreign culture.

Creation Care

The holistic movement uncritically promotes the idea that climate change is a major crisis facing mankind. Creation care has been emphasised by the Lausanne movement and the writings of John Stott and Chris Wright. In the essay, 'Mission and God's Earth', Wright expresses the view that 'a biblical theology of mission, flowing from the mission of God himself, must include the ecological sphere within its scope and see practical environmental action as a legitimate part of biblical mission'.[13] He asserts that 'creation care embodies justice because environmental action is a form of defending the weak against the strong, the defenceless against the powerful, the violated against the attacker and the voiceless against the stridency of the greedy'.[14] He concludes that 'there is no doubt that a major contributor to contemporary environmental damage is global capitalism's insatiable demand for more'.[15]

The environmental agenda of holistic mission is perfectly in line with the teachings of the Roman Catholic Church. Pope Francis' environmental encyclical, 'On the Care of Our Common Home', is a call to care for the earth, and a rallying point for the environmental movement that is sweeping the Church. In an address at the university of Molise, Southern Italy, Pope Francis said: 'This is our sin: exploiting the earth and not allowing her to give us what she has within her.'[16]

Yet Scripture is clear that God has created the earth for mankind to develop and use in order that human life might be sustained. Scripture tells us that God has created the world to be populated by mankind. Men and women, created in the image of God, are commanded to have dominion over God's creation. The earth and its rich resources have been created by God for man (the only creature made in the image of God) to develop and use. And the resources of God's world are sufficient to supply the needs of mankind. The people of God, who read and study Scripture, understand their God-given responsibility to be good stewards of the earth. They know that mankind was given dominion over all creation, and is responsible for taking care of it (Genesis 1.26; 2.15; Psalm 8.6-8). They also know that Scripture teaches that God is in control of the climate. While Christians are to be good stewards of God's creation, we should not allow politically-driven hysteria to dominate our view of the environment.

Ecumenism

A central aim of the holistic movement has always been to achieve the organisational unity of the visible Church. The spirit of ecumenism cultivated at Edinburgh 1910 gradually led to the formation of the World Council of Churches in 1948. The overt political agenda of the WCC and its sympathy for liberation theology, even condoning the use of violence to achieve political liberation, made it unpopular among evangelical Christians, who soon recognised that it was a deeply compromised organisation, and certainly not friendly to sound doctrine. To keep evangelicals on the ecumenical bandwagon, Billy Graham and John Stott convened the Berlin 1966 World Congress on Evangelism that included charismatics and liberals. Working together again, Billy Graham and John Stott created the Lausanne Congress of 1974, with the ostensible aim of world evangelism. But the Lausanne movement, despite its differences with the political agenda of the ecumenical WCC, soon revealed its own *evangelical* ecumenical agenda, working freely with the Roman Catholic Church and theological liberation proponents from South America, like Rene Padilla and Simon Escobar.

Missiology follows a deeply ecumenical agenda. It has been eager to work with every doctrinally deficient brand of Christianity, and even the Church of Rome. Indeed, the real agenda of missiology is to replace biblical Christianity with a postmodern contextualized, culturally relevant, worldview-sensitive version of the Christian Faith that is void of biblical truth.

A consequence of the Lausanne movement was that the doctrines of the Reformation were increasingly regarded by evangelicals as divisive to Christian unity. The long-term plan of Lausanne is now bearing fruit as the Reformation is largely forgotten by evangelicals, and unity with Rome is firmly on the agenda. Significantly the three major components of ecumenism, namely, the WCC, the Lausanne movement, and the Church of Rome were each prominent players at the Edinburgh 2010 celebration of holistic mission.

The ultimate aim of the ecumenical movement is to bring together the *political* ecumenism of the WCC and the *evangelical* ecumenism of Lausanne into one visible world Church.

The True Mission of the Church

In chapter 1 we saw that the true ministry of the Church, as commanded by Christ, is to preach the gospel of salvation. By examining Paul's ministry, recorded in Acts and in his letters to the churches, we gain a clear understanding of the mission of the Church. The apostle Paul was Christ's chosen vessel to preach the gospel to the Gentiles, to kings and to the children of Israel (Acts 9.15). Paul wrote: 'For necessity is laid upon me; yea, woe is unto me, if I preach not the gospel!' (1 Corinthians 9.16).

On the day of Pentecost, when Peter had received the gift of the Holy Spirit, he boldly preached Christ, repentance and the remission of sins to the gathered crowd. About three thousand souls were added to the Church. At the gate of the temple in Jerusalem, when Peter and

John healed a man lame from birth, Peter preached to the amazed Jews: 'Repent ye therefore, and be converted, that your sins may be blotted out…' (Acts 3.19). In the book of Acts there are over thirty references to the apostles preaching the gospel to both Jews and Gentiles. By examining the ministries of Paul and Peter, we gain a clear understanding of the mission of the Church. The risen Jesus opened the minds of the disciples that they might understand the Scriptures. He said to them: 'Thus it is written, and thus it behoved Christ to suffer, and to rise from the dead the third day: And that repentance and remission of sins should be preached in his name among all nations, beginning at Jerusalem' (Luke 24.46-47).

So there can be no doubt that the mission of the Church is to preach Christ as the Saviour from sin to all nations. Christ is the Lamb of God who takes away the sin of the world (John 1.29). The gospel message is repentance and remission of sins. 'This is a faithful saying, and worthy of all acceptation, that Christ Jesus came into the world to save sinners' (1 Timothy 1.15). God commends his love toward us in that, 'while we were yet sinners, Christ died for us. Much more then, being now justified by his blood, we shall be saved from wrath through him' (Romans 5.8-9).

A Biblical Perspective

An essential teaching of Scripture is the defence of the Gospel of Truth. It is a vital duty of the first importance. The New Testament epistles exhort believers to earnestly contend for the true Faith. And the reason we are to do so is because the spirit of antichrist is in the world and waging a ruthless and determined campaign against the gospel of salvation (1 John 2.18-19). The apostle Paul warned of ravenous wolves that would enter into the Church and of false men who would arise from within the Church (Acts 20.28-30). Jude and Peter both refer to ungodly men who will creep surreptitiously into the Church and turn the grace of God into licentiousness (2 Peter 2; Jude 4). The command of Scripture is to *expose* and *oppose* false teachers, not to ignore, excuse or dialogue with them.

What has been discussed concerning the downgrade of Christian missions should be of the utmost concern to all true believers, but none of us should be overly surprised or dismayed. The story actually begins in the Garden of Eden. It was in the Garden created by God that man was first tempted by the serpent to distrust God's Word, and thus aspire to godhood. The serpent, Satan, introduced into the mind of the woman the question: Did God really say? The result of this temptation was that Adam and Eve disobeyed God's Word (Genesis 3.1-6). The consequence was that God put permanent enmity between the seed of the serpent and the Seed of the woman, that is God's Seed – Christ (Genesis 3.15). From this time on human history would be dominated by relentless spiritual warfare between the two seeds. As such, Satan's cause is to accuse, slander and attempt to destroy the true Church of God. God's curse did not end with the serpent. He punished the disobedient man and woman with physical and spiritual death, and cursed the creation (Genesis 3.13-19). As a result mankind is in bondage to sin until redeemed by the blood of Christ (Romans 3.21-26), and the creation is fallen until redeemed and re-created by God himself in Christ (Revelation 21; Romans 8.19-22; 2 Peter 3.10-13). Additionally, God placed a permanent barrier between man and the Garden so that he could never become like God or enjoy paradise on earth (Genesis 3.22-24). Life on earth is dominated by the consequences of mankind's sinful, fallen nature. For man to be reconciled to God he needs a Saviour; he needs to be redeemed by the blood of Christ; he needs to be born again of the Holy Spirit. Even the creation itself waits with eager longing for this redemption (Romans 8.19).

Error of the Holistic Gospel

Over the past century and longer the Church has been tempted to challenge God's Word. The higher critics asked, 'Does God's Word really say that?' Later, various theologians asked, 'Is not the Great Commission to turn stones into bread—to feed, clothe and house the poor, and to heal the sick; and to save the world by our great good deeds? Is not that the real gospel?' More recently academic missiologists have insisted that the gospel is a 'holistic gospel'—a commission from God to 'transform' the kingdoms of the earth, solving social, political, environmental and economic problems. The natural heart of man is determined to be like God and to bring in the Kingdom here on earth, rather than waiting to receive it from God in the world to come.

In open defiance of the Great Commission the holistic mission movement has replaced the gospel of Christ with its own social gospel of good works. It has taken up the ancient temptation of the serpent that man can, of his own efforts, restore the creation and bring in the Kingdom of God. As noted in chapter 5, the early prophet of the social gospel, Walter Rauschenbusch, defined the Kingdom of God as, 'the ideal human society to be established', saying that 'the ethics of Jesus taught the true social conduct which would create the true society'. He saw the Kingdom of God not as a matter of individuals getting to heaven, but as a campaign to transform life on earth into the harmony of heaven. However, in stark opposition, Scripture says, 'Wherefore we receiving a kingdom which cannot be moved, let us have grace, whereby we may serve God acceptably with reverence and godly fear' (Hebrews 12.28). In addition, the Lord Jesus said, 'Whosoever shall not receive the kingdom of God as a little child, he shall not enter therein' (Mark 10.15). It is clear in Scripture that the Kingdom of God – like salvation, the promises of God and the blessings of faith – is something that man *receives,* not something that he earns or achieves by his own efforts.

The promise that man can by his own efforts transform life on earth into the harmony of heaven is proved false by the clear teaching of Scripture that 'the day of the Lord will come as a thief in the night; in the which the heavens shall pass away with a great noise, and the elements shall melt with fervent heat, the earth also and the works that are therein shall be burned up' (2 Peter 3.10). Believers are not called to transform the creation of themselves, rather we are called to 'look for new heavens and a new earth, wherein dwelleth righteousness' (2 Peter 3.13). The false promise that man can restore the creation and thereby solve not only the physical but also the spiritual problems of mankind has a strong attraction for the natural heart of man. Its attractiveness can in no small way be explained by the fact that good works are not at all offensive to an unbelieving world, unlike the Cross of Christ (Galatians 5.11).

We should not be surprised or dismayed that the Church has fallen prey to the temptations it has, especially in the area of missions. Matthew 24.5 tells us 'many shall come in my name, saying, I am Christ; and shall deceive many.' We should not be surprised that Satan, the enemy of souls, is waging a subtle war on the Great Commission, seeking to destroy the true gospel of salvation from sin. We have documented the large number of professing Christians and Christian organisations that have fallen prey to his temptations and are leading many others astray.

The prophecy of Scripture is that in the last days perilous times shall come, and that false men shall arise having an outward form of godliness, but no true spiritual power attending it (2 Timothy 3.1-5). The time will come when sound doctrine will not be endured, but false teachers will turn away many from the truth; and so it will be vital for true teachers to preach the Word in season and out of season (2 Timothy 4.1-5). We should know that all these things are in accordance with God's overarching plan of redemption, and so have the glorious hope that even the gates of hell will not prevail against the true Church of Jesus Christ (Mathew 16.18). Our Saviour told us, 'And many false prophets shall rise, and shall deceive many. And because iniquity shall abound, the love of many shall wax cold. But he that shall endure unto the end, the same shall be saved. And this gospel of the kingdom shall be preached in all the world for a witness unto all nations; and then shall the end come' (Matthew 24.11-14).

With this certain hope believers should trust and persevere knowing that false teachers will be punished (Matthew 7.21-23). We should be wise and faithful servants (Matthew 24.45), trust the Word of God as it has been received, vigorously oppose and expose false teaching, and be good *stewards* of God's creation, rather than aspiring to be its *redeemer*. We should also be clear that God-honouring good works are the *fruit*, not the *objective*, of the Faith. Indeed, every true believer who has the new nature is zealous for God-honouring good works. Being kind and concerned about the welfare of others, and doing good deeds are an inseparable part of a Christian's life in Christ. On the Last Day the righteous will ask in delighted and humble surprise, 'Lord, when saw we thee an hungred, and fed thee? or thirsty, and gave thee drink?' (Matthew 25.37).

As I said in the Introduction, the purpose of this book is to warn the people of God of the rise of *heresy* in the Church. Holistic mission ranks as a heresy because it redefines the very meaning of evangelism and the actual gospel itself; in practice the salvation of precious souls becomes at best secondary in the great socio-political mission of the Church to transform the world into the Kingdom of God on earth.

Thus we must conclude that the holistic movement has disastrously distorted the message of the gospel. But believers should not be downcast, for our Lord forewarned us that in the last times the deception would be so great that, if it were possible, even the elect would be deceived (Matthew 24.24). God will never be without his witnesses to the truth. When Elijah cried out: 'I, even I only, am left; and they seek my life, to take it away', the Lord assured him, 'Yet I have left me seven thousand in Israel, all the knees which have not bowed unto Baal' (1 Kings 19. 14, 18). Moreover the Word of God is eternal and will never pass away. 'The grass withereth, the flower fadeth: but the word of our God shall stand for ever' (Isaiah 40.8). So let us take courage and remember that the gospel of Christ is the power of God unto salvation to everyone who believes (Romans 1.16).

(Endnotes)

1   J. Gresham Machen, *The New Testament:* An *introduction to its Literature and History,* Banner of Truth, 1976, p368, reprint 2009

2   Ibid. p369

3   Ibid. p370

4   Ibid. p370

5   *The Sword & Trowel*, November 1887, A Fragment Upon the Down-Grade Controversy by C. H. Spurgeon

6   J. Gresham Machen, *Christianity and Liberalism*, Victory Press, 1923, p17

7   Cited from: Chalmers W. Alexander 2. Discipline Found Wanting, What Happened To The Signers Of The Auburn Affirmation? "Exploring Avenues Of Acquaintance And Cooperation", https://continuing.wordpress.com/2011/05/10/discipline-found-wanting/

8   The *Lausanne Covenant*, paragraph 5, Christian Social Responsibility

9   Joel James and Brian Biedebach, 'Regaining Our Focus: A Response to the Social Action Trend in Evangelical Missions', *The Master's Seminary Journal* [Spring 2014], p48

10   John Stott, quoting David Moberg in *Issues Facing Christians Today*, Marshall Pickering, published in Great Britain 1990, p8

11   David O. Moberg, *The Great Reversal –evangelism versus social concern*, Scripture Union, first British edition 1973, p20

12   David Bosch, *Transforming Mission*, Orbis Books, 1991, p565

13   Christopher Wright, 'Mission and God's Earth', an essay in *Perspectives*, p30

14   Ibid. p32

15   Ibid. p32

16   World, July 5, 2014, WORLD, Pope calls exploitation of nature a sin of our time

Index

A

Alexander, Chalmers W. 110, 112
All Nations Christian College 10
American Society of Missiology 222–224
Amsterdam 2000 Conference 215–216
Amsterdam Declaration 216
Anti-Western Ideology 328, 126, 129, 132,
133, 179, 195, 197-198, 215, 258,
259, 227, 278, 279
De-Westernizing the Gospel 244–246
Auburn Affirmation 103–116, 111

B

Berlin Congress (1966) 162-170
Christianity Today 163
Emperor of Ethiopia, Haile Selassie, 165
Henry, Dr Carl 163
Hubbard, David Allan 169
John Stott 165
Oral Roberts 166
Biedebach, Brian 5, 12
Billy Graham Evangelistic Association
152–161
Bosch, David 133, 219, 204, 219, 269,
278–281
Bready, J.W. 26
Briggs, Charles A. (1841-1913) 40, 59–67,
103, 110
*Whither? A theological question for our
times* 61–62
Bright Hope International 9
Bryan, William Jennings 107, 118

C

Carnell, Edward John 149
Chapman, Alastair 190
Charteris, Dr Archibald 52
Christianity and Liberalism (1923) 108
Christianity in Culture (1979) 270
Christianity Today 148· 151–161
Christian Leaders of the 18th Century 25
*Christian Message in a Non-Christian
World* (1938) 98

Christian Mission in the Modern World
(1975) 2
Chronological Bible Storying 217
Church Growth Theory 191
Church of England 8
Conference Jerusalem 1928 91–101
Consultation on World Evangelization (June
1980) 198–199
contextualization 131, 193, 221, 223, 227,
245, 257, 258, 268–282, 288, 326-327
Costas, Orlando 177, 199, 209
Creation Care 329

D

Davidson, Samuel (1806-1898) 40
Deception in the Church 320–321
De-Westernizing the Gospel 244
Downgrade Controversy 54–67
Driver, Dr S.R. (1846-1914) 40

E

Ecumenical Evangelism 157
Ecumenism 63, 81-82, 85-88, 97, 131, 134,
136, 157, 164, 168-170, 173, 176,
212, 223, 225, 229, 287, 290, 291,
295, 299, 330
Edinburgh 1910 Conference 86–101
Edinburgh Centenary Celebration 2010
284–301
Closing Celebration 296
Conference Talks 293
Ecological Perspective 289
Holistic Mission: God's Plan for God's
People 298
Pontifical Council for Christian Unity
294
The Common Call 296–297
The Environment 295
The Opening Celebration 291–292
Welcoming remarks of Cardinal O'Brien
292
Women in Mission 289
Words of Greeting from WCC 292
Words of Greeting from WEA 293
Eichhorn, Johann 38
England, Before and After Wesley (1939)
26
Error of the Holistic Gospel 333
Escobar, Simon 8, 177-179, 184

Eshleman, Paul 217
Essays and Reviews 50–67
Essentials: A Liberal-Evangelical Dialogue (1988) 21
Evangelical Missiological Society 224–225
evangelical revival 24–32
Evangelism and Social Responsibility, Grand Rapids (1982) 199–200
evangelization 174-175

F

Faith and Order Committee 90–101
First Presbyterian Church on West Twelfth Street 106
Ford, Rev Leighton 197
Fosdick, Harry Emerson 104–116
Freud, Sigmund 53
Fruit of Compromise 323–324
Fuller Theological Seminary 146, 148, 149–161, 169, 191, 192,195, 221-223, 232, 234, 270, 275, 304, 315, 322-323, 330

G

Godly Ambition (2012) 190
Graham, Billy 1, 124, 126, 146, 151, 157, 159, 162-164, 168, 173-74, 185, 189-191, 216, 233, 315
    puff Graham 152
Graham, Franklin 154
Great Commission 1-2, 17, 20, 30, 175-176, 181,203, 243, 262-263, 285
Great Reversal 20-21, 30
    sociological theory 22–32

H

Hague, Canadian Canon Dyson 37
Hearst, William Randolph 152
Henry, Dr Carl 150, 151, 163, 169, 173
Hesselgrave, David 3, 88, 224
Hiebert, Paul 275–278
    Critical Contextualization 275
higher criticism 33–49, 68, 72, 86, 91, 99, 102, 105, 107, 114, 281, 321
higher criticism in the USA 59–67
higher criticism on the mission field 42–49

History of the American Society of Missiology (2013) 222
Hocking Report 94–101, 103, 111
holistic mission 6–19, 12, 14–19, 20, 22, 30, 87, 97, 131, 134, 185, 205, 208-209, 214-215, 222, 227-229, 248, 255, 264-266, 284-285,290, 298
Holistic Mission: God's Plan for God's People (2010) 7, 227–228

I

Iguassu Affirmation (1999) 214–217
Independent Board for Presbyterian Foreign Missions 112
International Association of Mission Studies 225–226
International Congress for World Evangelization 2, 7, 173-185
International Fellowship of Evangelical Mission Theologians (INFEMIT) 208
International Missionary Council 89–101
Issues Facing Christians Today (1984) 20

J

James, Joel 5, 12
Johannine Commission 3-5
John Piper at Lausanne II 213–218
Johnston, Arthur 87, 88, 97
John Stott: A Global Ministry (2001) 190

K

Keller, Tim 13
Kingdom of God 4, 11, 21, 69, 76, 228, 242-248, 324
Kostenberger, Andreas 5
Kraemer, Hendrik, Dutch Reformed theologian 96
Kraft, Charles 270–275
    Carl Henry's Critique 274–275
    Christianity in Culture 273–275
    Mission to Muslims 271–273
Kuenen, Professor of Leyden 38

L

Larger Evangelism 97. 99–101

Lausanne Committee on World Evangelization (LCWE) 188–207
Lausanne Congress (1974) 172-187
  John Capon 177
  John Stott 175
  Latin American theologians 177–187
  Radical Discipleship Group 179–187
Lausanne Congress for World Evangelization 172–187
Lausanne Covenant 2, 6, 181–187
Lausanne III: Cape Town (2010) 302–318
  Environmental Agenda 314
  Lausanne's Feminist Agenda 313
  Lausanne's Religious Agenda 315
  Lausanne's Road to Rome 304
  Lausanne's Socialist Agenda 311
  Promoting the Visual Arts 306–307
  Storytelling the Gospel 307
  The Alpha Course 305
  The Cape Town Commitment 311
  The International Orality Network 310
  WCC at Lausanne III 304
  The Oral Bible 309
  The Real Agenda of the Orality Movement 311
  Tragedy of the Lausanne Compromise 315
Lausanne II Manila (1989) 210–212
Life and Work Committee 89–101
Life of Jesus (1835) 33
Lindsell, Harold 150

M

Macartney, Clarence E. 106, 110
Machen, J. Gresham 95, 103, 108–116
Machen on Social Reform 319, 319–320
Madras Conference 1938 97–101
Manila Manifesto 211–212
McGavran, Donald 222
McQuilkin, Robertson 272
Mencken, H.L. journalist 120
Mere Evangelism 327–328
Micah Network 9
Missiology 219, 326–327
Missiology in the UK 226–227
Missiology of Chris Wright 252–267
Moberg, David 20-24
modernism and liberalism 35–49
modern liberalism 109

Mott, John R. 83–101

N

National Vespers Hour 107
Neill, Bishop Stephen 97, 132
New Evangelicals 145–161
  Intellectual Respectability 157
  Social Activism 158
  Young and Worldly Evangelicals 154–161
Newman, Las 7, 314
Newbigin, Bishop Lesslie 97, 131,

O

Ockenga, Harold John 146–161
Oldham, Joseph Houldsworth 85–101
Oral Roberts: An American Life (1985) 167
Orthodox Presbyterian Church 112
Oxford Centre for Mission Studies (OCMS) 7, 209, 226-227

P

Padilla, Rene 7, 177–178, 180, 183, 191, 192, 194, 204, 209, 313
Perspectives on the World Christian Movement (2009) 234, 242, 248, 271, 274
Pickering, Ernest 154, 157, 159
Pierson, Arthur 83
Presbyterian Church 106
Priest, Robert J. 219–220
Princeton Theological Seminary 60, 63, 108, 112

R

Rauschenbusch, Walter 33, 68–80
  A Theology for the Social Gospel 71
  Christianity and the Social Crisis 71
  higher criticism 72
  committed socialist 72–80
Roberta Winter Institute 232
Roberts, Oral 166–171
Rockefeller, John D. 94, 106, 107
Ross, Kenneth 87, 286
Rowdon, Harold H 12
Ryle, J.C. 25

S

Samuel, Vinay 178, 199, 209-210
Schaeffer, Francis 182
Scopes Monkey Trial 117–121
   Bryan, William Jennings 107, 118-119
   Darrow, Clarence 118
   Linder, Douglas, Law Professor 119
Shall the Fundamentalists Win?' 106
Shall Unbelief Win? 106
Shenk, Wilbert R. 222
Sider, Ronald 180, 196, 198-199, 209, 247
Simple Lifestyle Consultation (March 1980)
      195–207
Smith, George Adam 40
Smith, William Robertson 40, 51–67
social activity, a partner of evangelism 201
social activity, bridge to evangelism 201
social activity, consequence of evangelism
      201
social gospel 83, 105, 324
socialism 73–80
social justice 196
socio-political action 6
Speer, Dr Robert E. 95, 111
Spurgeon, Charles Haddon 54–67
Stetzer, Dr Ed 221
Steuernagel, Valdir R. 211
Stott, John 1, 175–176, 188–
      190, 199, 210, 211–212
   betrayal of evangelical Christianity 30
   change of mind 20–32
   Christian Mission in the Modern World
      (1975) 2
   disagree with Billy Graham in public,
      189–191
   dislike of conservative Christians 21
   evangelism and social action a partner-
      ship 6
   historic Lausanne Covenant 181–183
   Johannine Commission 3–5
   John Stott at Berlin '66 165–166
   opening address to Lausanne 1974
      175–176
   radical change of mind 2
   social research 21
   sociological theory of the Great Reversal
      22–24
   socio-political action a Christian duty 6
   Stott and the Latin American theologians
      177–179
Strauss, David Friedrich 33

Student Volunteer Movement 78

T

Tear Fund 11
Temple, Bishop William 91
The Battle for the Bible (1976) 150
The Battle for World Evangelism (1978)
      199
The Cambridge Social History of Britain
      27
The Five Points 102–116
The Frontier Mission Fellowship 232
*The Fundamentals – a Testimony to the
      Truth* 36–49
*The Great Reversal: Evangelism Versus
      Social Concern* (1972) 22
*The Mission of God's People: A Biblical
      Theology of the Church's Mission*
      (2010), 261
*The Mission of God: Unlocking the Bible's
      Grand Narrative* (2006) 254
theological liberalism 34–49
theology of the social gospel 74–80
The Present World Situation (1915) 84
*The Second Evangelical Awakening in
      Britain* 29
Tingle, Rachel, British economist, 130, 269
Tinker, Rev Melvin 168
Toy, Crawford 64-66
*Transforming Mission: Paradigm Shifts in
      Theology of Mission* 278
true mission of the Church 15–19, 331
Tübingen School 33
two wings of a bird 201

U

undermining the Bible 321, 321–323
U.S. Center for World Mission (USCWM)
      234–235

V

Victorian People and Ideas (1973) 28

W

Wellhausen, Julius 38
Wesley, John 24
Westminster Confession of Faith 108
Westminster Theological Seminary 110,

113
Wheaton Statement (1983) 203–207
Whitefield, George 24
Willis, Avery 217
Willowbank Report: The Gospel and Cul-
    ture (1978) 191–207
Winter, Ralph 174, 222, 223, 231-248
  Age of the Earth 235
  De-Westernizing the Gospel 244
  Future of Evangelicals in Mission 247
  Intermediate Beings 237
  Mere Evangelism 241
  Ralph Winter at Lausanne 233–234
  The Kingdom of God 242–243
  Theology and Philosophy 235
  U.S. Center for World Mission (USCWM)
    234
  Winter and the Reformation 239–240
  Winter's Education 231–232
  Winter's Prehistory 236
  Works of the Devil 238
World Congress on Evangelism, Berlin
    1966 1, 162–171
World Council of Churches 122–144
  Aim of the WCC 122–144
  Bangkok 1973 131–144
  Brazil Assembly (2006) 140–144
  Canberra Assembly (1991) 137–144
  Church and Society Conference (1966)
    126–144
  Consultation on Racism (1969) 128–144
  Evanston Assembly (1954) 125
  Harare Assembly (1998) 138–144
  Mandela at Harare 138–144
  meaning of salvation 133
  Mission and Evangelism: An Ecumenical
    Affirmation (1982) 134–144
  Nairobi Assembly (1975) 134–144
  Neill, Bishop Stephen 132
  Newbigin, Bishop Lesslie 131
  New Delhi Assembly (1961) 125–144
  Potter, Philip 131
  Programme to Combat Racism (PCR)
    128
  Revolution of Reconciliation? (1992) 130
  Uppsala Assembly (1968) 127–144
  Vancouver Assembly (1983) 135–144
  Willem Visser't Hooft 124
WorldMissionary Conference, Edinburgh

1910 81–101
World Vision 11
Wright, Christopher 252-266
  Contextual Theology 257
  Creation Care 252–253
  Critique by Pastor Gary Millar 261
  Review by Pastor Mike Gilbart-Smith
    259–260
  The Mission of God 254–257
  The Mission of God's People 261–264
  Wright's Common Word 253–254

INDEX